FOR COMMUNICATION

BOVEN IN DE
VLUGGERVER...
5 CENT

16 VII

THE "ALPHA" POSTCARD

(For Address Only)

C000302897

THE Address to be Written
on this Side.

POST CARD—Carte Postale
Universal Postal Union—Union Postale Universelle

BRISTOL
MAY 27
26A

BRITISH GOODS
ARE B...

HALF PENNY

To—

S. K. Hathaway

28. Carlisle Ter

Tree Hac

Plymouth

Miss Green,
7, Mona Cottage

Miss M. Phillips
107 Elmcroft...
Wanstead

OUGHTON,
ESSEX

TUCK'
CARTE

Dear Mavis
mummy left her knitting
needle... I found it by the
front gate. So will take it
to Awley's in the morning
love to you both from

Copyright: The Medici Society Ltd., London
Art Publishers by Appointment to the late King...
Engraved and printed in Great Britain

A VIVIAN MANSELL & Co. Fine Art Publishers, London
Copyright. Printed in England

C.W.
FAULKNER
& Co
LTD

AWLEY
ISSEX

CORRESPONDENCE

Post Card

SALMON
SERIES
TRADE MARK

ADDRESS

PRINTED AND PUBLISHED BY J. SALMON LTD., SEVENOAKS, ENGLAND.

This pussy has sat a
Crown on...
The Sully...

THREE HALF

POST CARD

BRISTOL
MAY 28

# POSTCARDS FROM THE NURSERY

# Postcards from the Nursery

### The illustrators of children's books and postcards 1900-1950

by Dawn & Peter Cope

"IF YOU'RE EVER PASSING BY
PLEASE DROP IN AND VISIT I"

NEW CAVENDISH BOOKS

© New Cavendish Books

First published in the UK
by New Cavendish Books
November 2000

Book design by Peter Cope FCSD

Printed and bound in Thailand by
Amarin Printing and Publishing (Plc) Co.Ltd.

New Cavendish Books
3 Denbigh Road
London W11 2SJ

ISBN 1 872727 88 3

# Contents

*Left:*
*Artist: Agnes Richardson*
*Pub: Photochrom*
*Celesque Series*
*No. 1430*
*[c.1920]*

*Right:*
*Artist: Mabel Lucie Attwell*
*Pub: Valentine*
*Valentine's Attwell Series*
*A660*
*[1922]*

THIS ONE'S FOR <u>YOU</u>—DEAR.

# Acknowledgements

Many of the short biographies included in this volume have been compiled from the personal recollections and experiences of lifetime friends and relatives of the illustrators. We would like to acknowledge their time and effort in helping us with this project and thank them for the loan of beautiful photographs and other material in their possession. We have enjoyed sharing their memories and are delighted to have made their acquaintance. We wish to thank them for responding to our questions and requests without a hint of irritation:

James & Kate Anderson, Dora Banfield, Cecily Batten, Maureen Beazley, Phyllis Bishop, Kay & Victor Blundell, Dr G Bonner Morgan, Mary Bouet, Elizabeth & George Brassington, Jacqueline Burgers, Janet Bush, Judith Caspar, Anne Caulfield, Pam Chance, Trevor Cook, Hanna & Michael Cowham, Mrs Norah Driver, Charles Ellam, Norman & Dorothy Ellam, Pam Ellam, Tony Ellam, Eva Ewens, Sarah Gay, Peter & Chloë Greeves, Dorothy Green, Jean Gunn, Jean Hardy, Jill Hill, Grace Hogarth, Muriel Martin-Harvey, Julian Helps, Frank Hutchings, Dr A Kennedy, Christopher & Leni Lake, Richard Leared, Ailsa Le Page, Peggy McBride, David MacGregor, Peggy McGrillen, Mrs V Mancey, Lady Martin, Peter Mountford, Graham Mytton, Riet Neerincx, David Nicholson, Felicity Nicholson, Joan Nielson, Audrey Nunn, Anne Parry, Norah Pavey, Mr & Mrs C Pearn, Mr & Mrs R Pearn, Rosemary Pollack, Avis Prior, Philip Purser, Jan Reynolds, Margaret Reynolds, Elaine Richards, Marion Ricketts, Jeanette Robertson, Rita Russell, Jack Sammons, Lily Sanders, Miss J Savage, Eva Shackleton, Anne Shand, John Smallwood, Mrs I Smith, Jeannie Smith, Mrs J Smith, Donald & Joan Steele, Brian Stewart, Helmut Stoyer, Hilda Strickland, Angela Sturt, Stan Suggitt, James Symes, Nick & Joan Taylor, Joan Thain, Mrs G Trythall, Joan Tucker, Adèle Valsesia, Peter Walker, Kathleen Wheeler, Hilary & John Wickham, June Williams, Shelagh Wootton, Jean Wraith, Margaret Wray.

Thanks to the folowing organisations for assistance and permission to use material in this volume: Chris Beetles Limited, A&C Black, Blackie & Son, The British Library, Copyrights, Express Newspapers, First Church of Christ Scientist, Glasgow School of Art, Knowles Hill School, Newton Abbot, Liberty & Co, Manchester High School for Girls, Oxford University Press, North Somerset Museum Service, Roedean School, St Andrew's University, Start-Rite Shoes Limited, Westminster Public Library.

Special thanks to the following:

Ian and Patricia Aspinall for the loan of items from their collection, help with the detailing of information and support and encouragement throughout the project.

The Burrell Collection, Glasgow for the loan of the painting of Dorothy Carleton-Smith on page 106.

Bushey Museum & Art Gallery for the loan of photographic material on pages 23, 88 and 123.

Mrs Jillian Collins for the loan of material relating to Agnes Richardson.

Walt Disney UK for permission to use their material on pages 122 and 123.

Muriel and Brian Lamming for the loan of the photograph of Mary Tourtel and her family on page 240

Primrose Lockwood for providing extensive material on Joyce Lankaster Brisley.

Christopher Marshall for his drawings of Anne Anderson and GH Thompson on pages 76 and 238.

The Medici Society for permission to use their material throughout the book.

Derek Salmon and J Salmon Limited for their help and permission to use their material throughout the book.

Mark Schlossman for the jacket photograph.

Tony Warr for the loan of items from his collection and his advice and help with the detailing of information of Tuck artists.

Mark Wickham for the loan of his portrait of Mabel Lucie Attwell on page 85.

The York City Art Gallery for the loan of the painting of Chloë Preston photographed by Glen Segal on page 207.

# Preface

It seems like only yesterday, yet it was in 1974 that we first stumbled on an album of children's postcards. By then, we had been collecting children's books for two or three years. Like many book collectors, we were enchanted by the work of the great illustrators, who could transport their readers into a world far away from the cares and anxieties of everyday life.

We had bought our first children's book in 1971, a very shabby copy of the first edition of *A Apple Pie*, by Kate Greenaway, at a local Saturday market behind The Royal Standard public house in Blackheath.

The lives of all the other great gift book illustrators like Edmund Dulac, Kay Nielsen, Arthur Rackham and Charles Robinson, have been well documented, but our own enquiring natures began to lead us towards lesser known, but talented children's illustrators whose work provided the backbone of popular twentieth century children's illustration. Artists like Anne Anderson, Lilian Govey, Helen Jacobs and Millicent Sowerby intrigued us. They, and most of their contemporaries were women, which raised questions about their ability to cope with the pressures in a commercial world that was still very much a male domain. It is only in recent years that their talent has been acknowledged, yet their lives remain clouded in mystery.

In the summer of 1974, we spent a pleasant vacation in Cornwall. We stayed at a delightful cottage by the sea near Falmouth. But the weather was wet and we were unable to enjoy the cliff top walks and beachcombing excursions we had planned. One day we decided to drive to nearby Truro and browse around the flea market in the centre of town. Having wandered about for a while and found nothing of interest, we were attracted to the stall of a dealer selling general bric-a-brac, books and pictures.

Evening was approaching and we had seen nothing all day to catch our eye. But the dealer must have realised that we were not interested in anything on his stall. However, our conversation prompted him to invite us back to his home – an old farmhouse, a few miles out of town, tucked away in the countryside.

As we entered the house we were drawn towards an inviting maroon postcard album on his kitchen dresser, clearly bulging with postcards. He warned us that it was not for sale as he had only just bought it, but we were intrigued and curious. On examining a few loose cards at the front of the album we noticed that they had once been the property of two young children, Angela and Laddie Hathaway of Plymouth. Collected between 1923 and 1926, the cards had been sent to them regularly by their grannie from Bournemouth and their parents who seemed to spend a great deal of their time away from home.

As we carefully turned the leaves we saw, to our amazement, page upon page of postcards depicting nursery rhymes, fairy tales, fairyland fantasy, toys and games, and children at play. We recognised instantly the varied styles of many twentieth century children's book illustrators whose work fascinated us, but about whom we knew little. We had seen their illustrations in books, but we had no idea that they had access to the picture postcard as an outlet for their talent.

Needless to say, eventually a deal was struck and off we went with our prize. Little did we know then that our chance meeting with the Cornish dealer would be the beginning of a twenty five year quest to discover more about the illustrators whose lives and work have hitherto gone relatively unnoticed and largely undocumented.

We have often wondered what happened to Angela and Laddie Hathaway, the boy and girl who had carefully accumulated the wonderful album of postcards. Should we attempt to trace them to find out or should the course of their lives remain in our imagination, hoping that they enjoyed health and happiness?

"If You're Ever Passing By Please Drop In And Visit I"

*Left:*
*Artist: Phyllis Cooper*
*Pub: Raphael Tuck*
*Oilette Series 3482*
*Happy Land V*
*[1924]*

*Right:*
*Artist: Grace Drayton*
*Pub: J Asher & co*
*The Kismet Series*
*Calandar Card No.203*
*[1913]*

THE · THOUGHT · I · SEN[...]
MY · GARDEN ·
IN · THIS · LITTLE · CAR[...]
· · 🙝 · V 🙝 · 🙝[...]
"JUST · LONGING · DEAR[...]
THE · DAY · WE · M[...]
TILL · THEN · I'LL · SAY ·

## Little Treasures

We live in an age where letter writing is no longer the fashion. Just for a short while let's transport ourselves back to a time when children derived pleasure from sending and receiving warm messages of endearment on a postcard.

# A miscellany of messages

The touching messages on the backs of many nursery postcards contribute to our understanding of times past. The style of language and the content of the messages documents, for ever, aspects of the lives and characters of our forbears. Trivial messages, everyday messages of endearment and sentiment, leave an enduring memory of what it was like to be a child before the days of television and computers. Do you remember the simple pleasure derived from heartwarming dialogue and the receipt of a loving message on a postcard from an aunt or uncle? Exchanging messages with postcards was a wonderful way to keep in touch.

A SONG OF FLOWERS.

My dear Bunty
There are not many of *these* flowers left in the garden now though there are still many others. The country looks very beautiful in its autumn clothing and the different shades of green and brown are most wonderful... From Auntie Alice

My dearest May
I am pleased to hear you liked the postcard I sent you. How do you like this one? Very smart bathing costume, is it not?
Your old Daddie [Saturday]

[to Miss Mary Goodwin]
This is the picture of a little Dutch boy and it has come right across the big sea to you. I will try and bring you something nicer when I come home. With much love from your Auntie Connie. [18.10.18]

The Knight Errant.

[to Miss Marjory Hassall]
King Coal sends his love. He slept like a top and has been very good today. We have had great fun watching different animals coming from the show. Best love  [6.9.13]

THE FAIRY SHOEMAKER

My dear Connie
Don't you like the two tiny rabbits peeping around the tree trunk to see the Fairy Cobbler?... From Auntie [12.11.36]

OVER THE HILLS AND FAR AWAY

Dear Mary
...The little girl on this p.c reminds me of "Doll", don't you see a resemblance? Lots & lots of love and all good wishes from Auntie. [26.4.36]

"The Little Housewife."
Saturday

[to Miss Willycombe]
Hope you had a good day for blackberrying. Your tomatoes look very tempting. I have one every morn for breakfast. Apples and fruit don't keep. Best love & kisses [11.10.09]

WELL PASSED

[to Miss Joan Moore]
How do you like these little chaps? You must make up your own story for them. Lots of love & kisses from Dollie & Mummie XXXXXXXXX [21.08.15]

THE NEW LOVE

[to Miss Burdekin]
Hal, Rex & Lucy are sending you the toilet set with their love. I do hope darling, you will like the dolly I am sending you. Much love from Auntie Nellie. [22.03.11]

Friends in Trouble.

Dear Miss Dunkley
I am very sorry to hear you have met with an accident. We do not know what you have done, but many amusing suggestions have been made. But still we hope it is not very serious...
Love from Ethel  [02.08.13]

MARY, MARY, QUITE CONTRARY.
Mary, Mary, quite contrary,
How does your garden grow?
With cockle-shells, and silver bells,
And pretty maids all in a row.

For dear little Bubbles
With Nanna's love & kisses thanking Bubbles so much for the beautiful birthday blotter & the letter – so lovely. [10.02.19]

*COLUMN 1*

*Artist: Flora White*
*Publisher: J Salmon*
*No. 4343 [1936]*

*Artist: Aurelio Bertiglia*
*Publisher: Anon*
*Ser. 2002 [nd]*

*COLUMN 2*

*Artist: Rie Cramer*
*Publisher: Charles Hauff*
*Ser. 0129 [1923]*

*Artist: Agnes Richardson*
*Publisher: CW Faulkner*
*Ser. 1254 [1913]*

*Artist: Joyce Plumstead*
*Publisher: A Vivian Mansell*
*Ser. 2126 [1929]*

*COLUMN 3*

*Artist: Margaret Tarrant*
*Publisher: The Medici Society*
*The Springtime of Life [c.1935]*

*Artist: Anon*
*Publisher: Valentine*
*[c.1909]*

*Artist: Albert Ernest Kennedy*
*Publisher: CW Faulkner*
*Ser. 1404 [15]*

*COLUMN 4*

*Artist: Bessie Pease*
*Publisher: Guttmann & Guttmann*
*[c.1911]*

*Artist: Susan Beatrice Pearse*
*Publisher: CW Faulkner*
*Ser. 984 [1909]*

*Artist: Flora White*
*Publisher: J Salmon*
*No. 1095 [1917]*

**COLUMN 1**

*Artist: Anon*
*Publisher: A Vivian Mansell*
*Ser. 2114 [26]*

*Artist: Anon*
*Publisher: Raphael Tuck*
*No. 9855 [23]*

*Artist: Ethel Parkinson*
*Publisher: CW Faulkner*
*When George III was King*
*Ser. 226D [1903]*

**COLUMN 2**

*Artist: Eileen Hood*
*Publisher: Humphrey Milford*
*Ser. Farm Babies [1920]*

*Artist: Millicent Sowerby*
*Publisher: Humphrey Milford*
*Flower Fairies [1925]*

*Artist: Freda Mabel Rose*
*Publisher: Anon*
*Mabel Rose Series*
*No. 26 [nd]*

**COLUMN 3**

*Artist: Margaret Tarrant*
*Publisher: CW Faulkner*
*Ser. 923D [1909]*

*Artist: Ellen Jessie Andrews*
*Publisher: Raphael Tuck*
*No. 1822 [c.1906]*

*Artist: Margaret Tempest*
*Publisher: The Medici Society*
*Ser. Pkt 52/6482*
*Leap Frog*

**COLUMN 4**

*Artist: Linda Edgerton*
*Publisher: A Vivian Mansell*
*Ser. 1140 [1920]*

*Artist: Mabel Lucie Attwell*
*Publisher: Valentine*
*[1913]*

*Artist: Anon*
*Publisher: Raphael Tuck*
*Ser. 3328*
*Nursery Rhymes*
*[1920]*

Dearest Jane
Ask grannie if she saw any fairies fishing at Torquay like this. I hope you will soon get rid of your nasty cough & baby too, thank Grannie for her letter...
Lots of love Auntie Bee  [21.06.25]

[to Miss GG Glyde]
Boys & girls come out to play
Ask AB and she'll come to stay
And while away a Happy Day
And make 'em shout Hip & Hooray!!!

[to Mr Mattey]
Don't send me another telegram, as they always stop my 'heart'.
Hope all is well. 21.12.03

My dear Jean
I hope you like this card. I could not find any puzzles. Love from Daddy  [22.02.27]

[to CPM Phillips]
Do you think the little mouse is going to tell the time by this 'clock'? Grannie sends her love & a kiss to everyone.
Love from Auntie Mabel  [10.09.25]

Dear Lis
We have all got a moan on today. First, the shop was packed for 1hr with people waiting for doughnuts. We only let them have 6 each. Then Mrs Seaman came and said we were not to make any tomorrow & then when we do get them we are only to let 2 to go to each customer. Isn't it daft... Love Auntie Dollie  [06.05.45]

[to Miss AM Grist]
Daisy was invited to a fancy dress party - & this is how she went, dressed as a snowdrop. Of course she could not have the green leaf to stand on – that was just put in to make a pretty picture. Much love to you all from Auntie Allie  [1909]

To dear Hilda
Hoping you may have a cuddle with Father Christmas the same as this little girl. A happy Xmas and lots of presents.
With love from Auntie Maudie  [1907]

[to Miss Margaret Graham]
I'm sure you've never seen any squirrels having a game like these ones – even the birds look surprised. Lots of love, hugs and kisses from Mummie XXX  [03.09.41]

[to Miss Anne Loggin]
I hope your puff-puff is going like this keeping on the lines nicely. Thank you pet for your nice letters I do love them. Una & Jean have just gone to bed & send you lots of love and kisses. Nicki  [25.10.25]

Dear Auntie
I can't make many pies at Southport, because I am so sleepy at Southport. Not coming home yet. Your little niece Dorothy XXX  [15.07.13]

Dearest Baby
I hope you will like this card! - Are all the flowers in your garden withered? – Perhaps you will soon have some tulips and daffodils in the spring...Your loving Gran  [10.11.24]

[to Miss Goodchild]
Dear Goo
Thank you for the puzzle I play with it
nearly every day.
Love Cop XXXX.  [07.07.27]

Dearest Lovey Dovey
Here's one of the Land Girls come to look
at you. Be sure to let Boy have a look at
your book & be very good to him because
it is his birthday you know. You will be
having one soon & then you will get
presents. Love Auntie Glad XXX.  [2.10.20]

[to Master Alan Godwin]
Hello Chubbykins
Have you caught Mummy a nice crab yet.
Love to all. Mummy.  [26.8.26]

[to Master Eric Brill]
This little boy is fishing in a pail but I
don't think he is going to catch lunch –
his name is Simple Simon.
Fondest kisses. Grandma.  1.11.33

[to Miss Eileen Mitchell]
Dear Eileen
How do you like these wee children? They
have come to bring you Auntie's love and
hope you are better today.  [4.5.20]

[to Miss Daisy Faulkner]
What would you do if you met a little
black sheep like this when you were out
for a walk? Hope you & mother are better.
With love F Baker.  [1.9.27]

[to Lady Helen Gordon Lennox]
Have you got any of this kind? Is Joy with
you? Stutton. NB.  [24.9.03]

Dear Jacqueline
I hope you like this post-card, the mice are
going to play hop-scotch after tea. We have
not been on the beach lately, because it rains
so much. We are going to Birchington for
lunch today. Clarice sends her love to you
and so do Peggy and I. Yvonne.  [21.8.27]

[to Miss Barbara Rogers]
Isn't it boiling weather. I do hope you are
having a happy time & are all managing to
keep cool. You will find your toffee &
chocolate in the card drawer but go slow
with it or you will get spots again! Heaps of
love from Mummy.  [19.8.32]

My dear Doll
I hope you still like school and are keeping
quite well. You will be almost a grown up
girl when I come to see you again. Isn't this
a sweet little elf? I thought you would like
the ladybird too. Lots of XX's & OO's from
Auntie Alice.  [22.2.31]

[to Master Lewis Hathaway]
It was so kind of you to pick me those
pretty primroses, thank you very much.
Love from Jane.  [11.4.23]

[to Miss Lily Weston while in hospital]
My dear Lily
I wrote to your mother last night. I hope
she will see you today. I'm afraid I will not
be able to come & see you this week.
Hoping to have good news.  [6.12.05]

COLUMN 1

*Artist: Mabel Lucie Attwell*
*Publisher: Raphael Tuck*
*No. 4095*
*Grimm's Fairy Tales [c.1911]*

*Artist: Linda Edgerton*
*Publisher: EW Savory*
*Ser. 809 [c.1920]*

*Artist: Chlöe Preston*
*Publisher: Humphrey Milford*
*Peek-a-Boo Gardeners*
*[1926]*

COLUMN 2

*Artist: Linda Edgerton*
*Publisher: A Vivian Mansell*
*Ser. 1170 [1920]*

*Artist: Linda Edgerton*
*Publisher: A Vivian Mansell*
*Ser. 1096 [1919]*

*Artist: Linda Edgerton*
*Publisher: A Vivian Mansell*
*Ser. 1159 [1920]*

COLUMN 3

*Artist: Florence Upton*
*Publisher: Raphael Tuck*
*Ser: 1281 [1903]*

*Artist: Lilian Amy Govey*
*Publisher: Humphrey Milford*
*The Mouseykins [1926]*

*Artist: Rie Cramer*
*Publisher: Humphrey Milford*
*Joyous Days [1932]*

COLUMN 4

*Artist: Millicent Sowerby*
*Publisher: Humphrey Milford*
*Flowers and Wings*
*[1920]*

*Artist: Millicent Sowerby*
*Publisher: Humphrey Milford*
*Peter Pan Postcards*
*[1920]*

*Artist: Florence Hardy*
*Publisher: CW Faulkner*
*Ser: 501C [1905]*

*COLUMN 1*

*Artist: Millicent Sowerby*
*Publisher: Henry Frowde*
*Ser: Happy Days [1915]*

*Artist: Anon*
*Publisher: Raphael Tuck*
*Ser. 3376*
*Nursery Rhymes [1922]*

*Artist: George Henry Thompson*
*Publisher: T Stroefer*
*Ser. 965 [nd]*

*COLUMN 2*

*Artist: Hilda Dix Sandford*
*Publisher: Raphael Tuck*
*Ser. 9102*
*Boys and Girls Come Out to Play*
*[c.1906]*

*Artist: Agnes Richardson*
*Publisher: Raphael Tuck*
*Ser. 3447*
*Once Upon a Time Series II*
*[1923]*

*Artist: Charles Folkard*
*Publisher: A&C Black*
*Ser. 80*
*Alice in Wonderland [c.1924]*

*COLUMN 3*

*Artist: Agnes Richardson*
*Publisher: Wildt & Kray*
*No. 5231 [c.1926]*

*Artist: Ethel Parkinson*
*Publisher: CW Faulkner*
*Ser: 915F [1909]*

*Artist: Ethel Parkinson*
*Publisher: CW Faulkner*
*Ser: 1674 [1919]*

*COLUMN 4*

*Artist: Ethel Parkinson*
*Publisher: CW Faulkner*
*Ser: 734F [1907]*

*Artist: Linda Edgerton*
*Publisher: A Vivian Mansell*
*Ser: 1067 [1917]*

*Artist: Florence Hardy*
*Publisher: CW Faulkner*
*Ser: 1399 [1914]*

[to Miss Tiny Lintott]
I hope you are getting on well. I am sending you & Patsie the same post card as I would not like you to think that hers was nicer than yours. Much love & a large hug from Patsie's Mummy. [29.6.26]

[Miss Edna Maude Bingham]
Poor Tommy, if he had gone to your school he would have learned more. Love APH. [05.08.22]

What do you think of this funny PC? I am sending you a monkey next week & you will have to give him some food as he will be hungry. From Laddie with love. [1907]

[to Miss Nan Evans] Dear Nan
I am seriously annoyed with you. Please don't write to me again. Fond love Annie. [21.08.08]

[to Angela Carmen Hathaway]
So glad to hear you have an Oxo dolly, also that you like your frock. Please thank Mummie for her letter & I will write soon. Much love Grannie. [9.07.25]

[to Miss DM Easton]
My dear Dol. Did you ever see any funny fish like this at Barmouth? When Betty comes home perhaps she would read to you about them, for I think she has the book. I hope you are enjoying finding Teddy Tail & Kitty Puss still. Lots of love from Auntie Alice. 16.11.30

[to Mr K Wells]
If you were a piper's son you would have to dress like Tom. I think Josie would like to dance with one of the rabbits. It would be very nice to see you all Monday next. [5.07.28]

[to Captain Holmes]
Delighted I'm sure! May Morrie come too? Hope you & mother are keeping well. Nellie.

[to Miss Ivy Treagues]
Dear Ivy
Ralph thanks you very much for the pencil box. He loves it & works hard at the pencil sharpener. We wish you a Happy Xmas. Yours FGB. [22.12.30]

[to Miss Walpole]
Dear C
Eight Little Dutchies. Mrs P is boiling Xmas puddings this evening – Friday. It looks like Xmas doesn't it? [30.11.07]

[to Miss Lorna Rolfe]
When you get this you must sing for your supper like I used to when you fed me with lots of bread & butter. Do you remember when I sat on Mummy's bed one night? Lots of love Auntie Jan. [1.2.21]

[to Mrs Weaver]
Come over Sunday afternoon if possible. I have some important & bad news to tell you. Love E. [1914]

# A prelude to the postcard

Illustrated picture postcards first appeared towards the end of Queen Victoria's reign. Industry was expanding rapidly and the population was on the increase. There was peace at home, middle-class prosperity and a growing sense of confidence amongst the people, creating an atmosphere in which art and design could flourish.

The years of Art Nouveau, Realism, Impressionism and Naturalism had made their mark in art around the turn of the century. The great diversity of styles and subject matter in painting meant an increasingly decentralised art world, leading to a wider patronage. The new machine age, which began in the latter part of the Victorian era, brought with it a rapid advance in printing techniques, and constant improvements in printing processes, which meant that high quality colour printing was now available to a mass market. The great works of art, once accessible only to wealthy patrons, were now reproduced for all but the very poorest in our society.

The Victorians were proud of their artistic heritage. Artists were well schooled in drawing and painting techniques, fastidious about fine detail and the handling of a rich colour palette. Confident in their ability, artists developed a visual language accepted by people of widely differing social and educational backgrounds.

### Advances in printing techniques

Although advances in photography took work away from many artists, colour printing more than made up for this loss by providing new media outlets. Mass produced greetings cards and picture postcards are just two examples of new media created by the printing boom in the latter part of the nineteenth century.

In children's literature, the improved colour printing techniques provided illustrators like Kate Greenaway (1840-1901) and Walter Crane (1845-1915), with opportunities to create their classic children's books in high quality colour, a far cry from the black and white wood blocks or the crudely coloured illustrations which had previously accompanied children's stories. These fine artists and their peers whetted the reader's appetite for more. The Edwardian era saw an explosion of beautifully printed and bound illustrated books – the special limited editions illustrated by Arthur Rackham, Kay Nielsen, Edmund Dulac and others, that are treasured today.

### An era of change

The expansion of communications via road, rail and sea made it easier for artists to receive their training on the continent if they wished. They were also able to live and work outside London and yet retain their

*LEFT HAND PAGE*

*Below left:*
*Artist: Anon*
*Pub: Anon*
*Schneewittchen und die 7 Zwerge*
*(Snow White and the 7 Dwarfs)*
*Card no. 3514*
*[1899]*

*Above left & right:*
*Artist: Anon*
*Pub: Anon*
*Herbst/Sommer*
*(Spring/Summer) [2 of 4]*
*Card nos. 14465 / 14484*
*[1901]*

*Below left & right:*
*Artist: Anon*
*Pub: T Stroefer*
*Aquerelle Postkarte Serie IV*
*Nos. 310 / 312 (Kinder)*
*[1900]*

*RIGHT HAND PAGE*

*Left column:*
*Artist: Anon (English)*
*Pub: Misch & Stock*
*Series 125 [2 of 6]*
*Buds & Blossoms*
*[1904]*

*Centre column:*
*Artist: Anon*
*Pub: CW Faulkner*
*Series 326 [2 of 6]*
*[1903]*

*Right column:*
*Artist: Anon*
*Pub: Millar & Lang*
*National Series [2 of 4]*
*[1902]*

ROSES.

Ride a Cock-horse to Banbury Cross.

CORNFLOWERS.

It's very nice.

popularity by exhibiting regularly at the increasing number of galleries and exhibitions made available to them by the expanding art market and the patronage of the emerging art societies.

The first illustrated postcards depicting popular children's themes appeared in Germany around 1898. Others soon followed, but unfortunately they were usually unsigned, so the names of many of the talented artists who created them are likely to remain unknown.

European artists like Alphonse Mucha (1860-1933), Henri Cassiers (1858-1944) and Raphael Kirchner (1876-1917), who had done so much to develop poster art, were among the first to attract the attention of the British public with their lively and colourful postcard imagery.

Colourful and picturesque postcards flooded into the country from abroad and British manufacturers found it hard to compete with the continentals on level terms. They maintained that they could not create the same pictorial impact on the 'court sized' card, 4½" x 3½", which had been allowed in England since 1895.

There was a public outcry for change and in 1899, legislation was passed to permit private manufacturers to produce cards up to 5½" x 3½", the maximum size permitted by the European Postal Union.

The craze for postcards was just part of an enormous change in society. The death of Queen Victoria in 1901 heralded a new beginning. The Edwardians abandoned Victorian formality to indulge their tastes for the splendid and extravagant. Mass travel, foreign holidays, greater mobility and the emergence of large department stores belonged to the Edwardian era. People had little time for social graces such as letter writing and welcomed this informal way of keeping in touch with friends and family at half the cost of sending a letter. These rapid changes were noted by a perceptive contributor to *Girls' Realm* in 1900, who commented: *"The picture postcard is a sign of the times. It belongs*

*to a period peopled by a hurried generation which has not many minutes for writing to friends. What with the express trains going at a mile a minute, with telegrams and telephones, the world has become a small place. We go all over it, we have acquaintances in all parts of it. When we rush from Rome to Paris, do the galleries of Italy in one week and those of Holland the next, fly off to the Holy Land and take in Mount Olympus on our way, how can we pause to do more than send a signal of safe arrival and a sign of remembrance to our numerous acquaintances? The picture postcard is with us. It suits us. It meets our needs. It helps us to keep in touch with those we have left behind and gives them a glimpse of the places that for the time being form the background of our lives. I can imagine a future generation building up by their help all the life of today - our children, our pets, our adventurous youths, our famous old people, our wild and garden flowers, our outdoor delights, our life of sport, and our life of stress and strain, our national holidays, our pageants, and traces of the drama of our political life, are all to be found thereon."*

## Postcard legislation and the postal services

The British Post Office lagged far behind its European counterparts in permitting picture postcards to be sent through the post. At first, handwritten messages were barred from the address side of the picture postcard. Then, in 1902, an Act of Parliament was passed which proved to be the catalyst which pre-empted a picture postcard explosion. The Act permitted the writing of messages on the back of postcards. It stipulated five words only at first, but soon that rule was relaxed and the floodgates opened to set in motion a craze that gripped the nation for the first two decades of the twentieth century.

The popularity of postcards was supported by a highly efficient postal service. Up to six deliveries per day were not unusual and a card posted at any UK location was ensured delivery within twenty four hours. One could expect a

card posted in London in the morning to arrive at its destination in the afternoon, enabling people to inform friends and relatives of their imminent arrival with confidence . *"I shall be arriving on the 3.15 train this afternoon"*, was not an uncommon message.

The variety of picturesque themes available made collecting postcards as popular as sending them. For a few pence a beautifully printed picture postcard could be purchased, from fine art reproductions to bathing belles; from rustic scenes to ribald humour; artistic landscapes, animal and flower studies, stage celebrities, heraldry, transport, shipping, railways, glamour, woven silk designs and of course, traditional children's themes – the list is endless.

## Postcards and advertising

Sir John Everett Millais (1829-1896) was held in high esteem by many of his peers and had earned his reputation as a very popular genre artist and painter of children. One of his most famous pictures, *Bubbles*, painted in 1886, caused a sensation. It was bought by Pears, manufacturers of soap products, who realised the huge commercial potential in children's art. Somebody in the company had the idea of adding a small bar of soap in the foreground of the picture, and asked a disgusted Sir John to undertake the task. The picture was transformed instantly into a universally familiar advertisement. Following this success, Pears seized the opportunity of applying Millais' creation to a range of other advertising media, including the popular *Bubbles* picture postcard.

Many publishers and manufacturers, recognising the popularity of nursery themes in children's books, began to market a wide variety of high quality nursery items, from paper ephemera and greetings cards to building bricks, china, fabrics, furnishing and consumable products. Unwittingly, *Bubbles* demonstrated the power of the picture postcard as a medium for advertising children's products.

"BUBBLES."
By Sir John Millais, Bt., P.R.A.
After the Original in the possession of Messrs. Pears

OLD MOTHER HUBBARD SHE WENT TO THE CUPBOARD,
TO GET HER POOR DOGGIE A BONE,
BUT WHEN SHE GOT THERE THE CUPBOARD WAS BARE,
AND SO THE POOR DOGGIE HAD NONE.

Above left:
Artist: Joyce Mercer
Adv: Pascall Broadway Toffee
[1921]

Below left:
Artist: Phyllis Cooper
Adv: Ovaltine
No. P118 [1 of 6] [c.1924]

Above centre:
Artist: Linda Edgerton
Adv: Robinson's Groats
[1 of 6] [1920]

Below centre:
Artist: LEF
Adv: Wright's Coal Tar Soap
[1 of 5] [1903]

Above right:
Artist: Anon
Adv: Price's Candles
[c.1912]

Below right:
Artist: Anon
Adv: Price's Regina Shaving stick
[c.1915]

LEFT HAND PAGE

Above:
Artist: Sir John Everett Millais
Adv: Pears Soap
Bubbles
[c.1907]

Below:
Artist: John Hassall
Adv: Henri Nestlé
[c.1905]

# Advertising books with postcards

As well as being used as an advertising medium to help sell general products, publishers used postcards to promote books, ranging from the highest quality 'gift books' to run-of-the-mill volumes. Here are a few examples.

Postcards of illustrations by the great twentieth century illustrator Arthur Rackham were published by Heinemann to promote their expensively produced 'gift books' *Rip van Winkle* (1905), *Alice in Wonderland* (1907) and *A Midsummer Night's Dream* (1908). Two of the three cards shown here have standard pre-printed names and addresses of two major London retail outlets printed on the backs, namely, *The Times Book Club* and *Mudie's Select Library*. This suggests that Heinemann distributed the cards to the retailer, who in turn enclosed the postcards in mailings to their customers, to elicit book orders.

It is interesting to note that the illustration of *The Mad Hatter* in the *Alice in Wonderland* postcard, is a remarkable self-caricature of Arthur Rackham himself.

In 1909 Harrap published the *Rubaiyat of Omar Khayyam* illustrated by Willy Pogány (1882-1955), the Hungarian illustrator, who arrived in England *en route* to America in 1905 and stayed for ten years. Publication of the book was accompanied by a blaze of publicity, including decorative calendars published by Liberty & Co and a set of twelve duotone postcards issued by the publisher.

Publishers Wells, Gardner & Darton used postcards to promote their books – *The Children's Poets*, (a set of six postcards) *The Railway Children* by E Nesbit and *Plants We Play With*, written and illustrated by HR Robertson are shown here.

It is not uncommon for publishers to issue postcards from their books. Several illustrations from books by Dorothy Wheeler and Charles Folkard were issued in *Black's Beautiful Postcard's* series, while all except one of the postcard illustrations by Henriette Willebeek le Mair, published by Augener, can also be found in her books.

"ANIGHT MY SHALLOP, RUSTLING THROUGH
THE CITRON-SHADOWS IN THE BLUE."
*From "Tennyson"
in the Children's Poets.*
*(Wells Gardner, Darton & Co. Ltd.)*

"*The engine-driver took the little engine and looked at it.*"

### The Railway Children.
By Mrs. E. NESBIT. Illustrated by CHAS. E. BROCK. Large crown 8vo, cloth, 6/- Uniform with "Oswald Bastable and others."
"Mrs. Nesbit has never written a better story than 'The Railway Children.'"
—*Punch.*

London : WELLS GARDNER, DARTON & Co., Ltd.

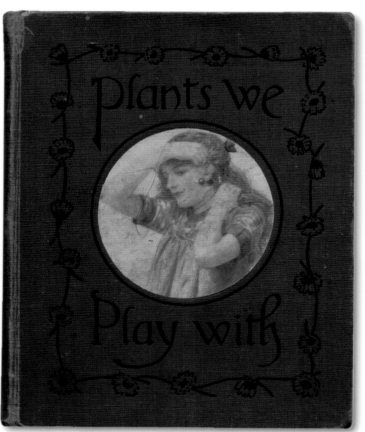

Plants We Play With *by HR Robertson [nd]*

LEFT HAND PAGE

*Above left:*
*Artist: Norman Ault*
*Pub: Wells, Gardner & Darton*
*The Children's Poets, 'Tennyson'*
*[1 of 6]*
*[nd]*

*Below left:*
*Artist: Charles Edmund Brock*
*Pub: Wells, Gardner & Darton*
*The Railway Children*
*[1907]*

*Above right:*
*Artist: HR Robertson*
*Pub: Wells, Gardner & Darton*
*The Plants We Play With*
*[nd]*

RIGHT HAND PAGE

*Top row:*
*Artist: Willy Pogány*
*Pub: Harrap*
*Rubaiyat of Omar Khayyam*
*[3 of 12]*
*[nd]*

*Below left:*
*Artist: Arthur Rackham*
*Pub: Heinemann*
*Rip Van Winkle*
*[c.1908]*

*Below centre:*
*Artist: Arthur Rackham*
*Pub: Heinemann*
*Alice in Wonderland*
*[c.1908]*

*Below right:*
*Artist: Arthur Rackham*
*Pub: Heinemann*
*A Midsummer Night's Dream*
*[c.1908]*

And when the Angel with his darker Draught
Draws up to Thee—take that, and do not shrink.

And as the Cock crew, those who stood before
The Tavern shouted—" Open then the Door ! "

Indeed the Idols I have loved so long
Have done my Credit in Men's Eye much wrong.

REDUCED FROM ONE OF 51 COLOURED PLATES IN
RIP VAN WINKLE
ILLUSTRATED BY ARTHUR RACKHAM, R.W.S.
PUBLISHED BY WM. HEINEMANN. PRICE 15s. NET

REDUCED FROM ONE OF 13 COLOURED PLATES IN
ALICE IN WONDERLAND
ILLUSTRATED BY ARTHUR RACKHAM, R.W.S.
PUBLISHED BY WM. HEINEMANN. PRICE 6s. NET

REDUCED FROM ONE OF 40 COLOURED PLATES IN
A MIDSUMMER NIGHT'S DREAM
ILLUSTRATED BY ARTHUR RACKHAM, R.W.S.
PUBLISHED BY WM. HEINEMANN. PRICE 15s. NET

# The rise of women artists

### Women artists in Victorian society

There have been many talented women artists over the centuries, but only a few have been accorded the recognition they deserve. They have faced the prejudices and barriers to choice and freedom that women have had to endure well into the twentieth century.

The Victorians regarded those women artists who were serious about their work as social misfits, endangering conformity and the clearly defined perceptions of the woman's role in society. Challenging male domination was an emotive issue that faced dogged resistance.

The 1850s was a time when women were facing an uphill struggle to improve art education, gain membership to national art institutions, like the Royal Academy and secure wider opportunities to exhibit their work. Radical changes in perceptions

of the women's role in society had to be overcome before women could compete with men as professional artists.

Art training has always held the key to women's success as artists. To gain access to life drawing classes, they had to challenge established codes of feminine propriety and sexual conduct.

### Women urged not to rock the boat

The demand for women to restrict their artistic endeavours to what was perceived as naturally feminine, increased as the nineteenth century progressed. In spite of the difficulties involved, censuses of the period show that almost one third of painters, sculptors and engravers in the UK were women. Yet, their representation in galleries was minimal and they rarely received critical acclaim or recognition. The Society of British Artists was formed in 1823 and women accounted for an increasing number of its exhibitors.

However, not one woman was elected to membership until the start of the twentieth century. The creation of the New Watercolour Society in 1832 showed a slight improvement. Of the sixty five members elected, eight were women. However, since exhibition space was reserved exclusively for members, very few women artists were in a position to exhibit their paintings.

In 1856 the Society of Female Artists was founded to extend the opportunities for women which hitherto had been so difficult to come by, and to recognise both professional and amateur female artists. Nearly one hundred and fifty women artists exhibited at the Gallery in Oxford Street, London, in the first year. In the previous year just over one hundred women had exhibited at the Royal Academy, the majority in the miniature painting section which tended to be dominated by female artists.

Many women worked in watercolour, but their virtual exclusion from membership of the leading watercolour societies made it difficult for them to gain recognition in this sphere. As a result, watercolours formed the majority of the work displayed at the Society of Female Artists' rented galleries.

Approximately three hundred women showed exclusively at the Society which became a seeding ground for new talent. It's existence played an important part in the lives of women artists by providing them with an opportunity to display and sell work and from 1867, a subscription scheme was introduced to provide a fund for professional members in cases of extreme hardship. The name was changed in 1899 to its present name the Society of Women Artists.

### Fighting for the chance to compete with men on equal terms

Many young male artists started their creative lives in an artist's studio where they learned their trade in much the same way that any apprentice would learn his craft. Others learned their skills by attending an art school or academy.

*The painting celebrating its founding,* The Academicians of the Royal Academy, 1771-72, *by Johann Zoffany, shows a group of artists and male models. Neither of the two women members are portrayed. Instead they are depicted in portraits hung on the studio wall, as women were legally excluded from being part of any group which included a nude figure of either sex.*

Nameless and Friendless *by Emily Osborn in 1857 (right) illustrates the problems women artists faced when trying to make their way in the male dominated world of commercial art. The painting depicts a young woman entering an art dealer's premises in an effort to sell a painting or drawing from her portfolio. It shows the dealer studying her work with contemptuous disinterest, while the other male customers show more interest in the young woman. The painting emphasises the isolation and helplessness of the single female in the patriarchal society of the time and particularly in the art trade where the woman's role was considered to be that of the subject or muse, not the maker or purveyor of art.*

*Right: Female students in a life drawing session at the Herkomer Art School, Bushey, Herts in 1900. A few years earlier women would have been prohibited by law from drawing the male figure, even in this semi-nude state.*

Young artists were taught that figurative historical works based on biblical or classical themes were of great importance and they were trained in the art of producing such prestigious masterpieces. Women were prevented from following either of these forms of training. They were banned from life drawing classes and from studying alongside men to the detriment of their training. As a result, women were excluded from competing with male artists at the highest level. The only way a woman could improve was to arrange for costly private tuition.

The founding of many art schools in the mid-nineteenth century and women's access to professional training, led to an increase in the number of women in the graphic arts. Often, they worked together, sharing models and providing mutual support to surmount the social barriers faced by even the most determined of their number.

A few private art schools eventually offered life classes to women, but it was not until 1893 that the Royal Academy relaxed its rules pertaining to women drawing live models. Even then, models were required to be partly clothed to 'preserve the modesty and delicacy of the female artists'!

Hampered by the social climate and denied formal training, women artists had to concentrate on the less prestigious areas of art, restricting their creative talents to the 'gentler' and naturally feminine arts – watercolour, miniature painting, portraiture or embroidery.

In 1860 one Leon Legrange wrote in the *Gazette des Beaux Arts*: *"…let men busy themselves with all that has to do with great art. Let women occupy themselves with those types of art which they have always preferred, such as pastels, portraits and miniatures. Or the painting of flowers…"*

## Women, art and the family

In the past, education has been deemed less important for women than for men. Women were conceived as being morally and spiritually superior to men and their creative powers were to be directed towards rearing children. They were expected to marry and those who did not were often stigmatised. During the nineteenth century the image of the ideal family achieved great importance. The family was seen as a strong social unit where the man presided over and provided for his family, while the woman attended to the children's needs and managed the home. Husbands often deprived women of their rights of freedom and choice within marriage and expected them to conform to their stereotyped roles.

Learning to paint, draw, embroider or play the piano were just some of the social skills young women from middle and upper class families were expected to acquire. They were often taught by impoverished gentlewomen (governesses) and, unless they came from an artistic family, had little opportunity to develop those skills which were seen as merely social accomplishments and not intended as a basis for a career.

In fact, women were not expected to compete with men, they were expected to obey them and this is the basis upon which Victorian society was founded.

## A time for change

The early to mid nineteenth century saw the beginning of widespread social and economic developments. A period of educational reform for women was on the horizon and many women artists emerged – women who wished to do more than 'dabble' in the arts. Many wanted to make significant contributions to literature and art. Other talented artists saw it as a way of earning a living – as a job on which their very lives depended.

By the latter half of the nineteenth century, wars had left many women without potential partners and women of marriageable age outnumbered men. Families could no longer afford to support dependent female relatives and unmarried or widowed women were forced to support themselves.

*Olive Hockin (1880-1936) was a fine painter of landscapes and writer of children's stories and a close friend and inspiration to the well-loved children's illustrator Anne Anderson.*

*Olive studied at the Slade School of Fine Art – an assertive woman holding feminist beliefs. Around the time of World War I, the struggle for female suffrage became so strong that Olive gave up painting to fight for the cause.*

When educational reforms eventually began to take place, reactionary voices still surfaced, maintaining that too much learning decreased femininity and that employment for women spelled unemployment for men.

Outmoded rules denying women parity in art training were gradually relaxed, so they could compete on a more equal basis. Amid growing confidence, more and more committed women artists chose to pursue careers in art at the expense of their domestic roles, leading the way for others to follow.

Greatly improved printing techniques that took place towards the end of the nineteenth century, enabled Kate Greenaway to enjoy success as the first universally popular children's illustrator. She inspired other women like Hilda Cowham and Mabel Lucie Attwell to carve out successful careers in commercial art and so a chain reaction began.

Streamlining printing and production processes meant more newspapers, books, magazines, annuals, greetings cards, postcards and games for children. This in turn created an explosion of full-time and part-time job opportunities in commercial art, that women were not slow to recognise.

Children's books and greetings cards provided a popular new medium for many artists and miniaturists whose art careers were put in jeopardy by the emergence of photography. It provided opportunities for women who wished to illustrate part-time, combining work with domestic duties.

Events took place in the eighteen nineties, like regular competitions in the applied arts run by *The Studio* magazine, which many young female artists entered as an early step in their professional careers.

For many, children's illustration was an introduction to the commercial world. A fee of two to three guineas for a set of six postcard illustrations, including forfeit of copyright, was an attractive proposition for young women artists or those women at home with a family.

Children's illustration was a sector in which women had the potential to excel.

One widely accepted view of the time was quoted by the editor of *Girls Realm* in 1903: *"There must be some inherent quality in women which makes them so peculiarly happy and successful in that little corner of art which covers the picturing of toy and children's books. Is it, I wonder, some fairy mixture of imagination and motherliness, touched with the dexterity of the artist, that helps them not only to realise but also to depict those things that most readily appeal to the heart of the child?"*

While this may have been partly true, due to the prevailing attitude, it is more likely that practical considerations were paramount and this was the type of commission most easily found by young women who needed to earn a living.

It is a curious paradox that it is male illustrators, like Arthur Rackham, Edmund Dulac and the Robinson brothers whose names are most familiar to us. These fine artists built their reputations on creating expensive 'gift' books targeted at adults. Yet, for all their skills of draughtsmanship, it has been mainly women artists, with their innate understanding of childrens' desires, who have created the styles and fashions in children's art through the twentieth century.

Publishers are partly to blame for the anonymity of most of their artists. They did little to promote them, and in turn, the artists considered themselves lucky to be allowed to sign their work.

As women's suffrage and the feminist movement gathered pace in the nineteen twenties, the tide of social acceptance turned and new fields of creativity were opened up for women artists.

Art is an all-consuming passion for the committed and most women were still constrained by their sense of deep-seated guilt for fear of neglecting their domestic responsibilities in favour of their careers. Many of the women featured in *Postcards from the Nursery* chose not to marry. With a few notable exceptions, the majority of those who did, discovered how incompatible a career in illustration and the management of household duties can be.

Those women with sufficient courage, achieved success in the art field against all odds, with a mixture of talent, skill and perseverance, unaware of one anothers' efforts or of the effect they would have on future generations. The images they created remain in our memories, but until today, many of those illustrators have remained unheralded.

*Left: After World War I, many women growing in self-confidence like Eileen Hood, the animal painter, actively sought work, either by responding to advertisements or writing to publishers and agencies. Many summoned up the nerve to hawk their portfolios around the premises of potential clients, demonstrating a great deal of perseverance and commitment and risking regular rebuttal.*

# Popular children's themes

*LEFT HAND PAGE*

*Artist: Ethel Parkinson*
*Pub: CW Faulkner*
*Ser. 580F*
*[1905]*

*RIGHT HAND PAGE*

*Above left:*
*Artist: Anon*
*Pub: W&AK Johnston*
*Series 81/1 [1 of 6]*
*[1903]*

*Above right:*
*Artist: Anon*
*Pub: Misch & Stock*
*Series 122 [1 of 6]*
*Cradle Songs*
*[1903]*

*Below left:*
*Artist: Anon*
*Pub: Delittle, Fenwick & Co*
*Series 31 [1 of 6]*
*Nursery Rhymes*
*[1903]*

*Below right:*
*Artist: Anon*
*Pub: W&AK Johnston*
*Nursery Rhymes*
*Series 81/3 [1 of 6]*
*[1903]*

It is difficult to think of a subject which does not appear on postcards – the list of themes is endless. Publishers of children's postcards covered all the best loved children's themes imaginable; nursery rhymes, games and pastimes, scenes from fairyland and more, as we shall discover.

Pictures are of paramount importance in books for the very young as Iona and Peter Opie observe in *The Oxford Dictionary of Nursery Rhymes: "When reading to our children we have repeatedly found that a rhyme in a nursery rhyme book is uninteresting to a child unless it is accompanied by an illustration. The child looks at the sea of print and says 'Nothing on that page', meaning that there are no pictures on that page, so he turns over until he comes to a picture."* So what could be better than a beautiful illustration on a picture postcard, accompanied by a short rhyme or message, to attract a child?

## Nursery rhymes

Nursery rhymes were handed down by constant repetition from generation to generation. Although books of infant rhymes had been published during the eighteenth century, the first comprehensive collection of nursery rhymes was *The Nursery Rhymes of England* by James Halliwell in 1842, followed by his *Popular Rhymes and Nursery Tales* in 1849. These volumes and others that followed were illustrated with wood or steel engravings, often hand coloured. However, the introduction of colour printing on a commercial scale gave illustrators scope and freedom to develop more varied and inventive styles and techniques to reinvigorate the traditional nursery rhyme imagery.

When picture postcard publishers started to think seriously about themes to capture a child's imagination, it comes as no surprise that they should have chosen the nursery rhyme – an important feature in the traditional language of childhood. Original and worthy themes for children's

projects are always emerging, but none has eclipsed the traditional nursery rhyme for popularity. It is a theme that has been instilled into all of us from an early and impressionable age.

At the turn of the century, nobody knew whether postcards for children would catch on in the same way as view cards, fine art, landscapes and military themes had done. Many publishers like Raphael Tuck, Valentines of Dundee, Delittle & Fenwick and Ruddock issued perennial favourites – nursery rhymes and fairy tales, in their early attempts to test the reactions of the younger market.

## Fairy tales

Fairy tales have been handed down by word of mouth over the years, their origins often blurred and indistinct through the passage of time. Their popularity was established by Charles Perrault (1628-1703), the Brothers Grimm (1785-1863 and 1786-1859), Hans Andersen (1805-1875) and others who collected and compiled the early fairy tales and anthologies.

The Victorians particularly liked mystical tales. The introduction of high quality colour printing towards the end of the nineteenth century increased their interest. and enabled more illustrators to add to a heritage of rich and varied fairy tale imagery. Ever since, the magic and enchantment that fairy tales contain has captured the imagination of children the world over.

The first illustrator to popularise the Brothers Grimm was George Cruikshank (1792-1878). His illustrations of Grimm's *German Popular Stories* 1823 introduced elves, fairies and goblins into English children's literature.

Traditional fairy tales were regarded as instructive as well as entertainment for children and their parents. Victorian parents placed a great deal of importance on 'moral values' – a subject that features in GK Chesterton's *All Things Considered* 1908: *"If you really read the fairy tales, you*

*will observe that one idea runs from one end of them to the other – the idea that peace and happiness can only exist on some condition. This idea which is the core of ethics, is the core of the nursery tales".*

Such was the popularity of fairy tales during the nineteenth century that traditional tales were staged as Christmas pantomimes and used as themes for toys and games. Nursery rhymes and fairy tales became trade marks for nursery ware and began to appear on every ephemeral item imaginable, from china to fancy tins and boxes, greetings cards, colourful scraps and picture postcards.

The fairy tale theme, with its sense of mystery and enchantment, is one of our favourites. The examples shown opposite, along with others that appear in the book, epitomise the range of styles and wealth of imagery to be found in postcard illustration.

## Fairyland

Victorian Britain was enchanted by the concept of fairyland. There were several eminent romantic and fairy painters who drew their inspiration from many quarters. William Shakespeare's *A Midsummer Night's Dream* and *The Tempest* and Edmund Spenser's *Faerie Queen* provided a rich source of subject matter. The theatre, pantomime, opera, and in particular, romantic ballet wielded a huge influence on artists of the day. The ballerina, clothed in white, sensually wafting across a stage, amidst spellbinding and ever-changing scenery filled the imagination with flights of fancy. Famous theatrical productions of *The Tempest* record Ariel astride a dolphin and riding on the back of a huge flying bat and the stage filled with all manner of elves and fairies.

The most influential contributory factor was the dawn of spiritualism in the middle of the nineteenth century. People craved escape from the drudgery of everyday hardship. Many resented the inexorable march of scientific discovery,

Merry & Christmas Greetings. The Sleeping Beauty

PUSS IN BOOTS

The Yellow Dwarf.

The Yellow Dwarf was a doubtful friend
He caused two lovers untimely end
And from their graves, in wind and weather,
Two fair trees grew and mingled together.

HANS ANDERSEN'S FAIRY TALES.
"THE LITTLE MATCH SELLER".
BEST WISHES FOR A HAPPY XMAS

LEFT HAND PAGE

*Above left:*
*Artist: Anon*
*Pub: Raphael Tuck*
*Christmas 8097 [1 of 6]*
*[1905]*

*Above right:*
*Artist: Anon*
*Pub: W&AK Johnston*
*Fairy Tales [1 of 6]*
*[1903]*

*Below left:*
*Artist: Anon*
*Pub: Misch & Stock*
*Series 120 [1 of 6]*
*Fairy Tales & Pantomime Stories*
*[1903]*

*Below right:*
*Artist: Sydney Carter*
*Pub: Hildesheimer & Co*
*Hans Andersen's Fairy Tales*
*[1 of 6]*
*[1903]*

RIGHT HAND PAGE

*Above left:*
*Artist: Walter Crane*
*Pub: Gesch (European)*
*No. 1350*
*[1900]*

*Above right:*
*Artist: Margaret Tarrant*
*Pub: CW Faulkner*
*Series 923F [1 of 6]*
*[1909]*

*Below left:*
*Artist: Fred Spurgin*
*Pub: Raphael Tuck*
*Oilette Series 3032*
*In Fairyland [1 of 6]*
*[nd]*

*Below right:*
*Artist: HGC Marsh*
*Pub: CW Faulkner*
*Series 1400 [1 of 6]*
*I do Believe in Fairies*
*[1914]*

felt stifled by religious dogma and were confused about changing attitudes towards sex. The Romantic and Pre-Raphaelite movements in art were manifestations of these concerns. People wanted to believe in the existence of fairies and so developed an insatiable appetite for the supernatural. Spiritualism enabled painters to draw inspiration, not only from the theatre and literature, but from the newly discovered passion for the supernatural and the unseen.

In the work of John Anster Fitzgerald (1823-1906), one can see the birth of flower fairies, as in *Fairies in a Bird's Nest* c.1860. Richard Doyle's (1824-1883) *Under the Dock Leaves: An Autumnal Evening's Dream,* 1878, combines a naturalistic woodland setting with a stream of delicate ethereal fairies drifting across the foreground, a scene popular with twentieth century children's illustrators. *Elves and Fairies: A Midsummer Nights Dream* 1856, by John Naish (1825-1905), depicts fairies with butterfly wings and an elf riding a moth amongst brilliantly coloured geraniums. Surely this was a picture from which later illustrators like Helen Jacobs, Hilda Miller and Millicent Sowerby drew inspiration. Naish had Pre-Raphaelite leanings as did Sowerby's father, illustrator John G Sowerby.

One of the most important originators of fairy art in this country was William Blake (1757-1827). His was the notion of equipping fairies with diaphanous butterfly wings, a concept harking back to the winged Psyche in ancient Greek vase paintings. Later, Victorian painters, including Richard Dadd (1817-1886) and Dante Gabriel Rosetti (1828-1882), reinforced the concept of the gnomes, goblins and winged fairies to a point where it was difficult to deny their actual existence.

However, fairy painting went out of fashion towards the end of the nineteenth century. Although examples of fairy tale imagery are plentiful, there is a paucity of of fairies in books and on postcards through the Edwardian era. It was not until the first and perhaps the greatest

Poppy

Each flower has its leaf, each bird has its mate
I'm lonesome; here's hoping I've not long to wait!

FORBIDDEN FRUIT.

*Fairy Frolic.*

The Duet.

twentieth century book illustrator, Arthur Rackham (1867-1939), explored the theme, that their popularity returned.

Rackham's work had a tremendous impact on many illustrators following in his wake. His unique qualities lie in his ability to create a strange mix of reality and fantasy which imbue the illustrations with a hypnotic and evocative power. His fairy subjects executed with deft draughtsmanship, often depict shadowy imagery, spiky trees with gnarled features resembling witches and grotesque and mischievous goblins; a recipe that is bound to strike fear and excitement into the hearts of his readers. He recaptured the essence of the great Victorian fairy painters and their allusions to the unseen and the occult. His fine illustrations for books of fairy tales around the turn of the century reached their peak with JM Barrie's *Peter Pan in Kensington Gardens* 1906. This work set a yardstick that others followed in later years. Rackham's work was a huge influence on the Australian illustrator, Ida Outhwaite (1889-1961), whose illustrations for *Elves and Fairies* 1916, written by her sister Annie, proved to be very popular.

Further interest in fairyland was fuelled in 1920 when Sir Arthur Conan Doyle, a champion of the supernatural, publicly supported the existence of *The Cottingley*

*Fairies*, caught on camera in a Surrey garden. The faked phographs were a clever hoax, an illusion; but such a strong fairyland culture had grown up that the nation was ready to believe that there really were fairies at the bottom of their gardens after all.

Conan Doyle, son of Victorian fairy painter Charles Doyle (1832-1893) and nephew of Richard Doyle, later mounted an exhibition of his father's work in London.

In the early twentieth century, menacing gnomes and hob-goblins largely disappeared and illustrators like Cecily Mary Barker and Margaret Tarrant, concentrated on the less menacing and more decorative, gentler aspects of fairy painting. In more recent years, JR Tolkien, Maurice Sendak and Brian Froud have revived the mystery and malevolence of fairies and goblins.

**Games, pastimes and novelties**

As far back as anyone can remember, boys and girls were encouraged to play games. As well as being fun it is a natural part of the learning process – learning to mix, learning to compete and so on. Battledore and shuttlecock, hide and seek, ring-a-ring-a-roses and many more traditional games, familiar to children and parents for generations, feature prominently in the work of postcard illustrators throughout

If you want to see a fairy
You must choose a grassy mound
And sit very still and listen
Till you hear a rustling sound.

FAIRY LAMPS.

LEFT HAND PAGE

*Above left:*
*Artist: Thomas Maybank*
*Pub: CW Faulkner*
*Ser. 1323  [1 of 6]  [1913]*

*Above centre:*
*Artist: Ida Outhwaite*
*Pub: A&C Black*
*Series 71a*
*from Fairyland*
*[1931]*

*Below centre:*
*Artist: Beryl Haig*
*Pub: AM Davis*
*Fairy Whispers Series 944*
*[1 of 6]  [nd]*

*Above right:*
*Artist: Constance Symonds*
*Pub: CW Faulkner*
*Ser. 1645  [1 of 6]  [1918]*

*Below right:*
*Artist: René Cloke*
*Pub: Valentine*
*René Cloke Postcards No. 3331*
*[1 of 6]  [1936]*

RIGHT HAND PAGE

*Above left:*
*Artist: Anon*
*Pub: Raphael Tuck*
*Oilette Series 9855*
*When All is Young*
*[1 of 6]  [1911]*

*Centre left:*
*Artist: Louis Wain*
*Pub: CW Faulkner*
*Ser. 454  [1904]*

*Below left:*
*Artist: Hilda Miller*
*Pub: CW Faulkner*
*Ser. 1857  [1925]*

*Above right:*
*Artist: Hilda Dix Sandford*
*Pub: Raphael Tuck*
*Girls and Boys Come Out to Play*
*Oilette Series 9102  [1906]*

*Centre right:*
*Artist: Millicent Sowerby*
*Pub: Henry Frowde*
*Ser. Playtime  [1917]*

*Below right:*
*Artist: Reg Maurice*
*Pub: Regent Publishing*
*Ser. No 3593  [c.1922]*

A SKIPPING MATCH.

SCARLET RUNNERS.

LOUIS WAIN. Blind man's buff.

BLINDMAN'S-BUFF
Blindman's-Buff is a glorious game,- scampering wild and fast,
However you run, its all the same, you're sure to be caught at last.

Battledore and Shuttlecock.

REG. MAURICE.

HERE WE GO ROUND THE MULBERRY BUSH.

the period. Like nursery rhymes and fairy tales, images of games and pastimes are perennially popular. So, from a commercial point of view, publishers were confident of their success with a theme much loved by grown-ups as well as children.

Throughout the period, riddles, though not common, can be found on the postcard. Riddles and riddle rhymes have been part of our juvenile heritage for well over 300 years and some are known to date back to the Middle Ages. A riddle combined fun with the exercising of young minds and thus provided edification, a prized virtue around the turn of the century.

### Toys, dolls, teddy bears and amusements

By 1904 the Edwardian era was heralding a golden age for children. JM Barrie's creation of *Peter Pan*, the boy who never grew up because the spectre of adult life was less attractive than childhood, portrays a shift in attitude. Children were no longer meant to be seen and not heard. Victorian strictures were lifted and children now became symbols of innocence.

Paper engineering was at its zenith in Edwardian days. The publishers Ernest Nister and Raphael Tuck led the way in producing the most intricate of 'movable' children's books and panoramas. Transformation books, as they were called, had their origins in and were inspired by complex 'transformation scenes' in Victorian theatre, in which spectacular scenery would be rapidly transformed by elaborate stage machinery. Nister and Tuck also produced colourful embossed 'scraps' and novelty ephemera that children used with great delight to build up scrapbooks. *Father Tuck's Panorama Series* of toy booklets, just some of hundreds of their productions, featured stories of *Cinderella, Robinson Crusoe, Little Snow White,* and other fairy tale characters.

Paper dolls became more and more popular, particularly in America, following the introduction of *The Heavenly Twins* of

1893 by Raphael Tuck. Presented with fanciful names like *Lovely Lily, Fair Frances, Playful Polly* and *Artful Alice,* they are fine examples of this popular pastime where cut out models could be adorned with different changes of hats and dresses.

*Father Tuck's Panorama, Little Snow White. No. 7006 [c.1907]*

LEFT HAND PAGE

Above left:
Artist: Anon
Pub: Stewart & Woolf
Ser. 694 [1908]

Above right:
Artist: After Florence Upton
Pub: Birn Brothers
Ser. S10 [1 of 6]
[nd]

Below right:
Artist: Fritz Hildebrandt
Pub: Raphael Tuck
Oilette Series 9792
The Teddy Bear Series 1
[1909]

RIGHT HAND PAGE

Above left:
Artist: Anon
Pub: Woolstone Brothers
The Milton Dressing Figures Series
No. 602 [1 of 6]
[c.1904]

Below left:
Artist: Linda Edgerton
Pub: A Vivian Mansell
Ser. 1186 (press-outs)
Little Red Riding Hood
[1 of 6] [1920]

Above centre:
Artist: George Piper
Pub: E Mack
The Surprise Packet
Working Toy Models Series 052
No. 053 [1 of 6] [1920]

Below centre:
Artist: E Wilson
Pub: Davis & Carter
Toy Models Series E11
No. 3318 [1 of 6] [c.1919]

Above right:
Artist: William Ellam
Pub: E Mack
The National Packet
Six Mechanical Figures Series 064
No. 067 [1 of 6] [1920]

Below right:
Artist: May Bowley
Pub: Raphael Tuck
Oilette Series 3399
Toy Rockers [1 of 6]
[c.1923]

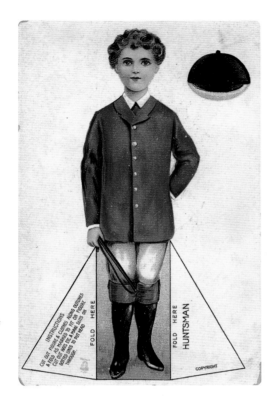

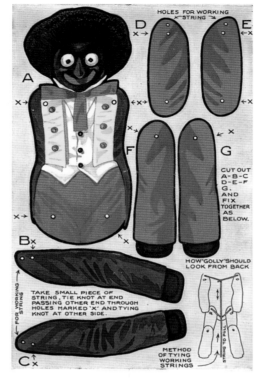

Due to the demand for paper dolls on both sides of the Atlantic, many publishers brought out sets of cut-out dressing dolls and cut-out toy models on postcards.

British toymakers enjoyed a surge in popularity at the turn of the century. Firms like Britains, Hornby and Bassett-Lowke were producing model soldiers, trains and Meccano sets. Model aeroplanes appeared on the market even before the first real plane had flown successfully.

English and American dollmakers began to compete with their German rivals and dolls' houses were mass produced along with dolls' house pieces which could be bought for a penny per item at Hamley's and many stores and toyshops up and down the country. The Golliwogg stories illustrated by Florence Upton (1873-1922), the teddy bears of the early nineteen hundreds and the 'Kewpie' all-bisque baby doll of 1912, gave rise to further popularity to be documented on postcards.

In the wake of President Theodore Roosevelt's refusal to shoot a captive bear in 1902, the first Teddy Bear was produced by an American toy company. From then on, the market has been saturated by the cuddly animal and loved by children everywhere. Many children's books have been based on toy bears – most notable perhaps is *Rupert Bear* by Mary Tourtel and to demonstrate his universal popularity, this little bear is to be found on several series of postcards published in Holland in the nineteen thirties.

### Animals dressed as humans

Animals with human characteristics have always played a part in children's literature; from tales passed down over generations to characters in today's children's books.

The Bestiaries used by monks in the fifth century, to teach spiritual truths, contained descriptions of fabulous creatures which must have enthralled and fascinated people of the period. *Aesop's Fables*, folk-lore and the old fairy tales all

include descriptions of animals or beasts with human characteristics. Over the years these mannerisms have changed in keeping with the spirit of the times, from the 'fierce bad wolf' in *Red Riding Hood* to the *Fierce Bad Rabbit* in Beatrix Potter's panorama published in 1906; from the horrifying beast in *Beauty and the Beast* to the gentle creatures drawn by Margaret Tempest for *Little Grey Rabbit* in 1929.

The symbolic qualities of animals have very ancient roots and by endowing animals with human traits their characters are altered or misrepresented; their loveable features are exaggerated and their natural wild instincts are often ignored.

*The Select Fables of Aesop and Others* produced in 1784 by Thomas Bewick, with woodcut illustrations, was the forerunner of many such books. In 1806 *The Butterfly's Ball and The Grasshopper's Feast* written by William Roscoe for *Gentleman's Magazine* and later reprinted in book form, continued the theme of creatures with human characteristics; many successors in the same genre appeared in the first part of the nineteenth century.

Walter Crane's *Nursery Pictures and Toy Books*, in the 1860s and 1870s, and *Randolph Caldecott's Picture Books* in the late 1880s followed the tradition. In America, *Uncle Remus: His Songs and Sayings*, a book personifying animal folk tales by Joel Chandler Harris was published in 1880 and appeared in England about a year later.

John Tenniel was principally a political cartoonist and was associated with *Punch* for fifty years. He had a gift for fantasy and humour which inspired the illustrations for Lewis Carroll's *Alice in Wonderland* published in 1865 and *Through the Looking Glass* in 1872. The fantasy animal characters – *White Rabbit, Cheshire Cat, Dormouse, Mock Turtle* and *March Hare* contributed to perhaps the best-loved children's book of all time. These characters have since been interpreted by many illustrators in many styles in books and on postcards, including, two sets of seven published by Fuller and

Richard in 1907, with the original Tenniel illustrations. In 1921, a delightful, but very different set, depicting Alice as a typical child of the twenties was illustrated by Kay Nixon and published by CW Faulkner from their book of the same name. In the same year, A&C Black published *Songs from Alice in Wonderland* illustrated by Charles Folkard and at the same time, published a set of 6 picture postcards in the *Black's Beautiful Postcards* series, depicting selected illustrations from the book. Folkard, a fun loving individual, created *Teddy Tail,* the mouse with the Eton collar, for the *Daily Mail* in 1915 – yet another example of the popularity of anthropomorphism and further evidence that young children do naturally identify closely with animals.

Louis Wain's cats in human guises achieved popularity on both sides of the Atlantic and postcard publishers clamoured for his services, while in contrast Beatrix Potter's gentle *Peter Rabbit*, first published in 1900, became one of the most enduring and popular characters in children's literature, but remained unpublished in postcard form until the Victoria & Albert Museum issued a selection in the nineteen fifties.

Many other notable illustrators have used the dressed animal formula with great success. Margaret Tempest's illustrations for the *Little Grey Rabbit* series have helped to sell millions of copies of the books. Lilian Govey, one of the Oxford University Press's major children's artists, illustrated such postcard series as *The Mouseykins, The Little Mouse Family, Nursery Rhymes from Animal Land* (from a book of the same name) and *Pleased to See You*, which she created in conjunction with Alan Wright, husband of Anne Anderson. More recently, Molly Brett, René Cloke and many of their contemporaries, have illustrated children's books, greetings cards and postcards depicting small furry woodland creatures playing children's games. This popular theme is best summed up in the words of Molly Brett –

*"animals doing the things that children do."*

Little Miss Muffet.

Mother Rabbit is off to the market, you see,
To buy you good wishes and much jollity.
S.H.

*LEFT HAND PAGE*

*Above:*
*Artist: Louis Wain*
*Pub: Alpha Publishing*
*No. 895 [nd]*

*Below:*
*Artist: Alan Wright*
*Pub: Regent Publishing*
*Ser. 1010*
*[nd]*

*RIGHT HAND PAGE*

*Above left:*
*Artist: Anon*
*Pub: Nister*
*No. 477*
*[c.1902]*

*Centre left:*
*Artist: Cyril Cowell*
*Pub: Bamforth & Co*
*The "Squirrelquins"*
*Series: No.1*
*[nd]*

*Below left:*
*Artist: Charles Folkard*
*Pub: Valentine*
*Valentine's Art Series*
*Teddy Tail*
*[1922]*

*Above right:*
*Artist: GH Thompson*
*Pub: T Stroefer*
*Series 965 [1 of 6]*
*[nd]*

*Centre right:*
*Artist: AE Kennedy*
*Pub: CW Faulkner*
*Series 1195*
*[1912]*

*Below right:*
*Artist: Doreen Parr*
*Pub: George Reynolds*
*In School*
*[1939]*

THE THREE LEGGED RACE.

## Humour and riddles

There's always a place for humour, although ribald humour was not well-received by Edwardian parents. Although zany things happen in traditional nursery rhymes like *'...the cow jumped over the moon',* anything less than edifying in Edwardian households was frowned upon. Humour of a more subtle kind was allowed, as were riddles, which were regarded as educational.

It was not until the much loved Mabel Lucie Attwell (1879-1964) came upon the scene that tongue-in-cheek child humour became popular, when people needed cheering up during World War I. Along with her many imitators, she became synonymous with humorous postcards, although paradoxically, she insisted that her cards were designed to appeal to adults to send to adults and not for children at all. She always maintained that her chubby children were but visual metaphors and that their remarks would have passed over the heads of the innocents in the nursery.

"You would'nt know your little girlie down here."

"THE COMPLETE ANGLER."

Scouts on the Warpath—Approaching the Foe.

SORRY, I'M MUCH TOO BUSY TO WRITE

**Dutch children**

The popularity of travel and holidays abroad around the turn of the century created popular trends. Holland, one of our closest neighbours was especially popular. People began to return home with souvenirs ranging from Delft pottery to clogs and wall hangings, reminding them of their holiday in the Lowlands. This precipitated such a huge demand for Dutch pictures and postcards, that publishers imported work by authentic exponents of Dutch art and as a consequence scenes depicting Dutch children painted by British and foreign artists were plentiful between 1905 and 1910. The usual ingredients for these pictures were romantic young couples in traditional costume in typical Dutch landscape settings.

Unsurprisingly this was a favourite theme of Florence Hardy (1867-1957), whose family had a home on the Franco-Belgian border, where her father Thomas Bush Hardy painted seascapes.

ZUIDER ZEE

It is the Miller's daughter, and she has grown so dear.

My big Brother

HOLIDAY

## Seasonal festivals

All the traditional images of Christmas that we revere today came about during the Victorian era. Christmas was hailed as a time of celebration, reflection and charity and as the nineteenth century wore on celebration became more intense and the commercial aspects of Christmas came to the fore. The first 'christmas tree' was introduced in 1840 and even by 1860 images of christmas trees and santas were still rather novel.

The first christmas card is said to have been designed in 1843 by Sir John Horsley, then over the next twenty or thirty years, a thriving and profitable industry emerged. Soon, a bewilderingly large selection of card designs bedecked Victorian homes at Christmas and by 1880, the Post Office was reporting a massive increase in post at Christmastime brought about by the christmas card. By 1881 Raphael Tuck were said to have been producing around 700 different christmas card designs per annum. At that time the company was working hard to gain and increase public interest in the christmas card. In 1880 the company had launched a competition to encourage new designs and invited a panel of eminent artists to judge the entries, of which there were almost 1000. Prizes were given and Tuck were able to choose new aspiring artists to join their already eminent team of artists and ditty writers.

One writer worthy of mention is Helen Marion Burnside (b.1843). She became totally deaf at the age of twelve due to an attack of scarlet fever. She is said to have written over 6,000 christmas sentiments and birthday verses, along with stories for *Girl's Own* and *Woman's Magazine*. She also painted and exhibited a number of pictures at the Royal Academy.

Valentine cards were equally popular at that time and inevitably greetings cards for other festivals and occasions followed including Easter, New Year and Halloween, their popularity soon spreading to America and the rest of the world.

Looking back at the elaborate and intricate christmas card designs that were often produced by Victorian artists – the materials used, the paper engineering, the complex production techniques – one often wonders at the ingenuity of it all. It signified the mood of change and growing confidence of Victorian society, but the intricate designs soon became over-elaborate.

The introduction of the picture postcard as a medium for sending seasonal greetings heralded a fundamental change in design and illustration. Now, designs were to be inherently simple, forcing artists to adopt a fresh approach, concentrating on the quality of the imagery rather than overelaborate decoration and this in turn produced a wealth of fresh styles and ideas.

This new medium appealed particularly to those young aspiring illustrators who were keen to express their new artistic skills and ideas. Miniature painters too, suffering a reduction in their patronage due to the growth of photography, saw in the postcard a fresh outlet for their skills.

Christmas has always been a time for children, and publishers, recognising this, made sure that there was a wide variety of designs to suit all ages. Edwardian artists contributed greatly to today's perception of the image of Santa Claus and all the decorative trappings of Christmas. Each year Raphael Tuck, the leaders in greetings card production, selected artists they regarded as most suitable to execute designs for the juvenile market. Often, they chose Ellen 'Eddie' Andrews, sisters May and Ada Leonora Bowley and later, Agnes Richardson, to execute Christmas postcards designs, while CW Faulkner, another prominent publisher of greetings cards, regularly commissioned Florence Hardy and Ethel Parkinson from their pool of illustrators to fulfil that task. Amazingly, in the space of a small rectangle, these artists captured the essence of Christmas and this familiar imagery, still fresh and relevant today, has been passed down to us through the generations.

With loving Christmas Greetings. From H.I.R.

Christmas Greetings

A Happy Christmas

Little Snowflakes – pretty things!
Just like little Fairies' wings!
Sometimes come at Christmas,
But dear Santa Claus you know,
Never, never fails to show
His dear face at Christmas.

*LEFT HAND PAGE* (CONT.)

*Above left:*
*Artist: Anon*
*Pub: Raphael Tuck*
*Christmas Series No. 1744*
*[1903]*

*Below left:*
*Artist: Agnes Richardson*
*Pub: Raphael Tuck*
*Oilette Series C1420 [1 of 6]*
*[1924]*

*Above right:*
*Artist: Ellen Andrews*
*Pub: Raphael Tuck*
*Oilette Series C1822*
*[c.1906]*

*Below right:*
*Artist: Ivy Millicent James*
*Pub: CW Faulkner*
*Series 922B [1 of 6]*
*[1909]*

*RIGHT HAND PAGE*

*Above left:*
*Artist: Anon*
*Pub: Harrods*
*[1912]*

*Centre left:*
*Artist: Anne Anderson*
*Pub: EW Savory*
*Series 624 [1 of 4]*
*[1917]*

*Below left:*
*Artist: Florence Hardy*
*Pub: CW Faulkner*
*Series 1107 [1 of 6]*
*[1911]*

*Above right:*
*Artist: Helen Marsh*
*Pub: CW Faulkner*
*Series. 1086 [1 of 6]*
*[1910]*

*Centre right:*
*Artist: Millicent Sowerby*
*Pub: Henry Frowde*
*Happy Little People [1 of 6]*
*[1915]*

*Below right:*
*Artist: Ada Leonora Bowley*
*Pub: Raphael Tuck*
*Oilette Series 3781*
*[1910]*

Homeward.

CHRISTMAS CHEER

WINTER

TWO CAVALIERS

CHRISTMAS GREETINGS
A perfect Christmas a glad New Year.

### Patriotic postcards in wartime

A sinister aspect of picture postcards was their value as weapons of propaganda in time of war. World War I touched everyone, from the oldest in society to the very youngest. Everybody was expected to contribute whatever they could to the war effort. Many illustrators who were unable to fight were deployed as war artists, briefed to 'tug at the heart strings of society' through their artwork. They contributed by exploiting patriotic themes depicting brave little patriots expressing morale boosting and heart warming messages.

The fervour stirred up by our political leaders and the media drove many artists, who by nature were the gentlest of souls, into contributing in this way. Those who refused to do this type of work for political reasons, risked being ostracised. Those with no strong reservations and those who were politically naïve, may have been unaware of the full implications of their actions. When briefed by a publisher to illustrate a patriotic series featuring children, they may have been afraid to say 'no', for fear of being regarded as a fifth columnist or risking the loss of future business, which would almost certainly have been the case. Although unacceptable in today's society, using young children to re-enact aspects of war had public support. Uniformed flag waving toddlers could be construed as harmless

fun, but more sinister scenes showing little patriots ganging up on others, impersonating the enemy, often went too far. Children were exploited as visual metaphors to portray adult fantasies. They appeared as gallant war heroes winning girls' hearts, as Red Cross nurses, war casualties and flag waving patriots, often making jibes at conscientious objectors and those who chose not to volunteer, very much in the spirit of '*What did you do in the War, Daddy?*'

Often the couplets supporting the illustration carried a strident message:

*Tommy and Jack, two plucky British boys,*
*They share alike in courage and in toys.*
*As brave as lions and as tough as leather,*
*Brothers in arms, they'll stand or fall together.*

The order was, that in time of war, even if artists' propaganda briefing guidelines are not issued, the pervading message has to be made clear: "*We are Good. They are Bad*".

### Children's fashions

At the turn of the century, children's fashions were slow to change. Despite the Edwardians' desire to break away from the strict social régime of Victorian days, there was little liberation for the children of 1900. Girls and boys remained encumbered by dresses abounding in frills and flounces, allowing them little freedom and even less comfort. For the boys sailor suits with white duck trousers

THE HERO

Back to Blighty

Never mind! I strafed 'em!

BROTHERS·IN·ARMS
TOMMY AND JACK, TWO PLUCKY BRITISH BOYS,
THEY SHARE ALIKE IN COURAGE AND IN TOYS
AS BRAVE AS LIONS, AND AS TOUGH AS LEATHER,
BROTHERS IN ARMS, THEY'LL STAND OR FALL TOGETHER!

"A Call to Arms" at Cleveleys

BRITISH

were still in evidence well into the new century.

A postcard illustrated by Helen Jackson confirms what Graham Greene, born in 1904, wrote in his autobiography *A Sort of Life*: "*My age was then about four, and I wore a pinafore, and had fair hair falling around the neck. My elder brother with a proper masculine haircut, an adult of seven, stares fearlessly towards the box-camera while I still have the ambiguity of undetermined sex*".

Children's clothing had previously been influenced by popular illustrators of the day, like Kate Greenaway. Now postcard illustrators began to document new styles in children's clothes as they appeared. A revolution in girls' clothing was fostered by Liberty & Co at the turn of the century when they introduced the loose and unrestricting aesthetic style made up in lawns and fine cotton, but it was in the 1920s that a real change occurred.

World War I was a watershed for children's dress. Girls went into the war period still stiffly and formally attired, yet emerged in loose and easy clothes, with bobbed hair, socks instead of stockings and simple, bar shoes instead of laced up boots.

The emancipation of women led to a new freedom in their dress and this in turn led to the liberation of children from the elaborate clothes worn by an earlier generation. Hats became less popular and the introduction, in the mid-twenties, of new man-made fibres, like rayon, facilitated easy carefree fashions for the young ones.

Phyllis Cooper postcards show long waisted dresses with sashes and short pleated skirts, accessorised with a large hair bow, popular attire for young ladies at that time. This trend for comfortable, relaxed clothing continued through into the thirties. Girls wore simple yolked dresses, nursery prints or polka dots and white ankle socks, while boys wore shorts and hand knitted jerseys.

The accompanying postcards show the rapid change in styles that covered only a twenty five year time span.

WHICH HAND WILL YOU HAVE ? *Painted by Helen Jackson*

*Loving Greetings*

OFF FOR A SPIN.

"ALWITE DEARWEE I'LL BE THERE."

WE HAVE BUILT A GOLDEN CASTLE FOR THE FAIRY KING AND QUEEN, AND SOON THEY'LL COME A-RIDING UP THE ROAD ACROSS THE GREEN.

# The magic of the painting book

Publishers went to great lengths to ensure that the needs and desires of children were well catered for with novelty ideas. Cut-out postcards, gramophone record cards and jig-saw puzzle postcards were all very popular, but perhaps the most appealing by-product of the postcard was the painting book.

The postcard painting book contained a number of postcards printed in colour and outline equivalents for youngsters to paint or crayon. It was a very natural way of introducing children to colouring materials and to examining closely and observing how the pictures they loved were created.

Often compiled from postcard designs already published, thousands of different painting books were produced during the period 1900–1950, by most of the popular artists and prominent publishers.

The *Flower and Fruit Postcard Painting Book*, published in 1914 (below), contains an entry form to the *Raphael Tuck & Sons' Painting Competition for Boys and Girls and Amateurs*. The name and address of the entrant had to be filled in and pasted onto the back of the page sent in for the competition. These prize competitions were immensely popular and attracted tens of thousands of entries.

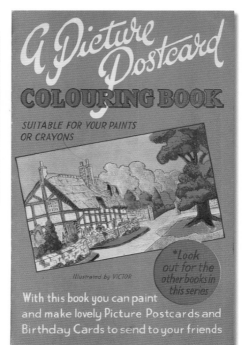

LEFT HAND PAGE

*Below left:*
*Artist: Catharina Klein*
*Pub: Raphael Tuck*
*Flower and Fruit Postcard*
  *Painting Book*
*[Flower and Fruit Series 4065]*
*[c.1913]*

*Above centre:*
*Artist: Hilda Cowham*
*Pub: Raphael Tuck*
*Father Tuck's Postcard*
  *Painting Book*
*No. 2534  [c.1907]*

*Below centre:*
*Artist: Louis Wain*
*Pub: Valentine*
*Zooland Postcard Painting Book*
*No. B494  [c.1908]*

*Above right:*
*Artist: Harry Payne*
*Pub: Raphael Tuck*
*Father Tuck's 'Patriotic' Series*
*Sons of the Sea Painting Book*
*No 3532  [c.1910]*

There's no doubt – painting books sold in their millions. In October 1914, a reviewer from the trade press enthused: *"The steadily lengthening evenings are devoted by an increasing number of children to the delightful pastime of painting, and all such are indebted to Messrs. Raphael Tuck & Sons for the charming series of Paintbox Painting books, about sixty of which have thus far been published.*

*These complete with palette, paints and brush are supplied to retail at 1/6d each. New designs are being constantly added and the collection now includes practically every conceivable subject. Each book contains sufficient colour to paint every picture in the book, so that all the little artist requires besides is a glass of water. Oval palettes are cut through the upper portion of the pages, with novel and most attractive effect, and the colours are thus ready for use, the brush being inserted in the book."*

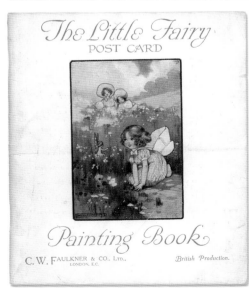

# Publishing children's postcards

Some publishers focused on specific subjects like photographic views, while others had a more general and varied list. As the demand for postcards increased, all tastes were catered for, including children.

This section is designed to provide a flavour of the world of children's publishing.

## The Art & Humour Publishing Co.

Maurice Spurgin, brother of Fred Spurgin (1882-1968) set up Art & Humour in their home town of Birmingham in 1915, as an outlet for his brother's work. Fred, real name Izydor Spungin, was of Jewish/Latvian origin. The new business freed Fred from the constraints of demanding art buyers, leaving him free to decide what to illustrate.

Prior to this venture, he had worked for Inter Art and many other publishers. He was a versatile artist with a flair for children's illustration.

Relatively quickly, The Art & Humour Publishing Company built up an extensive list of postcards and low cost annuals

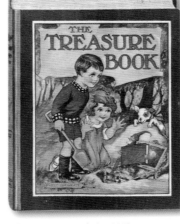

The Treasure Book *[c.1918]*

and children's books. Many of the books were designed by Spurgin himself, although another notable contributor was Gracie Marsh Lambert, who illustrated books in the *Cut-Out Series* and *Broidery Series*.

Art & Humour was especially keen on painting books, including postcard painting books, with titles like *Simple Sue & Brother Bill's Postcard Painting Book, Little Jack Horner's Postcard Painting Book* and *Funny 'ol Fings Postcard Painting Book*. The company claimed: *"Our collection of painting books has been carefully designed to appeal to all tastes and the imagination of the young mind…"*.

Humour and happiness were the corner stones of his art. Spurgin's rosy-cheeked goggle-eyed kiddies won the hearts of many but sadly not enough. The company foundered in 1924 and despite refinancing, the short-lived business finally closed down two years later.

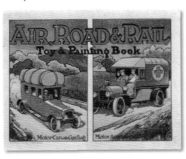

Air, Road & Rail Toy & Painting Book
*[1918]*

## Augener

Augener was a London-based music publisher run by Willy Strecker, a German, well connected with publishers in Europe. It was through one of his Dutch contacts, Nijgh & Van Ditmar of Rotterdam, that he made a chance contact with a little known twenty year old illustrator from The Hague by the name of Henriette Willebeek le Mair. They met over the co-publication of a Baby's Diary in 1910. She had not yet established herself as an illustrator of note, as this was only her second book. But Strecker took an immediate liking to her individual style that had distanced itself from the 'prettiness' of the Victorian illustrators. Through her illustration, he brought a fresh new dimension to his rather crusty music books.

Between 1911 and 1917, Henriette Willebeek le Mair designed and illustrated five important children's music books, the illustrations of which were reused in a series of small rhyme books and those in turn were also published as postcards. The relationship sadly came to an end when Willy Strecker, viewed by the authorities as an alien, was interned in 1917.

Essentially, Henriette was the only illustrator of note to work for the firm and the only reason we still remember the name of the publisher today.

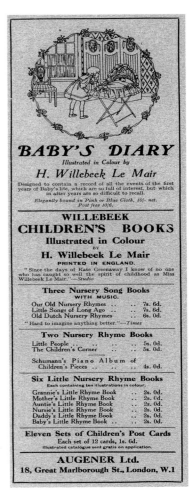

*Advertisement in* The Bookman *[1924]*

The Garden City.

I WISH YOU WERE HERE
TO FILL IT.

## A&C Black

A&C Black was founded in 1807 and has been a leader in the publication of illustrated books since the beginning of the twentieth century. Black had an impressive list that covered travel, natural history, scripture, animals & birds, flowers & gardens and juvenile books. The publication of their books was augmented by a series of picture postcards entitled *Black's Beautiful Postcards*, which first appeared around 1920. The series which was not extended after 1930, contained ninety four sets, the majority of which are painted landscapes, and are reproduced from their books. The postcards which retailed at 6d for a packet of six, also served to promote the books.

Many of Black's books for children published between 1920 and 1930, rank as classics of their time. The work of illustrators Ida Outhwaite, the Australian fairy artist, Charles Folkard of *Teddy Tail* fame and Dorothy Wheeler, noted for her illustrations of Enid Blyton's stories, all feature in the postcard series. Charles Folkard's *Mother Goose's Nursery Rhymes* (1921) is featured in series 43; Dorothy Wheeler's *English Nursery Rhymes* (1916) is featured in series 44, 44a, 45 and 45a; Folkard's *Songs from Alice in Wonderland* (1921) is featured in series 80 and *Mother Goose's Nursery Tales* (1923) is featured in series 91 (including

two designs by his co-illustrator JH Hartley. Ida Outhwaite's *Elves and Fairies* series 71, 71a, 72, 73, 74, 75, 76, 79 is comprised of pictures from *The Enchanted Forest* (1921), *The Little Green Road to Fairyland* (1922), *Little Fairy Sister* (1923), *Fairyland* (1926), *Blossom* (1928) and *Bunnie & Brownie* (1930).

Three Blind Mice

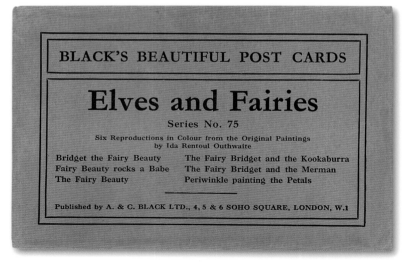

The Butterfly Chariot.

## Delittle Fenwick & Co

William Delittle and John Fenwick predicted the forthcoming boom in the postcard market and established this art printing and publishing company in 1903. They designed and printed in York, their own somewhat highly coloured and garish postcards, but the designs were eyecatching and extensively advertised. By 1904, the business had expanded so rapidly, new premised had to be found. The company specialised in art cards covering a broad range of themes including nursery rhymes, dutch dolls and fairy tales, such as those illustrated opposite.

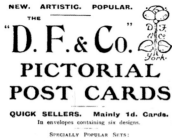

*Left:*
*Artist: Charles Folkard*
*Pub: A&C Black*
*English Nursery Rhymes*
*Series 43 [2 of 6] [c.1926]*

*Above right:*
*Elves and Fairies Ser. 75 packet*

*Centre right:*
*Artist: Ida Outhwaite*
*Pub: A&C Black*
*Elves and Fairies*
*Series 75 [1 of 6] [c.1926]*

*Below right:*
*Artist: Anon*
*Pub: Delittle Fenwick & Co*
*Ser. 37 [1 of 6]*
*Fairy Tales [1903]*

## CW Faulkner & Co

Charles William Faulkner was a sound businessman with a traditional outlook. He studied art and oil painting, before setting out on a career in fine art publishing.

As a young man, Faulkner entered the wool trade in Manchester, before joining publisher Albert Hildesheimer at Jewin Street, Aldersgate and later formed CW Faulkner & Co at the same address when the partnership with Hildesheimer was dissolved in 1895. A disastrous fire destroyed the premises in 1897 and the business was rebuilt at Golden Lane where it remained until the nineteen thirties.

The advent of the postcard occurred while the rebuilding of the company was taking place, but this did not deter Faulkner from building a team of skilled illustrators to satisfy public demand. Charles Faulkner had a keen eye for pretty young ladies and in the nicest sense, did a great deal to encourage and further the careers of the many young artists who knocked on Faulkner's door.

CW Faulkner employed many of the best loved children's illustrators at some time during their careers. The list includes: AE Kennedy, Hilda Dix Sandford, Ethel Parkinson, Florence Hardy, Sybil Barham, Gracie Marsh Lambert and Ivy Millicent James. This group accounted for over half of the total output of Faulkner's postcards aimed at a young audience. Other notable children's artists who worked for the company include Anne Anderson, Molly Brett, René Cloke, Alice Cook, Hilda Cowham, Joyce Mercer, Hilda Miller, Phyllis Palmer, Agnes Richardson, Millicent Sowerby and Margaret Tarrant. The work of these illustrators covers a broad range of themes and styles and contributed to the success of Faulkner as one of the most highly regarded fine art publishers of calendars, greetings cards, prints, books and picture postcards in the business.

Until World War I, most of Faulkner's publications were printed in Germany by the chromolithographic process. The quality of the printing and the smooth, resilient card, was exquisite. When war intervened, the company was forced to cease printing in Germany, and as British printers simply could not match the quality of their German counterparts, particularly during wartime, production standards plummeted. The former printing process using up to twenty individual colours was never viable again and although standards had improved by the mid-thirties, it was too late to halt the demise of a boom in children's postcards that had lasted for more than thirty years.

In all, Faulkner published over two thousand sets of picture postcards between 1900 and 1940, about one sixth of which was aimed at the juvenile market. As was normal throughout the trade, postcards were usually packaged in envelopes containing six different designs. Faulkner displayed the title of each set on the outer packet only. As the original packets are scarce, the record of the titles of the series remains incomplete.

*Left:*
*Artist: Anon*
*Pub: CW Faulkner*
*Unnumbered Series*
*[1903]*

*Right:*
*Artist: Florence Hardy*
*Pub: CW Faulkner*
*Series 780D*
*[1907]*

*A boatload cruising down the Thames. The annual summer outing for staff at CW Faulkner & Co [1906]*

CW Faulkner built its reputation on the production of a wide range of stationery products. Postcards were just one item in a very long list. At it's peak, around the outbreak of World War I, the company's products included, greeting cards, books, dairies, postcards, playing cards, jig-saws, a varied assortment of games, framed pictures, painting books and motto cards wedding cards, programmes, and menus.

*A set of playing cards, published by CW Faulkner in 1904 illustrated by John F Bacon.*

The company published a wide range of items for children, ranging from painting books and postcards to card games and party games. The illustrations for most of Faulkner's books, including painting books, utilise illustrations that are also published in their series of postcards.

Not Too Apparent Apparel.
*Series Q15. A Can You Solve? party game.*
*[c.1935]*

*Card games:* Fairyland Snap *and* Our Pets Snap *by AE Kennedy [c.1950]*

Peter Pan Postcard Painting Book
*by Sybil Barham [c.1918]*

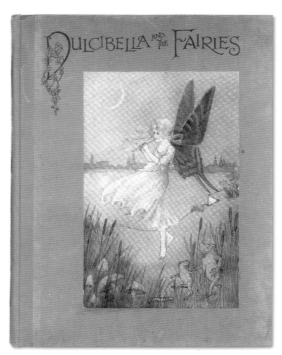

Dulcibella and the Fairies, *illustrated by Hilda Miller*
*(illustrations reproduced in postcard series 1690 and 1693)*

The Story of Fairy Bluebell *illustrated by Constance Symonds*
*(illustrations reproduced in postcard series 1645).*

*RIGHT HAND PAGE*

*Left column:*
*Artist: John Tenniel*
*Pub: Fuller & Richard*
*The Wonderland Postcards*
*Series 2 [1 of 7]*
*[1910]*

*Above right:*
*Artist: Willam Ellam*
*Pub: Gale & Polden*
*Children's Cut-Out Series*
*[c.1920]*

## Fuller & Richard

In 1910, Fuller & Richard, wholesale stationers in Windmill Street, London, published a range of children's stationery, comprising children's notepaper, invitations and postcards. Favourable reaction ensued in the trade press: *"Messrs Fuller & Richard, 41 Great Windmill Street have followed up their 'Wonderland' stationery by two packets of postcards reproducing the original designs of Sir John Tenniel to 'Alice in Wonderland'. Each packet contains seven cards and sells for 6d, so that there are fourteen of the pictures in all. The cards are antique toned boards and worked in sepia. Each illustration is accompanied by an extract in a young child's handwriting and the effect is quite natural and out of the common. Friends and confidantes of Alice are so numerous and they are so loyal to her that a considerable sale is assured to the postcards devoted to her adventures wherever they may be shown. Already the demand is large and should be greater during the Christmas season."*

*Trade advertisement for* The Wonderland Postcards. *[1910]*

*Goody Two Shoes, Fairyettes series, illustrated by William Ellam. [c.1920]*

Ernest Aris was a major contributor to Gale and Polden's children's book list. The son of artist Alfred Aris, he attended the Bradford School of Art and later, the Royal College of Art in London. He began his career as a portrait painter, but 'drifted' into commercial art and became a successful and prolific writer and illustrator of children's story books, specialising in animals. Whilst he drew humorous postcards, we have not yet identified any children's themes by him. He worked for many other publishers, notably Humphrey Milford and Partridge.

## Gale & Polden

Gale & Polden, established in 1885 and publishers of picture postcards since 1901, were connected with the armed services through James Gale, an ex naval officer and founder director of the company. Their location in Aldershot enabled them to build their business success through the contracts they won supplying print to the army. They will be best remembered for publishing outstanding military postcards by Ernest Ibbetson and Harry Payne.

Although military and aviation themes were their speciality, by 1916 they offered a large list of children's painting books, children's stories and postcards, including Hilda Cowham's *Good Old Nursery Rhymes* and a series featuring *Wee Peter Pug, Sir Timothy Tapertail, Dapple the Wooden Donkey, Woodfolk Market, Billie Rabbit, Little Miss Duck,* and *Bunnikin Brighteyes* all written and illustrated by Ernest Aris (1882-1963), the creator of hundreds of animal stories for young folk.

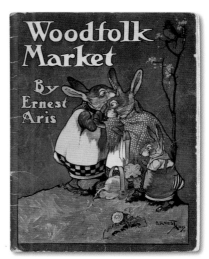

*Woodfolk Market, illust. by Ernest Aris. [1916]*

## Liberty & Co.

Liberty & Co. was established one hundred and twenty five years ago and built up its reputation by importing luxurious and exotic merchandise from the Far East. In the early years of the twentieth century Liberty sold high quality stationery, postcards, greetings cards, calendars and diaries, often decorated with eastern themes and printed onto high quality textured paper.

An extremely popular version of *The Rubaiyat of the Omar Khayyam*, illustrated by the Hungarian emigré Willy Pogany, was published in 1915 by Harrap, amidst a blaze of media hype. It was absolutely perfect for Liberty, who acquired exclusive rights to publish Pogany's Omar Khayyam pictures on a wide range of stationery items.

Hilda Miller made her reputation as an illustrator through her work for Liberty. for whom she designed postcards, greetings cards and calendars in a unique style. Her understated palette of pastel colours created an exclusivity to her designs. The children she depicted, dressed in smart fashionable clothes, emphasised the beauty of Liberty's children's garments.

*248*

USE **LIBERTY** FABRICS

(4) **CLYTHE COTTON.** A new fabric especially made to withstand hard wear and continual washing, particularly suitable for children's garments and for holiday wear. It is guaranteed fast colour and unshrinkable. In a range of new designs and colourings. 36 ins. wide. 1/11 a yard.
PATTERNS POST FREE                    LIBERTY & CO LTD REGENT ST LONDON

PUBLISHED BY LIBERTY & CO., LONDON & PARIS

BORN ON A MONDAY FAIR OF FACE

BORN ON A SATURDAY WORK HARD FOR A LIVING

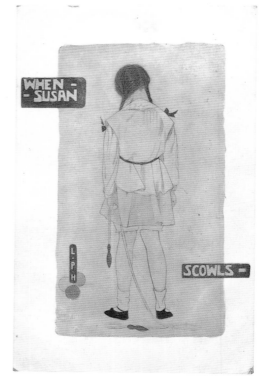

WHEN — SUSAN

SCOWLS —

LEFT HAND PAGE

*Centre left:*
*Artist: Anon*
*Pub: Liberty & Co*
*[c.1918]*
*One of a number of postcards*
*advertising fabric for children's*
*clothes.*

*Below left:*
*Artist: Anon*
*Pub: Liberty & Co*
*[c.1909]*

*Above centre & right:*
*Artist: Anon*
*Pub: Liberty & Co*
*Days of the week*
*[c.1908]*

*Below centre:*
*Artist: Anon*
*Pub: Liberty & Co*
*[c.1909]*

*Below right:*
*Artist: Lilian Price Hacker*
*Pub: Liberty & Co*
*Susan*
*[1910]*

*Above left:*
*Year book & diary*
*Artist: Willy Pogany*
*Pub: Liberty & Co*
*[1915]*

*Above:*
*Greetings card & envelope*
*Artist: Alison Atkins*
*Pub: Liberty & Co*

*Above:*
*Calendar for 1918*
*Artist: Hilda T Miller*
*Pub: Liberty & Co*
*[1918]*

*Left:*
*Postcard*
*Artist: Hilda T Miller*
*Pub: Liberty & Co*
*[c.1912]*

### Vivian Mansell

Alfred Vivian Mansell started out as a dealer in fine art. He entered the market later than most, but established his fine art publishing business in London during World War I and found a niche by publishing stylishly artistic postcards. From his Chapel Street premises came a constant stream of cards featuring beautiful gardens, royalty, greetings, children and animals. Mansell's trained eye for spotting creative talent enabled him to publish illustrated postcards, for all ages and tastes. Like any company that traded in fancy stationery, postcards, greetings cards, booklets, puzzles and games, the younger market was perhaps Mansell's main target audience.

Aided by the contacts he had built up during his time as an art dealer, he conducted a continuing search for talented artists, whose work enabled him to run a successful business through the inter-war years and beyond.

His children's illustrators included Linda Edgerton, whose naïve style appealed to the very youngest and Ethel Brisley, who had established her reputation as a portrait painter and miniaturist, having exhibited regularly at the Royal Academy, painted child studies. Ethel's sisters, Nina, a writer and illustrator of children's stories and Joyce, the creator of *Milly Molly Mandy*, illustrated children at play. Susan Beatrice Pearse, illustrator of the *Ameliaranne* stories, Hester Margetson, the daughter of painters William and Helen Margetson, Joyce Averill and Mary Horsfall made up a strong team of artists.

Despite a late entry into the fine art publishing market the company continued to publish good quality postcards through World War II.

*" I'm Coming "*

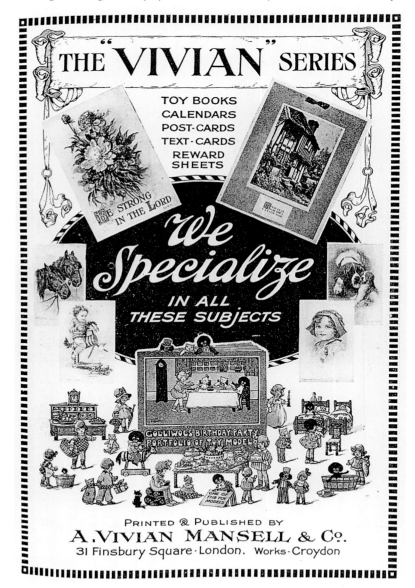

*Trade advertisement for Vivian Mansell publications [1921], featuring toy models by Linda Edgerton, the creator of several inventive sets of 'press-out' postcards for this publisher during the period.*

*Alice in Wonderland*

## The Medici Society

The Medici Society was founded in 1908 to publish at the lowest price possible a selection of accurate, direct reproductions of paintings by the great masters, obtained by 'its special method of photographic collotype in colours without screen and printed on pure hand made linen papers.' *"All subjects are chosen for their artistic value and beauty. It is part of the aim of The Society to bring together in one collection the masterpieces of painting from all over the world, so that in themselves the Medici Prints form an educational series of considerable importance, apart from their decorative appeal to all lovers of art."*

By the nineteen twenties the Society realized the need to diversify and extend their repertoire into Christmas cards and calendars, while maintaining their reputation for high quality artistic work. The nineteen thirties saw the introduction of Birthday and Easter cards as Medici realised that appealing to a young audience was becoming a source of significant revenue.

The Society had published postcard reproductions of Old Masters paintings as early as 1912 but in 1920 Margaret Tarrant, perhaps the most familiar name amongst all the twentieth century Medici illustrators, was the first of a group of young artists to provide illustrations for prints, greetings cards and postcards for children. Her favourite themes were fairy subjects, nursery rhymes, religion and young people enjoying the countryside. Her religious and fairy pictures are so familiar, they have become synonymous with the Medici Society and its guiding principles.

Other prominent illustrators made significant contributions to the Medici Society's children's list. They include Molly Brett, flower painter Hilda Coley, Muriel Dawson, Racey Helps and Margaret Tempest, who painted nursery friezes and postcards featuring rabbits, squirrels and teddy bears, but is best known for her illustrations for Alison Uttley's *Little Grey Rabbit* Series dating from 1929.

**PACKET No. 1. Price 9d.**
*also* with Birthday Greetings, No. 1 B

### NURSERY RHYMES
Pictures by MARGARET TARRANT

Jack and Jill
Blow Wind Blow
Little Boy Blue

Rock-a-bye Baby
Wee Willie Winkie
Little Jumping Joan

Little Jumping Joan

**PACKET No. 2. Price 9d.**
*also* with Birthday Greetings, No. 2 B

### MAGIC OF CHILDHOOD
by MARGARET TARRANT

A Sylvan Melody
Sea Joy
An Autumn Melody

Woodland Friends
Magic Music
The Daisy Chain

Sea Joy

**PACKET No. 3. Price 9d.**

### THE DEVOTIONAL SERIES
by MARGARET TARRANT

Love amongst the Snows
Everybody's Brother
In the quiet Night

Windflowers
Love that melts the Snow
'Thou visiteth the Earth'

Windflowers

**PACKET No. 4 Price 9d.**
*also* with Birthday Greetings, No. 4 B

### FAIRIES IN OUR GARDEN
by MARGARET TARRANT

Cherry Fairies
Snapdragon Fairies
Poppy Fairies

Honesty Fairy
Larkspur Fairy
Raspberry Fairies

Larkspur Fairy

**PACKET No. 5. Price 9d.**
*also* with Birthday Greetings, No. 5 B

### FAIRY HOURS
by MARGARET TARRANT

"Do you believe in Fairies?"
The Goblin Market
The Fairies' Market

The Gates of Fairy-
Peter's Friends [land
Fairy Secrets

The Fairies' Market

**PACKET No. 6. Price 9d.**
*also* with Birthday Greetings, No. 6 B

### FAIRIES OF THE COUNTRYSIDE
by MARGARET TARRANT

The Scots Pine Fairies
The Wood Anemone Fairies
The Pearblossom Fairies

The Gorse Fairies
The Honeybee Fairy
The Waterlily Fairies

The Gorse Fairies

**PACKET No. 7. Price 9d.**
*also* with Birthday Greetings, No. 7 B

### OUT O' DOORS
by MARGARET TARRANT

The Caravan
The Wind's Song
Dream Ships

Autumn Sprite
The Goatherd
Our Lady of the Buttercups

The Caravan

*The first seven sets of children's postcards by Margaret Tarrant advertised in The Medici Society trade catalogue [1935]*

Little Jumping Joan

Here am I Little Jumping Joan,
When nobody's with me,
I am all alone.

THE FAIRIES' MARKET
Margaret W. Tarrant

### Humphrey Milford / Henry Frowde and Hodder & Stoughton

During the reign of Edward VII, the Oxford University Press was keen to venture into children's publishing. The firm predicted a huge market for juvenile books, as several of their major publishing competitors were already enjoying a boom in the children's 'gift book' market, publishing prestigeous and beautifully bound books of fairy tales for the drawing rooms of the wealthy in Britain and abroad. These sumptuous, vellum bound volumes were illustrated and signed by the cream of British book illustrators of the day.

However, they realised that such a venture could be damaging to their reputation as serious academic publishers *par excellence*. So, they reached an agreement with Hodder & Stoughton, successful publishers of 'gift books', to create a joint publishing venture for a children's books division called Henry Frowde and Hodder & Stoughton and headed by James Elie and Charles Le Strange, recruited from publishers Blackie & Son.

Elie and Le Strange attracted artists and writers to Milford who had achieved success with Blackie – talented female illustrators like Angusine MacGregor and Rosa Petherick, who as a student, won second prize in a national competition to design a postcard, sponsored by *The Studio* in 1898.

*Rosa Petherick's prize winning postcard design in the Studio magazine competition. [1898]*

But the course of events meant that the venture did not go quite according to plan. With the euphoria of the new century fading and the prospect of instability in Europe looming, the days of the vellum bound gift book were numbered and by the time war broke out in Europe the market for expensive books had all but disappeared.

In spite of early setbacks, from 1909 the firm developed a very successful children's publishing operation, broadly divided into three categories – books for boys, books for girls and books for the very young. When Henry Frowde retired in 1913, he was succeeded by Humphrey Milford who in 1917 withdrew from the arrangement with Hodder & Stoughton, when he felt the children's publishing section of OUP was ready to stand alone. Over a thirty year period, the venture published a vast quantity of books in all shapes and sizes, ranging from miniature boxes of books to thick board, untearable panorama playbooks, annuals for all ages and adventure books for boys and girls – perhaps the most exciting children's list ever assembled.

A feature of Milford's publications was it's *Postcards for the Little Ones* series, which began under the imprint of Henry Frowde and Hodder & Stoughton in 1913 and continued under Humphrey Milford in 1917. The formula for the series was simple – to reproduce popular traditional themes, endearing to children and parents alike – rhymes, fairy tales, games and pastimes, scenes from fairyland and children's pets.

The *Postcards for the Little Ones* series, consisted of seventy four sets. Most of the sets were painted by artists whose rosy-cheeked children, blithe and carefree in idyllic settings, skilfully transporting their young audience into a fantasy world. Of the major contributors, Millicent Sowerby painted twenty nine sets in the series, Susan Beatrice Pearse, thirteen sets, Lilian Govey, six sets and Eileen Hood the animal artist contributed seven sets.

The series includes sets derived from illustrations originally commissioned for books, like *Golden Days* by Millicent Sowerby and *Joyous Days* by the Dutch illustrator, Rie Cramer. Illustrations were

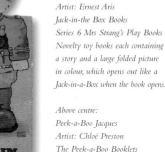

Books published
by Humphrey Milford

*Above left:*
The Tale of Jack in the Box
Artist: Ernest Aris
Jack-in-the Box Books
Series 6 Mrs Strang's Play Books
Novelty toy books each containing
a story and a large folded picture
in colour, which opens out like a
Jack-in-a-Box when the book opens.

*Above centre:*
Peek-a-Boo Jacques
Artist: Chloë Preston
The Peek-a-Boo Booklets
[c.1919]

*Above right:*
Captain Peek-a-Boo
Artist: Chloë Preston
The Peek-a-Boo Booklets
[c.1919]

*Centre:*
Lucy Locket's Play Book
Artist: Isobel Saul (cover)
Mrs Strang's Playbooks
[c.1922]

*Below left:*
Nursery Rhymes
Artist: Grace Lodge
The Tippenny-Tuppenny Books
[1932]

*Below centre:*
The Tippenny-Tuppenny Fair
Artist: Anon
The Tippenny-Tuppenny Books
[1936]

*Below right:*
Cheep-Cheep and Peep-Peep
Artist: Anon
The Tippenny-Tuppenny Books
[1931]

*Below left:*
*Artist: Susan Pearse*
*Pub: Humphrey Milford*
*Jolly Games [1 of 6]*
*[1926]*

*Above centre:*
*Artist: Ruth Sandys*
*Pub: Humphrey Milford*
*Old Street Cries*
*[1927]*

*Below centre:*
*Artist: Norman Hartridge*
*Pub: Humphrey Milford*
*A Child's Garden*
*[1924]*

*Above right:*
*Artist: Lilian Govey*
*Pub: Humphrey Milford*
*The Mouseykins*
*[1926]*

*Below right:*
*Artist: Millicent Sowerby*
*Pub: Humphrey Milford*
*Flower Children*
*[1920]*

created for at least two series of postcards which also appeared in a stiff board book entitled the *Fairy Frolic Playbook*.

Six different designs usually comprised a set which were contained in a fragile colour tinted envelope with a single colour printing on the front. Great care was taken in the preparation of the cards. Nearly all were printed in four colour letterpress with an additional gold printing for the verse and borders. Some of the sets carried two or three word captions, but the majority had four line rhyming couplets, often written by Jessie Pope, a talented children's writer, who also worked for Blackie & Son.

The *Postcards for the Little Ones* series has always been a particular favourite of ours. The style of illustrations and the images capture perfectly the atmosphere of a middle class nursery in the nineteen twenties. This beautifully produced series of around four hundred and forty cards, is a convenient size to collect and is detailed at the back of this book.

### Ernest Nister

Nister is particularly notable for its beautiful children's publications. The variety, the quality and the quantity were amazing, from transformation and 'circling surprises' books, to greetings cards, postcards, novelty items and scraps. Nister's artists attended design in all its aspects, creating imagery in a rich and colourful traditional style.

Ernest Nister, like Raphael Tuck, was a central European. It is no coincidence that through the latter part of the nineteenth century and into the twentieth century, the quality of work of both companies was exquisite: concepts, design, quality of production – everything was considered in fine detail and the end product surpassed any of their British competitors.

1n 1877, Nister had bought a small lithographic business in Nuremburg and developed it into one of the world's largest fine art printing plants in the world. He employed over 600 people deployed throughout the company – at the printing works and in the English and American publishing businesses.

Ernest Nister's obituary in 1909 reflects, *"His productions in the field of artistic printing are among the best that have appeared on the market, and through their technical and artistic perfection, have done much to build up the reputation which the firm has gained, of being one of the leading fine art publishers."* There is no doubt that the standard of chromolithographic printing in Germany was superior to anywhere else in the world at that time. Even CW Faulkner, a truly British company, was unable to achieve the printing quality in this country and was forced to go to Germany to achieve the quality to match the fine art publishers across Europe.

Nister employed many of the best writers and commercial artists of the day, although, unfortunately for latter day biographers, much of the artwork was unsigned, making it almost impossible to attribute the work. It seemed that the company's policy was to herald its publications as the work of a production team, rather than the work of individual writers and artists.

Had World War I not intervened and had the company not been forced to close in 1917 due to its German origin, would it have been able to adjust to the styles and tastes of the twentieth century? The question is hypothetical and although a vain attempt was made to reopen the business after the war, it never regained its position as one of the major forces in fine art publishing in Britain, when the hookline was: *"If anyone can do fine printing, Nister can".*

*LEFT HAND PAGE*

*Artist: Anon*
*Pub: Ernest Nister*
*No. 465*
*[1902]*

*RIGHT HAND PAGE*

*Above left:*
*Artist: GH Thompson*
*Pub: Ernest Nister*
*No. 461*
*[1902]*

*Centre left:*
*Artist: Anon*
*Pub: Ernest Nister*
*No. 459*
*[1902]*

*Below left:*
*Artist: Anon*
*Pub: Ernest Nister*
*No. 530*
*[1902]*

*Above centre:*
*Artist: GH Thompson*
*Pub: Ernest Nister*
*No. 467*
*[1902]*

*Below centre:*
*Artist: Anon*
*Pub: Ernest Nister*
*Series 200 No. 6*
*[c.1908]*

*Above right:*
*Artist: Anon*
*Pub: Ernest Nister*
*No. 331*
*[1902]*

*Below right:*
*Artist: GH Thompson*
*Pub: Ernest Nister*
*No. 415*
*[1902]*

## The Photochrom Company

The Photochrom Company, with Swiss origins, was established towards the end of the nineteenth century. The company forged its reputation with its own unique production process of 'view' postcards and by 1906 claimed to hold a quarter of a million negatives. The head office of the company, one of the most prolific of postcard publishers, was in London, but the printing works was in Tunbridge Wells, the home town of the two principals, Messrs F & A Wilde.

Photochrom published a broad range of illustrated postcards, many of which were for children. They employed many Of the best freelance artists including Mabel Lucie Attwell, Gracie Marsh Lambert, Agnes Richardson, George Studdy and Flora White and this press statement from the *Stationery Trades Journal* of October 1912 illustrates the high esteem in which the company was held. *"The Photochrom Company have just issued three sets of cards in colour by Miss Agnes Richardson, who has gained an enviable position as one of the most popular artists of the postcard world. The series are entitled* Birthday Greetings, Dutch Kiddies *and* Piccaninny Series *and they are all of and for children. In the first named set the charming little figures are the centres of pretty incidents which are daintily portrayed, while the funny groups in the others furnish a humorous contrast. There is point in all the drawings and the wording is peculiarly apt. The sets are being well taken up by the trade, and we would advise all our readers to order a supply without any delay so as not to be without some attractive cards which are bound to sell in large numbers."*

## Ruddock Limited

In its heyday, Ruddock claimed to be one of the largest publishers of view cards in the north of England and then in 1903, published a charming set of seven nursery rhyme postcards, one of the earliest series of its kind. In 1905, Boots Cash chemists bought their remaindered stock, sliced 6 mm off the cards to remove the Ruddock imprint and added their own.

LITTLE JACK HORNER.

*With fond love and good wishes for Christmas.*

**Comic Rooster.**

Cut out model and the white slots in the flaps. Carefully score and bend all dotted lines. Now lock body together by fitting the slots in the chest flaps into each other so that the black edge of each fits inside the other flap. Fold head at comb, lock it together, and fit it over neck. Fold tail, cut slot in it, and peg it on back slot. Bend feet out for a stand. —Copyright.

## Salmon of Sevenoaks

Salmon is one of the very few publishers of picture postcards established before the turn of the century and still thriving in business today. Nowadays, the firm produces a broad range of good quality gift items including calendars, greetings, picture postcards, stationery notelets and guide books.

Like many general publishers, Salmon split their postcards into three categories – 'photographic views', 'watercolours' and 'fancy' postcards. The 'fancy' series was a category covering everything except views and watercolour paintings. It comprised a broad range of themes, including postcards for children. Salmon started to include children's themes in it's 'fancy' postcard range around 1910.

Amongst Salmon's early contributors were Agnes Richardson, Gracie Marsh Lambert, Charles T Howard, Mabel Lucie Attwell and Cecily Mary Barker. But the most prolific of Salmon's children's artists was Flora White, whose work was ever present until 1935. She painted nursery rhymes, classic fairy tales, months of the year, elves and fairies, patriotic postcards and greetings postcards series of all types, many of which were extremely popular and remained in print for years.

Salmon's output of children's postcards was modest until after the first world war, by which time only about one hundred designs are in evidence. Frederick George Lewin (1861-1933), a prolific and most versatile artist, included children's themes in his vast repertoire exceeding 350 designs for Salmon alone. But like Salmon contemporaries Vera Paterson and Freda Mabel Rose, he tended to use children as a visual metaphor to amuse adults.

Salmon enjoyed close business ties with other publishers with juvenile lists – Mack and James Henderson in particular. The exact form of the relationship has not been unravelled, but a comparison of the backs of the cards of the two companies shows close similarities and it appears that the two businesses shared the same serial numbering system in part. Evidence exists that Salmon printed many of Mack's cards and possibly Henderson's too.

In 1918, Mack with its *Toy Town* series and Henderson with its *Toy Models* series published extensive cut-out series. Shortly afterwards Salmon published several amusing series of their own illustrated by WH Ellam, who had created many of the Mack cut-out cards. Furthermore, just after World War II, Salmon republished cut-out toy postcards from Henderson's *Toy Models* series – further evidence that some of the activities of the three companies may have been linked.

Salmon have always kept a keen eye on trends in public taste managing to 'move with the times' and maintain a profitable margin on picture postcards even today, where others have failed. Phyllis Palmer, René Cloke and Madge Williams worked through the war and on into the fifties, but then Salmon recruited Lorna Steele, Enid Bond and others, whose work reflected the styles of the fifties and sixties. By 1960, the company had secured postcard publishing rights to print children's TV characters Andy Pandy, Bill and Ben, Noddy and Sooty at a time when the era of heavily marketed media inspired characters was really getting underway.

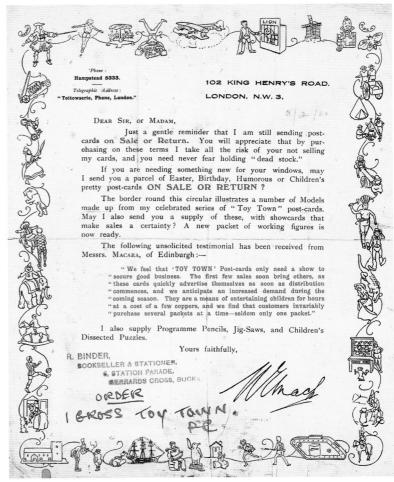

*A business link with Salmon – E Mack flyer promoting Toy Town series of cut-out postcards [1920]*

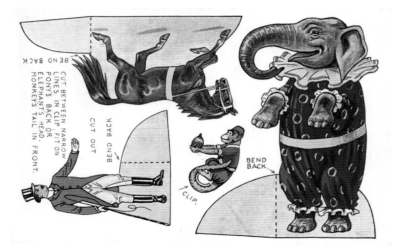

LEFT HAND PAGE

*Right:*
Favourite Fairy Tales, *by Anne Hope, illustrated by Flora White, published by J Salmon [nd]. The illustrations for this little volume are taken from the fairy tale postcard series illustrated by Flora White in 1920.*

*Below:*
Tommy Tinker and Tip-Toes *by Anne Hope, illustrated by Louis Wain. The six illustrations for this volume are taken from The Cats' Academy series of postcards, published by E Mack.*

*Left top & centre:*
*Artist: William Henry Ellam*
*Pub: J Salmon*
*Ser. 2931*
*The Children's Circus [1923]*

*Left bottom:*
*Pub: E Mack*
*Ser. 046*
*The Cats' Academy [1920]*

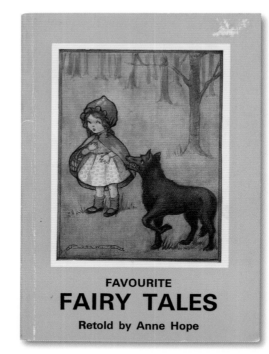

RIGHT HAND PAGE

*Above left:*
*Artist: Anne Anderson*
*Pub: EW Savory*
*Ser. 624 [1 of 4]*
*[1917]*

*Centre left:*
*Artist: Anne Anderson*
*Pub: EW Savory*
*Ser. 688 [1 of 4]*
*[1918]*

*Below left:*
*Artist: Linda Edgerton*
*Pub: EW Savory*
*Ser. 635 [1 of 4]*
*[1917]*

*Above right:*
*Artist: HGC Marsh Lambert*
*Pub: EW Savory*
*Ser. 868 [1 of 4]*
*[1920]*

*Below right:*
*Artist: Linda Edgerton*
*Pub: EW Savory*
*Ser. 807 [1 of 4]*
*[1919]*

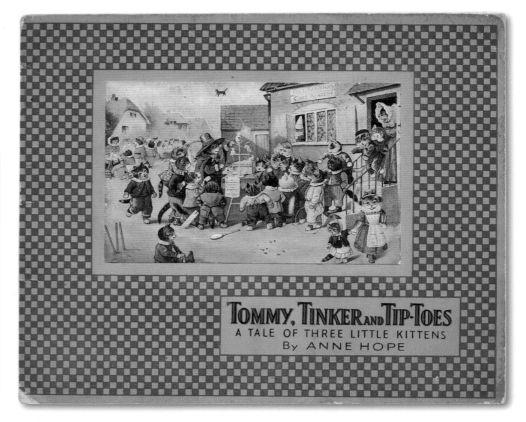

The patient Fisherman.

## EW Savory

Two characteristic features of children's postcards published by EW Savory are that they were generally made up into sets of four, rather than six and printed onto soft, off white, roughish stock which gives the appearance and texture of Whatman watercolour paper, making the postcard illustrations look like delightful miniature watercolours. This was the *Clifton Hand Coloured Postcard*.

This absorbent material must have appealed to a number of the best children's artists around, as many were attracted to Savory. It was a favourite of Anne Anderson, the prolific and much loved illustrator of children's books. She and her fellow illustrators would have provided Savory with black and white line artwork which would then have been printed and handcoloured by batteries of in-house artists. The beauty of the material meant that the paints would quickly soak in and dry. The Savory colourists made Anne Anderson's already pastel palette look even softer and enchantingly lyrical. In contrast, the absorbent material softened the bold outlines of Linda Edgerton and Helen Grace Marsh Lambert's designs to good effect.

However, the card was not very easy to write on. Its rough texture tended to clog up fountain pens and its soft composition meant that cards that went through the post, tended to attract grime and show signs of wear.

The work of Exeter-based painter Ethel Larcombe is also represented in the Salmon repertoire in the *Clifton Facsimile Colour Postcard Series*. One can only admire her sense of design and composition, coupled with her painterly skills of the Pre-Raphaelites. She is one of the most underrated British artist/designers of the twentieth century.

Postcards by these four artists date from the period 1917 to 1920. Savory also published work by other artists mentioned in this book, including Cecil Aldin, John Hassall, Eva Hollyer and FG Lewin.

## Raphael Tuck & Sons

Raphael Tuck & Sons contributed greatly to the high standards achieved by British fine art publishers in the years leading up to the turn of the twentieth century. Raphael Tuck, himself, was born in East Prussia in 1821, and moved with his family to England in 1865. In 1870 his three sons had joined him and made significant contributions in the development of the business and by 1875 the company was dealing in colourful chromolithographic sheet scraps for fancy box manufacture and decorative scrap books to house the collections of Victorian scrap collectors.

Rapid development continued and in 1893 the firm received the Royal Warrant. By this time it had expanded abroad and the company's creative flair shone out as it added books and calendars to its repertoire.

Tuck was constantly in search of new ideas and new talent. Adolph Tuck, who took over from his father in 1881, 'trawled' the country for artists and writers. He organised 'talent' competitions and one, in 1881, is said to have attracted up to ten thousand entrants, ending at the Royal Institute of Painters and Watercolours, where the entries were displayed.

*Folded greetings card. Raphael Tuck. [c.1895]*

He had many fine artists at his disposal – Royal Academicians like Sir G Clausen, H Stacy Marks, and EJ Poynter, all highly revered in their day. But Tuck had the sense to realise that female artists were more likely to create imagery in keeping with the desires of children, and so nurtured a group of highly talented

women artists to provide illustrations for publications for the younger market. Artists, like Ellen 'Eddie' J Andrews, the Bowley sisters, Maude Goodman, Helen Jackson and Ellen Welby were well established artists, having exhibited at Royal Academy Summer Shows. Their ideas, their deft skills and their rich palette

*Dear Arthur, of course you have heard all about 'The Three Bears' and little Goldenlocks, but I thought you would like to see the pictures of them, so I bought this card for you. Hoping you will have a Merry Christmas from your loving Grandma.*

*Goldenlocks & the The Three Bears. Folded greetings card, Raphael Tuck. [c.1896] (with sender's message above in italics).*

of colours were eminently suited to the new production processes, exploiting to the full Tuck's superb chromolithographic process operated at printing plants in Saxony and Bavaria, centres for the highest quality printing in the world.

Many of the early Tuck illustrations on books and greetings cards were unsigned, giving rise to debate as to whom certain work should be attributed. Often, the disciplined training of Victorian artists rendered their work stylistically similar, making the task of attribution even more difficult. Several notable examples of nursery rhyme and fairy tale postcards published around 1902, highlight the dilemma.

*Trade advertisement promoting Tuck's first packets of Dressing Dolls patented in 1894. [1895]*

*Below left:*
*Artist: Anon [German]*
*Pub: Raphael Tuck*
*Art Series 6093 [1 of 6]*
*[1903]*

*Below centre:*
*Artist: Louis Wain*
*Pub: Raphael Tuck*
*Christmas Series 8126 [1 of 6]*
*[1903]*

*Above right:*
*Artist: Anon [German]*
*Pub: Raphael Tuck*
*Series 537. No. 3471*
*Pantomimes [1 of 6]*
*[1901]*

*Centre right:*
*Artist: Maude Goodman*
*Pub: Raphael Tuck*
*Oilette Series No. 8651*
*Thinking of Somebody*
*[1905]*

*Below right:*
*Artist: Anon*
*Pub: Raphael Tuck*
*Christmas Series 1723*
*[1902]*

One of the first children's artists to contribute to the Tuck postcard repertoire was Helen Jackson, whose delicate genre paintings of children charmed the nation. She was a painter from Tulse Hill, south London and like her contemporary, Maude Goodman, had established herself as a fine artist before joining Tuck.

Tuck was at the forefront of postcard promotion to a public that was enchanted by its products. From time to time Tuck ran competitions open to the public, offering valuable prizes to entrants with the largest accumulations of their postcards, stirring a craze for sending, receiving and collecting. A bubble of popularity was created that one day would burst, but not before leaving a legacy to future generations.

Separate competitions were held for children. One in 1914 was called *Father Tuck's Painting Book Competition*. This invited the purchasers of various Tuck postcard painting books, containing beautifully printed colour vignetted cards, to colour

in the outline versions of the same scenes.

As the company entered the Edwardian era, Tuck saw the need to modernise. The refined Victorian renderings of the early days were beginning to look out of place as the new century gathered pace. Styles were changing and humour and creativity were in greater demand. Established cartoonists and illustrators like John Hassall, Dudley Hardy, Phil May and Louis Wain were hired along with aspiring new talent like Hilda Cowham and Chloë Preston, to support the esablished children's artists already on their books.

Tuck were always prepared to try something new. To stay ahead they had to be seen as the trendsetters, while others followed their lead. It was a tough challenge to create new novelty ideas on picture postcards, which were basically rectangular pieces of card. But Tuck succeeded!

Before the new century was ten years old, Tuck were publishing stereoscopic postcards, gramophone record postcards,

WASHING DAY

jigsaw puzzle postcards and cut-out, perforated and 'platform' press-out postcards. Around 1909 and following on from their Zag-Zaw Picture Play Puzzles, came Picture Puzzle Postcards and a craze for progressive puzzle parties. *The Daily Mail* enthused: *"In passing through Pullman cars on a journey one is likely to find half the travellers working at the puzzles and at meal times there are notices "Please do not touch" on partly completed puzzles. Similar notices are found in the saloons of Atlantic liners."*. Even *The Gentlewoman* commented: *"You are to be pitied if you have not yet tasted the delights of one of the most absorbing games that has ever captivated society. As an aid to the acquirement of concentration and quickness, picture puzzling is wonderful"*.

Tuck would often issue postcards to mark topical events. Two examples are *Ancient Egypt Up To Date* by Agnes Richardson, celebrating the disovery of Tutankhamun tomb in 1922 and *The Queen's Dolls House* series, published in 1924, to commemorate the gift from the nation to Her Majesty Queen Mary – a gift that was on display at the British Empire Exhibition in the same year. The series comprised eight sets of six postcards.

The market leaders, companies like Raphael Tuck, shaped the direction of children's publishing in this country during the twentieth century. Their vast range of high quality, affordable products and sophisticated mass marketing, reached a huge audience. For many years they kept coming up with innovative ideas for books, postcards, games, toys, calendars and a great deal more, leaving an indelible impression on the young, that would have remained with them into parenthood. Many popular illustrators like Hilda Cowham, Mabel Lucie Attwell, Phyllis Cooper and Gladys Peto went further. They did a great deal to advance a change in nursery fashions from the stiff and formal styles of the Victorians towards simple and relaxed styles with a great deal more flair and panache.

*Peggy and her Playmates, the shaped book from the Raphael Tuck 'Hurrah' Series of 1907 demonstrates the art of Hilda Cowham. She broke through frontiers of male domination and was the first woman to contribute cartoons to* Punch. *Her original approach transformed children's art in a very short space of time. Her influence on fashion was profound. She inspired new styles with her bold prints and bows and through this led women and children to a new freedom in their dress. She helped to create a climate where other female artists like Mabel Lucie Attwell could flourish.*

LEFT HAND PAGE

Above left:
Artist: Maud Goodman
Pub: Raphael Tuck
Art Series 143
No. 830
[1901]

Below left:
Artist: Helen Jackson
Pub: Raphael Tuck
Art Series 6752
[1906]

RIGHT HAND PAGE

Above left:
Artist: Ellen Jessie Andrews
Pub: Raphael Tuck
Art Series 6948
Flower Maidens
[c.1907]

Below left:
Artist: Hilda Dix Sandford
Pub: Raphael Tuck
Oilette Series 9220
Girls and Boys
[1907]

Above centre:
Artist: Chloë Preston
Pub: Raphael Tuck
Oilette Series 3505
Quaint Little Folk II
[1925]

Below centre:
Artist: Margaret Ethel Banks
Pub: Raphael Tuck
Oilette Series 3381
Dressing Dolls 1
[1922]

Above right:
Artist: Agnes Richardson
Pub: Raphael Tuck
Oilette Series 3496
Ancient Egypt Up-to-Date
[1924]

Below right:
Artist: Phyllis Cooper
Pub: Raphael Tuck
Valentine Postcard No. 102
[c.1925]

## Valentine & Sons

*"Valentine's Series are so attractive with their beautiful colours and their original designs, that it is not hard to understand how the post card craze developed".*

Daily Mail 1903

Valentine's of Dundee were one of the most prominent and prolific publishers of postcards from their inception through until 1960.

The business was formed in 1792 as a manufacturer of linen, but it never really succeeded, although its founder, John Valentine, tried to find a niche in the market by experimenting with pattern printing onto his products. His son James, who had trained as an artist, took over in 1832, when his father emigrated to America and turned Valentines of Dundee into a printing and publishing business. However, James's artistic leanings drew him towards the new art form – photography.

He excelled as a portrait and landscape photographer and was joined in the business by his own sons in 1863 and the business thrived, trading mainly in fancy stationery and greetings cards.

As soon as postal regulations permitted, the firm began to publish a vast range of photographic view postcards, many of which had been created by James, without cost to the business.

Flushed with success, and aware that foreign competition was threatening, Valentine decided to diversify its range. If they could achieve success with high quality photography, why couldn't they succeed with illustrated postcards? So from 1902, they quickly amassed a formidable list of contributing artists and illustrators. Louis Wain's *Seaside Cats*, Mabel Lucie Attwell's *Nursery Tots,* from around 1911, two of the best known names, feature amongst some early examples.

The company regarded the work of these two popular illustrators highly. Trade press sources in 1917 observed: *"Lucie Attwell Dolly Books – In the toy books and painting books by Mabel Lucie Attwell, Messrs*

*Advertisement in* The British Stationer *[1921]*

*Valentine & Sons have a series which are as welcome as they are fresh and amusing. The artist strikes a note which unfailingly appeals to many thousands. Among them is* Little So-Shy, *with a pink satin bow complete. Then there is* Ever So Nice Painting Book, *with numerous coloured pictures and outlines for painting, and many other titles. Running them close is* Tatters the Puppy, *also a shaped book by Louis Wain".* Further novelties from Valentine

arrived in the shops. 1922 brought press comment: *"It would be difficult to find at the price a more welcome present for a girl than the* Stitch Stitch, The Lucie Attwell Needlework Book *which is much more than a book. It is a collection of embroidery designs with a supply of vari-coloured silks and transfers tucked into pockets on the covers."*

The public continued to enjoy sending and receiving children's cards throughout

the twenties and into the thirties, bucking a trend that had seen a general decline since the outset of World War I. Valentine was one of the few companies who held the public's attention, by commissioning many of the best loved children's artists of the day, including Cecil Aldin, René Cloke, Hilda Cowham, Chloë Preston, Agnes Richardson, Harry Rountree, George Studdy (Bonzo) and Clarence Lawson Wood (Gran'pop).

Following the success of Chloë Preston's *Peek-a-Boos* books, Valentine published around eighty delightful postcard designs featuring her *Peek-a-Boo* kiddies, between 1923 and 1932. George Studdy's *Bonzo* and the Walt Disney series featuring *Mickey Mouse and Donald Duck, Snow White and the Seven Dwarfs* (1938), *The Water Babies* (1938), *Ferdinand the Bull* (1939) *Merbabies* (1939), and *Pinocchio* (1940), were all very popular in their time, but Valentine was unable to find a successor to the enduring popularity of Mabel Lucie Attwell's cute kiddies.

*Greetings card by Mabel Lucie Attwell [c.1930]*

*Above left:*
*Artist: Anon*
*Pub: Valentine*
*Xmas Postcard Series 635*
*[1904]*

*Below left:*
*Artist: May Bowley*
*Pub: Valentine*
*[1903]*

*Above centre:*
*Artist: Mabel Lucie Attwell*
*Pub: Valentine*
*No. 2828*
*[1934]*

*Below centre:*
*Artist: Chloë Preston*
*Pub: Valentine*
*Chloë Preston Series*
*No. 1531*
*[1929]*

*Above right:*
*Artist: George Studdy*
*Pub: Valentine*
*Valentine's Bonzo Series*
*[1927]*

*Below right:*
*Artist: Clarence Lawson Wood*
*Pub: Valentine*
*Valentine's Lawson Wood Postcards*
*[1935]*

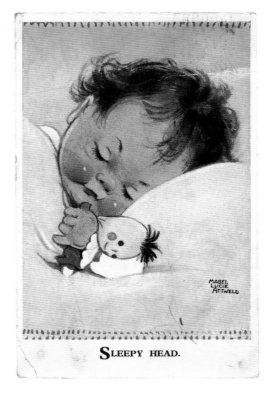

**Wildt & Kray**

The partnership of Wildt & Kray is best known for publishing highly decorative and embossed Christmas, New Year, Easter and birthday cards, dating from 1904.

Illustrated cards for children were not one of the company's main strengths, although notable contributors to the Wildt & Kray list included the work of Lilian Govey, Agnes Richardson and writer and author May Byron.

It is interesting to observe that the nursery rhyme illustrations by MLKK were copyrighted by the National Art Company in the United States in 1906 and assigned to Wildt and Kray around 1910. Rights to the designs on china objects were then assigned to Hart & Sons in the same year.

Postcards illustrating the traditional nursery themes of rhymes, tales and fairyland are far less in evidence in the United States, where the focus has always been on more decorative designs for greetings and festivals – also the speciality of Wildt & Kray.

Mistress Mary, quite contrary,
How does your garden grow?
With silver bells and cockle shells
and Pretty Maids all in a row.

Jack & Jill went up a hill
to fetch a pail of water.
Jack fell down and broke his crown
and Jill came tumbling after.

*LEFT HAND PAGE*

*Below left:*
*Artist: MLKK*
*Pub: Wildt & Kray*
*Ser. 1525. No. 311 [1 of 12]*
*[c.1910]*

*Above centre:*
*Artist: MLKK*
*Pub: Wildt & Kray*
*Ser. 1525. No. 309 [1 of 12]*
*[c.1910]*

*Above right:*
*Artist: MLKK*
*Pub: Wildt & Kray*
*Ser. 1525. No. 312 [1 of 12]*
*[c.1910]*

*RIGHT HAND PAGE*

*Artist: Chloë Preston*
*Pub: Valentine*
*No. 1530*
*'Just to Show you're not Forgotten'*

My loving wish I send you here,
A very merry Christmas, dear!
May there be frolic, feast, and fun,
For you and me and everyone!
MAY BYRON

*Advertisement in the* Stationery Trades Journal *for Nursery Rhymes series of China, Hart & Sons. [1910]*

# Cecil Aldin (1870-1935)

*A portrait of Cecil Aldin at the London Sketch Club by his great friend John Hassall.*

The first sentence in his autobiography of 1934 observes: *"On looking among the A's in Who's Who I see I am stated to have been born in the year 1870."* He goes on, *"My father had a craze for scrap books and some of these early attempts of mine have been kept. I only show one here as a warning to other parents whose children may have a painting complex."*

*"The earliest of all" – an indication that humour was to pervade most of his work.*

Throughout his life, Cecil Aldin had two strings to his bow. He remembered: *"Soon after I left school the career of an artist was vaguely indicated, although I had another alternative in mind which was to become a coachman…"* Horses, dogs and hunting were his all-consuming passion and his ability to draw enabled him to indulge to an even greater degree in his favourite pastime.

He was born and raised in Kensington. His mother Sarah, wanted him to enter the Church as a profession, but the wishes of his father Charles, a keen amateur artist, prevailed and he was sent the studio of Albert Moore (1841-1893) in Kensington. Although the studio was close to the Aldin's home, Moore's classical approach and interpretations of Greek art as an expression of ideal beauty in repose did not appeal to the youthful Aldin, so within a month he had moved on to study anatomy at South Kensington Art School. Later, he enrolled at Frank Calderon's School of Animal

Painting, at the artist's studio in Midhurst in the heart of the Sussex countryside, a situation much more to his liking.

In 1891 he considered himself a 'full blown' artist. The year gave rise to a triple celebration – his twenty first birthday, a studio in Chelsea and his second published drawing, that of a dog show, accepted by the *Weekly Graphic*. However, the next few years were not easy. He recounts, "…there began a slow dribble of dog drawings into weekly papers, at the cost of a great deal of shoe leather, trying to persuade editors to take them. When I was not walking up and down Fleet Street with my portfolio, I spent my days at the Zoological Gardens drawing the birds and animals".

In 1894, Aldin's Zoo sketches reached the *Pall Mall Budget* who commissioned him to illustrate Rudyard Kipling's *Jungle Stories* which were to be serialised in the periodical. Aldin called this *"his first real milestone towards a hunting career"*.

In those days Chelsea was a big artists' colony and Aldin, a convivial character, met and befriended many of his peer group, including Rex Whistler, Walter Sickert and William Nicholson and Jimmy Pryde, the Beggarstaffe Brothers. When he moved out to another bohemian quarter, Bedford Park, Chiswick, he relished the convivial company of all those we associate with the London Sketch Club – Tom Browne, Dudley Hardy, John Hassall, Phil May, Lance Thackeray and many more.

He soon realised that working for newspapers and periodicals meant that he needed a deft touch with the pen and a razor sharp wit to earn more and allow time for the recreational pursuits he loved.

Although postcard illustration did not pay particularly well, all these illustrators made it profitable by their speed of execution. It was also a medium through which they could express their rapier-like sense of humour, vying with each other in friendly competition.

During the eighteen nineties Aldin had been invited to stay at Chiddingstone by

Dendy Sadler, a fellow artist. Chiddingstone was a lovely village of fifteenth century timbered houses with dormer windows, no bricks and russet tiles, tucked away in the Kent Countryside. It was a slumbering tranquil place, far off the tourist track and Aldin fell in love with it.

*Chiddingstone at the turn of the century.*

Surely, Chiddingstone provided the inspiration for Aldin when he illustrated this set of nursery rhymes in 1898. The row of houses in *Ride a cock horse* is so reminiscent of Chiddingstone village. The church would have been at his back as he drew the scene, so he has included the tower of the fourteenth century building at the top of the picture on the opposite side of the road.

Although not typical of Aldin's subject matter, these postcards are classics of their kind, brimming with expression and vigour – the hallmark of his London Sketch Club friends. John Hassall's influence is clearly evident. The pictures appeared in *The Young Folks Birthday Book* (c.1904), published by Hills & Co, the London-based printers of calendars, greetings cards, menus and wedding stationery, who published books and postcards between 1903 and 1905.

Children amused Aldin and he recounts how he loved to tease them when they came to watch him sketch.
*"Did you see the circus ?"* he would say, murmuring that *"it had arrived at the far end of the village when he passed by an hour ago."* He reckoned it was a ploy that seldom failed to gain him peace and quiet to continue his sketching.

*Artist: Cecil Aldin
Pub: Lawrence & Jellicoe, London
'Billy's Little Love Affair'
from* The Doggy Book
Cecil Aldin's Painting Books Series
*[nd]*

*Right:*
*Artist: Cecil Aldin*
*Pub: Hills & Co*
*For the Empire Series*
*Nursery Rhymes*
*5092-97 [6 of 6]*
*[1904]*

# Anne Anderson (1874-1952)

Anne Anderson, (she was christened Annie), was born in London. At the time of her birth her parents were living at 31 Manor Place, Walworth, while her father James, was overseeing the installation of plant and equipment at the Oval gasworks, a familiar landmark to all cricket lovers.

James Anderson was an engineer and junior director of Henry Balfour & Co, an engineering firm based at Leven in Fife. His grandfather was a founder member of the company, which was established in the early part of the nineteenth century and is still thriving today. Balfour manufactured a wide range of products, from ships to mining machinery and carried out many major installations in the developing countries around the world.

Annie's father spent much of his working life representing his company in South America. Indeed, he and his wife Grace were married in Pernambuco, Brazil, in 1871. They had five children – James, born in Brazil, Annie, George, Jessie and David, later Sir David Anderson, a senior partner in the structural engineers, Mott, Hay & Anderson. The family were staunch Presbyterians and Annie was subjected to a rigid upbringing that was 'strictly in the kirk', an experience she grew to resent in later life.

She spent her early years in Scoonie with her family at their home named *Riverbank* and attended the local school.

The house was situated beside a man-made tributary leading from the River Leven into the Balfour iron foundry. Although built in a pleasantly verdant area, the large terraced property was close to Leven Dock and surrounded on all sides by the foundry, flax mills, sawmills and a rope works.

Annie's teenage years were spent in Argentina, while her father worked on an engineering contract for the Argentinian Government. It was in Argentina, during the mid-nineties, that she first met Olive Hockin (1880-1936), the niece of Glynne Williams, an entrepreneur involved in developing the railway at Rosario in the north of the country. A few years later, Annie met Guinivere Donnithorne, (Vere), an art school friend of Olive, with whom she shared a studio at Edwardes Square, Kensington. On her return to England, Annie lived for a while with Vere at her home in Palace Gardens, London.

Olive and Annie, (always called Nancy by those who remember her), were drawn to one another because they shared common interests. Neither suffered fools gladly and both were taciturn, utterly honest and fearless women who shared a love of the arts. Perhaps the most significant factor in their relationship was that while Nancy was endowed with a great deal of fortitude and strongly held

*Olive Hockin. [c.1920]*

beliefs, she was somewhat retiring by nature. She admired Olive for her dominant qualities of courage and endurance. She also admired Olive's passionate approach to the things she valued most – the arts, ski-ing (she was a ski-ing champion) and her dogged struggle for women's suffrage. She spent three months in jail for demonstrating her beliefs. Although Nancy was six years older, her sheltered upbringing meant that Olive was altogether more worldly.

Olive's character is accurately reflected in *Two Girls on the Land*, a poignant autobiographical novel published in 1918,

*Camping with Olive and friends in Pembrokeshire [1923]*

recording her personal experiences as a land girl on a Devon farm during World War I. Like Nancy, she also wrote stories for children, such as, *Mellifica the Honeybee*, a charming nature story, featured in *Cassell's Children's Annual* for 1921.

Nancy, Olive and Vere became lifelong friends. Olive attended the Slade School of Fine Art between 1901 and 1903 and again in 1910 and 1911, while Nancy and Vere enrolled as part-time students.

Nancy, was greatly taken by Olive's highly coloured pictures in the rich Rosettian fashion. Both women shared a love of mediaeval legend, Butcher and Lang's Odyssey, Burne Jones's memoirs, Morris's tapestried romances and the Utopia of *News from Nowhere*. Olive's paintings were widely appreciated and were shown at Royal Academy summer exhibitions between 1904 and 1915, the Society of Women Artists and other leading galleries.

"I wrote a letter to my love."

"My love is like a red, red rose."

LEFT HAND PAGE

*Above & below:*
*Artist: Anne Anderson*
*Pub: CW Faulkner*
*Series 1082 A/D [2 of 6]*
*[1910]*

RIGHT HAND PAGE

*Left column:*
*Artist: Anne Anderson*
*Pub: ETW Dennis*
*Nos. 4329/4330*
*[nd]*

*Centre column:*
*Artist: Anne Anderson*
*Pub: EW Savory*
*Series 524 [2 of 4]*
*[1917]*

*Right column:*
*Artist: Anne Anderson*
*Pub: EW Savory*
*Series 623 [2 of 4]*
*[1917]*

*Little Audrey showing the studio from the back garden drawn by Alan Wright. Pen and wash.*

Nancy began to develop her own style under the influence of Olive and the Pre-Raphaelites. Although her early work lacks the vigour and rich colour of her idols, she succeeded in developing a unique style which warmly portrays her animated characters in soft line and watercolour washes, ideally suited to the pages of books for young children. Her pictures illustrating fairy tales, the theme she loved best, are typified by pretty damsels with long blonde tresses and flowing gowns, drawn in fine line with unerring technique. Even wicked gnomes and goblins are tempered by a pervading sense of a compassionate female touch. Interwoven with all this are the influences of a number of her favourite contemporary illustrators including Arthur Rackham and Jessie M King. There is also a hint of the styles of Millicent Sowerby and Lilian Govey in her work both of whom were illustrating books for young readers with the publishers Henry Frowde and Hodder & Stoughton, by the time Nancy started working for the company.

Her popularity as an illustrator owed a great deal to her ability to identify closely with the market at which her illustrations were targeted. Alongside her fantasy drawings she was able to reflect the styles of the day in children's costume, even pre-empt them. Journalist Maleen Matthews observes: *"In her drawings you can find clothes for every season: long sleeved smocks and frocks with little boleros for spring; Christopher Robin*

*suits and short sleeved dresses and wide-brimmed sun-hats for summer. For winter, children are cosy in their knitted hats and scarves, coats and capes, fur-trimmed coats, coats with collars and cuffs to match and, as in the Little Busy Bee Book, buttoned leather gaiters to keep knees and ankles warm and dry."*

Her drawings of clothes influenced dress design in the twenties, providing enough detail for designers to lift children's costumes from the pages of her books and place them into shop windows.

She was an illustrator dedicated to her art. She had no children of her own, but through her work, created a family of hundreds of happy, bright and idealised children in the four hundred or so titles

*Miniature book from the 'Heads & Tails' Series. published by Humphrey Milford. [c.1924]*

*Cup & saucer from Royal Doulton teaset. [1924]*

that she illustrated or contributed to in a career that lasted nearly forty years.

Nancy worked for a number of postcard publishers including CW Faulkner, for whom she did her first postcard series in 1910. She also worked for ETW Dennis

*Artist: Anne Anderson*
*'A Voyage to Fairyland'*
*The Sleepy Song Book*
*Pub: George Harrap*
*[nd]*

*Artist: Anne Anderson*
*'She craftily untied the sack, and ran away with it'*
*Grimm's Fairy Tales,*
*The Knapsack the Hat & the Horn*
*Pub: Collins Cleartype Press*
*[nd]*

*Right:*
*Artist: Anne Anderson*
*Pub: EW Savory*
*Series 689 [complete]*
*[1918]*

*Below right:*
*Artist: Anne Anderson*
*Pub: EW Savory*
*Series 624 [1 of 4]*
*[1917]*

of Scarborough and Delgado of London. Most of the postcards she illustrated were published by EW Savory of Bristol, for whom she created around twenty sets, several of which were captioned for the French market. She also designed nursery china tea sets for Royal Doulton and the Staffordshire Tea Set Company.

Nancy maintained a keen interest in painting, particularly landscapes and in 1932 she exhibited a painting entitled *The Valley Farm* at the Royal Academy summer show. She often went out on sketching trips during the thirties, with her friend Cynthia Harnett (1893-1981), illustrator

and winner of the Carnegie Medal for the outstanding children's book of 1951, with her book *The Wool Pack*.

She met illustrator Alan Wright, her future husband, when both were working on projects for publishers Henry Frowde and Hodder & Stoughton. They married in 1912 and spent the rest of their lives at *Little Audrey*, Burghfield Common, in rural Berkshire. Their cottage was the gate house to *Audrey*, where Olive Hockin lived with her family until her marriage in 1922. The house was modestly named after Audrey, the country wench in Shakespeare's *As You Like It* – *"a poor thing, but mine own."*

# Florence Mary Anderson (1893-1972)

*Florence (left) with her brother John
(Squeaker) and sister, Margaret [1899]*

Florence Mary, the second of three children, was born in London in October 1893, to the Member of Parliament for St Austell, William McArthur, and his wife Florence. At the time of her birth, her father, a man of Irish/Australian descent, was a Lord of the Treasury and one of the Whips to the parliamentary Liberal party.

As a young girl, Florence lived with her family in Sloane Gardens, Kensington and was tutored by a governess. She grew up happily in an upper middle class London home with her sister Margaret and brother John, (always known affectionately as Squeaker) and developed an unusually strong bond with her father which was to last her through life.

In 1908, the family returned to Australia to deal with her father's business interests. During their three year stay Florence met and became engaged to James Anderson, a young army officer. He was often posted abroad on active service and she was still very young so marriage at that time was impractical. When the family returned to England, Florence enrolled at the Westminster School of Art.

Florence had a precocious talent for drawing and painting and while still a student, she illustrated *The Dream Pedlar* by Lady Margaret Sackville, published in 1914. Even then, she worked under the name of Florence Mary Anderson, although she did not marry James Anderson until he returned from war service in 1917. Over the next six years more books were to follow, including *The Travelling Companions* (1915), *The Cradle Ship* (1916), *The Magic Kiss* (1916) and *The Rainbow Twins* (1919), a story she wrote herself.

During her career as an illustrator she worked for many publishers including Simpkin Marshall, Harrap, Cassell, Nelson and Collins. She contributed regularly to *Little Folks* and many other popular children's annuals.

Her love of children and talent for drawing enabled her to compose colourful pictures of fairyland fantasy, mischievous gnomes, and other imagery familiar to the nursery. In 1921, the editor of *Little Folks* comments: *"Florence Mary Anderson is well beloved of my readers. Her fairies, gnomes and elves carry us right into the centre of Fairyland. She has a merry smile, a gladsome heart – and an eye for the prettiest tints in the fairy world."*

With maturity, came confidence and an awareness of the exciting possibilities to exploit bold, black and white linear pattern. She became an exponent of the woodcut, examples of which appear in her later books – *China Clay*, a Chinese anthology, (1922), *Woodcuts and Verses* (1922), *Tribute* (1923), a book dedicated to the memory of her father and *Come Christmas* (1927) by Eleanor Farjeon.

Illustrating children's books could not hold her interest indefinitely, and she reached a point where she decided to move on.

Art and the theatre had featured prominently in her life from an early age when her parents took the family to see many unforgettable West End productions. These memories fired her imagination and created a desire to work in this entirely different and exciting medium.

*Right:
Artist: Florence Mary Anderson
Pub: A Vivian Mansell
Series 2115 [3 of 6]
[c.1920]*

THE KEY TO THE MOON

THE MOONCHILD

WHITHER AWAY?

*Molly demonstrating a stage set. [c.1955]*

Florence was living in Oxford in 1923/24, when her determination to succeed in a new career was rewarded. She was approached by JB Fagan, a pioneer in stage lighting, to design the sets for Shaw's *Heartbreak House* at the Oxford Playhouse. It was here that Florence first met Tyrone Guthrie, one of England's most prominent directors and producers, who was 'starting at the bottom of the career ladder' a young scenery painter when this play was produced.

In 1925 she designed her first London production, *The Cradle Song* at the Fortune Theatre and later teamed up with Tyrone Guthrie to design stage sets for his early productions at the Westminster Theatre.

Although a few more books were to follow, *Mumbudget* (1928), an Irish fairy tale, written by her friend Helen Simpson and dedicated to her son Patrick, was one of her last illustrated books to be published. Despite the breakup of her marriage, her work in the theatre went from strength to strength and she collaborated with Guthrie on *The Cherry Orchard* and the *Importance of*

*'Stocking Time' from* Come Christmas *by Eleanor Farjeon, published by Collins. [1927]*

*being Earnest* at the Old Vic. She designed sets for other producers too, including Basil Dean, Dodie Smith and Irene Henschel. In 1937, she first met actress/producer Esmé Church and began a lifelong friendship.

After the war Florence teamed up with Esmé, then the director of the Bradford Playhouse, to develop and nurture the Northern Children's Theatre – established to entertain children and provide practical training for young Northern actors.

Here was a woman whose career was interrupted by a major philosophical change of direction, even to the extent that she reverted to her maiden name and called herself Molly McArthur Perhaps we will never know why she should suddenly move away from colourful and decorative fantasy illustration, so popular with children, and into a mode of bold, monochromatic and economical design. It was a philosophy that extended into her work for the stage, and one that was not always welcomed by producers who wanted a splash of opulence in their productions.

When Molly died in Oxford in 1972, her obituarist said of her: *"She had a remarkable eye for stage pictures which made a deep impression on the audience and long haunted the memory of those who saw them."*

*'When she laughed the wind laughed too' from* The Dream Pedlar. *[1914]*

# Ellen Jessie Andrews (1857-1907)

LEFT HAND PAGE

*Above & below:*
*Artist: Florence Mary Anderson*
*Pub: Little Folks*
*[c.1925]*

RIGHT HAND PAGE

*Far right:*
*Artist: Ellen Jessie Andrews*
*Pub: Raphael Tuck*
*Art Series 1156 II/IV/VI*
*Ping Pong in Fairyland*
*[3 of 6]*
*[1902]*

*Below:*
*Artist: Ellen Jessie Andrews*
*Pub: Theo Stroefer*
*Serie XXXIX (Mädchen) No.10*
*[1901]*

Ellen Jessie Andrews, otherwise known as 'Eddie', was one of Raphael Tuck's most senior children's artists. She was a fine painter of children and genre subjects and worked in the greetings card industry for over twenty years, illustrating children's books and cards, before her untimely death of a chronic illness in 1907. Ellen died at Napsbury Hospital, St Albans, where Louis Wain spent his final years over twenty years later. She was born in Camberwell, the third of four sisters, Emily, Elizabeth, Ellen and Emma. Her father, John James, a master mariner and Elizabeth his wife, hailed from Kent. They lived in Grimsby in the early years of their marriage while he worked on trawlers in the fishing industry. However, they settled back in Lewisham, London to raise their family. Their only son Allan, followed his father into shipping.

Very little has been documented about Ellen's life or where she trained as a painter. We know she was a prizewinner in a

*Greetings card from Outdoor Games Series. Tuck. [c.1903]*

Hildesheimer & Faulkner greetings card competition in the eighteen eighties, early in her career. She exhibited a picture at the Royal Academy in 1897, entitled *Two Little Maids from School* while living in Putney and then moved to Harlesden in 1902 where she spent the last five years of her life.

Ellen Andrews painted very much in the Victorian style and understandably, her work has been confused with other Tuck artists, notably Frances Brundage.

She was very disciplined in choosing her rich colour palette and favoured a predetermined selection of greens, blues yellows and reds – colours that are consistent throughout her captivating artwork.

*Greetings card. Tuck. [c.1903]*

Football. A Happy Birthday

Golf.

Hockey. Birthday Greetings

# Honor Appleton (1879-1951)

In twenty five years of collecting, we have discovered only two picture postcards illustrated by Honor Charlotte Appleton. These two, taken from a series of six, were published by Wells Gardner, Darton & Co, promoting their book, *The Children's Poets*, for which she contributed colour plates for the chapter on the nineteenth century writers, Jane and Anne Taylor.

These two rare cards have provided us with the opportunity of including one of the classic illustrators for young children of the period, for as her obituarist in the *Brighton Herald* observed in 1952: "*Few people have been able to capture so successfully the moods of children at work and play.*"

She was born in Brighton, the daughter of John Appleton, a vicar, and his wife, Georgina, who encouraged the creative talents in their daughters throughout their childhood. Honor had a younger brother, John and two elder sisters, Rachel and Alice Mary, affectionately known as 'Sissy'.

She was naturally talented and naturally methodical, a rare quality amongst artists. From an early age she kept sketch books, providing evidence that she trained herself throughout her formative years in the art of observation. Her ambition to enter the world of book illustration was achieved by her own painstaking application and the benefits of a thorough art training.

First, she attended the South Kensington Schools followed by Frank Calderon's School of Animal Painting in Midhurst. Calderon's insistence on minutely detailed anatomical studies of animals is highlighted in her sketch books that have survived.

In 1898, she achieved Honourable Mentions in three competition categories organised by the *Studio* magazine – two for book jacket designs and the other for the design of a bookplate.

At the age of twenty one she enrolled at the Royal Academy Schools, to take

*"Very handy when I have a big washing-day" from* Josephine and Her Dolls. *[1915]*

lessons in sculpture, drawing and painting. Her Royal Academy Schools sketch books demonstrate her awareness of the influences around her. They contain paintings of fairy children, in the styles of many of her contemporaries, including Mabel Lucie Attwell, Hilda Cowham, Annie French and William Heath Robinson.

While still in her second year at the college, her first book, *The Bad Mrs Ginger*, a Dumpy Book, was published in 1902, by Grant Richards. This was the first step of a successful career, in which she illustrated over one hundred and fifty books, and in particular, the *Josephine* series by Mrs HC Cradock, for which she is best remembered.

In her early years as an illustrator she worked with a soft palette of colours with predominantly blues, buffs and greys. The effect was like looking at life in the nursery through a fine gauze. There was a great deal of warmth poured into her paintings of children and the effect was serene and gentle, clearly observed with a female's eye. The paintings achieved a finely balanced counterpoint with the stark black and white drawings in her books. Gradually her colour palette became bolder and brighter. Whether this was from choice or pressure from her publishers remains a matter of conjecture. But some would say her paintings became more real, losing some of their magical quality.

She lived in Sussex all her life, never wishing to move far from home. To keep herself well informed she took the *Studio* magazine and after her training had ended, signed on as a correspondent to the Press Art School run by Percy Bradshaw, and subscribed to his series *The Art of the Illustrator* on contemporary artists, including Harry Rountree and Lawson Wood.

Honor Appleton was one of life's brilliant all-rounders, excelling in all she did, for although studious and unrelenting in her artistic pursuits, she was a keen sportswoman, playing for the Royal Academy Schools and later representing her beloved Sussex at hockey.

Ah, Mary! what, do you for dolly not care?
And why is she left on the floor?
Forsaken, and covered with dust, I declare
With you I must trust her no more.
*From 'Negligent Mary'
in the Children's Poets.
"Ann and Jane Taylor."*
*(Wells Gardner, Darton & Co., Ltd.)*

WASHING AND DRESSING.
If the water is cold, and the brush hurts your head,
And the soap has got into your eye,
Will the water grow warmer for all that you've said?
And what good will it do you to cry?
*From 'Ann and Jane Taylor' in the Children's Poets.*
*(Wells Gardner, Darton & Co., Ltd.)*

# Mabel Lucie Attwell (1879-1964)

*Mabel Lucie Attwell. [c.1910]*

When you think of a picture postcard, you can't help thinking of Mabel Lucie Attwell. She was an artist with a prolific output of ideas for picture postcards, books, calendars, china, posters, advertisements, bed linen, wall hangings, dolls and jig-saw puzzles – the list goes on. Mabel Lucie realised that to be a commercial success, it was not good enough simply to illustrate traditional nursery themes, but that it was essential to communicate and to address the issues and concerns that affect most people at some time in their daily lives.

Her ideas and pictures had vitality, wit and imagination and must have appeared to be a very modern innovation around 1911 when she started working for Valentines of Dundee. What an influence she has been on the work of numerous contemporaries. Her picture postcards were popular from the word go. Trade journal reviewers were quick off the mark to urge retailers to stock them, like this announcement from the *Stationery Trades Journal* in August 1911: "*Mabel Lucie Attwell, Valentine 2996 Baby Blossoms is a quite uncommon set of pictures, quaint and clever. We reproduce one of the subjects, a baby on a mountain top with address label and rubber comforter who says "I'se arrived! Did anybody ask for me."* or the review of February 1912 urging retailers:

"*Purchasers of the set of cards by Mabel Lucie Attwell in which occurred the delightful baby picture "I'se come", will at once snap up the new set by the same artist which Messrs Valentine & Son have just published. This is entitled "Nursery Tots" and gives six quaint imaginings, four of which we show on the miniatures page. This series is as pretty and fresh as any that have gone before; the colouring is delicate and the cards should be quickly placed in full view.*"

Her brand of humour really came into its own during World War I, proving to be a wonderful elixir for anxious relatives of unfortunate loved ones caught up in the fighting. But perhaps more important, the rosy faced, chubby children delivering those poignant patriotic messages, helped swell the ranks of young men volunteering for army service.

After the war had ended, sales of Mabel Lucie products, including picture postcards continued to boom if we are to believe the reviewer in the *Stationery Trades Journal* of

February 1924, who announced: "*Valentines' Mabel Lucie Attwell postcards are breaking all records for popularity. They were first published in small editions fifteen years ago and were found to sell well by the select few who recognised the refined humour and genius of this artist's work. Since then the sales have increased each year and new subjects are continuously being added, while the old designs still keep a permanent sale. An illustrated catalogue of Attwell postcards is now issued and is sent by the publishers to those in the trade, post free on application.*"

Born at Mile End in the East End of London, Mabel Lucie was the sixth in a family of eleven. Two of her sisters were particularly artistic. Emily, the eldest, became a fine watercolourist and Jessie, a younger sister, became an accomplished pianist. Mabel Lucie attended the Regent School of Art and Heatherley's, although she disliked the strictures of formal training and chose not to complete either course. She preferred to pursue the prospect of embarking on a commercial career.

*LEFT HAND PAGE*

*Above & below:*
*Artist: Honor Appleton*
*Pub: Wells Gardner Darton*
*Two of six postcards promoting*
*The Children's Poets [c.1912]*

*RIGHT HAND PAGE*

*Left:*
*Artist: Mabel Lucie Attwell*
*Pub: Raphael Tuck*
*Mother Goose*
*Series 4096*
*[c.1911]*

*Centre:*
*Artist: Mabel Lucie Attwell*
*Raphael Tuck & Sons*
*Grimm's Fairy Tales*
*Series 4095*
*[c.1911]*

*Right:*
*Artist: Mabel Lucie Attwell*
*Pub: Raphael Tuck*
*Mother Goose*
*Series 4096*
*[c.1911]*

SNOW-WHITE AND THE SEVEN LITTLE MEN

A Happy Easter

"J'se arrived!
Did anybody ask for me?"

DON'T CUSS—USE YOUR NIBLICK!

TO MY VALENTINE

Your heart loved ME
and mine loved YOU,
So now one heart
is made of two.

"I'SE DREAMING 'BOUT YOU."

ME AND MY GIRL.

*Above left:*
*Artist: Mabel Lucie Attwell*
*Pub: Raphael Tuck*
*Easter Series No 3715*
*[c.1911]*

*Below left:*
*Artist: Mabel Lucie Attwell*
*Pub: Raphael Tuck*
*Valentine Postcard Series*
*No 6 Innocence abroad*
*[c.1911]*

*Above centre:*
*Artist: Mabel Lucie Attwell*
*Pub: Valentine*
*Series 2996*
*Baby Blossoms Series*
*[c.1912]*

*Below centre:*
*Artist: Mabel Lucie Attwell*
*Pub: Valentine*
*Valentine's Attwell Series*
*No. 1090*
*from the Boo-Boos and Bunty's*
* Baby, published 1920*
*[1921]*

*Above right:*
*Artist: Mabel Lucie Attwell*
*Pub: Valentine*
*Valentine's Attwell Series*
*No. A395*
*[1921]*

*Below right:*
*Artist: Mabel Lucie Attwell*
*Pub: Valentine*
*Valentine's Attwell Series*
*No. 4425*
*[1938]*

*Artist: Mabel Lucie Attwell*
*Pub: Raphael Tuck*
Hans Andersen's Fairy Tales
*'Little Tuk'.*
*[1914]*

*Artist: Mabel Lucie Attwell*
*Pub: Valentine*
Just the Thing Painting Book
*'Attwell Kiddies' B352.*
*[c.1910]*

She married Harold Earnshaw, or 'Pat' as he was known, in 1908. He belonged to the London Sketch Club and she was fascinated by the spontaneous humour in the drawings of many of its members – John Hassall and Heath Robinson in particular. She also admired the work of Hilda Cowham, one of the first women illustrators to gain universal recognition.

Mabel Lucie started illustrating books in 1905 with her first publisher, W&R Chambers, for whom she worked on about a dozen titles. But it was with Raphael Tuck that enjoyed her first success. She was commissioned to illustrate six of the *Raphael Tuck Library of Gift Books*, edited by Capt. Edric Vredenburg, comprising *Mother Goose* (1910), *Alice in Wonderland* (1911), *Grimm's Fairy Stories* (1912), *Hans Andersen's Fairy Tales* (1914), *The Water Babies* in (1915) and *Children's Stories from French Fairy Tales* in (1917). The books were beautifully presented in boxes with mounted colour plates. Illustrations from *Grimm's Fairy Stories* and *Andersen's Fairy Tales* were reproduced in series of postcards. Other important books included *Peeping Pansy* by the Queen of Romania (1919) and JM Barrie's *Peter Pan & Wendy* (1921), published by Hodder & Stoughton.

From 1911 she enjoyed a lifelong relationship with Valentines of Dundee. A rapid and prolific worker, with a keen business sense, she made a meteoric rise to fame with her designs for postcards, calendars and greetings cards. Her *Mabel Lucie Attwell Annuals* first published in 1922, continued unabated until her death in 1974. At the peak of her career around 1929, she was producing twenty four new postcard designs annually, which sold in their millions. Valentines, her publisher, reported sales of half a million per month for just one design. It was the popularity of her postcards that first provided the impetus for the wealth of subsidiary merchandising material that followed in their wake.

She was a perfectionist and achieved success in part by the uncompromising

*Mabel Lucie Attwell painted by her grandson, Mark Wickham*

stance she would take with her publishers over the quality of her work. She was ably represented for most of her career by agents Francis & Mills, *'Business Managers to Leading Artists'* and one of the foremost agents of their day. They promoted her work and took care of all her contractual arrangements. She also designed posters, figurines and wall plaques and saw her creations turned into crockery patterns and soft toys.

Mabel Lucie Attwell was a household name by the nineteen twenties and few

British homes were without an Attwell plaque or biscuit-tin money box.

There were good times and bad for Mabel Lucie. The death of a married sister while only in her forties, the premature death of a son aged twenty, the divorce of her daughter Peggy and the disability and early death of her husband Pat were tragic events, yet, she had the strength and fortitude to channel these emotional upheavals into thoughts and ideas to help her audiences cope with the stresses and strains in their own daily lives.

# Margaret Banks (1899-1988)

*"Meet Miss Ethel Margaret Banks, Northampton lady artist whose works delight the nation's children. The thousands of our readers, young and old, who will at one time or another have been charmed and delighted by numerous pictures of bouncing babies, cuddly, curly haired children, and sporty little pets disporting themselves about the pages of sundry magazines, annuals and kindred publications for years past will, in but very few cases, have been aware that the lady responsible for the creation of these lovable little people is a Northampton resident".*
Northampton & County Independent *[1931]*

One of three daughters of the Rev EW Banks and his wife Edith, Margaret Banks was born into a very gifted family. Her grandfather was a Professor of Philosophy and Languages at Vienna University, her uncle, Sir Thomas Stevenson was a senior Home Office pathologist; and her sister, Winnie was a high-flying academic.

She was born and spent her early years at school in Brighton, although the family moved to Pattiswick, near Braintree, Essex, when her father took up the post of rector.

Her name hit the headlines while she was a pupil at St Mary's Hall, Brighton, a girls' boarding school. She was featured in *The Daily Mirror*, March 1913, aged 14. *"Schoolgirl Who Can Produce Sketches Full of Life and Expression"*, the headline read. *'All the little girl's pictures are wonderfully well drawn and painted, but what makes her work stand out is the fact that her sketches of people*

and scenes are full of life and expression, showing an appreciation of genuine artistic effect really remarkable in one so young. 'She began to use her pencil quite cleverly and spontaneously at the age of six,' her father said.

*'I like drawing and painting better than anything' she said. 'I always draw from imagination and have never copied any pictures. I look at children playing, or notice somebody in a room reading, and then I go home and draw them'. In twenty minutes while I waited, she sketched the dresses of five diferent periods – from 1860 to 1912. 'I always draw my own Christmas cards and sometimes I have been asked to illustrate menu cards'. Margaret prefers to draw pictures of a humorous turn. She loves drawing little imps.*

*She has been awarded the Royal Drawing Society's prize, which is competed for by many young artists, both in Britain and Canada."*

After Margaret's father died, she and her mother moved to Streatham in south London. Over a four year period she attended Lambeth Art School and when it closed in 1916 was moved to Clapham Art School. Before war intervened, Lambeth Art School had a fine reputation. Instruction was offered in drawing, painting, modelling and designing and was aimed at professional artists, designers, craftsmen and teachers. Many illustrious artists had attended the school, including Edmund Blampied, Arthur Rackham and Charles Ricketts.

Margaret attended Saint Martin's School of Art in Charing Cross Road, London. She had already been invited to work on children's book projects, prior to attending art school, but as soon as her training was complete, around 1920, she was contracted to a number of London's leading publishers, including Raphael Tuck & Sons. There, she designed paper-backed children's books, postcards and children's calendars and contributed regularly to Amalgamated Press titles including *Chick's Own, Tiny Tots, Bubbles, Bo-Peep,* and various annuals. Her accomplished drawings of children appeared regularly on covers of *Wife and Home* and the *Woman's*

Commenting on the liveliness of her work, a contemporary journalist writing in the Stationery Trades Journal remarked *"...she conceives the whole of the ideas for her sketches and most are purchased just as fast as they can be completed."* Margaret was only twenty two when she was commissioned to design several of Tuck's *Dressing Dolls* series, which are amongst today's rarest and most sought after children's postcards. Their rarity is due to the pleasure they have given to young children, with scissors at the ready, so that not too many cut-out postcards remain intact.

Margaret gave her own interpretation to Series 3381, *Dressing Dolls Series I,* Series 3384, *Dolls of Many Lands* and 3394, *Mechanical Dolls Series I.* Her fluent sense of draughtsmanship accurately reflects the popular styles in children's dress and makes these postcards poignant examples of nineteen twenties' artistry. Around 1930 she designed a weekly strip of cut-out dolls in *Bo-Peep* magazine.

Margaret Banks was a gifted portraitist and miniaturist. She was as proficient working in oils as she was in any other medium. While still at art school, she showed her potential as a painter by winning a national painting competition and shortly after she had graduated, a

of *The Church Times,* was exhibited at the 1920 Royal Academy Summer Exhibition.

It was said of her, *"...she is never so happy, as when, with the key of her perennially youthful imagination, she enters the magic realms of childhood's fancy and translates the simple beauty and happiness."*

*Unpublished artwork for Raphael Tuck cut-out series, created 25% larger than finished size.*

LEFT HAND PAGE

Artist: Margaret Banks
Pub: Raphael Tuck
Dressing Dolls Series IV
Dolls of Many Lands
Packet
Oilette Series 3384
[c.1922]

RIGHT HAND PAGE

Above & below left:
Artist: Margaret Banks
Pub: Raphael Tuck
Dressing Dolls Series I
Oilette Series 3381 [2 of 6]
[c.1921]

Above & below centre:
Artist: Margaret Banks
Pub: Raphael Tuck
Dressing Dolls Series IV
Dolls of Many Lands
Oilette Series 3384 [2 of 6]
[c.1921]

Above & below right:
Artist: Margaret Banks
Pub: Raphael Tuck
Mechanical Dolls Series I
Oilette Series 3394 [2 of 6]
[c.1921]

Dolly Dimple
and her frocks

LITTLE MISS AMERICA

The Little
Colleen

MECHANICAL DOLL Series

Little Pamela
and her frocks

LITTLE MISS BRITAIN

A Bonnie
Highland Laddie

MECHANICAL DOLL Series

# Sybil Barham (1877-1950)

Sybil Barham was born in Birmingham, the daughter of Francis Foster Barham, a bank manager, and his wife. Sibilla. However, the Barhams were a literary family. Her grandfather Charles was the brother of Thomas Foster Barham (1794-1869), a physician and author of many theological works. Her uncles were William (1802-1847), a poet, and Francis (1808-1871), a writer and journalist.

As a young girl Sybil and her family lived at 9 Bennets Hill, Birmingham. She had five brothers and sisters – Margaret Hilda, Harold, Charles, Muriel and Gertrude. It is likely that the girls in the family were taught by a governess, but in 1899 at the age of twenty two, Sybil was enrolled at the Herkomer Art School, where she studied painting for three years. There she befriended Kate Cowderoy, a

fellow student, who became a successful painter and illustrated for Raphael Tuck.

At the Herkomer Art School, Sybil found herself in an élite environment. To gain entry to the school, the quality of students' work had to be extremely high and many had attended other art schools prior to joining. A number of the students, like Lucy Kemp Welch, Mary Horsfall and Mabel Gear graduated and became well known animal painters. However, two thirds of the pupils were female and many ceased to practice when they married or other family demands were made on them. It was characteristic of the time that women were not expected to make a career as artists. Only the exceptionally talented were able to overcome this prejudice.

The women who chose commercial illustration were particularly fortunate in

that the rapid development of colour printing at the turn of the century provided an enormous boost to those who took up commercial art and chose to illustrate books, postcards and the like.

By the time she left art school, Sybil lived at the Priest's House, Bromsgrove and had become dedicated to painting. She exhibited at several major art galleries including Birmingham. Always preferring to work on relatively small formats, she decided that the new postcard medium would be well-suited to her style and started working for CW Faulkner around 1905. Her favourite subjects are of young people in twilight; soft browns, greens and blues being the prevailing colours of her choice. But many of the scenes she paints reveal a fascination for lanterns reflecting on faces and moonlight reflecting on water.

Most of her postcards are surrounded with dark brown borders, which at first glance convey a sombre tone to the paintings, but in reality, add depth and presence to her delicate and romantic style.

In all of Sybil Barham's paintings one sees a reflection of her idealistic nature and dreams of a gentle pastoral world – perhaps her interpretation of Utopia. Her softly drawn characters seem to waft sylph-like through her pictures with never a hint of violent movement – a refreshing sight for those caught up in a world speeding into the twentieth century.

Press reviews praised her genteel and delicate work highly. The *Stationery Trades Journal* gives a glowing review of CW Faulkner series 875: "*Beautiful Spring: ...stands prominent for its poetic feeling and imagination, artistic colouring and graceful treatment. This is a set of six drawings by S Barham depicting different phases of 'beautiful spring'. The pictures show a young girl gathering flowers by a brook or descending a hill. They are framed by a deep margin of broad grey which set the colouring most effectively. The set may be looked upon as one of the most charming that have been published for some time.*"

Sybil Barham worked almost exclusively for CW Faulkner, and her popular paintings, appeared on prints, postcards, greetings cards and calendars. Her postcards illustrate many of the popular children's themes, including nursery rhymes, games and pastimes, Browning's *Pied Piper of Hamelin*, Stevenson's *A Child's Garden of Verses* and Clifford Mills' *Where the Rainbow Ends*. Her favourite subjects were flowers and young maidens acting out visual interpretations from Shakespeare and other prominent writers – perhaps an association with her family's literary past.

She illustrated books and contributed to children's annuals and magazines throughout her career. She spent the later years of her life, painting at her home in East Durrant, Havant, in Hampshire, which she shared with Elizabeth (Bessie) Maynard, her friend and companion from their Herkomer days.

*A group of students at the Herkomer School [c.1900]. Sybil Barham is standing, third from the right at the back. Kate Cowderoy is second from the right.*

*Above left:*
Artist: Sybil Barham
Pub: CW Faulkner
Series 502B [1 of 6]
[1905]

*Centre left:*
Artist: Sybil Barham
Pub: CW Faulkner
Series 964 [1 of 6]
*Songs of Innocence*
[1909]

*Below left:*
Artist: Sybil Barham
Pub: CW Faulkner
Series 1218 [1 of 6]
*Where the Rainbow Ends
(Impressions of Mavis Yorke)*
[1912]

*Above left:*
Artist: Sybil Barham
Pub: CW Faulkner
Series 875 [1 of 6]
*Beautiful Spring*
[1908]

*Below centre:*
Artist: Sybil Barham
Pub: CW Faulkner
Series 1856 [1 of 6]
[1924]

*Above right:*
Artist: Sybil Barham
Pub: CW Faulkner
Series 1268D [1 of 6]
[1912]

*Below right:*
Artist: Sybil Barham
Pub: CW Faulkner
Series 1219 [1 of 6]
*Memories of Pavlova*
[1912]

WHAT ARE THE WILD WAVES SAYING ?

A Lantern Symphony

"When Daffodils begin to peer."

Where the Rainbow ends

Will-o'-the-Wisp tunes his pipe to the "Wind Song"

Evening Primroses.

The Bacchanale

# Cicely Mary Barker (1895-1973)

Cicely Mary Barker was born on 28 June 1895, the second daughter of Walter Barker, a partner in a seed supply company and his wife Mary. They lived comfortably in a sizeable Victorian house in a middle-class suburb of Croydon and due to the delicate state of Cicely's health her family cosseted and protected her from the outside world through out her childhood.

Walter Barker was himself a gifted watercolourist and so he encouraged Cicely in her own artistic development. He enrolled her at the Croydon Art Society, where they both exhibited from

*From* Flower Fairies of the Spring *published by Blackie. [1923]*

time to time and arranged for her to undertake an art correspondence course, so that she could work from home. One of her tutors and major influences was the illustrator Alice B Woodward (1862-1951).

As a small child Cicely spent hours painting meticulously the Kate Greenaway Painting Books she was given. She loved Kate Greenaway, who was one major influences and may account for her predelction for drawing ravishingly pretty children in idyllic rural settings, as her mentor had done some forty years earlier.

Walter died in 1912 at the age of 43, from a virus he had contracted from a corn sample he was testing. It was a devastating blow, but the family bore the loss with Christian fortitude. Dorothy, Cicely's elder sister, decided to train as a kindergarten teacher enabling her to earn a small salary.

In 1924, Cicely moved into 23 The Waldrons with Dorothy and her mother. It was a semi-detached Victorian villa and despite its close proximity to the centre of Croydon, it was in a select and private area. Artist Jean Burns, the present occupier remembers: "*Dorothy set up a kindergarten in the house, while Cicely, then aged 29, built a wooden studio in the garden. Before long she was painting the now famous Flower Fairies using children from Dorothy's classroom as models....In the studio there was a box of 'wings' for props, a stove for warmth and lots of paints and drawings.*"

Cicely is best known for her flower fairies – cleverly conceived images that combine childlike winged fairies in picturesque botanical costumes with which young children easily identified.

Deeply religious like her close friend, illustrator Margaret Tarrant, she was an ardent churchgoer and supporter of Christian causes. She designed a beautiful stained glass window to be seen at St Andrews Church, Croydon, and devoted a great deal of time designing cards for charity. Her love of nature and fondness for country walks, which she shared with Miss Tarrant, are reflected in her delicate

and observant drawings and her obsessive interest in countryside flower fairies.

Perhaps this rhyme, found in a bundle of her correspondence, was inspired by one of her walks in the Surrey countryside.

*"O what are these, so wee so queer?*
*I must not fear such tiny things!*
*I see their wings, like wings of bees;*
*I hear, I hear, a voice that sings*
*A tiny treble, thin and clear.*
*I'm hiding, crouching on my knees*
*Behind the mossy roots of trees;*
*I peep and peer – they're coming near!*
*The busy crowd a burden brings;*
*Now I can see each pointed ear –*
*O are you pixies? Tell me please!"*

As well as writing and illustrating children's books, she illustrated notable series of postcards for a number of prominent publishers.

Sadly, her death at Worthing in Sussex in 1973 occurred just before the 50th anniversary of her first book, *Flower Fairies of the Spring*, the first of a series which she wrote and illustrated and for which she will be best remembered.

Attractive young children dressed in gauzy botanical costumes cleverly entwined with the flower they represent was a simple concept borne out of a

*Text cards. Girl's Friendly Society. [nd]*

creative person's love of nature. Her extremely delicate work was enhanced by her use of watercolour which lends itself so well to the subject matter.

*Above:*
*Pub: J Salmon*
*No. 2478 [1 of 6]*
*[1922]*

*RIGHT HAND PAGE*
*Left hand column:*
*Pub: Harvey Fine Art Publishing*
*[3 of 6]*
*[1922]*

*Above centre:*
*Pub: CW Faulkner*
*Series 1644 [1 of 6]*
*Shakespeare's Boy Characters*
*[1918]*

*Below centre:*
*Pub: CW Faulkner*
*Series 1704 [1 of 6]*
*Shakespeare's Girl Characters*
*[1919]*

*Right hand column:*
*Pub: J Salmon*
*Children of the Allies Series*
*Nos. 921/924 [2 of 6]*
*[1915]*

THE KISS.

A JOY RIDE.

THE DANCE OF THE FAIRIES.

MOTH, PAGE TO DON ADRIANO DE ARMADO.

ARMADO— How canst thou part sadness and melancholy, my tender juvenal?
MOTH— By a familiar demonstration of the working, my tough senior.
ARMADO— Why tough senior? Why tough senior?
MOTH— Why tender juvenal? Why tender juvenal?

LOVE'S LABOUR'S LOST. Act I Scene II

JAPAN

AUDREY, THE GOAT-HERD.

TOUCHSTONE:- Truly, I would the gods had made thee poetical.
AUDREY:- I do not know what "poetical" is. Is it honest in deed and word? Is it a true thing?

AS YOU LIKE IT. ACT III SCENE 3

BELGIUM

Christmas Greetings.

# Doris Bowden (1900-1943)

*"She loved life, she loved people, she loved parties, she was clever, attractive and popular."*

Doris Harland-Bowden, like many of her peers, was an illustrator whose artistic career never really fulfilled its potential. Her father Lt Col. G Harland-Bowden was a successful businessman, MP for north east Derbyshire and a keen sportsman. Doris was equally versatile. She excelled at bridge and became a fine county tennis player. Her brother remembers, *"...when playing bridge, you couldn't let Doris score, because the whole score pad was soon covered with little sketches of fairies and pixies, etc"*.

From an early age she showed an exceptional gift for drawing. In her early teens, she attended St Albans School of Art near her home, but received little help as

*Watching cricket [c.1907]*

her drawing ability exceeded that of a Mr Groves, her tutor, who advised her to develop her own work. She took private drawing lessons from Madamoiselle de Lisle, tutor to Princess Mary, before enrolling at the Slade School of Fine Art in London.

Her educated upbringing and social skills enabled her to present her portfolio to publishers with confidence, resulting in commissions. Soon she was getting her designs into print. Her first cheque was for two guineas from Delectaland in Watford, makers of Vi-Cocoa and Freeman's Real Turtle Soup, for whom she designed and illustrated several delightful booklets.

Her brother remembers that Doris designed greetings cards for Raphael Tuck

*In the garden at Hazeldene, St Albans. [c.1910]*

and Delgado, and by 1920 was writing and illustrating stories on a regular basis. Work from CW Faulkner, *Little Folks, The Rainbow* magazine, *Leading Strings,* published by Wells Gardner & Darton, the *Graphic* and other publications followed. The first book she illustrated in its entirety was a version of *Fairies and Chimneys* by Rose Fyleman.

Doris Bowden's artistry captured the popular mood of the period. She illustrated for the sheer joy of it. Her pictures, though not beautifully drafted, contained all the ingredients that epitomise nursery life in the twenties and thirties, accurately reflecting the costumes, hairstyles attitudes

and pastimes of young children. Her drawing style was economical, but effective and she had a keen eye for observing the nuances of children at play. Sadly, for those who appreciated her artistry, her energies were gradually directed more and more towards social and domestic affairs and to her young family following her marriage to Stanley Osborne in 1926.

*Two greetings cards for Delgado. [c.1938]*

*An excursion in the family Rolls. [c.1913]*

*LEFT HAND PAGE*

*Above & below:*
*Artist: Doris Bowden*
*Pub: Hills & Co*
*Easter Greetings Series*
*[c.1927]*

*RIGHT HAND PAGE*

*Left:*
*Artist: Doris Bowden*
*Pub: CW Faulkner*
*Series 1811 [3 of 6]*
*[1923]*

*Right:*
*Artist: Doris Bowden*
*Pub: CW Faulkner*
*Series 1812 [3 of 6]*
*[1923]*

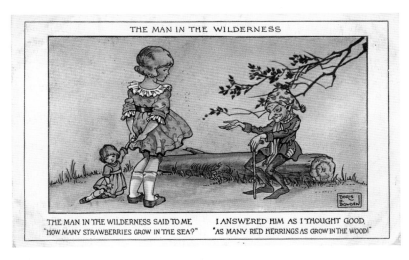

# Sophia May Bowley (1864-1960) & Ada Leonora Bowley (1866-1943)

*Above: Sophia May Bowley. 1908. Below: Ada Leonora Bowley. [c.1903]*

May and Ada Leonora, or 'Pep' as she was called by her family, were inseparable sisters. They lived and worked together all their lives, working primarily as artists for Raphael Tuck. From 1902, they shared a house in Croftdown Road, Highgate with 'Daisy' (Alice Ellen), another close sister. When Daisy died in 1938 and the sisters could not cope with the house, they spent the later years of their lives with their nephew's family in Herne Bay, as devoted to one another as ever.

During the girls' childhood years, the family frequently moved house – from Hackney, where May and her older sister Ellen were born, then to Hampstead where Pep was born, then to Bushey where their brother Leonard and sister Daisy were born, before settling at Burnt Ash Road, Lee, in south London, where other relatives of the family lived.

The sisters' grandparents had established themselves in London in the booming shipbuilding industry during the eighteen thirties and forties. Edwin, their father, was secretary of the British Empire Insurance Company. He recognised May's early and precocious creative talent. At the age of thirteen May had written three full length fairy tales, entitled *Prince Edwin and the Witch*, *Sybil and the Fairy of the Forest* and *Princess Shylie*. He arranged for them to be privately printed and published in paper wrappers and separately bound.

He continued to encourage the creative skills of his two daughters and enrolled them at art schools in south London. Edwin was honorary secretary to the local Blackheath School of Art in the mid eighteen eighties and although no records exist, it is likely that the girls attended the school during that period. May continued her art training at the élite Herkomer Art School between 1888 and 1891 and exhibited pictures at the Royal Academy Summer Exhibitions of 1890 and 1892. But any aspirations she had as a painter were dispelled when her father lost his job and the girls had to concentrate on

CINDERELLA

Old English Songs.     "SALLY IN OUR ALLEY."
" Of all the girls that are so smart
  There's none like pretty Sally,
  She is the darling of my heart
  And lives in our alley ;
  There is no lady in the land
  That's half so sweet as Sally."

supporting the family. May started work as a writer and illustrator, contributing to various Victorian magazines including: *Sylvia's Home Journal, Little Folks, Lady's Pictorial, The Tatler, St Nicholas, The Queen,* and *The Ladies Field Supplement*.

May's earliest postcard illustrations were for Valentine but it was through her contributions to magazines that her work came to the attention of Raphael Tuck around 1894. She introduced her younger sister to the firm and both joined the ranks of their senior artists. They illustrated annuals and books, including some of the most ingenious transformation books ever published. They also worked on novelty toys and games, greetings cards and postcards.

Raphael Tuck and his fellow directors maintained happy personal relationships with their artists and writers and offered encouragement whenever they could; but May and Ada were among their favourites.

With a rich palette of colours the sisters specialised in painting round faced, rosy cheeked and curly-haired children, happy in their nursery surroundings. They were regularly invited to design Tuck's Christmas postcards and excelled at traditional Christmas scenes, such as dancing around the Christmas tree and jovial santas with white bushy beards. They generated

*LEFT HAND PAGE*

*Ada Leonora at work in the studio at Croftdown Road, Highgate. [c.1903]*

*RIGHT HAND PAGE*

*Above left:*
*Artist: Ada Leonora Bowley*
*Pub: Raphael Tuck*
*Dressing Dolls II*
*Oilette Series 3382 [1 of 6]*
*[c.1921]*

*Below left:*
*Artist: Ada Leonora Bowley*
*Pub: Raphael Tuck*
*Nursery Rhyme Dressing Dolls III*
*Oilette Series 3383 [1 of 6]*
*[c.1921]*

*Above right:*
*Artist: Ada Leonora Bowley*
*Pub: Raphael Tuck*
*Fairy Tale Panorama*
*Oilette Series 3386 [1 of 6]*
*[c.1921]*

*Below right:*
*Artist: Ada Leonora Bowley*
*Pub: Raphael Tuck*
*Father Tuck's Toy Rockers*
*Oilette Series 3399 [1 of 6]*
*[c.1922]*

*May Bowley. Dollyville & Dollycot Villa.*
*Raphael Tuck Little Builders No. 300. [c.1908]*

BABY BUNTING

FATHER TUCK'S Fairy Land Panorama

THE FOREST

SQUIRREL HARE

LITTLE RED RIDING HOOD RABBIT

JACKDAW THE WOLF

RED RIDING HOOD

HANDY SPANDY JACK-A-DANDY

FOR INSTRUCTIONS SEE OTHER SIDE

CANDY

Peter paddling his canoe

round and round the lake.

FATHER TUCK'S TOY ROCKERS

all the excitement and anticipation that children love to enjoy on Christmas Eve.

Their styles are similar, but on close inspection one detects that Pep's pictures depict a greater air of mischievousness and fun, while May, perhaps on account of her more a formal art training, painted more conventionally happy children – a true reflection of their real-life characteristics.

The sisters became good friends with Edith Nesbit, whose writing was highly regarded by Raphael Tuck and whose home during the eighteen eighties, in Dorville Road, Lee, south London, was adjacent to Burnt Ash Road, where the Bowley family lived. The careers of Edith Nesbit and May, who was six years younger, had run in parallel. Both women had been obliged, somewhat against their wills, to turn to commercial art and writing to support their families and it is difficult to ascertain exactly how the friendship began. It may have been early in their careers when both women were submitting work to *Sylvia's Home Journal* or they may have met while working for Raphael Tuck, or more likely, they may have first met in the social circles of Lee, where they lived. We do know that in 1892 the sisters spent a vacation in Antibes in France, with the Blands, (E Nesbit's married name). Years later May had retained fond memories of the eventful trip and her impressions of the town, in those days spared all the trappings of commercialism – *"it looked like Nazareth from a distance."* she recalled.

May loved painting from nature and contributed to Tuck's postcard repertoire with two highly colourful illustrations of exotic 'press-out' birds entitled *Birds on the Wing* published in 1921, some of which first appeared in the book *Everything You Can Think Of* (c.1908). Around 1932, she painted an attractive series of postcards of British birds for Salmon of Sevenoaks.

In postcards, perhaps the innovative skills of the sisters are best demonstrated in several very original series of 'cut-outs', and 'press-outs' issued by Tuck between 1921 and 1923. Series 3383 *Nursery Rhyme Dressing Dolls* and series 3386 *Father Tuck's Fairyland Panorama* issued in 1922 were illustrated by Pep. Although unsigned, 'Pep' almost certainly illustrated series 3399 *Father Tuck's Toy Rockers* and series 3403 *Swinging Dolls,* issued in 1923. The concept for these designs dates back to the turn of the century when Tuck issued packets of *Doll Sheets* comprising paper dolls with several changes of costume, much to the delight of the children of the Edwardian period. Published in the nineteen twenties, these designs illustrated by May and Pep are re-issues from earlier projects, although the cut-out series illustrated by Margaret Banks are contemporary to that date. Certainly, series 3399 *Father Tuck's Toy Rockers* first appeared in *Father Tuck's Toy Rockers Modelling Book* in 1905. The Bowley sisters curtailed their association with Tuck before World War I.

They went on to work for other publishers, including Partridge and Dean & Co, but their artwork for Tuck typifies the company's colourful and innovative approach to children's publishing. They contributed hugely to Tuck's success. The books and postcards they illustrated were so attractive and brought such delight to so many, that they sold in their millions.

EVERYTHING YOU CAN THINK OF

*May Bowley.* Everything You Can Think Of *Father Tuck's Happy Times Series [c.1908]*

# Molly Brett (1902-1990)

Always a lover of nature, Molly Brett had a remarkable gift for observation, enabling her to make the animals she drew look thoroughly natural, while bestowing on them distinctly human characteristics.

She was one of the best exponents of twentieth century English anthropomorphic children's art, in the tradition of Peter Rabbit and Rupert Bear. She created a world where animals are in the ascendency, engaging in all sorts of human activities. In their world, life is always serene, time seems to stand still and thoughts of malice never enters the heads of her furry friends.

She developed her charming style at an early age and never really changed it throughout her career – a career that spanned more than seventy years.

Though she never married and had children of her own, Molly kept in touch with her youthful audience and spent time studying and sketching children in the local park and at the seaside. Her sympathetic personality and keen sense of humour provided her with a shrewd understanding of what they liked. When painting teddy bears, for example, she always borrowed old ones, maintaining that they did not acquire a personality until children had played with them.

Molly was born in Croydon in 1902 and attended school at Maybury House, Woking and Crofton Grange, Orpington,

before enrolling at the Press Art School in London. Her art education was positively encouraged by her mother, Mary Brett Gould, herself an accomplished animal painter. Molly took a correspondence course in book illustration which launched her into a lifetime of children's illustration.

She grew up in the verdant Surrey countryside and kept a wide variety of pets including a cow, a donkey, goats, bees, pigeons, guinea fowl and a large turkey that later became the hero in one of her books. She was so enchanted by animals that she was often to be seen with her sketchbook at the zoo, various local markets, or the Natural History Museum, London.

*'Eight Times Two' from* Leading Strings *pub. Wells Gardner Darton & Co. [1925]. One of Molly Brett's earliest illustrations.*

The colourful garden of Molly's cottage set in woodland Surrey, with its trees, flowers, goldfish pond, birds and squirrels, set the scene for many of her delightful pictures. She was a keen gardener, an active member of the Women's Institute and belonged to the Art Society and the Society of Authors.

In the early days she worked for Collins, Muller, Raphael Tuck, Warne, Wells Gardner & Darton and fine art publishers CW Faulkner, for whom she designed postcards and greetings cards. Her long and successful career was given a further boost in the nineteen fifties with an invitation to illustrate Enid Blyton's books for the Brockhampton Press. Although mostly in black and white, the opportunity enhanced her reputation in the publishing world.

Her first postcard illustrations featured fairies, a popular subject in the twenties and thirties. This was due in part to the much publicised *Cottingley Fairies*, and the great tradition of English fairy painting, dating from the eighteenth century. But before long, her early childhood influences led her back to animals. *"I like drawing animals in their natural settings best of all, but playing like children"* she once told us.

In the late twenties Molly forged a close relationship with the Medici Society, an enduring partnership that lasted for sixty years. The Medici Society's aim of providing the best reproductions possible at the cheapest price is a feature of the business that has attracted many of the best illustrators and Molly Brett was no exception. As well as illustrating stories for other writers, she wrote twenty one books for the Medici Society. In all the company published around five hundred of her paintings, prints, greetings cards and postcards. She never felt the need to be represented by an agent, always preferring to negotiate contracts with her publishers for herself.

In today's high tech environment, her style and choice of subject matter has taken on a quaint and whimsical charm, but her work will always pass the test of time. It contains humour and vitality in abundance, ensuring the allegiance of young children for years to come.

*'Making Them Grow' from* Leading Strings *pub. Wells Gardner Darton & Co. [1925].*

PIXIE PLAYTHINGS.          SYCAMORE SEEDS.

PIXIE PLAYTHINGS.          HONESTY.

*LEFT HAND PAGE*

*Artist: Molly Brett*
*Pub: CW Faulkner & Co*
*Series 2027 [2 of 6]*
*Pixie Playthings*
*[1932]*

*RIGHT HAND PAGE*

*Left column:*
*Artist: Molly Brett*
*Pub: CW Faulkner & Co*
*Series 1984 [2 of 6]*
*[1929]*

*Centre column:*
*Artist: Molly Brett*
*Pub: The Medici Society*
*Packet 168/169*
*Aesop's Fables*
*The Hare and the Tortoise*
*The Fox and the Grapes*
*[c.1953]*

*Right column:*
*Artist: Molly Brett*
*Pub: The Medici Society*
*Packet 145/177*
*[c.1950]*

# Barbara Briggs (1887-1976)

*Barbara Briggs in the nineteen twenties*

Barbara Briggs was the daughter of Isaac Briggs the younger, and his wife Sarah. Isaac the younger and his brother William were established in a worsted-spinning business in Wakefield, founded by their father, Isaac Briggs the elder, a remarkable entrepreneur who made his fortune in the eighteen forties as a railway contractor. He owned a house, *Sandal Cliff* at Sandal Magna near Wakefield, with a large garden and pastures, a coach house and stabling for his horses.

The Briggs family were musical and pillars of the local community. At some time in his early life, Isaac Briggs the elder had forsaken the Church of England and had become a keen Congregationalist. He and his family founded and maintained a church in the poor quarter of Wakefield, where he was pleased to provide the organ accompaniment at services.

Barbara and her parents lived at *Beechfield,* close to Sandal Magna and the rest of the family. She was educated at home by a governess and being an only child, she had a great deal bestowed upon her. But she had an overwhelming passion for animals and gained a reputation locally for being able to identify and heal their injuries.

Even as a young girl she had a natural talent for drawing and was mainly self-taught. Her love of animals naturally led her to drawing and painting them. She exhibited her pictures locally and in 1920 exhibited at the Walker Art Gallery, Liverpool and the Society of Women Artists in London. In the same year, she illustrated her first book, entitled *All About Pets*, in conjunction with fellow illustrator Savile Lumley. She also attracted the attention of publishers Humphrey Milford who commissioned her to illustrate animal pictures for the books and postcards published for their younger readers.

Having settled her father's affairs, in the wake of his death in 1926, she moved to London on a permanent basis and forged a successful working relationship with Eleanor Helme, writer and the first woman journalist to report on golf. Both Barbara and Eleanor were Fellows of the Royal Zoological Society and therefore qualified to embark on a series of substantial books about wildlife, the first of which, entitled *Friends of Field and Forest*, was published by the Religious Tract Society in 1926.

She illustrated several postcard series depicting dogs for publishers Geographia and Humphrey Milford. It takes an artist with a great deal of love and understanding of animals to create such perceptive studies. In contrast, the one series of children she illustrated for the Humphrey Milford postcards series was somewhat less assured.

Barbara Briggs remained in London illustrating books until 1938, when she emigrated to Canada and married John Woodward, a rancher from British Columbia. Living on a large stock farm, surrounded by animals and natural beauty, was her dream come true. Her reputation as an artist never dwindled and she continued to illustrate books in America under her maiden name for the rest of her life. Here was a woman descended from a wealthy family, with no need to work, save her desire to use her natural talents to help the preservation of wildlife as best she knew how.

*'The Fox / The Harvest Mouse' from* Friends of the Field and Forest. *RTS. [nd]*

*Left column:*
*Artist: Barbara Briggs*
*Pub: Humphrey Milford*
*Our Terriers [2 of 6]*
*[1926]*

*Right column:*
*Artist: Barbara Briggs*
*Pub: Humphrey Milford*
*The Busy Bees [2 of 6]*
*[1926]*

*Center column:*
*Artist: Barbara Briggs*
*Pub: Humphrey Milford*
*Our Dogs [3 of 6]*
*[1923]*

IRISH·TERRIER

ENTANGLED

BET LIKES HER CRACKER CAP SO GAY,
AND SAYS SHE'LL WEAR IT EVERY DAY.

SKYE·TERRIER

KNITTING

WINDY·WEATHER

WHEN JOHN GOES OUT TO DRIVE HIS HORSE
HE TAKES A GREAT BIG WHIP, OF COURSE.

# Nina Brisley (1898-1978) & her sisters

Nina Brisley was the youngest of three sisters, born in Bexhill, Sussex to Constance and George Brisley, by all accounts a rather tyrannical chemist, with unorthodox views on school education. As a result, the sisters spent much of their childhood at home. Joyce (1896-1978), the middle sister, recalled lying on the floor of their house reading the heavy volumes of the *Encyclopaedia Britannica* wondering what their friends were learning at school.

This strange situation, combined with their parents difficult marital relationship, created a close bond between the sisters Nina, Joyce and Ethel (1886-1961), also known as Tony. Ethel was the eldest by ten years or so and because of the lack of academic guidance, had taken to drawing and was beginning to earn money painting miniatures of friends and family. Nina and Joyce followed her lead and began to

*Joyce Lankaster Brisley. [1930]*

discover themselves by writing and sketching. Eventually, they directed their creative energies into the production of a homemade magazine called *The Wanderer*, produced monthly and passed around their circle of friends for a halfpenny a read, or a penny if you were over fifteen. It contained stories, pictures, verses and competitions that the girls had created. Their enterprise paid off. Through a family friend, the

magazines found their way to Lord Northcliffe, the owner of Amalgamated Press, then the world's largest magazine empire. He was impressed and put the girls on the bottom rung of the commercial ladder by introducing them to the editor of *Home Chat*, a popular weekly paper for the young.

The family split up around 1912 and before the female members of the family left for London, Ethel and Constance, her mother, joined the Christian Scientists, a movement that was to become important to all of them throughout their lives.

After spells living in Brixton and Streatham, south London, the family settled in Baron's Court and the girls pursued their artistic goals. They were a close knit family. Nina and Joyce attended Lambeth School of Art by day and practised writing and illustrating stories when they arrived home at night. All three sisters became accomplished painters and exhibited paintings at the Royal Academy. By 1920 they all belonged to the Christian Science movement and by the mid twenties Nina and Joyce were regular contributors to the *Christian Science Monitor* with verses and illustrations and later, stories.

It was in the *Monitor* that Milly Molly Mandy first appeared, written and illustrated by Joyce. A series ensued and in 1928 Harrap published *Milly Molly Mandy Stories*, the first of many books, readers, plays and omnibuses to be published.

Like her sister Joyce, Nina became involved with book illustration including a long series on girls' school life at the Chalet School in the Austrian Tyrol written by Elinor Brent-Dyer. She also liked to illustrate books for Elizabeth Clark and Elsie Oxenham.

Ethel was the serious artist. Specialising in portraits and miniatures she exhibited over forty pictures at the Royal Academy between 1910 and 1945. She illustrated a few books, one in 1938 in conjunction with Nina entitled *A Little Book of Bible Stories* by Elizabeth Clark.

*Milly Molly Mandy and her family in the* Christian Science Monitor. *[1925]*

However, both Ethel and Nina illustrated postcards for Vivian Mansell. The miniature format suited Ethel, who concentrated mainly on endearing child studies, while Nina's more exhuberent approach allowed her to present a wider variety of images of children at play. We have recorded only one set of six postcards, also published by Mansell, illustrated by Joyce, two examples of which appear opposite.

*Front cover,* The Children's Year, *pub. Blackie. [nd]*

*Above & below left:*
*Joyce Lankester Brisley*
*Pub: Vivian Mansell*
*Series 1156 [2 of 6]*
*[1920]*

*Above & below centre:*
*Ethel Constance Brisley*
*Pub: Vivian Mansell*
*Series 1005 [2 of 6]*
*[1915]*

*Above & below right:*
*Nina Kennard Brisley*
*Pub: Vivian Mansell*
*Series 1037 [2 of 4]*
*[1916]*

Cissy's small head is so be-decked with curls.
She thinks she is the luckiest of girls.

Do Come

"See-Saw"
Toby, you don't See-Saw a bit well

Ruth's hair is red; I fear this doth portend
She has a temper that she had best mend.

"I'm Ready"

"Hide and Seek"
Now don't you give me away

# Randolph Caldecott (1846-1886)

Caldecott was born in Chester, the son of an accountant and educated at King's School where he became head boy. From an early age he was devoted to the country and country pursuits. He spent much of his leisure time roaming the countryside. He loved to fish and shoot and frequented the meets of the hounds, markets and cattle fairs, all of which provided him with a bank of knowledge for his drawing in later years. In 1861 he went to work in a bank at Whitchurch, Shropshire, where for six years he seemed to have had time to indulge in his favourite country pursuits. When he was transferred to Manchester, he attended Manchester Art School, joined an art club and sketched scenes of life in a big Victorian city that must have seemed quite foreign to a country lad.

It was not until 1868 that he had his first drawings published, and then only in a humorous paper called *Will o' the Wisp*. He was bored by the bank and this minor achievement spurred him on to contribute sketches and cartoons to the *Graphic*, *Punch* and *London Society*, a fashionable magazine whose contributors included many notable artists and writers of the day.

In 1878 he met Edmund Evans, the reprographic genius behind the success of Kate Greenaway, who suggested that he should illustrate a series of colour books for children.

**Randolph Caldecott's Picture Books**
In 1914, scenes from *Randolph Caldecott's Picture Books*, were published by Warne in eight sets of six postcards, numbered from A1 – A6 to H1 – H6, a total of forty eight. They were re-issued in 1933 with slightly different set groupings. Cards from four of the books were never published. They were: *The Babes in the Wood* (1879), *The Farmer's Boy* (1881), *Mrs Mary Blaize* (1885), *The Great Panjandrum Himself* (1885).
*14 books contained 1 story and 2 books contained 2 stories – *Hey Diddle Diddle and Baby Bunting* and also *Ride a Cock Horse to Banbury Cross and A Farmer went Trotting upon his Grey Mare*.

| Postcard collection 1 | | | | |
|---|---|---|---|---|
| *The Diverting History of John Gilpin* (1878) | A1 | A2 | B1 | B2 |
| *The House the Jack Built* (1878) | C1 | C2 | D1 | D2 |
| *An Elegy on the Death of a Mad Dog* (1879) | A5 | A6 | B5 | B6 |
| Postcard collection 2 | | | | |
| *Three Jovial Huntsmen* (1880) | A3 | A4 | B3 | B4 |
| *Sing a Song of Sixpence* (1880) | C3 | C4 | D3 | D4 |
| *The Queen of Hearts* (1881) | C5 | C6 | D5 | D6 |
| Postcard collection 3 | | | | |
| *Hey Diddle Diddle and Baby Bunting* (1882) | E1 | E2 | E3 | E4 |
| *The Milkmaid* (1879) | E5 | E6 | F5 | F6 |
| *A Frog he Would A-Wooing Go* (1883) | G1 | G2 | H1 | H2 |
| *The Fox Jumps over the Parson's Gate* (1883) | G5 | G6 | H5 | H6 |
| Postcard collection 4 | | | | |
| *Ride a Cock-Horse and A Farmer went Trotting upon his Grey Mare* (1884) | F1 | F2 | F3 | F4 |
| *Come Lasses and Lads* (1884) | G3 | G4 | H3 | H4 |

The first of the sixteen *Picture Books* was begun and Caldecott was able to draw on the store of rural knowledge he recalled from his Shropshire days. Like many of the late Victorian illustrators, Caldecott posed the concept of a rural and pastoral world by dressing his characters in rustic eighteenth century English costume.

The *Picture Books* ranked second only in popularity to Kate Greenaway's children's books. His fresh and original technique of outline and applied flat colour had its keen admirers, especially Cecil Aldin. Caldecott turned to children's illustration late in life, having struggled for years to gain recognition as an illustrator. He began as a draughtsman and advanced his career through his contributions to *London Society*. Sadly, he died prematurely while in America seeking a cure for rheumatic fever from which he suffered.

The series of sixteen *Caldecott's Picture Books*, were first published by George Routledge between 1878 and 1885. In 1896 Routledge sold its children's book list which included titles by Caldecott and Kate Greenaway to the publisher Frederick Warne and subsequent reprints of the Routledge titles carried the Warne imprint.

*Postcards from the Randolph Caldecott Picture Books published by Frederick Warne [1914]*

*Above left:*
*The House That Jack Built Postcard C2*

*Below left:*
*The Queen of Hearts Postcard C5*

*Above centre:*
*The Diverting History of John Gilpin Postcard A2*

*Below centre:*
*Sing a Song of Sixpence Postcard C4*

*Above right:*
*A Frog He Would A-wooing Go Postcard G1*

*Centre right:*
*Bye Baby Bunting Postcard E3*

*Below right:*
*Come Lasses and Lads Postcard G3*

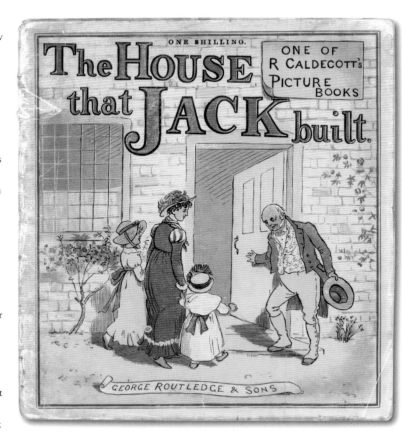

The House that Jack Built, *the first of 16 picture books, containing 33 illustrations engraved by Edmund Evans, published in 1878 by George Routledge & Sons*

*LEFT HAND PAGE*

*Above & below:*
*Artist: Marjorie Dexter*
*Pub: J Salmon*
*Series 3141*
*Numbers 3145/3146 [2 of 6]*
*[1926]*

*RIGHT HAND PAGE*
*Top row:*
*Artist: Marjorie Dexter*
*Pub: Valentine*
*Unnumbered series*
*Valentine's Series*
*[1925]*

*Bottom row:*
*Artist: Marjorie Dexter*
*Pub: J Salmon*
*Series 3765*
*Nos. 3765/3767/3769*
*[3 of 6]*
*[1931]*

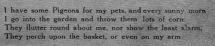

This is the Cat that killed the Rat.

— *The House that Jack built* —

*From the Original drawing by* RANDOLPH CALDECOTT

PUBLISHED BY F. WARNE & Cº

The dogs did bark, the children screamed,
Up flew the windows all;
And every soul cried out, "Well done!"
As loud as he could bawl

— *John Gilpin* —

*From the Original drawing by* RANDOLPH CALDECOTT

PUBLISHED BY F. WARNE & Cº

A Frog he would a-wooing go, Whether his Mother would let him or no.

— *A Frog he would a-wooing go* —

*From the Original Drawing by* RANDOLPH CALDECOTT

PUBLISHED BY F. WARNE & Cº

Bye, Baby Bunting!

*From the Original Drawing by* RANDOLPH CALDECOTT

PUBLISHED BY F. WARNE & Cº

The Queen of Hearts, she made some tarts,
All on a summer's day

— *The Queen of Hearts* —

*From the Original drawing by* RANDOLPH CALDECOTT

PUBLISHED BY F. WARNE & Cº

Was not that a dainty dish,
To set before the King?

— *Sing a Song for Sixpence* —

*From the Original drawing by* RANDOLPH CALDECOTT

PUBLISHED BY F. WARNE & Cº

Come Lasses and Lads, get leave of your Dads, And away to the May-pole hey.

— *Come Lasses and Lads* —

*From the Original Drawing by* RANDOLPH CALDECOTT

PUBLISHED BY F. WARNE & Cº

# Dorothy Carleton-Smyth (1881-1933)

*Dorothy Carleton-Smyth attending the retirement reception for Maurice Greiffenhagen (left), Professor of Painting at the Glasgow School of Art. [1929]*

The set of nursery rhyme postcards shown opposite was published by Valentines of Dundee early in 1904. It is the only series ever attempted by one of Scotland's most talented female artists. It is a coincidence that this series follows closely behind the only series of postcards illustrated by a contemporary from the Glasgow School of Art – six nursery rhymes by Jessie M King.

Dorothy Carleton-Smyth was a student at the Glasgow School of Art where she studied theatre and costume, stained glass, drawing and painting and at the age of twenty one she exhibited her stained glass window *Tristan and Iseult* at the Glasgow 1901 International Exhibition.

Taking a closer look at her postcard designs, painted two years later, one catches glimpses of her key strengths. The thick angular line and flat colours are reminiscent of stained glass. The costumes are impeccably detailed and the overall presentation has a staged and theatrical presence about it.

Dorothy was born in Glasgow of Irish and French heritage, with family origins in Fife. The sisters Dorothy, Olive, also an artist, and Rose a music composer, were the daughters of William Hugh Smyth and Elizabeth Ramage.

William Smyth was a jute manufacturer and moved the family to Manchester in the eighteen eighties when he became managing director of the Openshaw Oilcloth Company. Dorothy attended the Manchester School of Art for three years from 1895 to 1898.

An early mentor was Walter Crane, who had a visiting directorship at the school at that time. Crane and the Arts and Crafts movement were much revered by Fra Newbery, a committed socialist and principal of the Glasgow School of Art, which Dorothy attended between 1898 and 1905. During that time she won major prizes in the Board of Education National Competitions, namely: a bronze medal in 1899 for poster design, a silver medal in 1900 for book illustration and a bronze medal for stained glass design.

Her impressive career began as a portrait painter, but because of her fascination for exotic clothes combined with a love of the theatre she become the leading theatrical designer at the art school. Through a chance meeting with FR Benson, a prominent Shakespearean producer, she was appointed costume designer for his forthcoming tour, an entrée which enabled her to break into a jealously guarded closed shop of costume designers in London. Her success took her to France where she also worked for the Louis Verande and Paris Opera companies.

By 1910, she was designing stage costumes to great acclaim. She designed for Matheson Lang's production of *Othello* and John Martin Harvey's production of *Richard III,* and in 1914, enjoyed a major success with costumes for Granville Barker's production of *A Midsummer Night's Dream.* The critics dubbed them as *"futuristic".* On her appointment as Principal of Commercial Art at the Glasgow School of Art in 1914, Dorothy turned to teaching, concentrating on costume, lithography and illustration. She continued her portraiture, produced local plays in Glasgow and worked with Charles Rennie Mackintosh and others on decoration. She enjoyed success as a book illustrator for Blackie and Collins, worked in silver and designed panels for cruise liners. She also designed stone carvings, bronzes and murals and consolidated her reputation with writings and lectures and broadcast art talks for children on BBC radio, as *Paint Box Pixie.*

*Dorothy Carleton-Smyth,* Self portrait. *Oil on canvas. [1921]*

*Artist: Dorothy Carleton-Smyth*
*Pub: Valentine*
*Nursery Rhymes [6 of 6]*
*[1904]*

"JACK AND JILL WENT UP THE HILL
TO FETCH A PAIL OF WATER
JACK FELL DOWN AND BROKE
HIS CROWN,
AND JILL CAME TUMBLING AFTER"

*Valentine's Series—" Nursery Rhymes."*

"SIMPLE SIMON MET A PIEMAN
GOING TO THE FAIR;
SAYS SIMPLE SIMON
TO THE PIEMAN
"LET ME TASTE YOUR WARE"

*Valentine's Series—" Nursery Rhymes."*

"SING A SONG O' SIXPENCE   WHEN THE PIE WAS OPENED
A POCKET FULL OF RYE   THE BIRDS BEGAN TO SING
FOUR & TWENTY BLACK-   WAS NOT THAT A DAINTY
BIRDS,   DISH
BAKED IN A PIE!   TO SET BEFORE A KING?"

*Valentine's Series—" Nursery Rhymes."*

"HEY DIDDLE DIDDLE THE CAT & THE FIDDLE   THE LITTLE DOG LAUGHED TO SEE SUCH FUN
THE COW JUMPED OVER THE MOON   AND THE DISH RAN AWAY WITH THE SPOON"

*Valentine's Series—" Nursery Rhymes."*

"TAM TAM THE PIPER'S SON
STOLE A PIG AND AWAY DID RUN"
THE PIG WAS EAT
AND TAM WAS BEAT
AND TAM RAN ROARING DOWN THE
STREET"

*Valentine's Series—" Nursery Rhymes."*

"WHAT IS YOUR FORTUNE   "THEN I CANNOT MARRY
MY PRETTY MAID?"   YOU MY PRETTY MAID!"
"MY FACE IS MY FOR-   "NOBODY ASKED YOU
~TUNE SIR" SHE SAID   SIR" SHE SAID

*Valentine's Series—" Nursery Rhymes."*

# René Cloke (1904-1995)

*Walking on Wimbledon Common, [1975]*

René Cloke was an artist devoted to the creation of pictures for young children to enjoy. Her aim was to *"draw lively, colourful illustrations of animals, children and fairies to rouse the interest of every small person who opens one of my books".*

She was born Isobel Mabel Neighbour Cloke in Plymouth, Devon, the daughter of a bank manager. René had no formal art training, yet became one of our most prolific and admired children's illustrators.

Always in good health and full of energy, she worked as an illustrator for over sixty years, continuing until four months prior to her death, aged 90. As her career unfolded, she became noted for her distinctive and whimsical watercolours depicting fairies, flowers and animals.

Even as a young girl she was totally absorbed in drawing and painting and her persistence in approaching publishers eventually persuaded W & R Chambers of Edinburgh, to give her a chance and commission her to contribute pen and ink illustrations for *The Radiant Way* for infants, first published in 1933, a series aimed at achieving fluent reading, based on phonetics (the Initial Teaching Alphabet). This was followed shortly afterwards by *Mr Never-Lost* and *Maidlin to the Rescue* by Elsie Oxenham for the same publisher.

In the ensuing years, René illustrated many greetings cards and postcards, first, from 1934, with CW Faulkner & Co and then Valentines of Dundee, J Salmon of Sevenoaks and later with the Medici Society.

René enjoyed the postcard medium. She remembered *"...the predetermined space allotted for the picture enabled me to focus on making each illustration tell a vivid story".* She painted the most evocative fairyland scenes with captivating titles like: *Thistledown for Fairy Pillows, The Fairies Ferryboat* and *The Pixie Postman.*

The fairyland characters in her postcard illustrations of 1937 for CW Faulkner and Valentine are memorable for their naïve gracefulness and lightness of line. These designs executed by a self-taught illustrator near the dawn of her career are remarkable and rank with the best of her illustrious contemporaries engaged in similar work.

Through her long career as a writer and illustrator, her output of books, prints, postcards and greetings cards was enormous, with a break during wartime when she worked as a tracer for the War Office, mapping enemy installations.

In later years she illustrated books by Enid Blyton and wrote and illustrated books for leading publishers including Blackie, Collins, Ward Lock, Wheaton and Award Publications. Her popularity peaked in the nineteen eighties with many of her most popular titles being published and reissued at home and overseas.

She was a shy and modest person who shunned publicity, although kind and generous to those who knew her. From 1928 she lived in Wimbledon, south London, with her brother Douglas, an architect and sister Olive, the noted concert pianist, often returning to the West Country for walking holidays.

She worked from home in her first floor studio packed with children's books, overlooking a beautiful garden, where she could happily immerse herself in a world of fantasy.

*Greetings card published by Salmon. [c.1938]*

*Greetings card, pub. Noel Tatt. [1985]*

*"She found herself falling down a very deep well." from* Alice in Wonderland *[1943.]*

*Above left:*
*Artist: René Cloke*
*Pub: CW Faulkner*
*Series 2047 [1 of 6]*
*[1935]*

*Below left:*
*Artist: René Cloke*
*Pub: CW Faulkner*
*Series 2041 [1 of 6]*
*[1935]*

*Above centre:*
*Artist: René Cloke*
*Pub: CW Faulkner*
*Series 2019 [1 of 6]*
*[1934]*

*Below centre:*
*Artist: René Cloke*
*Pub: Valentine*
*René Cloke series [1 of 6]*
*No. 3717*
*[1937]*

*Right column:*
*Artist: René Cloke*
*Pub: Valentine*
*Art·Photo series [2 of 6]*
*Nos. 3533/3536*
*[1936]*

A MARCH BREEZE

The Pixie Pool.

AN ELFIN SERENADE.

THE PIXIE POSTMAN.

JACK FROST.

THE DREAM FAIRY.

# Phyllis Cooper (1895-1988)

*"Anyone who visits 'Northbourne', the house in Hatton Street, Wellingborough, where Mr WR Cooper lives, must know at once it is the home of an artist. Walls of his living room are covered with oil paintings, water colours and etchings, examples of his work."* Wellingborough Advertiser, Sept 1937 on the retirement of William Cooper, landscape painter.

*William Cooper sketching behind Grendon, near his home. [c.1937]*

William, the father of Phyllis Cooper was a fine landscape painter. As a young man, he studied painting at the South Kensington Schools and then in Paris for some years. He exhibited at the Royal Academy and other leading London galleries. He taught art at the Wellingborough Technical Institute for twenty eight years, but most of his working life was spent in commercial design and magazine illustration. He took the greatest interest in anyone who was interested in art and would take endless time and trouble in helping those who came to him for advice and tuition.

Phyllis was the eldest of four daughters; her brother was a film cameraman. Phyllis was always interested in photography, but her real passion was for drawing and painting.

Anyone living in Wellingborough who was thinking of a career in art, would attend Mr Cooper's class at the Institute. Not only did he develop Phyllis's natural

Snow White, *published by Juvenile Productions [c.1938]*

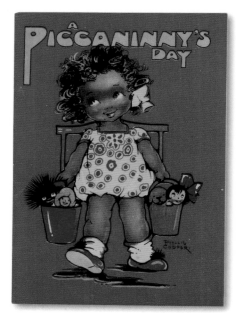

Piccaninny's Day, *publisher anon. [nd]*

*Above:*
*Artist: Phyllis Cooper*
*Pub: Raphael Tuck*
*Oilette series 3480 [1 of 6]*
*Happy Land III*
*[1923]*

*Below:*
*Artist: Phyllis Cooper*
*Pub: Raphael Tuck*
*Oilette series 3482 [1 of 6]*
*Happy Land V*
*[1923]*

Have you ever seen a sight so sweet ... In little boats of pearls and flowers,
As when the Elves and Fairies meet? ... They gaily spend the moon-lit hours.

A wish, a kiss and lots of love ... They never stop but march along
These dollies bring from me. ... As merry as can be.

Little Bow-Peep has found her sheep, ... See she comes to you to-day
So jolly she is feeling. ... Her little flock a-wheeling.

ability, but he also tutored her fellow illustrator Marjorie Dexter which is how the two girls became such great friends. They met one another frequently and shared thoughts on their work and which current fashions in art and design they should adopt.

When Phyllis moved to London to find work as a commercial artist, she stayed at the home of a lady artist in Hampstead Garden Suburb, who was a family friend.

In 1923, while still in her twenties, Phyllis forged a relationship with Raphael Tuck & Sons and immediately scored a success by creating the very striking *Happy Land* series of postcards. The series, comprising seven sets of six cards, (Happy Land I/VII), and two christmas series C2250/C2251, first appeared in 1923. She also created a series *Nursery Rhymes* in a similar style and provided witty captions for each series. The designs, all with an arresting black or navy blue background, show children at play, dressed in fashionable twenties costumes. Dolls and toys adorn the nursery settings and combine with the intricate art deco style decorations to epitomise the mood of the twenties. A subtle touch in the final set of six shows the dolls reversing roles and playing with the children's toys. These cards remained in print well into the thirties and were universally popular, so much so that the

*Phyllis in the twenties while working for Tuck*

makers of *Ovaltine* approached Phyllis to design an advertising campaign, including postcards, built around the *Happy Land* style.

Phyllis went on to illustrate postcards for Millar & Lang in a humorous style, but they lacked the impact and charm of her successful Raphael Tuck series.

In 1930 she married Andrew Buchanan, a documentary film producer and moved to Putney, then during the war drove ambulances in her home town. For Phyllis, post war Britain meant a new start. She felt she had achieved all she could in the field of children's illustration and that it was time to move on to a career as a writer. Her work included regular short articles for *Homes & Gardens* on the interiors and exteriors of interesting houses.

*Illustration from 'The Old Cobbler' Father Tuck's Annual. [1926]*

# Kate Cowderoy (1875-1972)

*Kate Cowderoy, seated far left, with a group of fellow pupils at the Herkomer Art School c.1901*

Kate Cowderoy, Sybil Barham and Alice L West, the noted bird artist, were in the same year together as students at the Herkomer Art School and became close friends. The three students all illustrated postcards during their careers.

By the time Kate enrolled at the school, it had gained a worldwide reputation through the extremely high standards of workmanship demanded by its founder, Hubert von Herkomer (1849-1914).

Herkomer, the noted portrait, landscape and figure painter, founded the school in 1883 with the financial assistance of Mr Eccleston Gibbs, who wanted Herkomer to teach his ward, Annie Slater. Herkomer had said that he was not prepared to give private tuition, but was willing to give his teaching to a school. So Eccleston Gibbs obliged by providing the school premises on his land. Herkomer's ethos was not to advance a particular style, but to encourage the unique qualities of each pupil.

Examples of Kate Cowderoy's postcards are scarce. It is unlikely that she illustrated more than a few sets. However, the designs illustrated here serve to demonstrate how the work of an aspiring but naïve student can be transformed with expert tuition. She offered a set of pictures, painted prior

to her student days, to Gottschalk, Dreyfus & Davis who eventually published them around 1905. The Christmas series was published by Raphael Tuck & Sons in 1903, the year Kate left the Herkomer Art School. It was also issued in France with a different series number. The defined style and attention to detail indicates her deft skill as a miniaturist, a talent she developed at the Herkomer Art School and for which she received many commissions.

Kate was born in Brixton, the daughter of Thomas a china merchant and his wife Isabella. Being the youngest child, Kate felt hampered by family members when trying to find studio space at home, but when she enrolled at the art school, her family moved to Bushey and extended their circle of artistic friends amongst the large colony of artists who lived in the area.

As a painter and miniaturist, she worked in oil, pencil and watercolour. She worked abroad in Karlsruhe and Paris and exhibited her pictures at the Royal Academy and the Paris Salon. She illustrated children's stories and in later life painted sunshades to be worn at Ascot and supplied handpainted silk to a friend's boutique.

Her studio collection is housed at the Bushey Museum, Bushey, Hertfordshire.

# Hilda Cowham (1876-1965)

*"I cannot tell you how I began to draw, for I never remember beginning at all. I always drew. When I was a child I used to make pictures of everything. I drew ships, I remember, with long reflections shining down into the sea. I stuck them up onto a mantelshelf and gazed at them. At that time I thought they were the most beautiful things in the world."*

Born in Westminster, Hilda Cowham studied art at Wimbledon College and Lambeth School of Art. In 1893, the *Studio* magazine started sponsoring design competitions that ran on a monthly basis for twenty years. Hilda Cowham entered several between 1893 and 1897 along with other aspiring young artists including Rosa Petherick, Helen Stratton and Alice Woodward. She never won, but gained two second prizes and four honourable mentions in pen and ink drawing, a fairy tale illustration and design for a calendar, christmas card and a book tailpiece. Perhaps her drawing was too free and avant garde to win, but the publicity she gained attracted interest in her fresh approach from many leading newspaper and magazine art editors and soon she was inundated with work.

Her drawing style was refreshing and spontaneous. Her early work for magazines in pen and brush is of great simplicity and reminiscent of the Japanese woodcut. Her whimsical style of drawing, showing traces of Japanese and Art Nouveau influence, are epitomised in *Curly Heads and Long Legs*,

published in 1914. The influence she had on Mabel Lucie Attwell and other nursery illustrators of her day, are plain to see.

Edith Young, writing in *Girls' Realm* in 1902 about the style and originality of her work, put it like this: *"…she is perhaps the only lady artist in her particular line of work who combines artistic ability with a dainty sense of real humour."*

Typical are her spontaneous and winsome images of children, drawn with simple, confident brush strokes with pastel colouring, conveying the freedom and naïvety of childhood, reflecting every parent's wish of how their children ought to be.

She contributed to magazines *Pick-me-up* and *The Queen* while still at school and by 1898, her illustrations appeared in *Little Folks*, a connection she maintained for many years. She enjoyed an association with Raphael Tuck throughout the Edwardian era, designing humorous postcards, including *1009 Write Away Series* in 1902, and early seaside humour with *1322/1323 Seaside Series I & II* in 1907. During this time and well into the twenties she contributed to annuals for Tuck, Blackie, Cassell and others. She wrote and illustrated

A Busy Day, *Pen-and-ink drawing of group. 2nd prize in Studio competition.[1895]*

books, the first of which, *Fiddlesticks,* was published by Pearson in 1900, but her best known works, *Blacklegs and Others* and *Curly Heads and Long Legs* were published in 1911 and 1914 respectively.

She was a celebrity in her time and in demand by magazine editors and advertisers alike. Postcard collectors are familiar with her designs for CWS and *Two Steeples* Jersey Boy and Girl underwear. These delightful drawings demonstrate her versatility and flair for fashion, which had surfaced in 1910, as clothes conscious mothers dressed their daughters in 'Hilda Cowham' styles.

She was one of the first women to draw cartoons for *Punch* and was soon considered one of the best female comic artists, following her success with the *Cowham Kid*. Her work appeared in many other periodicals including *the Graphic* and the *Daily Sketch*.

Around 1914 she developed the popular dolls, *Demure Dot, Nurse Norah, Madamoiselle, Saucy Sally, Motherly Molly* and *Little Miss Polly: the Hilda Cowham Kiddies*. The British Novelty Works, who produced the dolls for Dean & Son, announced them as the 'world famous' *Hilda Cowham Kiddies* in their advertising for the British Industries Fair in 1916.

From time to time throughout her career she illustrated children's postcards and greetings cards for many publishers including CW Faulkner, Inter Art, Ritchie, Tuck and Valentine of Dundee. In 1925 her designs featured on prestigious nursery china in the *Shelley Children's Ware* series. *Playtime, a second series,* appeared in 1927.

Hilda Cowham was also a painter of domestic scenes and landscapes and an etcher. She married Edgar Lander, himself a noted etcher and watercolourist. First, they lived in Marylebone, but by the mid twenties, had moved to an idyllic thatched cottage in the Chilterns at Chinnor where *"they would enjoy the summer days together with their pencils and pastels and brushes…in their summer retreat."*

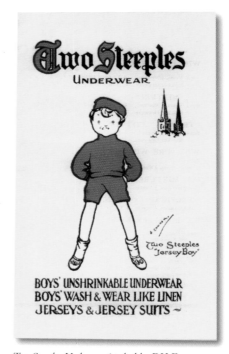

*Two Steeples Underwaer 'stocked by DH Evans for many years'. Leaflet containing fabric samples.*

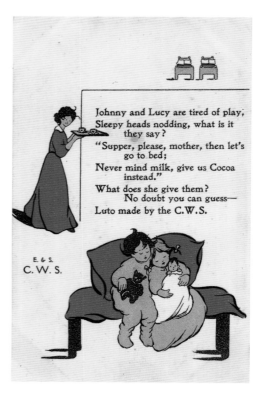

LEFT HAND PAGE

*Below right:*
*Artist: Hilda Cowham*
*Pub: CWS*
*[c.1912]*

RIGHT HAND PAGE

*Left column:*
*Artist: Hilda Cowham*
*Pub: Two Steeples Productions*
*[c.1912]*

*Above centre:*
*Artist: Hilda Cowham*
*Pub: CW Faulkner*
*Series 1618 [1 of 6]*
*Merry Moments*
*[1917]*

*Below centre:*
*Artist: Hilda Cowham*
*Pub: CW Faulkner*
*Series 1601 [1 of 6]*
*Fairy Revels*
*[1917]*

*Right column:*
*Artist: Hilda Cowham*
*Pub: CW Faulkner*
*Series 1918 [2 of 6]*
*The Land of Fairies*
*[c.1926]*

Two Steeples "Jersey Boy"

Love Laughs at Bolts and Bars.

BEDTIME.

Two Steeples "Jersey Girl"

A Jolly Christmas

Up in the Morning Early.

WHERE THE FAIRIES COME FROM.

# Rie Cramer (1887-1977)

Rie Cramer, the Dutch illustrator, was born in Indonesia, where she and her three sisters spent their early childhood. She returned to Holland with her family when she was nine years old and studied illustration at several art schools, including the Academy of Arts in the Hague. She found her inspiration in the flourishing tradition of English children's illustrators, particularly Kate Greenaway, Arthur Rackham and Walter Crane, while glimpses of Aubrey Beardsley are clearly visible in some of her work.

Her first book *Voor Meisjes en Jongetjs (For Little Girls and Boys)* was published in 1906 by W de Haan, Utrecht. It's immediate success prompted her follow up *Voor Jongetjes en Meisjes.* Between 1915 and 1917 she illustrated the classic tales of Andersen, the Brothers Grimm and *Mother Goose's Rhymes*. She was an artist with a prolific output and each year she produced at least one book of verses with illustrations.

Rie Cramer was an emancipated and widely travelled woman who moved in a social circle that included musicians, actors, dancers and painters. She enjoyed her latter years on the island of Majorca and returned to the Netherlands shortly before her death.

She wrote and illustrated books on Europe, was involved in advertising design, fashion drawings and even wrote plays and novels. In 1921 she married her first husband, the actor Eduard Verkade, resulting in closer ties to the theatre and logically to more theatre commissions, including scenery and costume design. This led to a change in drawing styles. Her dreamy, sensitive flowing lines and tints gave way to strong colours and heavy black contours.

Children everywhere have grown up with the songs, poems and delightful pictures by Rie Cramer. Like her Dutch compatriot, Henriette Willebeek le Mair,

*Illustration from* Russische Sprookjes

the style of her work is highly regarded by English audiences. Several of her books were published in English including *Little Picture Rhymes* and *Little Picture Songs* Augener, *Lentebloemen (Spring Flowers)* A&C Black, *The Snow Queen, Thumbelina* and *Goldilocks & the Three Bears* Blackie, *Favourite French Fairy Tales* and *Little Dutchy* Harrap, *Hans Andersons Fairy Tales, In The Garden* and *Little Mother* Humphrey Milford.

So universally popular is her work that British and Dutch publishers have issued the illustrations from many of her books as postcards.

*LEFT HAND PAGE*

*Artist: Rie Cramer*
*Pub: Charles Hauff*
*(Import from De Haan, Utrecht)*
*Series 0129 [3 of 12]*
*Above: 'Such a Lot of Apples'*
*Centre: 'The Little Nurse'*
*Below: 'Mother's Birthday'*
*from the book* Spring Flowers
*[1920]*

*RIGHT HAND PAGE*

*Top row:*
*Artist: Rie Cramer*
*Pub: W de Haan, Utrecht*
*Series 134 [3 of 12]*
*Months of the Year*
*[1922]*

*Bottom row:*
*Artist: Rie Cramer*
*Pub: Humphrey Milford*
*Postcards for the Little Ones*
*Series: Joyous Days [3 of 6]*
*from the books* Little Mothers
*&* In the Garden
*[1930]*

Susan at the dressing table,
Kneeling on a chair,
Shows her dollies, Meg and Mabel,
How to do their hair.

They're ready, Pamela and Pat,
For walking in the Square,
But neither of them wears a hat—
They've got such lots of hair.

October winds blow all around,
The leaves begin to fall,
And Cicely with leap and bound
Tries hard to catch them all.

# Muriel Dawson (1897-1974)

*Muriel Dawson in 1921, aged 24*

Muriel Helen Dawson was born in 1897, in Geraldine, near Christchurch, New Zealand. Her parents had moved there from Scotland a year earlier and opened a draper's shop. Muriel was the eldest child of four and from birth she was called 'Toby', a name she is thought to have inherited through her nine year old aunt!

From an early age, she loved the open countryside around their home which harboured a rich variety of wild life. She began to draw and paint and her father, William, recognised that his daughter's special talent was one to be properly nurtured.

Perhaps this was a reason why the family returned to England in 1913, enabling Muriel to receive a formal art education. They lived in Putney for a short while, then moved to Richmond where Muriel attended Richmond School of Art.

Clare, Muriel's youngest sister, was a delicate child, so during the Great War the family moved to Leigh-on-Sea for the benefit of her health. In 1919 they moved back to London and Muriel continued her studies at the Royal College of Art.

Upon graduation in 1922, she won a travel scholarship to Italy, a journey which was to have a profound effect on her life. While there, she injured her back and was nursed back to good health by nuns,

whose kindness and caring attitude resulted in her conversion to the Roman Catholic faith.

Soon after her return to England, she received her first commission, from publishers A&C Black to illustrate a new edition of Charles Kingsley's *Water Babies*. Later, Muriel established an enduring relationship with the Medici Society, for whom she painted many beautiful pictures of child life which were reproduced on postcards, calendars and greetings cards. Her prints and posters were also extremely popular and could be found on bedroom walls and in infant schools' classrooms up and down the country.

While working for the Medici Society, she took on commissions for book publishers, including Raphael Tuck. She will be remembered for many splendid covers for *Woman's Pictorial* magazine during the nineteen thirties. She also collaborated with her sister Clare, herself a gifted artist, on a number of religious book projects.

Muriel's style was her own. Typically she worked in charcoal and watercolour wash onto a textured base. The results were wonderfully free and natural and full of movement. As time went by her nature drawings, many of which are in the Natural History Museum, became more detailed and analytical.

*Cover for* Woman's Pictorial*, [May 1936]*

Just before the Second World War, she moved to Storrington, Sussex and built herself a studio in the garden where she continued to produce paintings for the Medici Society.

Muriel moved to Dartmoor during the early forties where she discovered that she relished all that the desolate moors had to offer – open space, freedom and an unspoiled natural environment. In fact, her overwhelming reason for moving to such a remote spot was her passion for wildlife. Here she could make accurate and beautiful drawings of animals in their natural habitat, a pursuit that was to become her sole preoccupation.

*'Toby's' response to repeated requests from one of her publishers for a photograph.*

Eventually, Muriel returned to the family's roots in Scotland and spent her latter years on the Shetland Islands, where she continued to draw from the wild. She was accompanied there by a menagerie of pets including cats, dogs, a rabbit and a goat which she took for walks regularly.

She became a well-loved figure in local society and when she died in 1974, the *Shetland Times* noted: *"...what Miss Dawson was doing was continuing a study of nature that started when she was a little girl in New Zealand and continued through a distinguished career that ended in Backlands Studio, Dale of Walls."*

My Book of Nursery Rhymes *and* Another Lovely Book of Nursery Rhymes *published by Raphael Tuck. [c.1935]*

*The pictures from the first book were also issued as birthday and Christmas greetings cards.*

*Above left:*
*Artist: Muriel Dawson*
*Pub: The Medici Society*
*Packet 19*
*The Happy Hours Series*
*The First Aconite*
*[c.1932]*

*Below left:*
*Artist: Muriel Dawson*
*Pub: The Medici Society*
*Packet 19*
*The Happy Hours Series*
*Welcome to Fairyland*
*[c.1932]*

*Above centre:*
*Artist: Muriel Dawson*
*Pub: The Medici Society*
*Packet 19*
*The Happy Hours Series*
*Tea Time*
*[c.1932]*

*Below centre:*
*Artist: Muriel Dawson*
*Pub: The Medici Society*
*Packet 19*
*The Happy Hours Series*
*Sleepy Head*
*[c.1932]*

*Above right:*
*Artist: Muriel Dawson*
*Pub: The Medici Society*
*Packet 19*
*The Happy Hours Series*
*Critical!*
*[c.1932]*

*Below right:*
*Artist: Muriel Dawson*
*Pub: The Medici Society*
*Packet 269*
*[nd]*

THE FIRST ACONITE    Muriel Dawson, A.C.A.

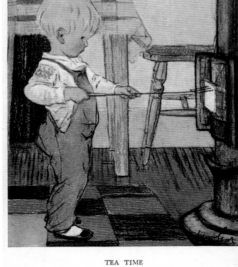

TEA TIME
by
Muriel Dawson, A.C.A.

CRITICAL!

SLEEPY HEAD

The Son of God is born for all
At Bethl'em in a cattle stall:
He lieth in a crib so small,
And wrapt in swaddling clothes withal.
*Old Carol.*

# Marjorie Dexter (1903-1992)

Green, Green Grass now while I tarry
Tell me true whom I shall marry
Tinker, Tailor, Soldier, Sailor,
Rich man, Poor man, Beggar man, Thief.

Imagine a picturesque, mature town house in the market town of Wellingborough, with mistletoe growing on ancient apple trees inside an idyllic walled garden. This was The Nook in Wellingborough High Street, the home of Ethel May and Roger Dexter and the birthplace of their two daughters Marjorie and Joyce. Roger Dexter owned a successful grocery business which he operated from another premises in the town, serving the local community for many years.

The girls attended Wellingborough Girl's High School where they were taught to draw by William Cooper, a prominent local artist and the father of their great friend and fellow illustrator, Phyllis Cooper. He was such an inspirational teacher that they even took extra tuition from his classes at the Wellingborough Technical Institute. With his strong influence and encouragement and the support of her family, Marjorie left school at seventeen and

began a correspondence course in art, working from home. In their spare time, Marjorie and Joyce loved to cycle out to neighbouring villages in Northamptonshire to sketch the cottages, farm buildings, woodland scenes and animals that captured their imagination, before returning home to tea. Although Marjorie was the more gifted artist of the two sisters, they both enjoyed drawing and being in each other's company, and would, on occasion, venture further afield together on their bicycles, on sketching holidays.

The first chance for Marjorie to display her skills as a commercial illustrator came at the age of sixteen when the local pastor asked her to design a front cover to advertise womens' meetings for his Wesleyan chapel magazine. Then in 1920, like many hopeful young artists, she moved to London to her cousin's house and attended the Slade School of Art. She was an attractive young woman, confident in her precocious ability

and was well received by publishers when showing them her portfolio. Persistence paid off. She was given opportunities to design postcards and greetings cards by a number of prominent postcard publishers, including Millar & Lang, Salmon and Valentine. During her career she also undertook other forms of commercial artwork and, in particular, forged a working relationship designing packaging for Joshua Margerison a soap products manufacturer.

Marjorie and Phyllis Cooper remained friends throughout their careers. Although they worked independently of one another, there were similarities in their artistic styles. One aspect was particularly noticable; they both worked very effectively in the popular nineteen twenties art deco style. Compare Phyllis's *Happy Land Series* for Tuck with Marjorie's happy children at play in her series for Valentine, both published in the mid-twenties. The floral patterns, the striking black backgrounds, the colouring and the children's dress designs have a great deal in common. Both women wrote the captions and rhymes for all their postcards, and both worked from time to time for Millar & Lang, although Marjorie's commissions were for Christmas greetings cards only.

Marjorie also drew in an objective, painterly style. It is easy to detect the influence of her childhood days, sketching country scenes with her sister Joyce, in her endearing series for Salmon of 1930, which depicts children and animals in harmony in pretty woodland settings. The girl playing with the animals in this series, is reminiscent of her sister Joyce, smartly dressed in nineteen twenties fashions.

During the nineteen thirties, Marjorie and her sister married brothers, Lance and Harold Mancey, whom they met in London. Marjorie continued to work commercially from her home in Bexley, Kent, until she was about sixty years old. A quiet and serene person in later life, she turned to her hobbies for recreation. She produced some wonderful wood cuts of local scenes, painted portraits, and played the piano.

One Crow sorrow. Two Crow's joy.
Three Crows a letter. Four Crows a boy.

# Walt Disney (1901-1966)

The unbridled expression of fun and humour of the strip cartoon began to emerge during the dark days of the first world war, as a result of newspaper editors' desire to cheer up the nation and win over the hearts and minds of younger readers. In Britain, Teddy Tail first appeared in the *Daily Mail* in 1915 and other papers followed suit, with Pip Squeak & Wilfred, Uncle Oojah, Tiger Tim and a multitude of other comic strips, eagerly consumed by millions of youngsters.

Cartoon characters appeared on the screen too, before Mickey Mouse was created by a team of seasoned animators led by Walt Disney, at a time when the film industry in America was bringing sound to films. Not even Felix, created by Pat Sullivan in 1919, could compete, for unlike Felix, Mickey Mouse had a voice!.

Mickey became an overnight success when *Steamboat Willie*, in which he starred, jazzing up a river trip, was premiered in 1928. Poor old Felix was tossed aside like the rest of his silent screen counterparts.

Throughout the thirties the fun and laughter generated by Mickey Mouse and his pals gathered momentum. When *Mickey Mouse Weekly* was launched in February 1936, British toyshops were full of a vast array of Disneyana for millions of children to enjoy. During the thirties and forties, Mickey Mouse and Donald Duck had their rivals, like Tom & Jerry and Bugs

Bunny, but none posed a serious threat to their universal popularity.

Mickey Mouse could not have arrived at a better time for the postcard trade. By 1930, postcard publishers were wondering how to bolster their flagging product. Children's postcard illustrators had been amusing children for three decades with many contrasting styles and themes. Yet, as time passed, the novelty of the postcard was fast becoming outmoded. Youngsters wanted something new. Disney characters gave children's postcards a new lease of life during the thirties and forties. This novel, brightly coloured imagery enabled children to relive through the postcard medium, for almost the first time, the animated adventures they had seen at the movies.

Valentine & Sons secured the valuable rights to publish Walt Disney postcards in Britain. These highly amusing cards featured Mickey Mouse and his playmates, Donald Duck, Minnie, Goofy and Pluto. They sold in their millions, helping the publisher maintain a success story to match marketing successes they enjoyed with Mabel Lucie Attwell, Chlöe Preston and George Studdy's Bonzo postcards of the nineteen twenties.

When the Walt Disney Studio moved into animated feature films, Valentines acquired reproduction rights for the UK, enabling them to reproduce stills from the films onto postcards. In 1938 Walt Disney released *Snow White and the Seven Dwarfs* – their first full-length animated feature and a turning point in the history of Disney Studios. The *New York Herald Tribune* was quoted as saying *"...it is one of those rare works of inspired artistry that weaves an irresistible spell around the beholder."* Published in the wake of such a successful movie, the postcard series was an enormous success. This paved the way for others, including *Gulliver's Travels* in 1939, *Pinocchio* in 1940 and *Bambi* in 1942. The success of these full length animated feature films was reflected in the great popularity of Disney picture postcards around the world.

ARRIVED SAFELY!

HERE'S WISHING YOU ALL THE LUCK !

YOU'LL NEVER KNOW HOW I MISS YOU

*LEFT HAND PAGE*

*Above & below:*
Pub: Valentine
*Walt Disney Postcard*
*No. 4019/4037/4444*
*[1937-1938]*

*RIGHT HAND PAGE*

*Above & below left:*
Pub: Valentine
*Snow White & the Seven Dwarfs*
*No. 4229/4232 [2 of 7]*
*Doc/Sleepy*
*[1937]*

*Above & below centre:*
Pub: Valentine
*Snow White & the Seven Dwarfs*
*No. 4175/4177 [2 of 12]*
*[1938]*

*Above right:*
Pub: Valentine
*Ferdinand the Bull*
*No. 4682 [1 of 6]*
*[1939]*

*Centre & below right:*
Pub: Valentine
*Pinoccio*
*No. 470/471 [2 of 6]*
*[1940]*

"DOC"

FROM THE
WALT DISNEY
FILM
SNOW WHITE

WALT DISNEY'S
Snow White and the Seven Dwarfs

SNOW WHITE DANCES TO THE MUSIC
OF THE DWARFS.

FROM WALT DISNEY'S
LATEST FILM
"FERDINAND THE BULL"

FERDINAND WOULDN'T FIGHT.
HE JUST SAT AND SMELLED THE FLOWERS.

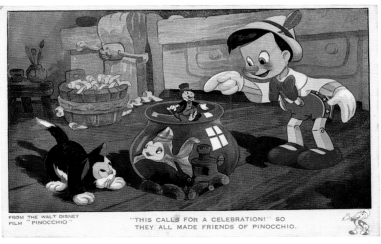

FROM THE WALT DISNEY
FILM "PINOCCHIO"

"THIS CALLS FOR A CELEBRATION!" SO
THEY ALL MADE FRIENDS OF PINOCCHIO.

"SLEEPY"

FROM THE
WALT DISNEY
FILM
SNOW WHITE

WALT DISNEY'S
Snow White and the Seven Dwarfs

"THE DAY THAT MY DREAMS
COME TRUE."

FROM THE WALT DISNEY
FILM "PINOCCHIO"

"SOON WE'LL GO TO BED" GEPPETTO SAID—
"BUT FIRST I MUST PAINT THIS FACE AND HEAD"

# Linda Edgerton (1890-1983)

Linda Edgerton was born in Wednesbury, Staffordshire in 1890 to William, an engineering inventor and Emma Amelia, a fine amateur watercolourist, engraver and leather worker. We know nothing of Linda's early life, but after the death of her father, Linda and her mother moved to Sutton in Surrey in 1917, where her newly married sister had settled.

Although Linda attended part-time classes at Sutton School of Art, she was mainly self taught. After moving to Sutton, she started to paint and illustrate nursery rhymes and having submitted samples to various publishers she was soon receiving regular commissions from Delgado, Vivian Mansell, EW Savory and Raphael Tuck to illustrate books and postcards.

Linda's simple naïve style struck the right note with parents buying books and toys for the very young. Her appealing little characters were ideally suited to playbooks and early learning primers. Nursery rhymes and fairy tales were by far her favourite theme and accounted for about half of her total output of postcards.

She wrote and illustrated many playbooks for Mansell and Tuck, which began to appear in bookshops at the end of the First World War, like: *The Colour Me and Cut Out Book, Dicky's Little Book of Riddles* and *Boy Blue and his Chum.*

Her work contained the combined ingenuity and artistic flair of her parents –

her father's mechanical genius and her mother's painterly skills. Her inventive streak led her into toy making. She made prototypes of many of the toys that appear in her postcards and even made more complex models, just to amuse her family. Many of her books and postcards were designed with perforation and simple mechanical movement for cutting out and making up as models. These ephemeral items are scarce today, as so many books were cut up by eager youngsters.

She attracted the attention of companies whose products were aimed at the very young. Robinsons, manufacturers of soft drinks, arranged to use Mansell series 1042, *Nursery Rhymes*, to advertise their Groats and Barley for weaned babies.

In 1924, Linda Edgerton's work was chosen by Shelley, the china manufacturers, for a nurseryware series. The set comprised six nursery rhyme designs supplied on a wide range of items including baby plates, egg cups, teaplates, jugs and beakers.

She designed extensively for Jacobsen, Welch, for whom she contributed to their ranges of Newton Mill Children's Stationery goods, with designs for games, note paper, notelets, invitations and a wide variety of other ephemeral material.

*Nursery mug, Shelley. [1925]*

Later in life, Linda befriended Glades Gibberd, the noted miniaturist and wife of architect Sir Frederick Gibberd. They became close friends and compared notes regularly on their respective artistic activities.

After her mother's death, Linda became disillusioned with commercial art and rejected a career that spanned more than twenty five years, preferring the solace of a

nunnery. She ceased to work as an illustrator in 1938 and joined St Catherine's Convent, near High Wycombe, Buckinghamshire, remaining there for the rest of her life.

Lovers of more sophisticated illustration might regard Linda Edgerton's work as repetitive and over simplistic and consider that her line work is somewhat crude in execution. But her naivety exudes a sense of childhood innocence that has an enduring and irresistible charm.

*The pictures below demonstrate Linda Edgerton's liking for drawing backgrounds to her nursery scenes from life. Left: Red Riding Hood's Cottage, published by Raphael Tuck c1920 and the actual Little Penn Cottage at St Gennys in Cornwall in 1999. Below: a 'press-out' postcard from Mansell series 1196 and above it a photograph of the farmhouse that stands on the road from Mount Bures to Fordham, Essex.*

*RIGHT HAND PAGE*

*Left column:*
*Artist: Linda Edgerton*
*Pub: E Savory*
*Series 811 [3 of 4]*
*[c.1918]*

*Above centre:*
*Artist: Linda Edgerton*
*Pub: A Vivian Mansell*
*Series 1160*
*Riddle Rhymes [1 of 6]*
*[1921]*

*Below centre:*
*Artist: Linda Edgerton*
*Pub: Robinsons*
*(from Mansell series 1042)*
*Nursery Rhymes*
*[1917]*

*Right column:*
*Artist: Linda Edgerton*
*Pub: J Salmon*
*No. 4116/4120 [4 of 6]*
*[1935]*

LOOK·OUT·OR·I·WILL·SNOWBALL·YOU!

OLD MOTHER TWITCHET HAD BUT ONE EYE
AND A LONG TAIL WHICH SHE LET FLY
AND EVERY TIME SHE WENT OVER A GAP
SHE LEFT A BIT OF HER TAIL IN A TRAP

JUST LOOK AT OUR SUNFLOWER

DO·YOU·WANT·THESE·DAFFODILS?

THERE·ARE·MORE·BLACKBERRIES·HERE

BA BA BLACK SHEEP HAVE YOU ANY WOOL
YES SIR, YES SIR, THREE BAGS FULL;
ONE FOR THE MASTER ONE FOR THE DAME
ONE FOR THE LITTLE BOY THAT LIVES IN OUR LANE.

FEEDING THE CHICKENS

# William Ellam (1858-1935)

William Henry Ellam was an illustrator with such an enigmatic character that few of those attracted by his beguiling nature could ever say they knew him really well.

His parents, William, a chemist and druggist, and his wife Isabella moved south from Lancashire, with their three children, Margaret, John and Lucy Ellen and settled in Baker Street in rural Enfield, North London shortly before young William was born on 23 December 1859. However, when he was only five years old, his father died, leaving the family with very little money. This meant that the youngsters had to start earning a living as soon as possible.

Young William Henry was interested in art and sculpture from an early age, yet he didn't take it up professionally until around the time of his first marriage. He was a bright and commercially focused young man and while working as a jobber at the London Stock Exchange in 1878, he won a medal at the Tottenham, Edmonton and Enfield Industrial Exhibition, having developed a keen interest in casting bronze and spelter figures.

By 1881 Henry, his mother and Lucy, the youngest sister, had moved to Lee in Kent. While living at Burnt Ash Hill in Lee, he met Elizabeth Tilley. They were in their early twenties when they married in 1882, near her home at Forest Gate, East London.

William Henry and Elizabeth set up home at Airdale Villa, Woodside Green, South Norwood. Over the next fifteen years they raised a family of eight – five boys and three girls – Leopold was born in 1883, Hugh in 1885, Gordon in 1886, Irene in 1887, Dorothy in 1890 and William, Ruby, and Douglas were born in the eighteen nineties.

By the time of his marriage he had become a full time commercial artist, continuing to produce sculpted figures to order. To maintain a large family, it became necessary for him to develop his drawing and painting skills and broaden his scope to take on advertisement illustration, humorous cartoons and handbills. He was a workaholic with a prolific output. By eighteen ninety one, he employed a live-in housemaid at their four-storey home at 64 Heathfield Road, Croydon, to support the needs of his wife, five children and his ailing mother. An early sign of Ellam's restless nature is highlighted by the constant changes of address in south London to which they moved during the eighteen nineties. In 1894, they lived at 11 Foulser Road, Tooting. By 1898, they were residing at 49 Enmore Road, Woodside and between 1899 and 1901 they were at 81 Lansdowne Road, Croydon.

The advent of the picture postcard could not have arrived at a better time, presenting Ellam with a wonderful opportunity to express his natural wit and accomplished artistic skills. It was his ideal medium. He was a gregarious and worldly personality, a fun loving man who was aware of current events and popular themes. Here was the chance for this politically aware artist, to exploit to the full his mischievous sense of humour and versatile range of painting skills.

After his first successes with Raphael Tuck in 1905, his services as a postcard illustrator were in great demand. He was such a versatile and amusing artist that he could turn his sharp wit to a wide range of themes. He lampooned politicians,

*WH Ellam's mother, Isabella [c.1888]*

*Above:*
*Artist: William Ellam*
*Pub: Raphael Tuck*
*Series 9562 [1 of 6]*
*Mixed Bathing*
*[1908]*

*Centre:*
*Artist: William Ellam*
*Pub: Raphael Tuck*
*Series 9684 [1 of 6]*
*Trunks Full of Fun*
*[1909]*

*Below:*
*Artist: William Ellam*
*Pub: Raphael Tuck*
*Series 9793 [1 of 6]*
*Teddy Bears at the Seaside*
*[1910]*

*RIGHT HAND PAGE*

*Below:*
*Artist: William Ellam*
*Pub: ETW Dennis*
*Puzzle 'Em Message Card series*
*[1 of 6]*
*[c1920]*

*A portrait of William Ellam's second wife Olga [1920]*

Fix these pieces up together in the order that is meant,
And 'twill tell the worried housewife how she soon can
make the rent.

The Puzzled 'em Message Card.          No. **4.**

illustrated trains, military men, hilarious dressed animals, original novelty postcards and from time to time made political comment, all with his own brand of incisive humour. His illustration knew no bounds, he could amuse children too. He was a great tease and loved to be in their company. Our selection of postcard imagery focuses on the designs he created to entertain his young audience.

His 1918 success in a competition sponsored by the *Worshipful Company of Makers of Playing Cards* demonstrates his versatility as an artist. He designed a pack of playing cards to be presented to King George V and Queen Mary to mark their visit to India. The press report stated that *"…two dainty boxes were presented – one to the King and one to the Queen – and each contained two packs of cards similar to those presented to the liverymen. Upon the backs of the cards is the design with which Mr WH Ellam of Sunnyside, George Lane, South Woodford won the company's prize in the last competition. It represents types of natives and animals in India and also depicts a soldier of the King George's Own Lancers. In the background is the Taj Mahal, erected by Shah Jehan in memory of his wife. The design of the card backs is surrounded by the Indian Crown."*

Winning this competition would have been regarded by Ellam as an honour. He was a confirmed royalist and ardent supporter of British tradition. Some of his work, particularly designs he did for the Up-to-Date Post Card Company, reveals his right wing leanings.

His astute wit and prolific output of artwork earned him a great deal of money, which he appeared to spend as soon as he earned it. He readily indulged his taste for fine clothes and high living, dressing with studied elegance in fashionable suits, hats, spats and carrying a silver-topped cane which was his hallmark. He sparkled in the company of women, yet in reality he was a solitary man, a prisoner of his own artistic thoughts and actions. But there was a serious side to Ellam's character. During

*William Ellam with examples of his cast sculptures [c.1930]*

wartime he volunteered his services as a war artist and produced a great deal of patriotic material including posters, advertisements and postcards. From the time of his youth he was fascinated by the military and he enjoyed drawing and painting military subjects. Many of his early sculpted figures depicted soldiers on horseback. As far as we know, he illustrated only two books – *Trafalgar* and *Waterloo*, companion volumes, published by Castell Brothers in 1905 to commemorate the centenary of the Battle of Trafalgar and the two famous military encounters.

Tragedy struck the family during World War I, when Ellam's wife Elizabeth was travelling to Ireland to visit their daughter Dorothy, who had married an Irishman in 1911. The ferry in which she was sailing across the Irish Sea, was hit by a German torpedo and she was drowned.

Before World War I, the family had been living at 47 St George's Road, Wimbledon, but by 1915 Ellam had moved out to South Woodford in Essex. In the intervening years, his children had married and left home and he suddenly found himself alone. But at the end of the War he met Gertrude Magdelina Olga de Kovrigin, the daughter of an heiress to a Russian estate who, due to the Communist

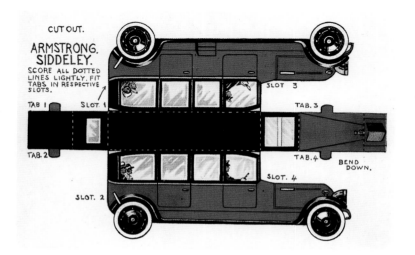

Cut out slots marked I in upper
picture, fit tabs of lower picture
in slots (from the back).
Cut out all white

WESTMINSTER
ABBEY

MODEL

SCORE AT BACK
BEND FORWARD

SCORE
BEND BACK

CUT OUT

SUPPORT
BEND BACK

take over in 1917, had been forced out of
her native country, unable to claim her
inheritance on the death of her husband,
and had settled in North London.

Olga was strikingly good looking. She
was a woman, who enjoyed taking on a
masculine appearance, with her short dark
hair and mannish outfits. Yet, her rosebud
lips defined by scarlet lipstick, maintained a
tantalisingly powerful aura of femininity.
Ellam found her irresistible and in 1920
the 61 year old artist and his 28 year old
bride, were married in London, soon to be
united with a son.

Troubled by family life, the restless
artist moved away soon after the marriage
into an apartment studio in Clapham,
where he continued his career through the
nineteen twenties. He was still able to earn
a comfortable living as an illustrator and
fulfil a dream he had to visit Australia.
Eventually however, age and poor health
caught up with him and he returned
home to spend his last years with his wife
and son at their rented Hampstead home,
to savour his colourful and eventful life.

Today, knowledgeable collectors are
still identifying postcards he illustrated and
discovering that his output could be
approaching a total of two thousand designs.

*William Ellam with wife Olga and his
mother-in law. [c.1932]*

# Charles Folkard (1878-1963)

Charles James Folkard was born in Lewisham, south east London, on 6 April 1878, the son of a printer. Brought up with an understanding of print 'in his blood', he was to become an accomplished and versatile illustrator.

Having first attended Dr Herrick's Academy for the Sons of Gentlemen, a local 'prep' school, he followed his father's footsteps to Colfe's School, Lewisham in 1892, where he became the co-publisher of *The Colfean*, the school magazine which is still published to-day. After Colfe's he attended evening classes in art at Goldsmith's Institute and in later years was often heard to say that he regretted not having more formal art training. By day, he was apprenticed to a firm of printers, but his humorous outlook and fascination with fantasy led him into conjuring, an ambition he had pursued from childhood. He achieved professional status and appeared regularly at charity shows, children's parties and concerts, well into the

nineteen thirties. Arthritis in his hands, which impaired his dexterity, forced him to retire from conjuring before the war.

While designing programmes for his own shows, he discovered his greater talent for drawing and decided to follow his brother Harry into the studio of newspaper group Harmsworth Publications, where he remained for a short while as a staff artist.

His life was not without its setbacks. His first wife Winifred died in childbirth in 1909, only two years after their marriage. But in 1910 he remarried and set up home in Eltham with his new wife Amelia and daughter Betty from his first marriage. Edward and Jane were the children of his second marriage and the family remained in the area until shortly before Charles Folkard's death.

Before World War I, Folkard had established himself as a freelance illustrator of children's books, working from a studio in Fleet Street. But he found too many

people dropped in for a chat and wasted his time, so he moved back to Eltham and worked from home.

His early successes included *Swiss Family Robinson*, 1910, *Pinocchio, Grimm's Fairy Tales* and *Arabian Nights*, 1911, *Aesop's Fables*, 1912 and *Swedish Fairy Tales*, 1913.

In 1915, Lord Northcliffe, proprietor of Harmsworth and Folkard's former employer, knowing of the artist's capabilities, called him in to discuss the creation of a children's strip to appear in the *Daily Mail*, to 'create a bright light in a dark war'.

It did not take long to come up with a character. The quick-witted Folkard is said to have invented *Teddy Tail,* the little mouse with the Eton collar, bow tie and cherry nose, on the train home from his meeting with Northcliffe, naming the cheeky animal after Edward, his son. It is thought to be the first of many strips for children to appear in any British newspaper. Folkard was not highly paid and soon tired of the work. Six cartoons a week kept him fully occupied and netted £600 a year. After a while he handed the work over to his brother Harry, freeing himself to work on book illustration. During the nineteen thirties, the *Mail* lured Herbert Foxwell away from *Tiger Tim* and encouraged him to remodel Teddy in the highly popular *Rainbow* style. This facelift meant that *Teddy Tail* ran in the *Daily Mail* until 1960, except for a short break during World War II – a favourite with successive generations the world over. The *Teddy Tail League* was formed in 1933 and four years later the list of members had swollen to eight hundred thousand!

As a young man Folkard had always admired the work of Arthur Rackham and Edmund Dulac. The accomplished pen, ink and watercolour technique he employed in his children's book illustrations, are reminiscent of Rackham. His illustrative style was confident and professional, with the rare ability to combine naturalistic detail with a strong element of caricature.

He enjoyed a long career illustrating

books of high quality, notably, *Mother Goose Nursery Rhymes* (1919), *Songs from Alice in Wonderland* (1921), *Granny's Wonderful Chair*, 1925 and *The Troubles of a Gnome*, 1928. Around 1926, his publisher A&C Black, selected twelve illustrations from *Mother Goose* and *Songs from Alice* to appear in their *Black's Beautiful Postcards* series – a series of ninety four sets of cards, most of which are devoted to Black's travel books. Although not designed specifically for the postcard medium, these illustrations are wonderful examples of the artist's work.

He was a gentle whimsical man, although his dark, deep-set eyes revealed an inner restlessness. He never stopped drawing – anniversaries, and birthdays were opportunities for him to send humorous hand-drawn greetings. He was kindly, generous and gave a great deal of his time to help with local theatrical activities, where he loved involvement with writing scripts, making props and painting scenery.

Colour Your Own Postcards. *[c.1920]*

*Above left:*
Artist: *Charles Folkard*
Pub: *Valentine*
Card number: *545*
*[1922]*

*Below left:*
Artist: *Herbert Foxwell*
Pub: *Teddy Tail League*
*[c.1936]*

*Above centre:*
Artist: *Charles Folkard*
Pub: *A&C Black*
*Alice in Wonderland*
Series 80 *[1 of 6]*
*[c.1926]*

*Below centre:*
Artist: *Charles Folkard*
Pub: *A&C Black*
*English Nursery Rhymes*
Series 43 *[1 of 6]*
*[c.1924]*

*Right column:*
Artist: *Charles Folkard*
Pub: *A&C Black*
*Nursery Rhymes and Tales*
Series 91 *[2 of 6]*
*[1930]*

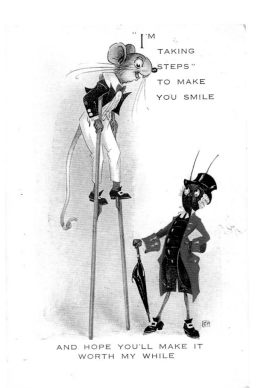

I look for Butterflies that sleep among the Wheat.

Little Bo-Peep.

Old Mother Hubbard

Tom, The Piper's Son.

# Maude Goodman (1853-1938)

*"Her work is uniformly dainty and highly finished, the colouring warm and well arranged, and the incidents such as one might see any day in a Kensington house. There is no attempt at the expression of passion. A girl reading a love letter, a child peering into an eight-day clock, a pretty face, or an interior with rugs and bric-a-brac, high-backed chairs and flowers, are the subjects associated with this artist."*

Art Journal, 1889

She was born Matilda Goodman in Manchester in 1853 to Louis, a cigar dealer, and his wife Amelia, who died while Matilda was very young. His second wife, Kate, who Louis married in 1859, bore a son named Victor, the following year. Kate, from a liberal London family, was much younger than Louis and was very supportive of Matilda through her formative years.

From an early age, Matilda had yearned to be an artist and showed a fondness for drawing, but her father was against the idea. A rich and self-made man, Louis expected his daughter to conform to society norms and be on hand to receive the many guests and visitors who came to their home. After her husband's death, Kate, being a Londoner by birth, took the family back to Pimlico and allowed Matilda, then in her late teens, to study drawing and painting at one of the fashionable South Kensington Schools.

There she won a number of prizes and

medals and, more importantly, while still a student, became known to Henry Wallis, an influential London art dealer who, seeing the commercial potential in her work, became her agent and encouraged her to exhibit at the Royal Academy. Her first picture was accepted in 1874 when she was twenty one years old.

Prompted by Wallis, Matilda realised that she would need to refine her provincial upbringing if she was to gain acceptance with society patrons, so decided to work under the name of Maude Goodman. Maude was a very popular name in literary circles in those days, made fashionable by the song, *Come into the Garden Maud* by Lord Alfred Tennyson from 1857.

After leaving art school she studied at home for a while before working in the studio of a Spanish painter based in London. By 1880 she had established herself as an artist, equally proficient in watercolour and oil and greatly admired by the social élite and her upper middle class patrons.

She excelled at painting inoffensive and charming genre paintings of small children living in privileged households with servants and nannies on hand. Her daintily created pictures recorded the refinement and sophistication of middle class home life with painstaking attention to detail.

In all she exhibited fifty two pictures at the Academy and countless more at other leading galleries in Britain and abroad. With the exception of 1896, when one suspects she was busy with commercial ventures, her work was shown at the Academy every year between 1880 and 1901. Her paintings were so popular that they usually sold at the private view, before the exhibition opened to the public.

In 1882 she married Arthur Edwin Scanes, an accountant, and bore two children upon whom the couple doted – Arthur Edwin Leigh and Maude Agnes Sybil. Both would pose as models for their mother's pictures. Her precocious young son is said to have commented: *"...I wish*

*that the Royal Academy Hanging Committee would admit photographs which would relieve me of the monotony of long sittings."*

Arthur was a literary man and an ardent supporter of his wife's work. He contributed to text and poetry for books she illustrated for Raphael Tuck, including *Flowers I Bring and Songs I Sing*, a compilation of poems, to which Edith Nesbit and Helen Burnside also contributed.

Describing a visit to her home at 7 Addison Crescent in 1902, a writer from the *Girl's Realm* observed: *"As I entered her house I seemed to step into one of her pictures. I was in an atmosphere of cool, delicate colouring, surrounded by quaint and pretty things. The Chippendale furniture that plays so large a part in her pictures was here; the Empire mirrors and tables, the white and gold panels that we are familiar with in the interiors she portrays, were all about me... My hostess came forward to greet me, a slender graceful woman, dressed all in white. There is a charm about Maude Goodman of an exquisite womanliness. Her manners are gentle and reserved, her voice low and sweet. By her side walked a small maiden,* (her daughter), *dressed in a picturesque olive green velvet frock, carrying a white kitten in her arms."*

Asked if she would advise girls to take up painting as a career, Maude Goodman replied: *"Yes, if they are prepared to study really hard. They must be prepared for days of heartbreak when nothing will come right. Oh! how often have I had fits of despair at the impossibility of realising what I wanted to do. Girls are much better in health and spirits if they have a serious occupation."*

That was nearly a hundred years ago, but in her time Maude Goodman was an inspiration to other women interested in taking up art as a career. She came to be regarded as the *"painter of youth and of the grace and charm of home. Young mothers, young girls, children, set amid graceful surroundings, are the subjects of her brush."*

It was a great coup for Raphael Tuck to acquire the artistic services of this gifted Victorian painter during the eighteen nineties, when her popularity was at its

*Top:* Months Go By Calendar for 1894. *Above: Two companion volumes:* Rosy Cheeks and Golden Ringlets *and* A Christmas Visit. *[1894]*

zenith. Around 1893 she was asked to execute a series of genre paintings to be reproduced as prints and used for books and calendars. In 1902 these pictures were issued as postcards. Another series of postcards entitled the *Maud Goodman Series,*

*Above left:*
*Artist: Maude Goodman*
*Pub: Raphael Tuck*
*Art Series 6747 [1 of 6]*
*Sing a Song of Roses*
*[1907]*

*Above centre:*
*Artist: Maude Goodman*
*Pub: Raphael Tuck*
*Art Series 6748 [1 of 6]*
*An Errand of Mercy*
*[1907]*

*Above right:*
*Artist: Maude Goodman*
*Pub: Raphael Tuck*
*Art Series 6748 [2 of 6]*
*In the Woods*
*[1907]*

*Bottom row:*
*Artist: Maude Goodman*
*Pub: Raphael Tuck*
*Art Postcards 831/834*
*Series 143 [2 of 12]*
*The Maud Goodman Series*
*[1901]*

(Tuck spelt it Maud and not Maude), sold in their millions.

Until her work was published by Tuck, it was accessible only to the elite and discerning members of the upper classes. Tuck brought the paintings of Maude Goodman and her contemporaries into the homes of audiences who would not otherwise have had the chance to appreciate them. It is interesting to note that the quainter titles of some of her pictures like *Want to see the wheels go wound* and *I love 'oo* – language which one associates with Mabel Lucie Attwell twenty or so years later – was coined in the Victorian era.

Only a privileged few of her audience would have shared such fine surroundings as those depicted in her paintings, but they were entering an age when ordinary people began to aspire to better living conditions. Henriette Corkran, writing in the *Girl's Realm* in 1902, sums it up: *"Maude Goodman is a chronicler to some, for others she points the way."*

# Lilian Govey (1886-1974)

*Lilian Govey in 1924, aged 38*

Lilian spent her childhood with her father Frederick, a letter sorter at the Post Office, her mother Amy Elizabeth, and three sisters, at Barretts Grove, Stoke Newington, east London, before moving to nearby Clissold Park. Even as a young child, she carried a sketch book wherever she went and drew everything that caught her eye. She attended drawing and illustration at art school in her teens and became a keen participant in local amateur dramatics.

By her mid-twenties she was highly regarded as an illustrator and writer of children's stories and verse, and worked for a number of prominent publishers including

*Miniature book from the 'Blinker Booklets'. Published by Humphrey Milford [c.1924]*

Hodder and Stoughton, Dean & Son, Harrap and Wells, Gardner & Darton. Due to a disagreement she had with the latter over the presentation of one of her books, she decided that all future work for them would be done under the pseudonym of JL Gilmour, so that the name of LA Govey would not be tarnished. The publisher Henry Frowde & Hodder and Stoughton, later to become Humphrey Milford, was

*Lilian (Lily to her family) in 1904, aged 18*

her major source of income and she was retained by them for many years. She was one of a select band whose sense of composition and colourful imagery flowed naturally off the brush and onto the pages of the books she illustrated. As proficient in pen and ink as watercolour, her work can be seen in many *Mrs Strang's Annuals* and playbooks and in several sets of postcards in the *Postcards for the Little Ones* series. Titles such as *The Mouseykins, A Day at the Zoo* and *Dreams and Fairies* reflect the themes at which she excelled.

Her style of drawing is reminiscent of her contemporary Anne Anderson and on occasion Lilian collaborated with Anne Anderson's husband, Alan Wright, the creator of the *Bunnykins* books, whose style was also complementary to hers. She become a well-known and successful children's illustrator with a substantial income, but decided to leave London

*Miniature book from the 'Heads & Tails' Series. published by Humphrey Milford [c.1924]*

during World War I to work in more tranquil surroundings. She moved with her friend Ethel Collett to a remote cottage at Older Hill near Midhurst in Sussex. While there, she developed an absorbing interest in spiritualism and earned a reputation locally as a faith healer. As her fame spread, she attracted a band of followers and devotees who camped around the cottage and expected her to provide for them.

At one time her curiosity was aroused by an ancient Roman road that passed close by and she started digging around for anything of historical interest. She heeded her 'spirit guide' concerning places to dig and uncovered a number of historical items, but never found the large cache for which she was searching. Eventually she shifted the foundations of the cottage rendering it unsafe. But despite pleas from the local council and her family, she stubbornly resisted pressure to leave and spent the last

twenty years of her life in a caravan on the site with her many cats. Always a bohemian, very generous and loved by local people, she attracted unusual situations. Even in her remote location she managed to capture a hapless German pilot, forced to bail out near her home during World War II. He surrendered without resistance when she approached him with her dog.

*Above: 'The Goose Who was Queen' from the Big Book of Bedtime Stories, pub. Humphrey Milford (nd). Below: Amateur dramatics: (Seated bottom right) Lilian with sister Dorothy; (standing behind left) Winifred with Ruby.*

*Above & below left:*
*Artist: Lilian Govey*
*Pub: Humphrey Milford*
*Postcards for the Little Ones*
*Dreams & Fairies [2 of 6]*
*[1924]*

*Above & below centre:*
*Artist: Lilian Govey*
*Pub: Humphrey Milford*
*Postcards for the Little Ones*
*A Day at the Zoo [2 of 6]*
*[1927]*

*Above & below right:*
*Artist: Lilian Govey*
*Pub: Wildt & Kray*
*Series 4021*
*[c.1915]*

WHEN CHILDREN OUGHT TO BE ASLEEP
THEIR PLAYTHINGS FROM THE CUPBOARDS CREEP,
AND WORKING HARD BY CANDLE-LIGHT,
THEY MEND AND WASH THEIR CLOTHES, ALL NIGHT.

FOR A CAMEL RIDE THE KEEPER KIND
PUTS ONE IN FRONT AND TWO BEHIND.
AND THEN HE LEADS US ON A CHAIN
ROUND THE DAHLIAS AND BACK AGAIN.

With Fondest Birthday Wishes
This comes to you with love from me
To say I hope to-day will be
The happiest birthday you could see
And lots of wishes warm and true
( More than these chicks,-now count them-do!)
I'm sending with my love to you

HUGH AND HILDA BY THE STREAM
THOUGHT AT FIRST IT WAS A DREAM.
TILL A FAIRY SAID TO HUGH
"NO — IT'S FAIRYLAND COME TRUE"

QUAINT OLD BIRDS, YOU'RE LOOKING COLD;
I WONDER MIGHT I BE SO BOLD
AND OFFER YOU, SO STILL AND WISE,
A PEPPERMINT DROP, OR A FEW BULLS'-EYES?

With Loving Birthday Wishes
I'm sending you this, with love and a kiss,
To wish you a birthday so bright,-
May each little minute have happiness in it,
From morning till tub-time at night!

# Lilian Price Hacker (1879-1948)

*Painting of Lilian Price Hacker by Arthur Hacker, entitled 'There was a veil past which I could not see' exhibited at the Royal Academy in 1910, only three years after their marriage*

Hacker was an established society portrait painter and the advances of such an eminent artist flattered Lilian who was then in her early twenties. The couple married in 1907, but sadly the marriage was unsuccessful and childless.

Although unhappy together, Arthur Hacker certainly helped Lilian develop a career in art through his contacts in art and commerce. Between 1909 and 1924 she exhibited fifteen pictures, mainly miniatures, at the Royal Academy Summer Exhibition, working from addresses in west London and Glynde in Sussex. Her preferred medium was watercolour and her soft and sympathetic style was extremely popular.

*Arthur Hacker c.1894*

these designs were reissued by Humphrey Milford in 1926.

The cover and title page of the book were treated in an oriental style in keeping with Liberty's practice of importing exotic merchandise from the East. It was a handsome and popular gift book which went out of print quite quickly with the onset of World War I.

Another boxed picture book published by Hodder & Stoughton, entitled *Numbers of Things*, was to follow in 1920, of which, a reviewer commented: *"...verses and pictures are by Lilian Price Hacker, whose work is distinguished by a rare charm and delicacy. There is a subtle harmony of colour running through* Numbers of Things, *reminding one of a world seen through a haze of golden light."*

Sadly, for lovers of her delicate imagery, Lilian Price Hacker ('Auntie Bill' to friends and family), withdrew from commercial illustration to focus her energy on the Christian Science movement, for whom she worked tirelessly for the rest of her days.

*Susan, published by Henry Frowde. [1912]*

Lilian Price Edwards was the third of five children (four girls and one boy) born to Edward Price Edwards and his wife Mary. The family lived at Sutton in Surrey and Edward was Secretary to Trinity House. Between 1900 and 1905 Lilian studied drawing and miniature painting at the Royal Academy Schools. She was clearly a talented student, winning two prizes and a silver medal for her drawing. It was there that she met Arthur Hacker, a fashionable Edwardian portrait painter, over twenty years her senior, who had taught at

the school since the eighteen nineties.

Arthur Hacker (1858-1919) was the son of a line engraver and studied at the Royal Academy Schools between 1876 and 1880. He took further tuition in Paris between 1880 and 1881 under Louis Bonnat, the internationally acclaimed portrait painter and close friend of Edgar Degas. As a young man he travelled widely in North Africa, Spain and Italy, often with his friend Solomon Joseph Solomon, a painter of dramatic classical scenes.

By the time the couple met, Arthur

Arthur Hacker had painted portraits of members of the wealthy Liberty family, founders of the high class emporium, established in 1875. In 1912, Liberty's published a series of six postcards and nursery wall plaques entitled *Susan*, in collaboration with Hodder & Stoughton who published a boxed picture book with the same title, written and illustrated by Lilian. The book contained twelve colour plates, with verses to accompany them. Only six of the twelve plates, which describe a little girl, Susan and her many moods, had been issued as postcards and

*Artist: Lilian Price Hacker*
*Pub: Humphrey Milford*
*Postcards for the Little Ones*
*Susan [5 of 6] & packet*
*[1926]*

# Evelyn Stuart Hardy (1865-1935)

Beatrice Evelyn Elizabeth Hardy was born into a family of artists in the Clifton area of Bristol in 1865. Her grandfather James, her father David, her mother Emily and her uncle Heywood, were all artists. She had a younger sister Mabel Dora and two brothers, David Paul Frederick Hardy (1862-1940) and Norman Heywood Hardy (1863-1914), all of whom became successful painters and illustrators.

Evelyn's father died in 1870, leaving the family virtually destitute. Emily just managed to make ends meet by painting, teaching and renting out rooms, so it is not surprising that Evelyn and her brothers, who all learned to paint at home, had to start work at a tender age. We are told that Evelyn received her first commission at the age of nine.

Her uncle, Heywood Hardy, was a successful animal painter, etcher and illustrator who hailed from Bristol, but who moved to London around 1870. His success led him to be elected to the Royal Institute of Oil Painters in 1883 and the Royal Watercolour Society in 1884 and he contributed to the *Illustrated London News,* the *Graphic* and other leading journals.

Heywood Hardy's reputation helped establish Evelyn and Paul as successful commercial artists in London during the eighteen eighties and nineties.

Paul was a prolific illustrator. As well as working for most of the prominent magazines of the day, he contributed to *Chums* from 1896 to the year of his death in 1940. He was also a metalworker with a keen interest in armour and became advisor to the armoury department of the British Museum in the nineteen twenties.

Evelyn enjoyed a successful career, starting off in the art departments of the *St James' Budget*, the *Sporting & Dramatic* and the *Gentlewoman*. Perhaps it is not surprising that in the wake of her brother's interest in armour she developed a keen interest in drawing military subjects, receiving technical instruction in the correctness of detail from a Captain Drake of the Royal Horse Guards.

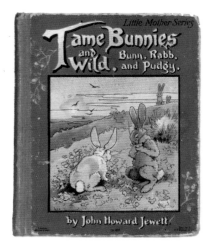

Tame Bunnies and Wild, *pub: Nister [nd]*

*I Saw Three Ships, from* Mother Goose's Nursery Rhymes *[nd]*

The story goes that her curiosity and dogged determination often got her into trouble. An editorial in *Pearson's Magazine* recalls that *"With officers and troopers of the 'Blues' she is an especial favourite and has found many models from life among them. At Aldershot on one occasion she was suspected of being a Nihilist and another time was taken for a French spy when making some sketches of a fort, but in each dilemma her soldier friends were quickly able to show that she was not a dangerous character and restored her confiscated studies."*

She worked extensively for Nister between 1894 and 1910 and became an important member of a team of illustrators who created some of the most inventive and exciting children's books ever created, rivalled only by Raphael Tuck and Lothar Meggendorfer in Germany. Her illustrations appear in many transformation and moveable books including *Push and Pull Pictures* and *Our Darling's Surprise Pictures*, as well as *Nister's Holiday Annuals* and many other Nister titles.

When Nister faced problems at the outbreak of World War I, Evelyn Hardy joined the publishers Shaw, where she illustrated a version of *Alice in Wonderland* and contributed to *Our Darlings Annual*. Perhaps her major work was a series of biblical paintings entitled *Friends of Jesus*, comprising a collection of 977 pictures, a selection of which appeared in a pocket bible published by Collins in 1971.

When and why did Evelyn Hardy add Stuart to her name? She adopted the name in the eighteen eighties. She never married and as far as we can ascertain Stuart was not part of her family name. So perhaps she felt more comfortable as a commercial artist using a more masculine name.

She lived in a cottage at Storrington, Sussex, near her brother David, until she died in 1935.

The postcard series entitled *The Circling Year*, illustrated on page 139, is set in the countryside she loved. This delightful series comprises twelve designs and is printed on a textured board to simulate a canvas finish.

*Left column:*
*Artist: Evelyn Stuart Hardy*
*Pub. Ernest Nister*
*Series 41 [2 of 6]*
*[1902]*

*Centre & right column:*
*Artist: Evelyn Stuart Hardy*
*Pub: McDougall's Educational Co*
*The Circling Year [4 of 12]*
*Top row: May, June*
*Bottom row: October, November*
*[c.1903]*

### The Fox and the Crow.

A CROW, having secured a Piece of Cheese, flew with its Prize to a lofty Tree, and was preparing to devour the Luscious Morsel, when a crafty Fox, halting at the foot of the Tree, began to cast about how he might obtain it. "How tasteful," he cried, in well-feigned Ecstasy, "is your Dress; it cannot surely be that your Musical Education has been neglected. Will you not oblige—?" "I have a horrid Cold," replied the Crow, "and never sing without my Music, but since you press me——. At the same time, I should add that I have read Æsop, and been there before." So saying, she deposited the Cheese in a safe Place on the Limb of the Tree, and favoured him with a Song. "Thank you," exclaimed the Fox, and trotted away, with the Remark that Welsh Rabbits never agreed with him, and were far inferior in Quality to the animate Variety.

*Moral.*—The foregoing Fable is supported by a whole Gatling Battery of Morals. We are taught (1) that it Pays to take the Papers; (2) that Invitation is not Always the Sincerest Flattery; (3) that a Stalled Rabbit with Contentment is better than No Bread, and (4) that the Aim of Art is to Conceal Disappointment.

### The Prudent Tiger.

A PRUDENT Tiger, having observed a Procession bearing the Remains of a Sainted Brahmin to the Tomb, communicated the Intelligence to his Wife, who said, "My dear, we are almost out of Meat, and though the Deceased, from the Austerities of his pious Life, was in poor Condition, I make no Doubt that among his surviving Friends we may encounter others more Succulent." "Miserable Tigress," exclaimed her Lord, "cannot you see that if we permit the Deceased to be canonized, Pilgrimages will be instituted to his Tomb, and the Producer and Consumer will be brought together in accordance with the True Principles of Political Economy? Rather let us, then, offer a Chromo for each new Pilgrim." This prudent Advice being followed, the Tiger enjoyed a Free Breakfast Table to the End of his Days.

*Moral.*—Beware of Breaking the Egg that Hatches the Golden Goose.

# Florence Hardy (1867-1957)

The childhood of Florence and her brother Dudley passed pleasantly in the artistic environment of their father's studio. They enjoyed his instruction and supervision and began to experiment with his brushes and paints.

Florence, (known as Florry in the early days), her elder sister Edith and Dudley Hardy (1866-1922), were born in Sheffield, the children of Thomas Bush Hardy (1842-1897), the prolific and popular painter of marine pictures and coastal scenes. A self-taught artist, he evolved a fluent and painterly style based on the Dutch landscape school. He made frequent trips abroad, often taking the family to their summer house near Boulogne, close to the English Channel, where he painted some of his most dramatic seascapes.

He was a gregarious man, with a wealth of experience and zest for life. He was a fine teacher and endowed all of his children with his creative talent.

The family moved down to Islington, London in 1870, where there was a larger market for Hardy's pictures and where Jessie, Frank (also a noted painter), Winifred and Dorothy were born. On arrival in London, Hardy took a clerical job with the Inland Revenue at Somerset

House, until he felt he could earn enough from painting to support his large family. With a brief interval of residence in Boulogne between 1877 and 1880, where Jacqueline, the sixth of his seven children were born, the family resided in London until after his untimely death.

Dudley was sent to study at the art academy in Düsseldorf at the age of 15. He matured into a fine painter and exhibited at the Royal Academy and other leading galleries in the late eighties and early nineties. Later, he became a member of the London Sketch Club, illustrated books and postcards and was a leading poster artist of his day, working for the D'Oyly Carte Opera Company and the Savoy Theatre. He may be best remembered for his humourous, satirical black and white sketches and cartoons for *Punch* and other leading journals.

Florence and her younger sister Jessie, trained as painters and miniaturists at the Sorbonne in Paris in their late teens. Then, for ten years, between 1887 and 1897, Florence exhibited her work at all the major galleries including the Royal Academy, the Royal Society and the Society of Women Artists.

In contrast to her father and Dudley, Florence was a painstaking and meticulous draughtswoman. Training as a miniaturist had taught her to be attentive to fine detail. She always made many preliminary sketches prior to her finished artwork. Often she would trace the outlines of her compositions before satisfying herself they were correct in every minute detail.

A year after the death in 1889, of his first wife Mary Ann, Hardy married Rebecca Purchas the daughter of a silversmith from Clerkenwell. Her pet name was Muriel and she bore him another child. She was twenty one, twenty eight years Hardy's junior. At that time they were renting a large family villa – number 32 Castelnau, Barnes. The house, befitting a painter of Hardy's standing, was described as *"...substantially*

*Florence (top left) with her sister Jessie [c.1890] (Seated) Winifred, Jacqueline and Dorothy.*

We care for nobody _ no _ not We!

When the Heart is young.

Which_?

*Artist: Florence Hardy*
*Pub: CW Faulkner*
*Series 1166 A/D/E*
*[3 of 6]*
*[1911]*

*Right:*
*A family group enjoying a holiday by the sea at TB Hardy's bungalow, 'Wicardenne', Kingsdown, near Dover in summer 1892. Hardy is in the centre, proudly looking at his two year old daughter. The group comprises Hardy's three eldest daughters, Edith, Florence and Jessie standing at the back in dark dresses. 'Muriel', Hardy's second wife with baby Barbara on her lap, surrounded by her sisters and brother, who could not resist moving his head, seated at the front in a sailor suit.*

*as well as ornamentally built...with a carriage drive up to the door."* The family employed several live-in servants and housekeepers.

Florence was set for a career as a painter, but several family misfortunes, including her father's premature and sudden death in 1897, forced her to turn her attention to commercial work. She had to help support the family, hitherto accustomed to a high standard of living.

Scout Quack and Dolly Dutch *published by SW Partridge & Co [c.1920]*

The advent of the camera reduced the demand for miniatures and so Florence turned to publishing as a source of regular income. Her miniaturist skills were satisfied by the new craze – the picture postcard.

Like most miniaturists she drew her child figures in outline with colour infill and had an innate sense of composition. Her scenes of children linking arms in a row or in formal groups are hauntingly memorable images.

Her love of costume is apparent in all her work. Often, she would choose to draw children in costumes from days gone by, reminiscent of Kate Greenaway. Delicately drawn, they looked like porcelain dolls with their demure and distant smiles. Her eye for detail is particularly evident in her early postcard designs for CW Faulkner. Many of her finest examples are Christmas postcards,

depicting children, skating or sledging, but you can be sure that they would not have a crease or even a speck of snow on their costumes.

Dutch boys and girls were another favourite Florence Hardy subject. It was a popular theme of the day, exploited by many artists, but she had memories from her own childhood of holidays across the Channel, which make her renderings of Dutch children in typical Lowland scenery, especially poignant.

The postcard provided her with a commercial alternative to miniature painting. She continued working, well into the nineteen twenties, contributing to *Little Folks* and other children's periodicals, but did not quite manage to achieve the quality and consistency she showed in her early postcard designs.

After World War I, Florence shared a flat with her sister Jacqueline in Hereford Road, Maida Vale. Sadly, she illustrated only a few children's books, most notably, a collaboration with Louise Rossel for a series of small books about *Scout Quack and Dolly Dutch*. Louise, who provided the verses, was the sister of Harry Rossel, a Belgian who worked in the diplomatic service and who was Florence's long time romantic partner.

*Auntie Flo with sisters Jessie, Jacqueline (standing) and friends at Ditchling [c.1948]*

Before World War II, at the suggestion of artist Frank Brangwyn, a close family friend, the sisters moved to Ditchling, Sussex, where they spent their later years.

*LEFT HAND PAGE*

*Tob row:*
*Artist: Florence Hardy*
*Pub: Meissner & Buch*
*Series: 1814 [2 of 4]*
*[1907]*

*Below left:*
*Artist: Florence Hardy*
*Pub: Raphael Tuck*
*Oilette Series E1159*
*Joyous Easter*
*[c.1907]*

*Below right:*
*Artist: Florence Hardy*
*Pub: Raphael Tuck*
*Oilette Series 9694*
*Young Hearts*
*[1907]*

*RIGHT HAND PAGE*

*Tob row:*
*Artist: Florence Hardy*
*Pub: CW Faulkner*
*Series 732 [2 of 6]*
*Childhood's Happy Time*
*[1907]*

*Centre row:*
*Artist: Florence Hardy*
*Pub: CW Faulkner*
*Series 779 [2 of 6]*
*[1907]*

*Boltom row:*
*Artist: Florence Hardy*
*Pub: CW Faulkner*
*Series 1238 [2 of 6]*
*[1912]*

Home again, home again, market is done.

My love is like a red, red rose.

# John Hassall (1868-1943)

John Hassall made his name as a cartoonist and artist designing some of the most striking and effective posters of his day, including the classic, *Skegness is so Bracing*. Many of his theatre posters were for fairy tale productions such as *Babes in the Wood*, *Little Red Riding Hood* and *Mother Goose*.

He loved children and had five of his own. He was twice married; first, in 1893 to Isobel Dingwell, by whom he had a son and two daughters; and second, in 1903, to Constance Maud, the daughter of a vicar. The son of this marriage was Christopher Hassall, poet, actor and playwright and the daughter was Joan Hassall, the renowned wood-engraver.

His child rearing days clearly put him in the mood for illustrating books and other ephemeral items for children. From 1900 onwards he illustrated hundreds. Here are just a few examples of the titles for publishers Blackie & Son alone: *Jack and the Beanstalk, Red Riding Hood, Beauty and the Beast, Blackie's Red Picture Book, Blackie's Blue Picture Book, Cinderella, Dear Old Nursery Tales, Travelling Musicians, Jack and the Giant Killer, Puss in Boots, Babes in*

the Wood, Aladdin and the Lamp, Hansel and Gretel – the list goes on and on. His cheerful, jaunty characters were drawn in bold outline with flat colour washes, ideally suited to the roughish, thick paper used for many of the popular children's books of the day.

Hassall's funny and expressive cartoon style drawings and bold colouring, had a great deal of impact on picture postcards and his work was in great demand by publishers everywhere.

*Hassall's Painting Book, published by Dean & Son. [nd]*

The first Hassall illustrations to appear on postcards were the humorous CW Faulkner series 72, 12 designs entitled *Fun and Frolic*, of 1901. After that he worked for various other publishers including EW Savory, Raphael Tuck, Valentine, Voisey and Wrench. In 1903, along with several of his colleagues from the London Sketch Club, including Tom Browne, Dudley Hardy and Phil May, he created for Davidson Brothers some of his most memorable postcard designs. *Nursery Rhymes Illustrated* shown opposite is perhaps one of his very best.

ONE, TWO,
BUCKLE MY SHOE,
THREE - FOUR,
SHUT - THE - DOOR.

ELSIE MARLEY'S GROWN SO FINE,
SHE WONT GET UP TO FEED THE SWINE,
BUT LAYS IN BED TILL AFTER NINE.
LAZY ELSIE MARLEY.

NEEDLES & PINS—NEEDLES & PINS,
WHEN A MAN MARRIES HIS TROUBLE BEGINS.

DICKORY, DICKORY DOCK,
THE MOUSE RAN UP THE CLOCK
THE CLOCK STRUCK ONE
DOWN THE MOUSE RUN
DICKORY DICKORY DOCK.

*LEFT HAND PAGE*

*Artist: John Hassall*
*Pub: Wrench*
*The Wrench Series [4 of 12]*
*[c.1907]*

*RIGHT HAND PAGE*

*Artist: John Hassall*
*Pub: Davidson Brothers*
*Series 3507 [6 of 6]*
*Nursery Rhymes Illustrated*
*[1907]*

# Racey Helps (1913-1971)

*LEFT HAND PAGE*

*Above:*
*Artist: Racey Helps*
*Pub: The Medici Society*
*Packet 190*
*Haymaking*
*[nd]*

*Centre:*
*Artist: Racey Helps*
*Pub: The Medici Society*
*Packet 221*
*Bunnies Picnic*
*[nd]*

*Below:*
*Artist: Racey Helps*
*Pub: The Medici Society*
*Packet 197*
*The Balloon Seller*
*[nd]*

*RIGHT HAND PAGE*

*Above right:*
*Artist: LM Hine*
*Pub: British Art Company*
*Fairies and Pixies packet*
*Rhymes by AM Stewart*
*[1924]*

*Bottom row:*
*Artist: LM Hine*
*Pub: British Art Company*
*Fairies and Pixies [3 of 6]*
*Rhymes by AM Stewart*
*[1924]*

Angus Clifford Racey Helps was born in 1913, of English-Scots descent and spent his childhood in the hamlet of Chalvey, Somerset. He was privately educated at a vicarage and later at Bristol Cathedral School, before entering the antiquarian book business and attending the West of England College of Art.

He began to write stories at school for a young cousin. Then, in the nineteen forties, having started writing again to amuse his own daughter and son, he achieved commercial success.

Racey's books, like *Barnaby in Search of a House* and *Little Mouse Crusoe* have been favourites with young children for many years and some of his characters are well known on both sides of the Atlantic and can be seen on greetings cards, postcards, as strip pictures in the Bristol Evening World and even jig-saw puzzles. He would often reflect on the many letters sent by children expressing their delight with his stories.

His anthropomorphic characters exist to play and enjoy life in a world totally unthreatened by predators. His approach was simple. Racey Helps always maintained that *"...boys and girls like excitement and adventure with a happy ending and that like animals they are closer to the ground than adults and therefore understand them better."*

He always tried to place himself close to the ground when drawing, a task made easier by his love of nature.

# Lydia Margaret Hine (1904-1964)

*Lydia Margaret Hine [c.1933]*

Margaret Hine, the second of four children of John McLennan Hine and his wife Lydia Emma, was born in Maryport, Cumberland in 1904, a member of the family of of Hine Brothers, ship owners. Her father was a marine engineer, educated at Dulwich College during the 1890s. He moved the family to Nottingham in 1910

on joining the Ocean Insurance Company. Sadly, he was killed at the Battle of Jutland in 1916 while serving on *HMS Invincible,* when Margaret was only 12 years old.

Prior to his death, John Hine had spent time away from home during the course of his work, but correspondence between father and daughter reveal that even as a child, Margaret loved drawing and painting. In 1922, knowing that her father would have wanted her to develop her artistic talent, Margaret was enrolled at Nottingham School of Art. In those days, students underwent formal training in drawing, painting and anatomy and her sketch books prove this to be the case. It was a forward thinking school led by Principal, Joe Harrison, a prime mover of progressive art education at that time.

Margaret was not a prolific illustrator, although her *Fairies and Pixies* series created for the British Art Company during the nineteen twenties is a wonderfully delicate example of fairy postcards to accompany

the many seasonal greetings cards she drew for the same firm.

Working from her Nottingham studio, she advertised her services as a designer of nursery pictures, flower studies, calendars and decorator of wood, glass, pottery, tins and lampshades in water-colour, pastel and black and white. Between 1923 and 1928

she exhibited at the Nottingham Art Gallery. In 1933, she married Eric Saywell, later to become a Baptist minister and bore two sons. Due to her husbands various postings, they lived in different parts of the country. Margaret continued to work as a flower painter and exhibited regularly at the Pastel Society until her death in 1964.

A Pixie made a chain of flowers,
And hung it in a tree,
And swinging there the whole day long,
He sang a little Fairy Song,
A.M.S.          As happy as could be.

A pretty Fairy Mother
Is searching all around,
The Pixies hate to go to bed,
They run away and hide instead,
A.M.S.          And never make a sound.

When Fairies find a tiny pool,
And long to make a boat,
They choose a Lily on the Pond,
And touch it with a magic wand,
A.M.S.          Then off they gaily float.

# Eva Hollyer (1865-1943)

Eva Hollyer was born Evangeline Grace Ellen Hollyer in 1865 in Walworth, South London. She was the first of a family of ten children to artist William Perring Hollyer and his wife Grace Emily, who had married a year earlier.

William Perring Hollyer (1834-1922) was a noted animal painter and is best remembered for his paintings of highland stags, cattle and sheep, which were popular pastoral subjects in the latter half of the 19th century. William's father Joseph Hollyer was a heraldic painter and coach builder of Dover who moved with his family to South London in 1851, before he diversified into the then new technology of using acid to etch glass. Several of Joseph's other children became artists in glass and several generations of Hollyers followed this trade or took up gold-leaf signwriting.

In her childhood, it appears that Eva's skills were more inclined to music than art, since the 1871 census records her at the age of six as being a pianist. Eventually, she became a painter and amongst her exhibited works were *Expectation* (1891), *A Tiff* (1892) and *The Course of True Love Never did Run Smooth* (1892). She also exhibited at the Royal Academy Summer Exhibition in 1891 (*Hurt*), 1894 (*Happy*) and 1898 (*Spring*). At this time the family were living in Cheshire. Her main interest was in figure painting and her sister Verna

would often sit for her. Several galleries house her pictures, notably the Walker Gallery in Liverpool which has twenty seven in its collection.

In 1906, at the age of 41, she married her 19 year old cousin, the artist Joseph Richard Hollyer, at Pontardawe in Wales. They both told 'little white lies' to the Registrar as the marriage certificate shows their ages as 35 and 22 respectively. It appears the marriage may have been a sham, as nothing more is heard of Joseph. It was a childless marriage and there is no record of Joseph's death, so he may have moved abroad.

After her marriage, Eva continued to paint and many of her paintings were reproduced as postcards. Her delightfully romantic Christmas scenes painted for EW Savory are signed with her pseudonym of Alice Martineau, possibly to avoid antagonising her better patrons. who may not have approved. These designs bear a striking resemblance to the early postcards of Ethel Parkinson.

Eva also illustrated postcards for Birn Brothers, Langsdorff and Raphael Tuck during the Edwardian period.

Eva and her sister Maud lived together through the twenties and thirties. Eva wrote a delightful article for *Woman's Magazine* in 1927 called *Our Property Venture* describing their home *(Wayside Cottage)* at Hagbourne,

LEFT HAND PAGE

*Below left:*
*Artist: Eva Hollyer*
*Pub: EW Savory*
*Series 702  [1 of 4]*
*[c.1905]*

*Centre/right columns:*
*Artist: Eva Hollyer*
*Pub: Birn Brothers*
*Series 2401  [4 of 6]*
*[1906]*

*Right:*
*Eva with her sisters*
*[c.1895]*

# Eileen Hood (1892-1970)

*Eileen Hood with a group of tounger family members. [c.1912]*

Eileen Hood was the second of four sisters born to Arthur Hood, a stockbroker and his wife Florence. Her early years were spent in the quiet, leafy London suburb of Streatham. Success at work around the turn of the century, enabled Arthur Hood and his family to move to a spacious home out of London, at Kenley in Surrey, where they lived for many years. Eileen enjoyed the benefits of a private education and later attended Roedean School where she joined the same class as Radclyffe Hall, author of *The Well of Loneliness*.

Although art was an extra-curricular subject at Roedean at that time, Eileen's natural drawing talent was nurtured by Sylvia Lawrence, head of art from the school's inception in 1885 until her

retirement in 1928. Even as a very young child, Eileen loved art and animals. Her sketchbooks show how she managed to develop a delicate technique which she practised at every available opportunity by drawing carefully observed portraits of animals and members of her wide circle of friends. As a young girl of twelve, she showed great promise by winning the *GF Watts Prize* at the Royal Drawing Society for an animal study.

A turning point in her appreciation of art took place at Christmas 1908, when Sylvia Lawrence presented her with the gift of a book for some excellent holiday work. The book was entitled *The Art of John M Swan RA* and showed plates of the powerful animal paintings of John Macallan

Swan, one of the most revered animal painters and sculptors of his day. An article in the *Art Journal* of 1894 recognises the classical qualities of Swan's skill as a draughtsman, combined with his ability to express the decorative aspects of his subjects through the delicacy of Japanese influences that were in vogue at the time.

The gift of this book had a profound effect on Eileen Hood's short but fruitful career as an artist. She was clearly touched by Swan's technique and confidently developed her own style influenced by many of his modes of expression.

Not long after leaving Roedean in 1910, her perseverence was rewarded when her work was accepted for exhibition at the Royal Institute.

Her first commercial commisions came from publishers Geographia, and then from Henry Frowde and Hodder & Stoughton for whom she painted several sets of postcards depicting farm animals, creatures in the wild and children with their pet dogs in their *Postcards for the Little Ones Series. Chums, Faithful Friends, Farm Babies, The Farm Team, Our Sporting Dogs, Trusty and True* and *Wild Life* are all series titles

*The left handed golfer practising her swing*

*A pencil sketch for* Trusty and True

that evoke the country life that Eileen loved. Each of these miniature paintings demonstrates a confidence and fluency that would not normally be associated with one so young. By 1917 she was contributing, along with other artists, to Mrs Strang's Annuals and playbooks for the very young, including *Little One's Own Playbook*, published by Humphrey Milford, successors to Henry Frowde and Hodder & Stoughton.

During the World War I work was hard to come by, yet in spite of this she seemed set for a successful career as an illustrator, until she met her husband to be, Charles Walker. Charles was a brilliant civil engineer, who was to become one of the founder directors of the De Havilland aircraft company. His laconic nature and disarming wit was the perfect foil for Eileen's assertive and fiery disposition.

Eileen and Charles married in 1916 and moved to Stanmore in Middlesex, so any thoughts that she may have had for a career in art were nipped in the bud. She no longer needed to earn a living and although she still enjoyed drawing and continued to keep a sketch book, she chose to express her passion for dogs by becoming one of Britain's leading breeders of Irish Setters. eventually rising to become an eminent member of the Kennel Club and a senior judge at Crufts.

*Left & centre column:*
*Artist: Eileen Hood*
*Pub: Humphrey Milford*
*Postcards for the Little Ones*
*Chums [4 of 6]*
*[1926]*

*Above right:*
*Artist: Eileen Hood*
*Pub: Humphrey Milford*
*Postcards for the Little Ones*
*Farm Babies [1 of 6]*
*[1926]*

*Centre right:*
*Artist: Eileen Hood*
*Pub: Humphrey Milford*
*Postcards for the Little Ones*
*Wild Life [1 of 6]*
*[c. 1919]*

*Below right:*
*Artist: Eileen Hood*
*Pub: Humphrey Milford*
*Postcards for the Little Ones*
*The Farm Team [1 of 6]*
*[1918]*

THOUGH WOLVES ARE FIERCE WHERE'ER THEY BE,
A WOLF-HOUND IS THE FRIEND FOR ME. ◦ ◦

THOUGH I'M IN CHARGE OF BOB, YOU SEE,
HE THINKS HE'S TAKING CARE OF ME'-

NOW DOGS, ATTEND TO WHAT I SAY —
A GAME OF CARDS WE'RE GOING TO PLAY.

TO WIN A HORSE'S HEART YOU'LL FIND
YOU MUST BE GENTLE, JUST AND KIND.

TWO'S COMPANY

# James Horrabin (1884-1962)

James Horrabin was born in Peterborough, the eldest son of James Woodhouse Horrabin, a cutler. He was educated at Stamford School and later attended Sheffield School of Art in his parents' home town. He started as a metalwork designer but later changed to drawing. He joined the art department of the *Sheffield Telegraph and Star* in 1906 and rose rapidly to Art Editor.

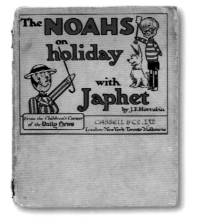

The Noahs on Holiday [*c.1920*]

Little did Horrabin know when taking up the position of Art Editor of Fleet Street's *Daily News*, in 1911, that he would be the instigator of one of the most popular cartoon features to appear during the inter-war years. *The Adventures of the Noah Family* began as a single panel in the Daily News on 13 June 1919. This jolly family of wooden toys, comprising Mr and Mrs Noah, their three children Ham, Skein and Japhet, lived at The Ark, Ararat Avenue in London, with their pet bear Happy.

As its popularity grew, the panel became a strip and was then reissued in book form, the first title being *Some Adventures of the Noah Family* published by the *Daily News* in 1920. The first *Japhet and Happy Annual* appeared in 1932 and continued until 1952.

The three postcards from a set of six illustrated below and published by Davis & Carter, date from 1921, shortly after the first compilation of Noah Family cartoon strips was published in book form. These *Toy Models* series E14 and series E16, Japhet's

Model Theatre, were two of seventeen Toy Models series first published by James Henderson, but inherited by Davis & Carter when Henderson closed down.

Horrabin was also the creator of *Dot and Carrie*, a popular adult strip first appearing in *The Star* newspaper in 1922 and later in *The Evening News* until 1962.

Horrabin, an active left-wing socialist, had careers in politics and the media. He was Labour MP for Peterborough (1929-31) and was a regular guest on radio, including, *The Brain's Trust, Questions Answered* and *Questions on the Year*. He also wrote and illustrated books and made appearances on pre-war television.

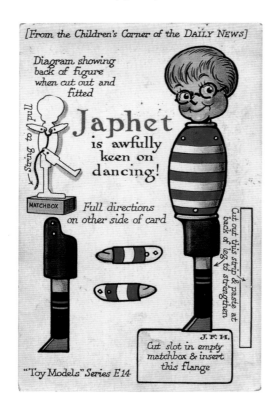

# Sydney Hulme Beaman (1887-1932)

LEFT HAND PAGE

*Above:*
*Artist: James Horrabin*
*Pub: Davis & Carter*
*Toy Models Series E16*
*Japhet's Model Theatre*
*Card no. 3347 [1 of 6]*
*[1920]*

*Bottom row:*
*Artist: James Horrabin*
*Pub: Davis & Carter*
*Toy Models Series E14*
*Card nos. 3333/3335/3336*
*[1919]*

RIGHT HAND PAGE

*Top row:*
*Artist: Sydney Hulme Beaman*
*Pub: Humphrey Milford*
*Postcards for the Little Ones*
*Toytown Folk [3 of 6]*
*[1930]*

Loud the Toy-town bagpipes play!
See – the piper comes this way!
Fido says "From what I hear
This poor Scotsman's feeling queer."

Here's St. George, the Toy-town Knight,
Ready for his dragon fight,
Dragon looks so small and thin
I feel sure St. George will win.

Cowboy Micky likes to ride
On his bucking horse astride.
"Fido – go away!" cries Mick.
"Mind yourself! You'll get a kick!"

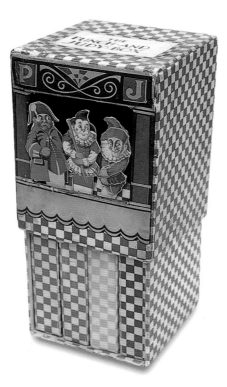

*"Whether they represent animals or humans, Mr Beaman's grotesque, square little figures are masterpieces of art. How he manages to put so much vigour and expression into them is nothing short of marvellous. All the old friends of the author's wireless talks are here met with again – the Mayor, Ernest the Policeman, the Magician, Larry the Lamb and all the rest of them…"* exclaimed a 1930 reviewer about *Wireless in Toytown* published by Collins.

Toytown is the series with which Sydney Hulme Beaman is readily associated. It owes a great deal to its success as a radio feature on *Children's Hour* and the way Derek McCulloch (Uncle Mac) portrayed Larry the Lamb. The stories were more about the individual characters, than the

plots, which were farcical and inept. It is the pompous mayor, the inept inventor and the fragile ponderous Larry the Lamb who will be best remembered by all those of us who were children either side of World War II. The feature lasted until the demise of *Children's Hour* in 1964.

Beaman was born in Tottenham, North London and attended Heatherley's School of Art. He started work as a toymaker and carved puppets and small wooden figures with jointed limbs, on which he based his first cartoon strip, published in the *Golder's Green Gazette* in 1923.

Credibility for these odd drawings drew strength from a current fad for 'Straight Line Caricatures', a style that influenced a number of illustrators during the nineteen twenties. It occurred by way of a natural extension of the *art deco* movement's simplification of form. Other children's illustrators like Joyce Mercer, Hugh Lofting and May Smith introduced *art deco* to children's illustration in a more creative way.

*Left:* The Punch and Judy Box, *published by Humphrey Milford [c.1925], containing four little books:* Punch and Judy, Three Little Plays, Banger's Circus *and* The Wet Day Book, *along with Toy Town characters by SG Hulme Beaman.*

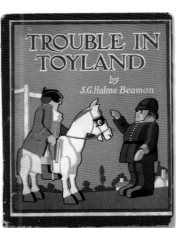

*Trouble in Toyland [1925] was one of four "quaint and amusing" hard-backed booklets in the* Toyland Series *published by Humphrey Milford. The other three titles were* Jerry and Joe, The Way to Toyland *and* The Wooden Knight.

# Helen Jackson (1855-1911)

Charles Wakefield Jackson was a successful builder and contractor. He was responsible for the construction of the Chappel Valley Viaduct in 1849, an impressive thirty two arched edifice which carried the Stour Valley Railway across the River Colne, near Colchester in Essex. He went on to become one of the main organisers of labour for the construction of the Crystal Palace in 1851.

*Charles Wakefield Jackson [c.1875]*

He and his wife Emily hailed from Gainsborough in Lincolnshire, but moved south when building contracts brought him to the London area. They settled at 76 Tulse Hill, before moving to a more substantial property at number 101 in the eighteen seventies. In those days this verdant neighbourhood was occupied by successful middle-class professionals and tradesmen.

By now, although retired, Jackson was a wealthy man with a family of four girls, Elizabeth, Helen, Harriet and Evelyn and two boys, George and Charles. Two other children had died as infants. They had three live-in servants and a coachman and his wife who occupied the adjoining coach house. Maria Best, a housemaid, remained in service with the family for most of her life.

Helen and her younger sister Evelyn were talented painters, specialising in genre and figurative subjects. Helen loved nothing more than to paint portraits of family and friends in her studio at home. In 1879 she was accepted into the Royal Academy Schools in London to study drawing and painting and between 1885 and 1904 exhibited seven pictures at the Royal Academy, one of which, entitled *Aurora*

*Emily Jackson, Helen's mother [c.1875]*

*Leigh*, (1887) is said to be a self-portrait and another *Evelyn*, (1893) is of her sister. She also exhibited work at most of the leading galleries in Britain.

Helen gave art lessons to aspiring artists, one of whom was Mary Drew, who lived locally at the time. Mary became an accomplished painter in her own right. Not only did she paint a portrait of Helen in 1898, she exhibited twenty three pictures at the Royal Academy between 1885 and 1901.

During the eighteen nineties, Helen contributed illustrations to Raphael Tuck, many of which appeared in books and postcards and some have been used for advertisements, such as *Treloar Mats, the Best Foor Coverings*. Examples of Helen's work, published at the same time as her work for Raphael Tuck can also be found on monochrome postcards published by William McKenzie.

Around the turn of the century, she suffered a stroke and spent her latter years in considerable pain, bringing a sad ending to her life. A short obituary in the *Art Journal* acknowledged her death in 1911.

*Painting of Helen Jackson by Mary Drew, oil on canvas. [1898]*

*Left: The back garden of Somerby, 101 Tulse Hill, painted by Evelyn Jackson. Somerby is a Lincolnshire village where Helen's parents did their courting. Above: The end of an era. Number 107 — one of the last Victorian family residences in Tulse Hill awaits demolition in 1999. Right: A decorative and embossed greetings card by Raphael Tuck, with a verse on the inside by Helen Burnside. [c.1895]*

With my Love.

*Above left:*
*Artist: Helen Jackson*
*Pub: Raphael Tuck*
*Art series 6749*
*The Little Mother*
*[c.1907]*

*Below left:*
*Artist: Helen Jackson*
*Pub: Raphael Tuck*
*Art series 6750*
*Only a Little Shower*
*[c.1907]*

*Above centre:*
*Artist: Helen Jackson*
*Pub: Raphael Tuck*
*Art series 6750*
*Home From School*
*[c.1907]*

*Below centre:*
*Artist: Helen Jackson*
*Pub: Raphael Tuck*
*Art series 6750*
*Heigho, Heigho! Here we Go*
*  Swinging To and Fro*
*[c.1907]*

*Above right:*
*Artist: Helen Jackson*
*Pub: Raphael Tuck*
*Art series 6749*
*I Love Little Pussy*
*[c.1907]*

*Below right:*
*Artist: Helen Jackson*
*Pub: Raphael Tuck*
*Art series 6749*
*Pussie's Portrait*
*[c.1907]*

THE LITTLE MOTHER. *Painted by Helen Jackson*

HOME FROM SCHOOL. *Painted by Helen Jackson*

I LOVE LITTLE PUSSY

I LOVE LITTLE PUSSY
    HER COAT IS SO WARM
AND IF I DON'T HURT HER
    SHE'LL DO ME NO HARM
SO I'LL NOT PULL HER TAIL
    OR DRIVE HER AWAY
BUT PUSSY AND I
    TOGETHER WILL PLAY
SHE'LL SIT BY MY SIDE,
    AND I'LL GIVE HER SOME FOOD
AND SHE'LL LOVE ME
    BECAUSE I AM GENTLE AND GOOD.

*Painted by Helen Jackson*

ONLY A LITTLE SHOWER. *Painted by Helen Jackson*

HEIGHO, HEIGHO! HERE WE GO SWINGING TO AND FRO!

*Painted by Helen Jackson*

PUSSIE'S PORTRAIT *Painted by Helen Jackson*

*Birthday Greetings*

# Helen Jacobs (1888-1970)

*"All those who have basked in the sunshine of the humours of WW Jacobs must be interested in the work of his accomplished sister, the gifted artist Miss Helen M Jacobs. The artist possesses that force of originality that is displayed in many clever designs and illustrations for fairy books, a line that denotes general skill in draughtsmanship and an imaginative charm that book lovers everywhere have good reason to admire."*
The Hippodrome, 1917

Helen Mary Jacobs was born and raised in Church Street, Stoke Newington, east London. As a young child and with the full backing of her literary family, she was encouraged to develop her natural flair for painting. They directed that she was to be excused drawing lessons at school in case she was mistutored and preferred her to be coached by them at home. So while the rest of her class drew and painted, she was given needlework exercises to do.

She went on to study at West Ham School of Art under the tutelage of Arthur Legge RBA. Here she painted from life and worked in pen and ink, at which she proved herself such a gifted exponent. At college she won many prizes for illustration for which she was presented with beautifully bound volumes by Dulac, Rackham and others whose work she admired. She blossomed into a fine artist and illustrator, constantly occupied with commissions from publishers and private individuals alike. Initial Contributions to annuals such as *Rainbow, Playbox* and *Little Folks* were followed by commissions from many of the major publishers, but one is left to wonder why she never achieved the prominence the high quality of her work merited. Many of her watercolours were exhibited in galleries all over the country including the Whitechapel Art Gallery and the Royal Institute. Her draughtsmanship was so accurate that she was approached by Lord Rothschild, a keen entomologist, to carry out a series of drawings showing various species of moth. The prominent process reprographic firm, The Grout Engraving Co. used her pictures for

*Helen Jacobs discussing a project with friend and writer Stella Mead. [1930s]*

*Illustration from* The Land of Happy Hours, *by Stella Mead, published by Nisbet. [1929]*

*Helen Jacobs' bookplate [c.1920]*

publicity on account of her colour and compositional sense and fine pen work.

Regularly, her work received favourable press comment. In 1929 a new series of fairy stories for Nisbet was reviewed thus: *"In* Princes and Fairies, *Miss Stella Mead has followed the thought of a child in telling these stories in a simple and attractively ingenuous manner. There is humour too...these are stories that children would love to read*

*Helen's elder brother, short-story writer WW (William Wymark) Jacobs (1863-1943). Very popular in his day, he is best remembered for his chilling horror story* The Monkey's Paw *[1902] and his humorous tales of London's dockland, published in* Many Cargoes *[1896],* Captains All *[1905] and* Night Watches *[1914].*

*many times, as they have the quality that captures a child's imagination. The illustrations, mostly by Miss Helen Jacobs, show a conception of the folks of fairyland that would lend an air of invitation to any child's book."*

'Jake', as she was lovingly called by those close to her, was deeply interested in education. She believed she could use her wonderful gift as an artist to help children. Nisbet, who published much of her work from the late nineteen twenties onwards, were best known for their school books, primers and readers for children. These were practical books, so their quality was only adequate; the colour reproduction, sadly, did not do justice to the precise beauty of the fairyland and fantasy paintings done by Jake in pen and ink and watercolour.

Devoted to illustrating books with an educational content, she was not a prolific illustrator of postcards, and the designs she created for CW Faulkner and James Henderson do not reveal her talent at its best. Her one series of postcards for CW Faulkner in 1922, Series 1764, 12 cards of fairyland scenes, representing months of the year, was created with her close friend and collaborator, the poetess VH Friedlander.

Sadly, too much space is devoted to the verse, so the fine pen work and delicacy of her illustrations is diminished. In contrast and perhaps in keeping with her lively sense of humour and her brother's literary style, her 'comical' designs for Henderson from 1919, drawn *à la* Attwell, demonstrate her dexterity and versatility as an illustrator.

Having spent most of her adult life in Winchmore Hill, Jake joined the staff of St Matthias Primary School in Stoke Newington. A former pupil of the school remembers her thus: *"Her bohemian appearance and eccentricities were the subject of endless amusement to staff as well as pupils. Now I often think of her with gratitude. She encouraged me to write and taught me to draw so that, through her, my recollections of school are profoundly happy ones."*

*" Does he bite ?"*

*"Be a man, for goodness sake!"*

*"Just between you and me."*

*"Tea time."*

*LEFT HAND PAGE*

*Above centre & right:*
*Artist: Helen Jacobs*
*Pub: James Henderson*
*Series K9 Kiddies*
*[c.1918]*

*Below centre & right:*
*Artist: Helen Jacobs*
*Pub: James Henderson*
*Series K10 Kiddies*
*[c.1918]*

*RIGHT HAND PAGE*

*Artist: Helen Jacobs*
*Pub: CW Faulkner*
*Series 1764 [6 of 12]*
*[1924]*

We are the Leprechauns of March,
With crocus spears to
point, and starch
To put into the golden frills
Of dancing, darling daffodils.

We are the airy April Sprites,
Who paint the orchard
pinks and whites,
And set out breakfasts, dinners, teas
For butterflies and bumble-bees.

We are the Fairies who in May
Splash every hedge
with flowery spray,
Light candles on the chestnut trees,
And spread the grass with
bread-and-cheese.

We are the singing Nymphs of June;
Linnets and larks
half catch our tune;
Where we have passed a lily blows,
Where we have kissed we leave a rose.

We are the Dryads of July,
Dreaming in trees
as you go by;
Hidden by branches all the day
And (when you're dreaming) out at play.

Jolly young Urchins all are we,
Proper to August
and the sea;
We curl the waves and smooth the sand,
And tempt you far away from land.

# Ivy Millicent James (1879-1965)

The seaside resort of Weston-super-Mare was the birthplace of Ivy Millicent James and where she lived for much of her life. Born on 12 July 1879, Ivy was the youngest of four children. Her Welsh father William had been a solicitor in the family firm in Merthyr Tydfil. Her mother Caroline came from Taunton. After their marriage in 1863, they lived in Bristol before moving to Weston in 1868. Ivy's elder sister Maud, of whom she was especially fond, went to Cheltenham Ladies College and on to the Slade School of Art, while Ivy, a delicate child prone to headaches, attended a local private school before enrolling at the new Weston School of Art.

Ivy was always fascinated by greetings cards. By the time she was twenty, she was catching publishers' eyes with her portfolio of Christmas card designs and by 1901 she was receiving numerous commissions from Delgado, Faulkner, Hills, Tuck and Valentine. Her drawings, mainly of children in clogs and coif-like head-dresses depicted in rural

settings are unmistakable – charming if a touch primitive. Her bold signature – I.M.J is highly visible. Following a disagreement, she parted company with Raphael Tuck and settled into a long and fruitful working relationship with CW Faulkner that extended to 1919.

The raw material for her designs was provided by the annual trips to the Continent, where the two sisters walked, sketched and visited churches and art galleries. These holidays provided the inspiration for the flowering of that idyllic world of children engaged in various rustic pursuits or as romantic couples set against village or mountain scenes. She loved to sketch from life – windmills in Holland and Belgium and mountain scenery in Switzerland are just two of her favourite subjects. Occasionally a landscape may be recognised on a card such as the Matterhorn on CW Faulkner series 1628.

Most of her themes depict everyday events. A few are topical and several cards

show boys smoking. Only one card gives a hint of the War – *The Latest News* (CW Faulkner series 1636a), where we see children in Dutch costumes reading the news in a London street!

Ivy's work certainly aroused favourable comment in the press. The editor of the *Stationery Trades Journal* commented in 1911 about her latest designs *Early Loves* (CW Faulkner series 1015): *"this series is quaintly conceived and charmingly coloured and shows the ups and downs of the sentimental association of two people in old fashioned country surroundings."*

Those who remember her describe her as strong-willed and intelligent; both she and Maud were active in the local branch of the Suffragette movement. The make believe life of her postcard children was an antidote to Ivy's busy round of visits to the hospital, to schools, her church work and her help with orphans. Her love of children was real and most of her efforts went towards the improvement of their lot.

LEFT HAND PAGE

*A watercolour copied from a phoographic postcard of the fountain at Baden-Baden, Germany, for a CW Faulkner postcard, but never published.*

RIGHT HAND PAGE

*Left hand column:*
*Greetings cards.*
*Ivy entered* The Studio *magazine design competitions on several occasions and in 1900, aged 21, won three honourable mentions for her designs. The first was for a christmas card. This success was followed by a prize for a book tailpiece and another for a decorative initial letter.*

*Artist: Ivy Millicent James*
*Publishers top to bottom:*
*Raphael Tuck. [c.1904]*
*G Delgado [c.1910]*
*CW Faulkner [c.1908]*
*Raphael Tuck [1904]*
*Raphael Tuck published Christmas postcards in this series entitled*
*Nursery Rhymes No. 9*
*[1904]*

*Centre column postcards*
*Above centre:*
*Artist: Ivy Millicent James*
*Pub. Raphael Tuck (US)*
*Dutch Children Series*
*Christmas Postcard No. 522*
*[c.1909]*

*Below centre:*
*Artist: Ivy Millicent James*
*Pub. CW Faulkner*
*Ser. 882*
*[1908]*

*Right hand column postcards*
*Above right:*
*Artist: Ivy Millicent James*
*Pub. CW Faulkner*
*Ser. 922*
*[1909]*

*Below right:*
*Artist: Ivy Millicent James*
*Pub. CW Faulkner*
*Ser. 1628*
*[1914]*

The Only Girl in the World.

# AE Kennedy (1883-1963)

*AE Kennedy. [c.1928]*

Albert Ernest Kennedy, or AE Kennedy as he was known professionally, was born and brought up in the Leyton area of London. He was one of nine children – six boys and three girls – several of whom grew up to be artists. Most prominent was Cecil Kennedy, the noted portraitist and flower painter, who exhibited pictures at the Royal Academy and leading galleries around the world. His father Thomas was a well known painter who worked in the style of JMW Turner and his brother Harley became an accomplished sculptor.

AE Kennedy's family was so large that his father could not afford to send him to art school. But he was surrounded by artists in the family and with their help, quickly developed a fluent illustrative style and embarked on his successful career.

Right from the start he liked drawing animals. He first made contact with CW Faulkner in 1912 and scored an immediate success with postcards illustrating his humorous dog characters *The Tubbies,* (Series 1215) to be  followed up with *More Tubbies* (Series 1216) and *Dancing Tubbies.* Faulkner urged him to keep drawing mischievous cats and dogs and he obliged. *Fifi* (Series 1241) and *Mike* (Series 1316) soon appeared – happy and playful animals cavorting around on postcards and displaying those human characteristics that

makes mimicking pets so amusing. Although painting animals was Kennedy's forte and the subject he enjoyed, he could turn his hand to other themes, as in *Nursery Rhymes,* Faulkner postcard series 1633 from1918, depicting traditional nursery characters.

His son remembers being taken to London Zoo regularly from their home in St Albans, where his father would sketch the animals, before returning to his studio to turn them into formal drawings for his work in progress.

During World War I he served in the Royal Naval Air Service and was stationed at various points along the south and east coasts of England, where from all accounts, he whiled away his time drawing aircraft. On leaving the forces, he returned to

*On holiday at Frinton with his wife and daughter Lesley. [July 1929]*

civilian life and joined CW Faulkner on a part-time basis, later becoming a director of the firm - an association he maintained throughout the inter-war years.

As a book illustrator, he worked for several publishers including Blackie, Collins and Faber. Perhaps his most memorable character was *Epaminondas,* a little black boy and the central figure in a series written by Constance Egan. After World War II, he forged a successful working relationship with Alison Uttley, visualising the characters for her books about *Sam Pig* and *Tim Rabbit.* A note from the author expresses her delight with his work. *"How delightful is the Sam Pig picture! This one is indeed most perfectly lovely, full of expression and joyfulness, gaiety and innocence."*

Another letter from an editor at Collins confirms Kennedy's professional approach: *"You amaze me! I have just received your parcel with those delightful drawings for our book on Big Game Hunting. To say I'm delighted is only putting it mildly, both at your remarkably good draughtsmanship and also the speed with which you have executed the commission. I will endeavour to be as speedy in paying for them and have today authorised payment."*

Although AE Kennedy will be best remembered as a children's illustrator, he was a truly accomplished painter of flowers and landscapes in watercolour.

*The House that Jack Built, from* Gay Gambols, *published by Blackie. [c.1915]*

*AEK and his wife near their home. [c.1938]*

*Artist: AE Kennedy*
*Pub: CW Faulkner*
*Unnumbered series*
*Three Little Kittens*
*[c.1912]*

RING A RING O ROSES

DING DONG BELL.

Ding, dong, bell! Pussy's in the well!
Who put her in? Little Johnny Green.

Who pulled her out?
Big Tommy Stout.

ALL IN TOGETHER.

HEY! DIDDLE DIDDLE!

Hey! diddle, diddle, the Cat and the Fiddle;
The Cow jumped over the moon.

The little Dog laughed to see such sport,
And the Dish ran away with the Spoon

ORANGES AND LEMONS.

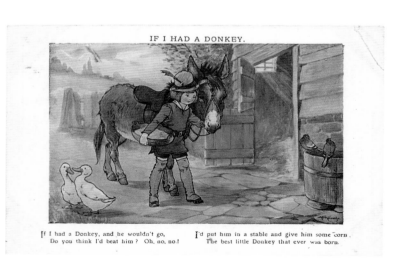

IF I HAD A DONKEY.

If I had a Donkey, and he wouldn't go,
Do you think I'd beat him? Oh, no, no!

I'd put him in a stable and give him some corn,
The best little Donkey that ever was born.

*LEFT HAND PAGE*

*Left column:*
*Artist: AE Kennedy*
*Pub: CW Faulkner*
*Series 1317 [3 of 6]*
*[1913]*

*Right column:*
*Artist: AE Kennedy*
*Pub: CW Faulkner*
*Series 1633 [3 of 6]*
*Nursery Rhymes*
*[c.1917]*

*RIGHT HAND PAGE*

*Left above:*
*Artist: AE Kennedy*
*Pub: CW Faulkner*
*Series 1195 [1 of 6]*
*[1912]*

*Left below:*
*Artist: AE Kennedy*
*Pub: CW Faulkner*
*Series 2055 [1 of 6]*
*[1935]*

*Centre column:*
*Artist: AE Kennedy*
*Pub: CW Faulkner*
*Series 1336 [3 of 6]*
*The Three Bears*
*[1913]*

*Right above & below:*
*Artist: AE Kennedy*
*Pub: CW Faulkner*
*Series 1538 [2 of 6]*
*[1915]*

Overbacks.

*Somebody's been eating my porridge !*

"PLEASE, SIR, I WASN'T
A'THROWIN' AT YOU SIR.
I WAS THROWIN' AT BILLY JONES."

*Somebody's been here !*

### LITTLE MISS MUFFET
Little Miss Muffet sat on a tuffet,
Eating her curds and whey ;
There came a great spider and sat down beside her,
And frightened Miss Muffet away.

*There she goes !*

"SNOWBALLS ! NO !
I HAVEN'T SEEN NO ONE THROW NO SNOWBALLS !"

# Jessie M King (1875-1949)

Jessie Marion King studied at the Glasgow School of Art and was a contemporary of Charles Rennie Mackintosh and the group of artists who together established what has come to be known as the Glasgow style.

In 1903 she designed a set of exquisite and unique nursery rhyme postcards for the Glasgow firm of Millar & Lang, best known for their production of comic and cartoon style postcards.

This venture was an attempt by Millar & Lang to establish, in their *National Series*, a British counterpart to the fine German cards that were flooding into this country at that time. They invited Jessie King, even by then recognised as the foremost Scottish illustrator, to design the postcards to be printed on a special textured card which simulated watered silk. The illustrations were the first she had attempted in watercolour. Until then, she had used colour very subtly, but for the postcards she used stronger colours applied over pen and ink. She made the nursery rhyme characters look majestic in long, sweeping gowns, with an angular line that was to become a hallmark of her later work. The cards were beautiful, probably the most attractive examples of nursery cards of the period, but possibly too sophisticated for their market and even at sixpence for the set, Millar & Lang had difficulty disposing of their stock. That may be why they are so scarce today.

Ride a cock horse *was shown at her first solo exhibition in London in 1905, along with* Little Boy Blue *from the series of postcards. Pen and ink on vellum. [1903]*

*Artist: Jessie King*
*Pub. Millar & Lang*
*The National Series*
*[1903]*

MARY·MARY·QUITE·CONTRARY·HOW·DOES·YOUR·GARDEN·GROW·

HARK·HARK·THE·DOGS·DO·BARK·
THE·BEGGARS·ARE·COMING·TO·TOWN·

LITTLE·BOY·BLUE·COME·BLOW·UP·YOUR·HORN·
THE·COWS·IN·THE·MEADOW·THE·SHEEP·IN·THE·CORN·

THE·QUEEN·OF·HEARTS·SHE·BAKED·SOME·
TARTS·ALL·ON·A·SUMMER·DAY·

ALL·THE·KING'S·HORSES·AND·
ALL·THE·KING'S·MEN·

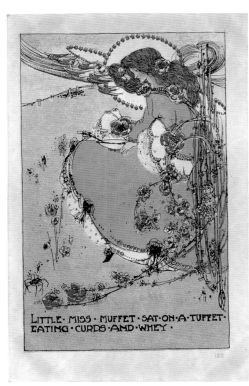

LITTLE·MISS·MUFFET·SAT·ON·A·TUFFET·
EATING·CURDS·AND·WHEY·

# Ethel Larcombe (1876-1940)

Laura Ethel Larcombe lived in Exeter all her life. She was the sixth child of seven, (three boys and four girls), born to John Samuel Larcombe and his wife Louisa. Ethel's parents ran a school in the centre of the city, originally called *St John's Hospital School and Orphanage*, but by the eighteen nineties it had been renamed *Samuel Larcombe's Boys School*. The school provided tuition for around twenty five boys aged between eight and thirteen, from Exeter and the neighbouring towns.

*Initial letter.* The Studio *design competition Honourable mention.* [1903]

*Greetings card.* [c.1895]

Coming from an educated and literary family, Ethel was surrounded by books at home and delighted in the illustrations of Kate Greenaway and Walter Crane, whose work was so popular during the years of her childhood. Her natural talent first led her to recreate Greenaway images in her early greetings cards, but as she grew up she became more interested in William Morris (1834-1896) and his circle. *The Arts and Crafts* movement embraced all the aspects of art and design that Ethel loved. Her resolve to work in the Morris style was strengthened when the *Kelmscott Chaucer* was published in 1896.

Clearly, she was interested in English literature, as her work is peppered with literary references from mediaeval times. Typically, she adapted older styles from the

gothic and rococo periods, with patterning and motifs taken from nature, She excelled in her use of exuberant and unrestrained form, colour and line. As time passed, she moved away from the mediaeval and into the more floral and decorative *Art Nouveau* style. She admired the work of Edward Burne Jones (1833-1898) and Dante Gabriel Rossetti (1828-1882) and trained herself to become a multi-faceted designer and illustrator.

By 1899, she began to enter national art and design competitions organised by *The Studio* magazine. These competitions started in 1893 and attracted aspiring young artists and designers, many of whom would later become successful in their respective fields, including Alice Woodward, Helen Stratton, Charles Folkard, Rosa Petherick and Ernest Aris. During the subsequent ten years, Ethel Larcombe won twenty three first prizes, seventeen second prizes and gained forty honourable mentions, winning over sixty guineas in prize money, (approximately £4,400 in today's currency). Her successes

*Greetings card, pub. Hills & Co.* [1900]

were achieved in a wide range of categories, from book plates and type design to advertisement design and book illustration.

Her work was greatly admired by Talwin Morris (1865-1911), the artist and book designer from Winchester in the south-west of England. He had joined Blackie & Son in 1893 as art manager and moved with his wife Alice to Dunglass Castle just outside Glasgow. His work came to prominence when he exhibited at the *Arts and Crafts* exhibition of 1896, alongside the 'Glasgow Four', Charles Rennie Mackintosh, Herbert McNair and Frances and Margaret Macdonald. This important exhibition caught the eye of Gleeson White, then editor of *The Studio*, and resulted in a series of articles about Morris and the Glasgow group which Ethel Larcombe undoubtedly would have read and which would have stiffened her resolve to succeed.

Her successes in *The Studio* magazine competitions, attracted Talwin Morris's attention, particularly as she worked very much in his style. Between 1904 and 1912, he invited her to work for Blackie and her assignments included about twenty delightful gilt book bindings for the publisher and its subsidiary, Gresham, including: *A Heroine at Sea* by Bessie Marchant, *The Lances of Lynwood* by Charlotte M Yonge, *What Katy Did* by Susan Coolidge and *The Clever Miss Follett* by JK Denny.

She was a member of the Society of Women Artists and designed greetings cards and bookplates for individual patrons. Success in competitions brought her talent to the attention of publishers seeking decorative design and illustration for books and greetings cards. These included: JM Dent, G Delgado, Hills & Co, AR Mowbray and EW Savory. Towards the end of her career she designed greetings cards for Carfax.

Ethel combined her design and illustration skills with great effect in the many striking postcards and greetings cards she designed. She continued to

*Ethel Larcombe in 1893*

*Greetings card, pub. Delgado.* [1901]

*Postcards right:*
*Artist: Ethel Larcombe*
*Pub. EW Savory*
*Series 567 [4 of 4]*
*[1917]*

illustrate professionally into the nineteen twenties, after which she helped her sisters run the school in Exeter which they had inherited from their parents.

Although extremely romantic in her art, Ethel never married. She was a fine Art Nouveau painter, who loved to combine extravagant imagery with familiar texts, where she could employ her undoubted skills as a typographer.

*Design for publisher's mark.* The Studio design competition. First prize. [1903]

*Greetings card, pub. Anon. [c.1899]*

Ethel Larcombe      "THE PRINCESS"

Ethel Larcombe      "WILD ROSES"

Ethel Larcombe      "THE SONNET"

Ethel Larcombe      "MY LADYE FAIRE"

# Hester Margetson (1890-1963)

While teaching in Oxford she met and married Michael Martin-Harvey, the celebrated actor. They had a country house close to her home town, and adjacent to the house of Susan Pearse the children's book illustrator, where they created a wonderfully happy-go-lucky artists colony, which lasted for many years.

Hetty was an introvert. She had a sensitive and retiring disposition and was not a great conversationalist, while her husband was outgoing and extremely temperamental. Yet they complemented one another perfectly, for he too was an accomplished dancer and loved art, especially pottery.

She adored fantasy, where she could explore in her mind carefree pursuits detached from the stresses and strains of life. In her art she dwelt entirely in a fantasy fairyland world with tiny gentle people in idyllic woodland settings, encountering dancing sprites and harmless animals. Her soft, pastel watercolours, popular in their day, reflect her sheltered background and love of freedom. They are sensitive and innocent, but naïve in execution. The Milford series *Fairy Wings* is typical. The designs depict sprites, floating free on the backs of benign creatures without a care in the world.

Hetty's nursery illustrations appeared in

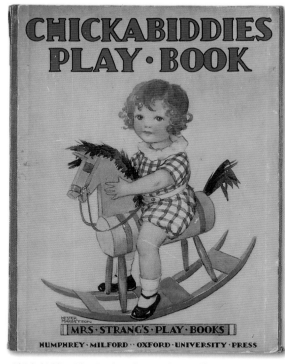

Chickabiddies Play Book, *pub. Humphrey Milford. [c.1920]*

*Mrs Strang's Play Books* published by Humphrey Milford. Also, she illustrated *Delia the Dutch Doll* for Blackie and contributed to books and annuals for Nelson and Ward Lock and illustrated postcards for A Vivian Mansell.

Hester Margetson spent her early life in the beautiful neighbourhood of Wallingford, a small market town in Oxfordshire. She was the daughter of William Margetson and his wife Helen, both noted painters and book illustrators. One of William's hobbies was dancing, so it was not surprising that 'Hetty' should follow closely in her father's footsteps, for throughout her life she was devoted to dancing as well as drawing.

Coming from a wealthy family, she

never had to rely on illustration for her living, yet had a natural love for portraiture in pastel and watercolour. As a young woman in her twenties, Hetty worked as a dancing teacher. Theatrical by nature, she revered Isadora Duncan, the pioneer modern American dancer, not only for her dancing, but also for her feminist beliefs. She was a keen disciple of natural motion in dance and loved to express movement in loose flowing tunics whenever the opportunity arose.

*In the Nursery from* Pretty Pets Play Book, *pub. Humphrey Milford. [c.1920]*

*A New House for Dolly from* Little Pets Play Book, *pub. Humphrey Milford. [c.1922]*

*Top row:*
*Artist: Hester Margetson*
*Pub. A. Vivian Mansell*
*Series 2129 [3 of 6]*
*[c. 1935]*

*Bottom row:*
*Artist: Hester Margetson*
*Pub. Humphrey Milford*
*Series Pretty Wings [3 of 6]*
*[1930]*

# HGC Marsh Lambert (1888-1981)

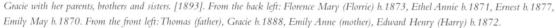

*Gracie with her parents, brothers and sisters. [1893]. From the back left: Florence Mary (Florrie) b.1873, Ethel Annie b.1871, Ernest b.1877, Emily May b.1870. From the front left: Thomas (father), Gracie b.1888, Emily Anne (mother), Edward Henry (Harry) b.1872.*

Helen Grace Culverwell Marsh, was the youngest of seven children born to Thomas Culverwell Marsh, a gentleman's outfitter, and his wife Emily Anne. During her childhood the family lived comfortably in a suburban neighbourhood of Bristol. 'Gracie', as she was known to those close to her, started to develop her talent for drawing as a very young child and grew up to become one of the most prolific children's illustrators of her time.

By the time of her marriage to Charles Theodore Lambert, a member of Coutts Bank, in September 1913, Gracie had already established a reputation as a children's illustrator and chose Marsh Lambert as her professional name.

Although a banker, her husband's real love was music and writing, a talent he had inherited from his mother, Genie. His family were members of the Plymouth Brethren and during his life he edited a Brethren tune book and composed a number of hymns. He became Gracie's source of encouragement and support and often helped with her work by providing text and, where required, music as well. *Songs for Wee Folk*, a book published by Gale & Polden and dedicated to their daughter Barbara, ascribes the musical content to CT Lambert.

Gracie was a highly active and lively personality, able to handle a prodigious output of work and still find time to raise

Teddy Bear's ride

*Advertisement in* The Studio. *[1909]*

HIDE AND SEEK.

LEFT HAND PAGE

*Above:*
*Artist: HGC Marsh Lambert*
*Pub: CW Faulkner*
*Series 962 [1 of 6]*
*[1909]*

*Below:*
*Artist: HGC Marsh Lambert*
*Pub: CW Faulkner*
*Series 1400 [1 of 6]*
*I Do Believe in Fairies*
*[1914]*

RIGHT HAND PAGE

*Above & below left:*
*Artist: HGC Marsh Lambert*
*Pub: CW Faulkner*
*Series 1086 E/F [2 of 6]*
*[1910]*

*Above & below centre:*
*Artist: HGC Marsh Lambert*
*Pub: AM Davis*
*Series 549 (Set No. 2)*
*Flower Fairies*
*[1915]*

*Above & below right:*
*Artist: HGC Marsh Lambert*
*Pub: Photochrom*
*Celesque Series Nos.*
*1458/1462*
*[c.1918]*

You can't hit me.

Carnation's sitting all alone
Like a princess on her throne;
She wears a crown upon her head
Of pink or yellow, white or red

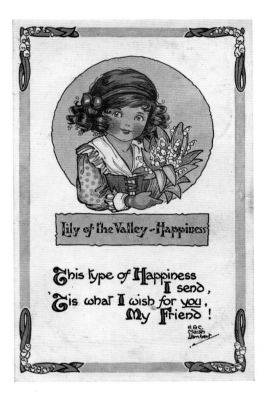

Lily of the Valley - Happiness

This type of Happiness
I send,
'Tis what I wish for you,
My Friend!

We've been roaming.

Forget-me-not is very shy,
And often lets you pass her by,
Yet if you'd stoop, she'd say to you —
"Please don't pass on but pick me —Do!"

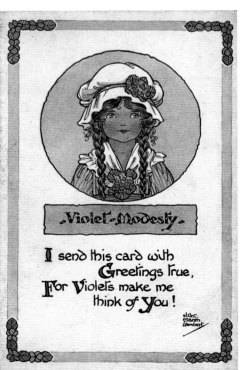

Violet - Modesty.

I send this card with
Greetings true,
For Violets make me
think of You!

*Left column:*
*Artist: HGC Marsh Lambert*
*Pub: CW Faulkner*
*Series 1686 [2 of 6]*
*[1919]*

*Centre column:*
*Artist: HGC Marsh Lambert*
*Pub: Ovaltine*
*Card Nos. P185/P188*
*[c.1922]*

*Right column:*
*Artist: HGC Marsh Lambert*
*Pub: Puritan*
*Series 1 [2 of 26]*
*[c.1921]*

*Gracie and her fiancé Charles Lambert (left) with friends. [1910]*

paper as it did on high grade stock. Her drawings were fluent, bold and confident and few could match the effectiveness of her distinctive black and white line. Yet her images of child life retained a sense of warmth, aided by her ability to compose her pictures and juxtapose her nurseryland characters so well.

Grace understood instinctively the needs of her publishers and always responded with speed and efficiency, to make her illustrations work on any surface from fine paper to the textured fabric of rag books.

*Gracie and daughter Barbara. [1921]*

tales, games, pastimes, little patriots (during wartime) and young romance.

Gracie was held in high esteem by advertisers too, who valued her arresting style on newsprint. She was commissioned by Puritan Soap and Ovaltine to design advertisements for nursery products, promotional booklets, postcards, novelty puzzles and games.

People who remember Gracie tell of her kindness and modesty and her dexterity as an artist, capturing in a quick sketch, those familiar heart-shaped faces and smiling eyes of the children she loved to draw – children who reflected her own happy and engaging personality.

Not only was she a skilled draughts-woman, but she had a keen and innovative mind. An active illustrator between 1908 and 1935, she did a great deal to make novelty books of all types – shaped books, dot-to-dot books, rag books and pop-up books – popular in the nursery through World War I and beyond.

Gracie and her husband lived in Sidcup, Kent for many years and later moved to their 'dream cottage' in Paignton, Devon, the county where she had loved to spend her holidays as a young girl.

a family. The couple had two children – Barbara born in 1919 and Roger born in 1923. Barbara was a very pretty child with fair, curly hair, who inspired Grace to create the little curly headed girl who appears in many of her drawings, and it was Barbara who 'modelled' for Gracie's early Ovaltine illustrations.

Gracie's great skill was painting images of happy and carefree children at play. She was quite down to earth and seldom indulged in flights of fantasy into fairyland. Some of her earliest advertisement designs depict cute kewpie-like characters, which she recreated in 1914, series 1400 for CW Faulkner, *I Do Believe in Fairies*. Even her two *Flower Fairies* series, published by

AM Davis in 1916 looked like children in pretty floral costumes.

Why was she commercially successful? She was one of a new breed of children's illustrators who managed to create fun-loving children at play with whom twentieth century children identified and who regarded pictures of sedate Victorian children from a decade earlier as a distant memory.

As World War I approached, paper became a scarce commodity and the popular press turned to lower grade paper at prices they could afford. A need arose for illustrators whose style would reproduce well on any material. Grace's simple yet unique style worked as well on poor grade

She was commissioned by many publishers operating at the popular end of the children's publishing market including Allday, The Art & Humour Publishing Co., Dean & Son and Gale & Polden. She also worked for Collins and Ward Lock and contributed to Little Folks and numerous annuals and compilation books.

Greetings and postcard publishers also faced austerity measures and were subject to the same constraints as their book publishing counterparts. Gracie's simple and uncluttered style lent itself particularly well to the highly popular postcard medium. During her career she turned her hand to almost all the children's themes imaginable, including nursery rhymes, fairy

*Advertisement for Colgate Dental Cream that appeared on the back of a paper backed painting book published by Colgate. [c.1928]*

# Joyce Mercer (1896-1965)

Amy Joyce Mercer was the youngest of four children born to a Sheffield solicitor, William Mercer and his wife Amy. Joyce was a precocious and extremely self-assured girl who liked nothing better than to withdraw to the studio at the top of the house that she had fashioned for herself. She would spend hours on end drawing, and studying the styles of the great illustrators of her day – Beardsley, Annie French, Jessie King, Nielsen, Rackham and Charles Robinson, all of whom influenced her as a designer and illustrator.

Such was her commitment for design that, although naturally left handed, she trained herself to be ambidextrous by drawing symmetrical designs with both hands simultaneously.

She attended the Girls High School in Sheffield and then enrolled at Sheffield School of Art where her tutors soon realised her extraordinary ability. Feeling unable to cope with such an extraordinary talent they sent her to Manchester School of Art, but the principal advised her to continue to develop her ability on her own, fearing that a general art course would hold her back. Self-disciplined and intellectually mature, she continued her studies at home.

It was not long before she realised that a move to London was inevitable if she was going to achieve her full potential and earn a full time living from her work. She found a flat in Neville Square and enrolled at Chelsea School of Art when she was about twenty three.

Apart from figure drawing and design she became keenly interested in costume which was to become such an important facet in her repertoire. She was fascinated by architecture too and would spend countless hours walking about London studying buildings.

Her ability to understand and draw the human form enabled her to handle convincingly the abstract figures which were to form the basis of her future work.

She became an ardent follower of the design-led illustration styles. Having been born into the era of *Art Nouveau*, her love of form and composition directed her towards the *Art Deco* movement, much in vogue during her student days.

Hutchinsons, the publishers, provided her with her first commercial opportunity by offering her the chance to illustrate the favourite stories of her childhood – Andersen's and Grimms' fairy tales. Charmed by these classical stories, she submitted several series of postcard designs to CW Faulkner, some of which were used also as high quality tasselled greetings cards. These are superbly confident examples of her interpretation of the *Art Deco* style. Although decorative, her figure work is remarkably convincing due to her sound knowledge of life drawing.

She had an acerbic wit and turned her hand to topical cartoons. During the thirties she contributed to *London Opinion, Punch, Bystander* and *Illustrated London News*. However, the cartoons lacked that special quality which made her early work so remarkable.

Pattern and design are always the primary elements in her work, closely followed by bright colour and dynamic composition. Although her illustrations are somewhat two-dimensional, they are full of energy. What mediaeval damsel would not swoon at this bold knight, dressed up like a peacock and mounted on his white charger, coiled like a spring and ready to leap into battle?

In her fifties Joyce became seriously disturbed by her experiences during World War II, when working in the dockland area of London as a member of the Women's Voluntary Service. She withdrew to Penrith in the Lake district to spend the last twenty years of her life in quiet isolation.

Joyce was a self-critical and forthright woman. She abhorred the popular and sentimental presentation of children and nursery themes as portrayed by many of her contemporaries. Her innate ability and devotion to design enabled her to develop her unique style, providing children of all ages with a fresh vision of classical themes. Her work has retained its freshness and originality due to her bold and courageous approach to design.

*Female nude. Sheffield School of Art. [1917]*

*Fragment from front cover of* Grimms' Fairy Tales, *published by Hutchinson. [c.1932]*

*Left column:*
*Artist: Joyce Mercer*
*Pub: CW Faulkner*
*Series 1959 [2 of 6]*
*[1927]*

*Centre column & above right:*
*Artist: Joyce Mercer*
*Pub: CW Faulkner*
*Series 1896 [3 of 6]*
*[1926]*

*Below right:*
*Artist: Joyce Mercer*
*Pub: CW Faulkner*
*Series 1960 [1 of 6]*
*[1927]*

RED RIDING HOOD

RIDE-A-COCK-HORSE TO BANBURY CROSS
TO SEE A FINE LADY RIDE ON A WHITE HORSE
RINGS ON HER FINGERS AND BELLS ON HER TOES
SHE SHALL HAVE MUSIC WHEREVER SHE GOES.

THREE WISE MEN OF GOTHAM WENT TO SEA IN A BOWL
IF THE BOWL HAD BEEN STRONGER MY SONG WOULD HAVE BEEN LONGER

JACK AND THE BEAN-STALK

THE QUEEN OF HEARTS

HER EYES THE GLOW-WORM LEND THEE
THE SHOOTING-STARS ATTEND THEE
AND THE ELVES ALSO
WHOSE LITTLE EYES GLOW
LIKE THE SPARKS OF FIRE ATTEND THEE
NO WILL O'THE-WISP MISLIGHT THEE
NOR SNAKE NOR SLOW-WORM BITE THEE
BUT ON, ON THY WAY
NOT MAKING A STAY
SINCE GHOST THERE'S NONE TO AFFRIGHT THEE

# Hilda Miller (1876-1939)

*Hilda Miller on her wedding day. [1907]*

Hilda Theodora Baker spent her early childhood in Edgbaston, Birmingham. As far back as anyone could remember, she wanted to become a painter, but none of her family were artistic and felt unable to give her any particular encouragement. Then, to her own credit she enrolled at Birmingham School of Art, where in 1902, she won a silver award in the Board of Education National Competition for the design of a gesso decorated box. She continued studies at the Slade School of Fine Art in London, until the family moved to Harpenden in Hertfordshire, when Hilda switched her studies to St Albans School of Art.

In 1907, she met and later married Andrew Miller, a representative of a Scottish woollen mill, with connections in the West End of London. He introduced her to Liberty & Co. for whom she designed calendars, advertisements, prints, greetings cards and postcards between 1910 and 1918. Before submitting her designs, she studied the work of contemporary Liberty illustrators and devised a delicate style to blend with the store's quality products. Her work projected a genteel and serene image to attract the store's high class clientele. Her well-groomed children were presented as little mannequins, creating an aura of wealth and well being.

The costumes, comprising panniered dresses, bonnets, cloche hats, bar shoes and elegant prints are of an earlier period, but they exude quality. The soft pinks, mauves, greens and oranges are applied in smooth pastel, with a few designs applied onto a slightly rougher textured surface.

It is interesting to compare Hilda Miller's Liberty style with her other work, which is clearly less constrained. Her postcard illustrations for CW Faulkner are more colourful, with a far greater sense of movement and vitality. In contrast to her Liberty designs, Hilda preferred a palette of blues and mauves, generally a hallmark of her style. *The Fairy Dance* from CW Faulkner series 1926 from 1927, displays passion and vigour in the dancing sprites, the designs displaying a delicate line and strong compositional sense. Her designs for *Little Folks Nursery Rhymes*, series 1784, from 1923 are drawn with the gracefulness of the nursery rhyme pictures by Henriette Willebeek le Mair, created about ten years

earlier. She was a versatile artist with the ability to switch from her Liberty style to fantasy themes with apparent ease.

Hilda illustrated an attractive volume of *Dulcibella and the Fairy*, one of the few books published by CW Faulkner, from which postcard series 1690 and 1693 are taken. She illustrated a small number of books for several other publishers, most notably, *Shoes; Stories for Children* for Cape [1920], *The Pageant of Flowers* for Thornton Butterworth [1922], done in conjunction with Lilian Govey and *The Rose Fyleman Fairy Book* for Methuen [1923].

She was shy and retiring, due in part to the deafness she contracted at an early age. Yet deafness may have encouraged her to develop her drawing ability as a means of expressing herself. Sadly her retiring nature combined with marital duties prevented her from becoming a more prominent illustrator, for she had the ability to draw beautiful nursery pictures with the utmost delicacy and sensitivity.

*Have you watched the fairies?*
*From the* Rose Fyleman Fairy Book
*Pen & ink. [1923]*

*Left column:*
*Artist: Hilda Miller*
*Pub: Liberty & Co*
*[1914/1917]*

*Centre column:*
*Artist: Hilda Miller*
*Pub: CW Faulkner*
*Series 1926 [2 of 6]*
*Fairy Lovers*
*[1927]*

*Above right:*
*Artist: Hilda Miller*
*Pub: CW Faulkner*
*Series 1784 [1 of 6]*
*Little Folks Nursery Rhymes*
*[1922]*

*Centre right:*
*Artist: Hilda Miller*
*Pub: CW Faulkner*
*Unnumbered card*
*[c.1922]*

*Below right:*
*Artist: Hilda Miller*
*Pub: CW Faulkner*
*Series 1857 [1 of 6]*
*[1924]*

*Fairy Flannel is the Skin of Peaches,* The Rose Fyleman Fairy Book, *published by Methuen. Pen & ink & watercolour. [1923]*

THE FAIRY DANCE

SLEEP, BABY, SLEEP!

Sleep, baby, sleep! | Thy mother shakes the dreamland tree,
Thy father guards the sheep, | And from it fall sweet dreams for thee.

THE FROG PRINCE.

FAIRY LOVERS

Tripping and Skipping with Shouting and Laughter.

# Olwen Morgan (1896-1960)

WEDNESDAY'S CHILD IS FULL OF WOE.

THURSDAY'S CHILD HAS FAR TO GO.

Of all the illustrators featured in this book, Olwen Mary Morgan is one of two true amateurs. Born in Burton-on-Trent, of Welsh descent, she was the daughter of a chemist and optician. The family moved back to South Wales when she was quite young, where her father established himself as a prominent member of local society. From time to time he broadcast on Welsh radio and loved nothing more than fraternising with celebrities who visited the area. Relatives remember Olwen as being a talented young artist and writer of poetry. They recall being shown some impressive pieces of artwork, including a memorable painting of *The Pied Piper of Hamelin*.

Publishers CW Faulkner encouraged aspiring artists to submit work with a view to publication. So it was in Olwen's case. Records show that she approached Faulkner in this way with her perceptive renderings of children for two series of postcards – a months of the year series, number 1782 and *A Week of Happy Days*, series 1850. The series were published in 1922 and 1924 respectively. Although never formally trained, Olwen's pictures compare favourably with

those of her more seasoned contemporaries and are eagerly sought by today's discerning collector. These watercolours dating from 1920, accompanied with simple rhymes, are beautifully observed cameos of children in their everyday lives – at play or revealing their many moods. We can find no evidence that any other illustrations of Olwen's were ever published in books or on postcards.

Any ideas Olwen might have had of pursuing a career as a commercial artist were short lived, when she met her husband-to-be, Eric Nicholls, then a railway manager, while on holiday in Egypt in 1924.

*Olwen (left) with husband Eric and soprano Mavis Bennett. [mid-1920's]*

SATURDAY'S CHILD WORKS HARD FOR A LIVING.

THE CHILD THAT IS BORN ON THE SABBATH DAY IS BONNY AND BLYTHE AND GOOD AND GAY.

*LEFT HAND PAGE*

*Artist: Olwen Morgan*
*Pub: CW Faulkner*
*Series 1850 [4 of 7]*
*[1924]*

*RIGHT HAND PAGE*

*Artist: Olwen Morgan*
*Pub: CW Faulkner*
*Series 1782 [6 of 12]*
*[1922]*

DULL NOVEMBER BRINGS THE BLAST,
HARK! THE LEAVES ARE WHIRLING FAST.

COLD DECEMBER BRINGS THE SLEET
BLAZING FIRE AND CHRISTMAS TREAT.

JANUARY BRINGS THE SNOW,
MAKES OUR FEET AND FINGERS GLOW.

AUGUST BRINGS THE SHEAVES OF CORN,
THEN THE HARVEST HOME IS BORNE.

WARM SEPTEMBER BRINGS THE FRUIT,
SPORTSMEN THEN BEGIN TO SHOOT.

BROWN OCTOBER BRINGS THE PHEASANT,
THEN TO GATHER NUTS IS PLEASANT.

# Kay Nixon (1894-1988)

Kathleen Irene Nixon was the youngest child in a family of nine and all her life had been interested in painting animals, birds and flowers. *"I've always loved animals; I was brought up with them."* Born in Woodside Park, North London, she studied at the Camden School of Art in 1911, and having obtained her teachers' certificate stayed on as the youngest teacher there, although she didn't care much for teaching. She recalled: *"In those days there was no school on Mondays, so I used to spend alternate Mondays at the Zoo and in the Natural History Museum. One week my animals would be still, and the next they would be on the move."*

In 1913 she decided to abandon teaching in favour of a book illustration course at the Birmingham School of Art, where she teamed up with an old friend, Dorothy Newsome Glenn, with whom she formed a long and fruitful collaboration. *"It was terrific fun working together like that, because she was good at buildings and scenes and people and I could do animals. So she did figures for me when I needed them and I did the animals for her."*

Teamwork paid off and soon they were receiving commissions for book and magazine illustrations. *"We went to London every six months with a parcel of things we'd worked on and go round the publishers."*

After World War I, when the couple had worked together as tracers at Armstrong

Siddeley, they enjoyed success with *Harraps' Nature Series*. They illustrated many of Enid Blyton's stories, including around twenty five covers for the *Sunny Stories* series of magazines, although it was not an experience that she remembered with great affection. *"I met her on a few occasions, of course; but mostly she just sent down to say what she wanted, and we simply got on with it."*

Kay always loved painting rabbits, so in 1923 she approached CW Faulkner with a series of paintings for *Alice in Wonderland*, which they published in book form and as postcards series 1760, *Alice in Wonderland*. Kay's portrayal of the White Rabbit demonstrates her skill as an animal painter. Although this is one of the few series of postcards by Kay Nixon ever published, the designs are memorable examples of *Alice* imagery. Perhaps she had a natural attraction to Alice, for as she herself said *"I'm quite mad of course; but then I was born on the fourteenth of August and people born on the fourteenth are allowed to do everything upside down."*

In the late twenties Kay and Dorothy were offered a commission from the Oxford University Press visit India to do a series of drawings life in the sub-continent. This event marked a turning point in her life and for the next twenty six years she spent a good deal of time there.

Before they had been there long, the girls were invited to design thirty four colour posters of animals and birds for the Indian State Railways and toured the country at their request. While in Bombay, Kay designed and painted a mural of wild ducks in flight for the Bombay Natural History Museum. She became the official artist to the *Times of India Press* and the *Bombay Weekly* and was commissioned by the Maharajah of Gwalior and others to paint portraits of their favourite racehorses.

It was while in India in 1927, she met and later married Victor Blundell MC, who was serving in the British army. They lived in India for twenty five years before returning home to Burwash, East Sussex.

*Pindi Poo and Pushti with their friend Mrs Bushy Tail from* Poo & Pushti, *published by Frederick Warne. [1959]*

Kay Nixon's renderings of Brer Rabbit for stories by Enid Blyton will be especially remembered, as will her series of books based on her own pets, written in the nineteen fifties – Pindi Poo, a mischievous dachshund and Pushti, a handsome Siamese kitten. Her animal paintings have been exhibited all over the world – in London, Melbourne, India, Singapore and in the Paris Salon.

*From* Oxford Annual for Baby, *published by Humphrey Milford. [1927]*

*The White Rabbit*

*Artist: Kay Nixon*
*Pub: CW Faulkner*
*Series 1819*
*Alice in Wonderland*
*[1923]*

"Oh dear! oh dear!" said the White Rabbit,
"I shall be too late."

The whole pack of cards rose up and came
flying down upon her.

The Mad Hatter came with a cup in one hand and a piece
of bread and butter in the other.

The Duchess tucked her arm affectionately into Alice's.

The Blue Caterpillar and Alice have an argument.

The Queen never left off quarrelling
with all the other players.

# Ida Rentoul Outhwaite (1888-1961)

*Ida Rentoul Outhwaite aged 25. [1913]*

Success came early to Ida Rentoul, one of six children born to John Lawrence Rentoul and his wife Annie, who had emigrated to Australia from Belfast in 1870. Rentoul was a professor in Hebrew and Greek at Melbourne University, before entering the Presbyterian ministry and eventually becoming Moderator General of his church in Australia. He was a fine scholar and an outspoken supporter of the oppressed. His wife was absorbed in art, literature and music and therefore it is no surprise that all six children were intellectually gifted, romantic and articulate.

Ida and her elder sister Annie grew up within the confines of the University in happy and secure surroundings. They listened spellbound to the fairy tales told by their parents at bedtime, which left a lifelong impression of fairyland and the world of make-believe. Hours spent dreaming up fairy stories and developing and refining a delicate style of drawing meant the sisters' first stories appeared in print when Ida was only fifteen. In 1903, six *Austral Greetings* cards appeared in *The New Idea*, with a title *The Ida Rentoul Series*. These were followed in 1904 by publication of Ida's for which first book, *Molly's Bunyip*, her sister Annie wrote the storyline. Scenes from the book were published as postcards in 1905.

Spurred on by the success of this book, the two sisters were encouraged to write more stories. Several other books ensued before Ida married Grenbry Outhwaite, a successful businessman. He proved to be a first class agent for her and introduced her to many influential people in Australian society, organised exhibitions and actively promoted her work.

Her illustrations were becoming hugely popular. When *Elves and Fairies*, the sisters' first major success was published in 1916, Ida was being compared with the established twentieth century gift book illustrators, Detmold, Dulac, Nielsen and Rackham. The book was greeted with acclaim, a handsome but expensive volume with numerous spellbinding black and white illustrations and full colour plates. All proceeds were donated to the Red Cross, and the book was a wildly successful best-seller, making the sisters Australian celebrities overnight. Their fame quickly spread to England where A&C Black published the sisters' other major successes.

The books – *The Enchanted Forest* (1921), *The Little Green Road to Fairyland* (1922), *The Little Fairy Sister* (1923), *Blossom* (1928), *Bunnie and Brownie* (1930) and *Fairyland* (1931) were to be accompanied with sets of postcards, entitled *Elves and Fairies,* in the *Black's Beautiful Postcards* series. Gift books of this type were very expensive, so postcards depicting scenes from the books, at least offered those unable to afford such luxuries a glimpse of Ida Outhwaite's exquisite fairy paintings.

Queen Mary was a great admirer of Ida's work and visited her exhibitions in London. The queen was fond of sending the *Elves and Fairies* postcards to friends, thus creating a vogue for them during the nineteen twenties. People were captivated by the graceful drawings and bought them to keep rather than to post, which is why many of the *Elves and Fairies* cards found by collectors today are not postally used.

However, by the time *Fairyland* was published by A&C Black in 1931, even these beautiful renderings of fairies were losing their fascination. Many people were being damaged by the effects of the Depression and in such a climate fairies seemed trite and expendable. Demand for expensive gift books waned, finally heralding a move away from the lavishly illustrated volumes which once had been so successful. Postcards were also losing their popularity as more and more people began to own telephones. A radical change was taking place as publishing was becoming geared to meet the needs of the mass market, a change to which many illustrators found it difficult to respond.

None of the books that followed caught the public's imagination like the *Elves and Fairies* books, but by then Ida had amassed a large income from the work she loved doing. She was a small woman, only five feet tall, but a mischievous and dynamic personality. She travelled the world with her husband and often came to England to meet publishers and arrange exhibitions. She loved children and had four of her own and regularly entertained their many friends at their large house near Melbourne. One could say that her life really was a fairy tale come true.

*Above & centre left:*
*Artist: Ida Rentoul Outhwaite*
*Pub: The New Idea*
*Austral Greetings [2 of 6]*
*[1903]*

*Below left:*
*Artist: Ida Rentoul Outhwaite*
*Pub: Anon*
*From Molly's Bunyip*
*[1904]*

*Above & below centre:*
*Artist: Ida Rentoul Outhwaite*
*Pub: A&C Black*
*Series 75*
*Elves and Fairies*
*from Little Fairy Sister*
*[1925]*

*Above & below right:*
*Artist: Ida Rentoul Outhwaite*
*Pub: A&C Black*
*Series 73*
*Elves and Fairies*
*from Bunny and Brownie*
*[1925]*

*The Moonboat, from* Bush Songs from Australia *published by George Robertson. [1910]*

The Ida Rentoul Series.

Contemplative
Bunnies.

The Ida Rentoul Series.

Daddy
Cookatoo.

110° in the shade.

Periwinkle painting the Petals.

It was very
difficult—at first.

The Fairy Bridget and the Kookaburra.

Round the grass-tuft glided a pearly shell.

# Phyllis Palmer (1893-1989)

*Phyllis Palmer in her teens. [c. 1910]*

Phyllis Miriam Palmer was born on 21 October 1893, the second daughter of Thomas Palmer, printer and stationer of Grantham, Lincolnshire and his wife Beatrice. The family lived above the shop in Vine Street in the centre of town. As a schoolgirl, she shone at English, but was bored by the art lessons: *"...drawing meant making pencil copies of cones or cubes..."* she complained. Eventually she persuaded her parents to let her attend Nottingham School of Art. Even there she was bored by the formal, more disciplined aspect of the course and longed for the hour at the end of every daily session when the students were allowed to draw from imagination: *"Something you saw on your way to school today"* might be the suggestion. She would choose favourite fairy stories from her childhood and for them evolved a delicate, romantic style in pencil and watercolour.

After finishing art school around 1913, she worked from home and sold her first postcard designs to Alphalsa Publishing Co (Alpha). The cards, drawn around 1917 and unsigned by Phyllis were decorative and sentimental illustrations to such themes as *The Love Letter* and *The Farewell*. A little later, she drew a series of more jocular cards for Vivian Mansell signed, Phyllis M Palmer. She recalled: *"a little girl sits at a*

*table with a tiny dog in the chair next to her. The caption is "Now Fido – say your grace!"* Whatever the source of the idea, the little verse or quip below the picture was always her own work.

In 1917 Phyllis married Jack Purser, her childhood sweetheart. Jack had enlisted in the army, having been working in France before the war, and when that was over he and Phyllis lived in Paris where she continued with her drawing. While she was there she painted a new set of postcard designs and sent them home to her mother who always took a keen interest in her art career. The designs were submitted to Salmon of Sevenoaks who accepted them at a guinea apiece. So began a long relationship with Salmon who continued to publish her cards for the rest of her life and still have one set in print today.

In 1921, Phyllis and Jack returned to England and started a family. In 1934 they settled in Hoylake, Wirral, having enjoyed homes in Kingsdown, Ingrave, Letchworth and Leamington. In spite of her distant home location, she continued to supply Salmon and also sold designs to Photochrom in Tunbridge Wells. As well as postcards, she designed greetings cards, valentines and even gift tags.

The years before World War II were her most productive as a postcard illustrator but the end of the war brought Phyllis her happiest and most fruitful years as a painter. She still worked occasionally for Salmon but, as fashions changed and the popularity of postcards dwindled, she decided to take up her formal art training again. She exhibited and sold her work through local galleries and had a painting accepted for the permanent collection at the Williamson Art Gallery, Birkenhead.

As an illustrator, her distinctive style is often compared with Mabel Lucie Attwell. However, on close inspection, the two artists are quite different. Mabel Lucie's kids are cute and chirpy, while Phyllis's little characters stir the emotions with their vulnerability.

*"Every Girl does her bit!"*

BE PREPARED

THERE'S NOTHING EXCITING TO TELL YOU
THERE'S VERY LITTLE TO WRITE
'CEPT THAT I THINK OF YOU DAILY
AND DREAM OF YOU 'MOST EVERY
NIGHT!

I MIGHT HAVE BEEN A KING'S SON
BUT ON THE OTHER HAND
I MIGHT HAVE BEEN A COBBLER'S
WHICH ISN'T QUITE SO GRAND!

A LITTLE BIRD TOLD ME!

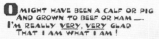

O MIGHT HAVE BEEN A CALF OR PIG
AND GROWN TO BEEF OR HAM —
I'M REALLY VERY, VERY GLAD
THAT I AM WHAT I AM!

'twould be nice to see your face again !

# Ethel Parkinson (1868-1957)

*Ethel Parkinson. [c.1945]*

Mary Ethel Parkinson, the daughter of Walter Parkinson a master draper and his wife Maria, was born in Hull in 1868, the youngest of three sisters. Her sisters Emilie and Lydia were considerably older, fourteen and twelve years respectively. Ethel was taught to paint by Lydia, who had established herself locally as a painter of some repute.

In her early teens Ethel experimented with Lydia's oil paints by applying them onto glass and wood. Local people liked her painted jars and boxes when she offered them for sale at fêtes and bazaars, which strengthened her resolve to pursue art as a career.

Around 1880 Ethel's father took over a general merchant's business in south east London and the family moved to a house in Greenwich. But it appears that they could not adjust to life in the south and returned north fairly quickly.

However, while in Greenwich, Ethel first met her husband-to-be Walter Chapman, a man from the Deptford area training to be a solicitor. The buzz of life in London appealed to Ethel and she vowed to return as soon as she could.

Ethel was a very independent woman and, as good as her word, returned in 1900 and found 'digs' in Moreton Street, Westminster. With only half a crown left

in her purse, she marched into the offices of CW Faulkner in Golden Lane with her portfolio of drawings and in her forthright manner, demanded to see the managing director, Charles Faulkner. He was impressed by the quality of her samples, her strong personality and her businesslike approach and offered her a job on the spot. Their northern backgrounds formed the basis for a strong and fruitful bond which was to last until Faulkner's tragic accident in 1915. Both were down-to-earth people who respected hard work and honest endeavour.

Inspired by Charles Faulkner's support, Ethel worked tirelessly and almost exclusively for Faulkner for about twenty years. She designed over three hundred greetings cards, postcards, painting books, wall plaques, calendars and prints, many of which were syndicated to Europe through Faulkner's connection with German publishers Dondorf and Munk.

She didn't care for the classical themes, like nursery rhymes, fairy tales and fairyland. She favoured themes about courtship, Dutch children, traditional Christmas scenes and people in olden day costumes. Her formal style, well suited to

*Greetings card, pub. CW Faulkner. [c.1904]*

the small format greetings card and postcard was reminiscent of those artists with a grounding in miniature painting. Her dainty characters adopt fixed expressions, revealing only enigmatic smiles, but her compositional sense and costume detailing is immaculate.

Sometimes, Charles Faulkner or one of his colleagues would suggest themes for her to illustrate. Travel and exploration were favourite pursuits for the Edwardians. The *Arctic Series* 941, a subject quite out of character for Ethel Parkinson, was almost certainly inspired by the American Robert Peary's successful journey to the North Pole in 1909, although he wouldn't have encountered the penguins she depicts. A set of illustrated songs published in 1905, Series 448, may have been an attempt by Faulkner to challenge the popularity of the Bamforth Song Card.

One of Ethel's favourite themes was Dutch children. She certainly played her part in helping to satisfy the public's desire for anything Dutch – a craze fired by the quantity of souvenirs that came flooding into the country when people started taking their summer holidays abroad.

*Dutchie Doings*, a story about childlife in Holland, published by Blackie in 1908, was a typical example of this popular theme and one of the few books she illustrated. The story was written by her supportive husband, Walter Chapman, whom she married in 1905. She had not liked him particularly when they first met, but on meeting him again a few years later she recognised in him attractive qualities she had not noticed before.

In those days, people were fascinated by piccaninnies, or black children. The fad may have been fuelled by the immensely popular *Little Black Sambo*, the story of a little Indian child, written by Helen Bannerman, published in 1899. Series 1173, by Ethel Parkinson features piccaninnies. Perhaps this and similar series by other artists was Faulkner's attempt to target a popular market of the day.

*Greetings card, pub. CW Faulkner [c.1903]*

*Sambo and Susannah*, a companion volume to *Dutchie Doings*, published by Blackie at the height of this particular fad in 1907 is a story about two black children, illustrated by Ethel Parkinson, with words supplied by May Byron, whose writing supported the work of so many talented illustrators .

November 1915 was a black month for CW Faulkner & Co. Charles Faulkner was killed by a train on a railway crossing at Hatch End, Middlesex. He had been visiting an artist on a dark winter's evening and had not heard a train approaching as he crossed the track.

The support and inspiration that Ethel had relied on so heavily was gone. Although she continued to work for the company after his death, she found it hard to adapt her style to the needs of the early twenties as her commitment was waning.

She turned to her secure family life with her husband and son Hubert, gradually withdrawing from the commercial scene to concentrate on flower painting and gardening, at their home in Bromley, Kent.

*Above left:*
*Artist: Ethel Parkinson*
*Pub: CW Faulkner*
*Series 226D [1 of 6]*
*When George III Was King [1902]*

*Below left:*
*Artist: Ethel Parkinson*
*Pub: CW Faulkner*
*Series 670A [1 of 6]*
*[1906]*

*Above centre:*
*Artist: Ethel Parkinson*
*Pub: CW Faulkner*
*Series 569D [1 of 6]*
*When the Heart is Young [1905]*

*Below centre:*
*Artist: Ethel Parkinson*
*Pub: CW Faulkner*
*Series 1674 [1 of 6]*
*Children's Carnival [1919]*

*Above right:*
*Artist: Ethel Parkinson*
*Pub: CW Faulkner*
*Series 1157F [1 of 6]*
*Happy Days in Holland [1911]*

*Centre right:*
*Artist: Ethel Parkinson*
*Pub: CW Faulkner*
*Series 941B [1 of 6]*
*The Arctic Series [1909]*

*Below right:*
*Artist: Ethel Parkinson*
*Pub: CW Faulkner*
*Series 1167 [1 of 6]*
*Friends or Foes [1911]*

A Lady of Fashion, 1813.

Safety in Numbers.

Follow the man from Cooks!

To wish you a Merry Christmas
and a Happy New Year.

CLOWN AND ITALIAN MAIDEN.

A Trying Moment

# Rollo Paterson (1892-1978)

Vera Paterson and Reg Paterson were one and the same person. In fact, both were the *noms de plumes* of Rollo Paterson, born in Australia to Patrick Paterson, the son of a rich industrialist from Stirling, Scotland and his wife Ellen Chester. Ellen was a composer and pianist, while Patrick had made a fortune as the owner of a large tannery. When Rollo was only three, he returned to Stirling, where he stayed with his paternal grandparents, before being sent off to college in Edinburgh at the age of eight. Even at this tender age, his school reports indicate that he was indifferent to everything unrelated to drawing and painting. It is even said that he managed to

talk the headmaster into letting him have extra curricular art tuition, to master the basic drawing and painting techniques that were to underpin his remarkable career as an artist and illustrator.

At 16, he spent his first two years out of college working at an architect's office in Stirling. But his sights were firmly set on painting and he left the architect and his family on his eighteenth birthday and set off for London to become a painter.

His versatility as an artist enabled him to survive. When he arrived in London he painted theatre sets and posters, turned his hand to newspaper cartoons and undertook humorous picture postcards – in short, he

was prepared to turn his hand to anything that would earn him the money he needed to exist as a painter. In his free time he loved travelling on a bus or the Underground observing his fellow passengers and sketching them as they went about their daily tasks. It was through his work in the theatre that he met and married his first wife at the age of twenty two and for a while he settled down with the theatre company painting scenery.

In 1915, he volunteered for army service in World War I, although his health had been affected by his struggle for survival over the previous four years. While waiting for the outcome of medical tests, he passed the time painting soldiers in his regiment. In the end however, he was sent on community service making artificial limbs for those unfortunate enough to get injured in the fighting. The end of the war also saw the end of his marriage, and he was off again, this time to Llandudno in North Wales to join a circle of painters, established in the region. One of those painters was Florence, who was to become his second wife and a huge influence on his life. She dedicated herself entirely to supporting him in his work and spent a great deal of time modelling for him.

When he arrived in Paris with Flo for the first time in 1919, he introduced himself to many of the bohemian artists living on the Left Bank, including the Italian artist Amadeo Modigliani, who became a close friend until the young artist's premature death from tuberculosis in 1920. A great admirer of Modigliani's work, he came to regard him as his mentor. Like Modigliani, Paterson was in awe of many contemporaries including, Cézanne, Toulouse-Lautrec and Picasso.

Paterson was a landscape and portrait painter, but he majored on the female nude, modelling himself on Modigliani's own preoccupation with strong linear rhythms, elongated forms and free use of large flat areas of bold colour.

As restless as ever, Paterson and Flo

travelled through France, heading for the Riviera and the Alpes Maritimes. Passing many fairground caravans parked at several popular resorts, prompted him to think that a caravan would be the perfect vehicle for him to move from place to place with all his equipment and look for fresh scenery and subject matter to paint. So he set about building his own caravan which he towed all over France.

On his travels with Flo, he met an artist who introduced him to the benefits of making his own pastels, a medium that had always appealed to him. Apart from the vast range of intense colours that can be obtained, pastels don't fade. So, from then on, he always made his own from soils that he researched at length. Between 1919 and 1938, he seldom moved away from oils and pastels. Right up to World War II he stayed in France, with periodic sorties back to England to keep in touch with his publishers and undertake commissions. He favoured postcards for which he had developed a lighthearted style of his own, signing some of his comic designs Reg Paterson and others, Vera Paterson.

He was a man with a great sense of humour. He regarded postcards as potboilers and deliberately cast Vera Paterson in the role of creator of Mabel Lucie Attwell look-alikes. His plan was a success as he worked through the thirties and the World War II period for Regent Publishing, Salmon and Valentines.

Rollo and Flo returned to Llandudno at the outbreak of war and he continued his work. He found no shortage of models, for apart from Flo, whose lithe and delicate body was ideal for his style, there were numerous nurses at a nearby hospital who were only too pleased to sit for him and forget the horrors of war for a while.

In 1948 Paterson returned to France and travelled to Barcelona in 1952. A greatly admired artist in Spain, he settled in Malaga and remained there for the rest of his active life, before failing health forced his return to Britain two years before his death.

*Above left:*
*Artist: Rollo (Vera) Paterson*
*Pub: Valentine*
*Mail Novelty Postcard*
*No. 1964*
*[nd]*

*Below left:*
*Artist: Rollo (Vera) Paterson*
*Pub: J Salmon*
*Series 5125*
*No. 5125*
*[1953]*

*Above centre:*
*Artist: Rollo (Vera) Paterson*
*Pub: Regent Publishing Co.*
*No. 127*
*[1929]*

*Below entre:*
*Artist: Rollo (Vera) Paterson*
*Pub: Anon*
*Humoresque Series*
*No. 2710*
*[c.1931]*

*Right hand column:*
*Artist: Rollo (Vera) Paterson*
*Pub: J Salmon*
*Series 5249*
*Nos. 5251/5254*
*[1955]*

A Cheery P.C. From
**DUNFERMLINE**

A GOOD SPORTS MODEL.

IT'S A SECRET I PROMISED NOT TO TELL —
AND GOSH, NOW I CAN'T REMEMBER IT

MY HEART BEATS ONLY FOR YOU AND ME,

I HOPE YOU'RE THINKING WHAT I HOPE YOU'RE THINKING.

YOU CAN ALWAYS TELL A VISION —
BUT YOU CAN'T TELL HER MUCH

# Susan Beatrice Pearse (1878-1980)

Susan Beatrice Pearse, 'Trissie' to all who knew her well, was born in Kennington and grew up with two brothers and sisters. Her father William was a journalist and Susan remembered that much of her childhood was spent in the country at Fair Oak, near Eastleigh, Hampshire, the home of her paternal grandparents.

She attended the New Cross Art School between 1897 and 1901 and achieved notable successes in the Board of Education National Competitions for book illustration and poster design in 1898, book illustration in 1900 and in 1901, book illustration and decoration for a day nursery.

In 1902, Susan entered the Royal College of Art, South Kensington, to study watercolour painting and went on to exhibit at the Royal Academy, the Royal Institute, the Society of Women Artists and galleries in Paris and Vienna.

While still a student at the College, she met and eventually married the noted young portrait painter WE Webster.

Although still dreaming of becoming a painter, Susan Pearse found commercial success as a children's illustrator. Some of her earliest illustrations were postcard designs published by CW Faulkner dating from 1908 – delicate and detailed studies of children at play, reflecting her painterly upbringing.

She retained a link with CW Faulkner and postcard illustration for several years, until she began a long association with Henry Frowde and Hodder & Stoughton, from whom she received her earliest book illustration commissions, *The Pendleton Twins* by EM Jameson in 1908 and *A Little Silver Trumpet* by LT Meade in 1909. She was also contributing to *Little Folks* at that time and it was through Hodder & Stoughton that she first came into contact with Arthur Mee in 1915. In that year she contributed to *Arthur Mee's Gift Book* and went on to make significant contributions to his popular *Children's Encyclopaedia* for many years.

She was a petite and vivacious woman with whom it was a joy to work. In 1910 she embarked on another long-term association with *Playbox Annual*, for whom she illustrated many lively covers.

Her appeal has been in her ability to convey childlike expressions of joy and wonder on the faces of her young characters.

*Ameliaranne Goes Touring. [1941]*

*The only way.*

*Home from Market.*

Artist: Susan Beatrice Pearse
Pub: CW Faulkner
Series 798A/B
[2 of 6]
[1908]

*Poster for Start-rite Shoes. [1930]*

Her delightful postcard illustrations for Humphrey Milford, for whom she did some of her most enduring work, are typical of her sensitive portrayal of the very young in their many moods – none more so than her designs for the Milford series *Holiday Time, Jolly Games, Playmates, Little Helpers* and *By the Seaside.* The series titles themselves suggest the fun and zest she generates in her drawings.

She had a distinctive and simple style of great charm. Many of the little books she illustrated for Humphrey Milford have now been forgotten, but *what a find* when a collector discovers one of these little treasures at a book or antique fair!

She will be best remembered as the illustrator of the poster for *Start-Rite* shoes – a simple and memorable concept that still plays a key role in the company's marketing. Her illustrations for the *Ameliaranne* series of books, created by the author Constance Heward in 1920 were another major achievement. The series of twenty books spread over thirty years demonstrate her use of clear, delicate colour.

Although she enjoyed Chelsea life, she loved to withdraw to Nottingham Fee, her little studio in Blewbury, tucked away in the Berkshire countryside.

A contemporary described it thus: *"The cottage is very small, with a steep conical roof, a blue door and two little windows with blue check curtains. By the side of it there is a wooden building with a gabled roof and a very big window. Within, at her work is Miss Susan Beatrice Pearse, illustrator of children's books".*

Until her sudden death in 1980, aged 102, her energy and appetite for life never faltered. She continued to divide her time equally between Broom Villa in Parsons Green and her Blewbury studio. Always a bohemian at heart, she was happiest when in the company of her artistic friends who included fellow illustrator Hester Margetson and her husband, actor Michael Martin Harvey and author Kenneth Grahame, who lived nearby.

A writer for the *Christian Science Monitor* in the twenties describes lyrically, typical subject matter at which Trissie excelled: *"...these young folk of hers go climbing up their hill of dreams clad in their nighties, each holding its little candle, while the big moon rises above the castle towers; or a joyous boatload, they voyage to the happy islands, balloons flying and toy ships trailing. Often, too, they frolic over flowery meadows with skipping lambs, fall fast asleep on quilts of blossoms, fanned by the lightest wing of gorgeous butterfly."*

*"Miss Susan Beatrice Pearse, illustrator of children's books at work under the thatched roof and within the blue door of her studio, which nestles among meadows and streams in the English countryside."* Christian Science Monitor

*Ameliaranne and the Green Umbrella, by Constance Heward, illustrated by Susan Pearse and published by Harrap in 1920.*

Such Good Scholars.

LEFT HAND PAGE

*Below:*
*Artist: Susan Beatrice Pearse*
*Pub: CW Faulkner*
*Series 1243D*
*[1 of 6]*
*[1912]*

RIGHT HAND PAGE

*Left hand column:*
*Artist: Susan Beatrice Pearse*
*Pub: A Vivian Mansell*
*Series 1172*
*[2 of 6]*
*[1922]*

*Centre column:*
*Artist: Susan Beatrice Pearse*
*Pub: Humphrey Milford*
*The Busy Day*
*[2 of 6]*
*[1923]*

*Right hand column:*
*Artist: Susan Beatrice Pearse*
*Pub: Humphrey Milford*
*Jolly Games*
*[2 of 6]*
*[1926]*

Cinderella

Little Red Riding Hood

# Gladys Peto (1890-1977)

Gladys Emma Peto had a highly individual style which owed a great deal to the influences of the *Art Deco* movement. As a student, she was also extremely fond of the powerful linear style of Aubrey Beardsley, being particularly excited by his use of strongly contrasting black and white imagery. She was born in Maidenhead, Berkshire and attended Harvington College, Ealing, before entering the Maidenhead School of Art in 1908 and London School of Art, Kensington in 1911. Gladys was always looking to improve herself and enrolled on a design course with the John Hassall Correspondence School towards the end of World War I.

*Gladys Peto with Isola Strong, a young girl who modelled for her drawings for Gladys Peto's Children's Annual. [1923]*

Gladys became a pithy diarist and writer and a highly versatile artist and designer. Her design and illustrative work was in great demand during the twenties, but her commercial success was due largely to her own versatility, enabling her to turn her hand to a variety of different design disciplines including advertising, posters, fabrics, ceramics, costumes and scenery as well as book and postcard illustration. During the nineteen twenties and thirties it was considered fashionable to be seen wearing a *Gladys Peto* dress.

She developed a technique that mastered the art of achieving impact in monochrome when executing drawings for reproduction onto the thick absorbent paper used for thirties children's annuals. She was able to apply large contrasting areas of black and white with exciting, bold contrast. Other confidently stylised colour renderings of children at play are executed with a delicacy and application of colour reminiscent of Dutch illustrator H Willebeek le Mair.

*LEFT HAND PAGE*

*One of six* Alice in
Wonderland Handkerchiefs
*by Gladys Peto [c.1925]*

*RIGHT HAND PAGE*

*Top row:*
*Artist: Gladys Peto*
*Pub: Salmon*
*No. 3993/3995*
*[1932]*

*Bottom row left & centre:*
*Artist: Gladys Peto*
*Pub: Salmon*
*No. 3996/3997*
*[1932]*

*Bottom row right:*
*Artist: Gladys Peto*
*Pub: Allenburys*
*[1920]*

" You May Lead a Horse to Water, But You Can't Make Him Drink. "

IT'S AN ILL WIND THAT BLOWS NOBODY GOOD.

"It Never Rains, But it Pours."

"A Rolling Stone Gathers No Moss."

Like le Mair, Gladys Peto concentrates on elegant design. Her rather self-conscious children show little emotion, but are posed to show off the clothes they are wearing to the best advantage. The quality of the production of the books she illustrated did not, in the main, match up to her skills as an artist. Yet, such was her popularity, that several story books and annuals bore her name during the twenties and thirties, like *Gladys Peto's Children's Annual* and *Gladys Peto's Bedtime Stories*. Her earliest achievements included book illustrations for the works of Louisa M Alcott in 1914 and a satirical illustrated diary for *The Sketch* from 1919 to 1926.

Her love of travel is highlighted in many of her books. She lived in Malta, Egypt and Cyprus between 1924 and 1928, where her husband Colonel CL Emmerson was stationed. This experience prompted her to write and illustrate lighthearted travel books on Egypt, Malta and Cyprus. The couple lived in India between 1933 and 1938, before finally settling in Northern Ireland in 1939, where Gladys had several successful exhibitions of Irish watercolours. Latterly she devoted her time to cultivating and selling rare cottage perennials and primroses of which up to the last, although crippled by a stroke, she took pleasure in drawing with her left hand.

# Joyce Plumstead (1907-1986)

*Joyce Plumstead . [c.1930]*

Joyce Plumstead was the third of five children born to William Plumstead, chief surveyor with Prudential Assurance Company, and his wife Ethel May of Higham's Park, London. Her mother was a keen amateur flower and landscape painter who nurtured Joyce's natural flair for art and throughout their lives they enjoyed going on painting expeditions together.

As a teenager, Joyce fitted out a studio at home to provide a retreat where she could withdraw whenever she wanted to enter her own fantasy world of art.

When the family moved to Buckhurst

Hill in 1923, Joyce attended Walthamstow High School and from 1925, she studied general art subjects at Leyton School of Art and was regarded as a star pupil. She was inspired by the teaching of L Gordon Andrews ASAM, principal at the school through the inter-war years.

On leaving art school, Joyce was introduced to Raphael Tuck & Sons by a contact of her father. She was employed as a staff artist for a while but, preferring the freedom of freelancing, showed her portfolio around the London publishers.

During the thirties she contributed regularly to Dean & Sons' *Monster Books* and illustrated postcards for Vivian Mansell with quaint titles like *The Fairy Shoemaker, The Pixie's Airmail* and *Little People of the Seashore*. Her delicately drawn images depict her carefree fairyland children – half child, half fairy, gambolling around in the sunshine – a sentimental view, but an overwhelmingly popular one in the nurseries of the nineteen twenties and thirties.

Her marriage to banker Vernon Land, in 1935, lasted only a few years then Joyce moved from her house in Woking to a cottage near Sherborne in Dorset in 1950. Like many people in her position, with two sons to care for, she never realised her full potential as a artist, but she continued to work on greetings cards for the Medici Society and books for Dean & Sons whenever she could. In 1965, she wrote and illustrated *Giggles the Spotted Donkey*, a story for young children.

Joyce learned about painting landscapes from her friend Pasco Holman RWS, a former teacher and noted painter of seascapes. She and her mother spent many happy hours painting in Portisham, Dorset, where he lived. Joyce also enjoyed going on painting holidays in Devon, organised by Jack Marriott, the artist renowned for his striking posters for Union Castle and the Great Western Railway. Latterly, she lived in Lyme Regis, where she continued to enjoy her life painting delightful portraits and landscapes.

*Tim the newspaper boy from* Giggles the spotted Donkey. *[1965]*

*LEFT HAND PAGE*

*Artist: Joyce Plumstead*
*Pub: A Vivian Mansell*
*Series 1004*
*Little People of the Seashore*
*[3 of 6]*
*[c.1938]*

*RIGHT HAND PAGE*

*Artist: Joyce Plumstead*
*Pub: A Vivian Mansell*
*Series 2126*
*[1936]*

THE PIXIE'S AIRMAIL

FAIRY CLOCKS

THE ELFIN RIDER

FAIRY UMBRELLAS

THE FAIRY SHOEMAKER

AUTUMN LEAVES

# Chloë Preston (1887-1969)

*Left:*
*Chloë Preston*
*photographed by*
*Dorothy Wilding*
*[1920's]*

Chloë was born into an aristocratic family. Her father, Henry was the heir to Moreby Park, a huge estate close by the River Ouse, running south from York on its journey towards the Humber Estuary. This is the magnificent property that the family were to move into on the death of Chloë's grandfather – the property she was to inherit years later. Her mother, Beatrice, was one of nine children of Archbishop Thomson of York and Chloë, born Beatrice Zoë in 1887, had a brother Tom who was exactly a year older.

The two children grew up together in splendid surroundings at Middlethorpe Manor, a fine Queen Anne style house close to York racecourse – a happy, affluent family who wanted for nothing. As Mary Hillier points out in her book, *Chloë Preston and the Peek-a-Boos*, *"It is easy to find details of their own childhood reflected in the simple adventures of Chloë Preston's Peek-a-Boo books"* – the quality clothes they wore, the balls they attended, the games and parties, the joys of riding and hunting – these and other events are essential to the *Peek-a-Boos*, a series of fifty or so books and booklets illustrated between 1910 and 1932.

As children, Chloë and Tom were great mates. Then Tom was sent to Eton while Chloë remained at home to be educated. Tom was a convivial fellow and a good mixer. Like members of his family before him he joined the army; he was awarded the MC and bar for bravery in World War I. Chloë volunteered as a hospital auxiliary during the war and worked in Sheffield.

Chloë and Tom were both artistic, creative and confident. Chloë was a self-assured young woman and Tom was a secure and well balanced boy who did not feel threatened by his sister's assertive nature; in fact they got on very well together. They were happy to bounce ideas off one another and we are told they created the *Peek-a-Boos* concept together. We do know that Tom wrote some of the adventures. However, he had a career in the army to attend to, leaving Chloë to

develop the *Peek-a-Boos* into a commercial success – a success he was not to share.

A reviewer of *The Peek-a-Boos in Town* of 1913, enthused: *"Some two or three years ago the Peek-a-Boos suddenly burst on an unsuspecting world and since that time their adventures have appeared with regularity…This book is at least as funny as its predecessors and the pictures as funny – which means that Miss Preston is keeping up a remarkably high level".*

Chloë was a forthright woman who more than held her own in dealings she had with publishers, manufacturers and those who had been granted subsidiary rights to produce *Peek-a-Boo* merchandise. She enlisted the services of her uncle Sir Basil Thomson, a seasoned businessman, to act as her agent in the early days. It was through his overtures that Chloë was introduced to publishers Henry Frowde and Hodder & Stoughton.

His advice got her started, but before long she was handling her own business dealings with confidence.

*Frontispiece from* The Peek-a-Boos Among the Bunnies. *[1912]*

17 March 1914, Middlethorpe Manor: *"In answer to your letter about the calendars I shall be pleased to accept your terms – 10% royalty in the case of calendars sold at 2/6 upwards and 5% on calendars issued at a lower price. I hope they will undersell the gentleman who is pirating them!!"*

1 Feb. 1918, Moreby Park: *"I have received your letter and will let you know what I decide to do about the people who want to use 'Peek' designs in the course of a day or two…"*

6 Feb. 1918, 1 Elvaston Place, SW [Sir Basil Thomson's London address]: *"Referring to your letter, you speak of "usual arrangements between you and ourselves" – I've not been able to look up our correspondence so will you kindly let me know what these were? I should be ready to sell the permission to use the Peek-a-Boo designs on china ware to this firm* [The Paragon China Company] *…provided they specify for my approval the designs…"*

24 Feb. 1918, Moreby Park: *"…I think we had better ask the terms you suggest – namely £1/10/6* [the firm offered £1] *per subject and that they be guaranteed the sole use of the* <u>*subjects they choose*</u>*…I am afraid I have not much faith in "English" ventures!! (Publishing – of course I don't include!) but in "fancy goods" they never seem to do the quantity or have the push that the Germans had – though I suppose it is treason to say so!…"*

By now, Chloë's letters are beginning to show her suspicions and anxiety of any successful author – dealing with pirating and plagiarism.

21 April 1921, Moreby Park: *"…By the way, I have been trying to trace (unsuccessfully, I'm afraid) the matters of some china plates, mugs etc. with drawings from "The Peek-a-Boos in Camp". Have you come across any? A friend of mine bought some in a shop in Southampton and the man there said they were* <u>*German*</u> *made but "*<u>*pre-war*</u> *stock" (it was about 1920)*

*– This is ridiculous as the* <u>*book*</u> *did not come out till the second year of the war!! Do you think it is those people who asked you about Peek designs and then said the terms were too high? I will go round when I get to London & try & find a shop who sells them. An aunt of mine had one given (she has lost it now) & thinks it was got in London. I feel I should get something out of it – or if they have used the designs without permission I could go for them whoever they are."*

14 May 1921, Moreby Park: *"I received the cheque all right but they have not included the payment of the booklets* [4 booklets]*. I don't know what you usually pay but I think I should have at least 2 guineas each – as they are a great effort for me to do!…I find that the china with drawings from the "Peek-a-Boo's Camp" was made in Germany! – I first saw it during the War – so they somehow managed to get it back into this country…"*

10 Oct. 1921, Moreby Hall: *"I'm afraid I*

don't see your point of view about royalties from the china. When my uncle Sir Basil Thomson used to do my "business" with you – he was much surprised when I told him you took some of the royalties. I explained to him that you negotiated and drew up the agreement – in fact – acted as my "agent". We agreed that you should have one third of the royalties. He disapproved – as he said that my copyrights were my own to do what I liked with – however, I told him I wished to leave it at that. I cannot see your argument about the drawings being use from "your" books. You must realize that one can sell the same designs for different purposes – it is done every day…"

13 Dec. 1924, Moreby Park:
Yes, by all means let us allow the Germans & Austrians to have the Peek books. I'll be willing to accept 5% royalty. I'm afraid I shan't be able to do any more Peek-a-Boos as I've more work than I can do comfortably! – & find press work & postcards & commercial etc. pays so much better than books that I'll have to stick to it as long as there's any demand for my stuff. I see the books still "massed" in Harrods this year. I can't think why anyone wants them – I should have thought they'd be tired of them".

8 Jan 1927, Moreby Park, York: "Yes, I think it would be quite a good idea to make panorama books of the Peeks. Raphael Tuck does it with some drawings I sent him long ago and they seem very popular with children [Tootsie Wootsie Kiddies]. It makes a little change for smaller children. I fancy there is rather a "slump" in children's books from all accounts – you have been having so much trouble with strikes etc! My most paying 'line' is soft toys – it beats all ordinary publishing work hollow!"

Oct 1928, Moreby, York: "I will certainly be willing to accept half receipts of anything that can be got out of the American people! I am afraid it _will_ be a difficult thing now, everyone seems to be "pirating" Peek-a-Boos!…".

One senses, reading the correspondence,

Ready, aye Ready!

To Wish you
a Happy Christmas

True Blue

To Wish you
a Happy Christmas

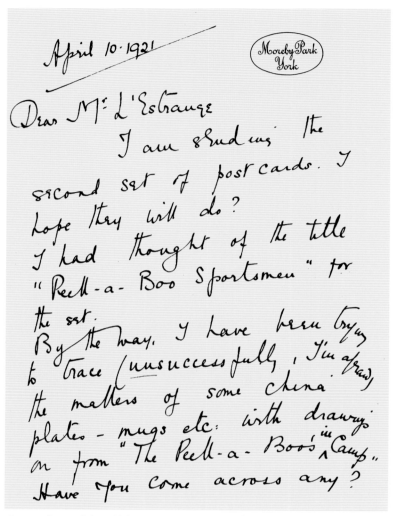

*Correspondence with her publisher concerning* Peek-a-Boo Sportsmen. *[1922]*

that by 1928 Chloë is growing tired. Her letters are disconsolate, with an air of resignation about them. She seems to be venting her angst on the publisher for years of stress that the publishing world had heaped upon her, by informing him that other types of work are better rewarded. People flouting her copyrights, loss of public interest in the *Peek-a-Boos* and the looming Depression seemed to have tested even her steely disposition.

This is in stark contrast to the woman, who, ten years earlier had been brimming with tenacity and business acumen.

In those days, she had not been a woman to put all her eggs into one basket. In an effort to capitalise on the *Peek-a-Boos'* success, in 1916 she began to experiment with a new idea – The Chunkies. *"Do you know the Chunkies? They are jolly little people with jointed arms and legs…and the pictures are just splendid - coloured of course as well as plain"*, said an eager reviewer in 1921.

*The Chunkies* enjoyed a number of adventures together between 1916 and 1922, but never achieved the popularity of the *Peek-a-Boos,* although they were used to raise funds for wounded war veterans.

*LEFT HAND PAGE*

*Artist: Chloë Preston*
*Pub: Henry Frowde*
*Hearts of Oak*
*From The Peek-a-Boos, [1910]*
*[1915]*

*RIGHT HAND PAGE*

*Artist: Chloë Preston*
*Pub: Humphrey Milford*
*Peek-a-Boo Sportsmen*
*[5 of 6 with packet]*
*[1921]*

Says the Peek-a-Boo sportsman "Beware, shooting rabbits is very good fun!"
Says Bunny "Right-o! But take care that you use the right end of the gun."

This Peek-a-Boo fisherman-look, has a bite on the end of his hook!
So for supper a Peek-a-Boo fish will be cooked on a Peek-a-Boo dish.

This Peek-a-Boo can swim and float upon the water, like a boat,
And see, his sister shows with pride the way to dive in from the side.

The Peek-a-Boos go driving past "Hooray" they cry "gee up!"
And though the spotted horse runs fast, still faster runs the pup.

This Peek-a-Boo gallops his horse, he's a very good rider, of course.
The dogs don't object to the pace because they are having a race.

**AFTERNOON TEA**

Peterkin Perkins and Annabel Joy
Had for a present a simply sweet toy!
Just try and guess what that toilet could be,
A dollie's wee teaset you plainly can see
P'raps if you're good - oh, as good as can be,
May be they will ask you for afternoon tea!

*MARJORIE F. SEYMOUR*

**TOO BUSY**

No! I can't play with you yet! - dolly's busy too;
Wait a little while, now doggie do!
I must write this postcard to a little friend of mine,
And send it with my loving greetings true!

*MARJORIE F. SEYMOUR*

**IT CAN'T BE DONE!**

Apples red, and apples green - biggest apples ever seen;
We should like to give you one - but, alas! it can't be done!
So we send you on this card, loving wishes by the yard,
We both hope they'll find you well; and that's all we have
to tell!

*MARJORIE F. SEYMOUR*

**FAIRY KISSES**

Balloons are fairy kisses so they say,
I've bought some and I'm sending them today,
Sending them by Dobbin true,
In the hope they'll all reach you,
But as we had but little money,
We could only buy a few ——!

*MARJORIE F. SEYMOUR*

**OH! SO NAUGHTY!**

There was a fluffy Peke with a flowered collar gay,
And he looked very proud and very haughty - o!
He made me write his greetings, because he felt too grand,
Which I think was very, very naughty - o!

*MARJORIE F. SEYMOUR*

**FAIRY JEWELS**

There's nothing like a garden to make one bright and jolly,
Be it filled with summer flowers or mistletoe or holly.
For every night the Fairy Folk just whisper to the dew
To hang a jewel on every leaf and make it shine for you,
I'm sending one along to say "All happiness the livelong day."

*Left column:*
*Artist: Chloë Preston*
*Pub: Raphael Tuck*
*Series 3461*
*Quaint Little Folk*
*[2 of 6]*
*[1923]*

*Left column:*
*Artist: Chloë Preston*
*Pub: Raphael Tuck*
*Series 3505*
*Quaint Little Folk II*
*[2 of 6]*
*[1924]*

*Left column:*
*Artist: Chloë Preston*
*Pub: Raphael Tuck*
*Series 3520*
*Quaint Folk*
*[2 of 6]*
*[1924]*

*"Dobbin did nothing but go on puffing" from* Chunkies' Adventures. *[1921]*

By 1920, Chloë's fame had spread. Her services were in demand from several publishers and manufacturers, including Valentine's and Raphael Tuck. Tuck needed a family as successful as the *Peek-a-Boos*. Chloë came up with the *Tootsie Wootsie Kiddies* around 1920, producing artwork for a concertina style book, referred to in her letter to Milford in January 1927. But the idea did not catch on. It is events like these that chip away at an artist's morale and confidence and over the years they took their toll.

At home, a rift that had been festering between Tom and the family over his marriage in 1917 and his legitimacy as heir to the family fortune, came to a head on the death of his father in 1924. Tom's marriage in 1917 had not met with the approval of his parents. Even worse, it was alleged by some that he had been born just out of wedlock and should not succeed his father as the heir to the Moreby estate.

Sadly, poor Tom was disinherited and Chloë found herself the heiress to wealth and property. She now owned a huge estate covering several miles and including villages which housed many tenant workers and their families. But she didn't want the worry of managing it, so she sold it – much of it to the tenants – and left her brother and his family a modest legacy to occupy and maintain the house.

Chloë was now a fabulously wealthy and independent woman – rich beyond her dreams. She maintained her flat in Chelsea for a while and then moved to Falmouth in Devon to stay with friends. She finally

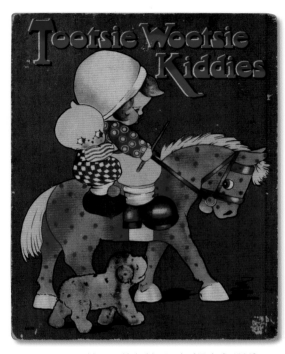

Tootsie Wootsie Kiddies, *published by Raphael Tuck. [c.1920]*

left England in 1932, with her friend Norah McCaw. This heralded the start of a new life in Monte Carlo and the laying to rest of the *Peek-a-Boos*. They had been her children for many years and she had been devoted to them, fiercely protective of them against predators. Now, after what seemed to be a period of turmoil in her life, it was time to start afresh.

Chloë had always enjoyed postcard design and, as she claimed in letters she wrote to her publisher, she generated more income through postcard designs than she did through books.

In 1921, Chloë created the *Quaint Little Folk* for Raphael Tuck, a successful three set series for the postcard and greetings card markets. Valentine's published over a hundred of her postcards between 1923 and 1932, along with numerous greetings cards. Humphrey Milford published *The Peek-a-Boo Gardeners* in 1920 and *The Peek-a-Boo Sportsmen* in 1921, with

Peek-a-Boos in Winter, *published by Henry Frowde and Hodder & Stoughton [1911]*

accompanying rhyming couplets on each card provided by Jessie Pope, a popular contributor to children's books and annuals. Two 'patriotic' wartime postcards were published under the Hentry Frowde imprint in 1915, taken from Chloë's first book, as part of a set entitled *Hearts of Oak*. Other notable postcards by Chloë included a set of six coy little children illustrated for the British Art Company around 1923.

*May Byron in 1912*

### May Byron

May Byron (Mary Clarissa Gillington) (1861-1935), was one of the most able journalists and writers of children's books of her day. Her writing supported the work of many of Britain's foremost illustrators at the beginning of the twentieth century and she was commissioned to provide the words for many of the *Peek-a-Boos'* and *Chunkies'* adventures. Her name lent real credibility to any books she wrote.

May was the daughter of a cleric from Yarmouth, Isle of Wight. She married an architect and lived in Streatham, south London for many years. She was famous for her cookery books, but her repertoire was extraordinary. She was a music critic, writer of lyrics and librettos, anthologies in prose and verse, and books on nature and religion.

"YOU MUSN'T LOOK AT ME LIKE THAT!"

"COULD YOU BE TRUE TO EYES OF BLUE
IF YOU LOOKED INTO EYES OF BROWN?"

THREE CAN BE A CROWD!

A STORY AS OLD AS THE HILLS.

I'M COMING ROMPING HOME.

*Above left:*
*Artist: Chloë Preston*
*Pub: Valentine*
*Chloë Preston Series*
*No. 1142*
*[1926]*

*Below left:*
*Artist: Chloë Preston*
*Pub: Valentine*
*Chloë Preston Series*
*No. 1145*
*[1926]*

*Above right:*
*Artist: Chloë Preston*
*Pub: Valentine*
*Chloë Preston Series*
*No. 1167*
*[1927]*

*Centre right:*
*Artist: Chloë Preston*
*Pub: Valentine*
*Chloë Preston Series*
*No. 1169*
*[1927]*

*Below right:*
*Artist: Chloë Preston*
*Pub: Valentine*
*Chloë Preston Series*
*No. 1233*
*[1928]*

The portrait on this page is a painting of Chloë Preston in 1909, aged 21, by American, James Jebusa Shannon in oil on canvas on the occasion of her 'coming out'. The picture was exhibited at the Royal Academy in 1909. The portrait on page 200 is a photograph by Dorothy Wilding, the most fashionable of all the society photographers of the nineteen twenties.

### James Jebusa Shannon (1862-1923)

He was born in Auburn, New York on 3 February 1862 of Irish parents.

He arrived in London aged sixteen and studied at South Kensington School from 1878 until 1881. He received a Gold Medal for figure painting and established a successful portrait painting practice. He placed a large mirror behind himself so that his sitters could see the reflection of the painting as he worked. He believed that *"the artist should find a bond of sympathy – physical, pictorial or spiritual with his sitter to make heedful selection of expression, pose, accessory, in accord with that bond and supremely to leave the mark of his own personality on that portrait."* Several of his portraits won awards and his style was considered by some to rival that of James Sargent.

### Dorothy Wilding (1893-1976 )

She was born in Longford near Gloucester on 10 January 1893, the fourth daughter of a commercial traveller by his second marriage. Largely self-taught, she saved enough to open her first London studio aged 21. She believed in *"doing her job through the eyes of a painter"* and adopted a logo of an artist in a beret, which she employed throughout her career. Her theatrical and extrovert approach to 'camera portraits' led to her photographing the rich and famous in society and the world of entertainment. The portrait of Chloë Preston, taken in the mid-twenties was personally signed indicating that she had paid a great deal of personal attention to the portrait.

*Miss Chloë Preston, portrait by James Jebusa Shannon (1862-1923), oil on canvas. [1909]*

# Eugenie Richards (1873-1941)

Born on 13 July 1873, Eugenie Richards was the eldest of four children – two brothers and two sisters – born to Samuel Richards and his wife Mary.

Eugenie was raised in a family involved in the design and manufacture of lace, Nottingham's major industry at that time. Friends and other family members were equally revered lace draughtsmen and designers in the city. These early influences steered Eugenie and her younger sister Daisy towards an interest in the applied arts.

Eugenie was a remarkably talented and multi-faceted student at the Nottingham School of Art & Design. She continued her studies there for about ten years and her achievements in the annual Board of Education National Competition were remarkable. Between 1901 and 1909 she received 16 awards and commendations, a record unsurpassed over the competition's twenty two year period. Eugenie's record was exceptional due to her range of abilites and the areas in which she won prizes – children's book illustration, stained glass, alphabet design, showcards, life drawing, wallpaper, friezes, majolica plates, nursery decoration, portrait painting, and the illuminated page.

The competition culminated in an annual exhibition held in South Kensington and was regarded as a 'shop window' of young designers making the transition from students to practitioners. *The Studio*, reporting the 1903 show, commented effusively on Eugenie's work: *"Some strong ornamental plaques were shown by Eugenie Richards – one of the chief and most deserving prize-winners of the year. What Cecil Aldin does for nursery tiles, this student has done for nursery plates, treating them very much in the style of her poster work which we shall note elsewhere…"* Later in the review her work is again highly praised: *"…some designs for the decoration of a nursery were admirably conceived from the decorative standpoint… as were her designs for colour prints for children's books…"* Her work was influenced by the Arts and Crafts Movement and the great poster artists of the day, John Hassall and Dudley Hardy.

On completing her studies, she took up a position as a teaching assistant at the art school, under the leadership of the principal, Joseph Harrison.

'Joe' Harrison was one of the most powerful influences in design education in his day. He was the son of a missionary and born in Nottingham. As a young man he spent some time as a master at the Leicester School of Art before being appointed Principal of Nottingham Art School in 1881. He was Head of the Art School when Laura Johnson (Dame Laura Knight) and Harold Knight were students there.

*Eugenie on the beach with a nephew. [c.1900]*

Joe Harrison made radical changes in the way art and design was taught in England and his influence affected many of the young artists and designers recorded in this book. Courses became more structured and focused on vocational training for the applied arts, preparing students for jobs. His success was well documented in the reports of inspectors of the Department of Science and Art, who commended him on his 'systematic' teaching of design. He was an imposing character and a source of inspiration for many.

Eugenie and Daisy were among those who came under his influence and were beneficiaries of his teaching philosophy. His inspiration combined with his love of the lace industry, was a great source of encouragement for them.

One of Eugenie's earliest commissions came from Boots the Chemist, great patrons of design and the arts. At the turn of the century they sold stationery and around 1904 commissioned Eugenie to illustrate a set of of six nursery rhyme postcards. It was a theme that she enjoyed and the cards sold well. But in trying to adhere to the brief and provide pictures that would appeal to the very young, she compromised the fluid and assured line of her prize winning nursery rhyme designs.

Eugenie was well-known locally as a contributor to the annual exhibition of the Nottingham Society of Artists between 1909 and 1919. Her favourite subjects included portraits, nursery rhymes and miniatures in watercolour, pen and ink, pencil, crayon and charcoal.

She worked as a book illustrator for publishers, including Sissons & Parker for whom she worked on paper-backed penny books for the very young in the *Humpty Dumpty Nursery Rhyme Readers* series and the twopenny *Humpty Dumpty Books*. She worked for Dean & Son, Methuen on a series of Rose Fyleman fairy books and contributed to Blackwell's *Joy Street* and books published by Blackie and Simpkin Marshall.

Life at art school had a profound effect on both sisters for different reasons. In 1920, Daisy, now the art school librarian and a lifelong admirer of Joseph Harrison, married him three years before he retired from the art school. At 40 years of age, she was 33 years his junior, but due to his longevity, they enjoyed eighteen years of married life together.

Eugenie is remembered as an awesome and domineering woman who spoke in resounding patrician tones, enunciating every word and emitting an intimidating air of grandeur. In her heyday she could be seen striding round Nottingham in a cloak and flowing gown – very much the professional artist.

Towards the end of her life, Eugenie sold her house and joined her sister and brother-in-law. Although middle class and comfortably well off, all three of them had working class roots and held socialist beliefs, as demonstrated by their record for supporting generously those in society less fortunate than themselves.

Simple Simon. *National Art Competition entry. [1903]*

*Artist: Eugenie Richards*
*Pub: Boots Cash Chemists*
*Pelham Series*
*[1910]*

SIMPLE·SIMON·MET·A·PIEMAN·GOING·TO·THE·FAIR
SAID·SIMPLE·SIMON·TO·THE·PIEMAN·LET·ME
TASTE·YOUR·WARE···SAID·THE·PIEMAN·TO
SIMPLE·SIMON·SHOW·ME·FIRST·YOUR·PENNY
SAID·SIMPLE·SIMON·TO·THE·PIEMAN
INDEED·I·HAVE·NOT·ANY

DUNCE·DUNCE·DOUBLE·D
HE·CAN'T·SAY·HIS·A·B·C

MARY·MARY·QUITE·CONTRARY
HOW·DOES·YOUR·GARDEN·GROW
SILVER·BELLS AND COCKLE·SHELLS
AND PRETTY·MAIDS·ALL·OF·A·ROW

TWO·BONNY·BLUE·EYES
A·DEAR·LITTLE·NOSE
A·PRETTY·LITTLE·MOUTH
AND·HER·NAME·IS·ROSE

DICKY·BIRD·DICKY·BIRD·COME TO ME
YOU·SHALL BE·HAPPY·JOYOUS AND FREE
YOU·SHALL BE ALL THE WORLD·TO ME
DICKY·BIRD·DICKY·BIRD·COME TO ME

A·LITTLE·COCK·SPARROW·SAT·ON·A·TREE···SINGING·SO
BLITHE·SO·HAPPY·WAS·HE···A·LITTLE·BOY·CAME
WITH·HIS·BOW·AND·ARROW···AND·SAID·I·WILL·SHOOT
THAT·LITTLE·COCKSPARROW···HIS·HEAD·WILL·MAKE·A
VERY·NICE·STEW·HIS·WINGS·WILL·MAKE·NICE·PIE·TOO···BUT
THE·LITTLE·COCKSPARROW·SAID·THAT·WILL·NOT·DO
SO·HE·OPENED·HIS·WINGS·AND·AWAY·HE·FLEW···

# Agnes Richardson (1884-1951)

"May I have the pleasure?"

Hawthorne for Hope

Kate Agnes Richardson, one of the best-loved artists of popular children's themes was born in Wimbledon, the year that Maud Watson won the first Ladies Singles Tennis Championship. She was the youngest in a family of eight. Raised in a household in which her father and brothers worked in print, young Agnes was aware of opportunities open to her in drawing, painting and commercial art. Her mother died when she was only six, so naturally, she grew up in the company of the male members of her family.

One of her brothers, Robert, a keen painter, helped Agnes (she never used her first name) set her mind on becoming an illustrator. Her interest was heightened by watching Robert and his friend Arthur Savage painting in the attic studio at their Darlaston Road home. They let her experiment with various paint mediums and with their encouragement and help from her teachers at school, she entered art competitions whenever she could. She

loved competing and was often amongst the winners. In 1902, the *Girls Realm* awarded her a diploma for a drawing of *Simple Simon Met a Pieman*.

On leaving school she attended drawing classes at Lambeth School of Art, close to her home. On completion of the course she took a job in a printer's studio, while she hawked her portfolio around London publishers. It was difficult at first, but her personality and eagerness brought its reward. Her ambition to become an illustrator of children's books was gradually realised, but it was postcard publishers who first took a keen interest in her style and before long she had become a major illustrator of postcards and popular children's books and annuals.

Her earliest postcards for CW Faulkner and dating from 1910, indicate her interest in young romance, a recurring theme throughout her career. These charming watercolours depict youthful couples in costumes from an earlier period, but

A little walk.

Springtime of Love

*LEFT HAND PAGE*

*Left hand column:*
*Artist: Agnes Richardson*
*Pub: CW Faulkner*
*Series 1155B/E*
*True Little Lovers*
*[2 of 6]*
*[1911]*

*Right hand column:*
*Artist: Agnes Richardson*
*Pub: CW Faulkner*
*Series 1265E/F*
*Love's Language of Flowers*
*[2 of 6]*
*[1912]*

*RIGHT HAND PAGE*

*Left hand column:*
*Artist: Agnes Richardson*
*Pub: Raphael Tuck*
*Series 3484*
*Wee Pierette*
*[2 of 6]*
*[1924]*

*Above centre:*
*Artist: Agnes Richardson*
*Pub: Raphael Tuck*
*Series C7131*
*[c.1924]*

*Below centre:*
*Artist: Agnes Richardson*
*Pub: Raphael Tuck*
*Series C1421*
*[c.1924]*

*Right hand column:*
*Artist: Agnes Richardson*
*Pub: Raphael Tuck*
*Series 3496*
*Ancient Egypt Up-to-Date*
*[2 of 6]*
*[1924]*

MOST IMPORTANT!
Three little puppies - one little maid,
Dressed in her best - looking so staid,
Errand's important - she's coming to say
Please take my greetings on this happy day!

A MERRY CHRISTMAS FROM US ALL
A BRIGHT NEW YEAR FROM GREAT AND SMALL
THE VERY BEST OF CHRISTMAS CHEER
AND LOTS OF FUN, WE WISH YOU, DEAR.

IT'S QUITE THE CUSTOM -
ON THE NILE!

TO TELL YOU SO!
Under the mistletoe kisses are sweet,
(Pierrot may have one just for a treat!)
You're far away, but I love you, you know,
(Here comes a wee card a-telling you so!)

CHRISTMAS GREETINGS
A World of love and kindness
To make you glad and gay
And here's a hearty greeting
For merry Christmas Day.

I SPHINX
I'M FORGOTTEN!

HEARTY CHRISTMAS WISHES.

Only a wee expression,
Only a word or two -
But oh, what a long succession
Of joys they are wishing you.

WHEN YOUR SHIP COMES HOME.

HAPPY CHRISTMAS WISHES.

When this little card you see
You'll know I think of you-
so think of me.
And if you wish me what I wish you,
'Twill be a happy time for two.

YOU CAN'T HELP LIKING
THE SCOTCH.

*LEFT HAND PAGE*

*Left hand column:*
*Artist: Agnes Richardson*
*Pub: Inter-Art Co.*
*Comique Series*
*Nos. 6760/6762*
*[1929]*

*Centre column:*
*Artist: Agnes Richardson*
*Pub: Photochrom*
*Celesque Series*
*Nos. 1383/1430*
*[c.1916]*

*Above right:*
*Artist: Agnes Richardson*
*Pub: Millar & Lang*
*Nos. 3416*
*[1924]*

*Below right:*
*Artist: Agnes Richardson*
*Pub: Millar & Lang*
*Unnumbered*
*[1924]*

*RIGHT HAND PAGE*

*Artist: Agnes Richardson*
*Pub: Wildt & Kray*
*Series 5231*
*[c.1927]*

THE QUEEN OF HEARTS.
The Queen of Hearts, she made some Tarts
All on a Summer's day,
The Knave of Hearts, he stole those tarts
And took them right away.

LITTLE BO - PEEP.
Little Bo - peep has lost her sheep,
And cannot tell where to find them;
Leave them alone, and they'll come home
Bringing their tails behind them.

showing touches of the Attwell style. As her career developed, a coy brand of humour emerged that made her brightly coloured pictures of rosy cheeked children, very popular with young people.

One of her earliest series of postcards for CW Faulkner, the *Agnes Richardson Series* 996, attracted positive response from trade press in April 1911: *"…quaint and fanciful child pictures by one of the most appreciated younger artists."* In 1913 the trade press enthused over her *True Little Lovers* series 1155 from CW Faulkner: *"It is a long time since a series of pictures of this kind has been issued, so quaintly pretty, and with such harmony of treatment. It seems a shame to put them in the post."* Her *Love's Language of Flowers* series 1265 elicited a similar response: *"…lovely colouring on dark ground, of children in the country and on the water carrying Chinese lanterns, whose variegated light contrasts effectively with the evening sky and sombre surroundings."*

As well as children, she loved pets and often included them in her compositions. Along with the traditional children's themes she exploited topical events. Some of the most telling and emotive examples of her work are the images of little patriots bringing cheer and a feeling of optimism to everybody during the dark days of World War I. Another vivid example of her sense of topicality is the discovery of Tutenkhamun's tomb in 1922, which prompted her to depict her rosy-cheeked children in sphinxian backgrounds for Raphael Tuck's series 3496 *Ancient Egypt Up-To-Date*. Her happy and carefree children may be too sugary for some, yet most will agree that many of her postcards, particularly those for Raphael Tuck, are notably striking and well composed with bold background colouring and inventive borders, demonstrating a real design talent. In all her work her sense of unbridled fun and humour keeps shining through.

She was extremely prolific and for the next forty years Agnes Richardson was a familiar name in nurseries up and down the country, as a major contributor to many annuals for the very young. During the nineteen thirties her popularity was such that *The Agnes Richardson Book* published by Birn Brothers in 1936 and the *Agnes Richardson Annual* were best sellers. She also wrote children's stories including *The Dainty Series* (four volumes) [1924] and *Chubby Chums* [1932]. She designed a series of posters for London Transport in 1921.

In 1911 she married her childhood painter friend Arthur Savage. Marriage and raising a family did not quell her output of work or her desire to bring joy and happiness to millions of children with her own brand of jolly humour. She was one of relatively few illustrators who managed to combine a hectic working schedule with devoted motherhood. She loved her own children and delighted in sharing with them another magical gift. Her daughter Priscilla remembered: *"We were lucky children and took a tremendous interest in everything she did, especially the stories she used to tell us."*

From Rêves d'enfants (Infant's dreams)
Published in France (c.1930)

# Jennifer Rickard (b.1912)

Jennifer Margaret Rickard remembers that as a schoolgirl living in Eastcote, Middlesex in the nineteen twenties, she excelled at art. Her mother was an accomplished amateur painter who was happy to see her attend Harrow School of Art for four years, after leaving school. One of Jennifer's four brothers, Stephen, was also very talented. He attended Kingston School of Art and the Royal Academy Schools and has followed a career as a noted sculptor and glass engraver.

*Jennifer Rickard on her wedding day. [1948]*

In her youth, Jennifer had admired a number of children's illustrators, in particular, Honor Appleton and Margaret Tarrant, whose work inspired her to take up a career in illustration.

By the beginning of the nineteen thirties, talented and determined women artists were beginning to assert themselves in the commercial world. Precedents had been set by others who had gone before, like Beatrix Potter and more recently, Mabel Lucie Attwell and Hilda Cowham, so, like many other aspiring college leavers, Jennifer Rickard set off confidently to hawk her portfolio around London's publishing houses and found some success.

Her talent for illustration was recognised by a neighbour who introduced her to Newnes, publishers of magazines and mass market children's books. This was her first real break. She was one of a number of young artists chosen to illustrate covers of Enid Blyton's *Sunny Stories*. Others included Kay Nixon, Sylvia Venus, Nora Unwin and Dorothy Wheeler. At two guineas per cover and one shilling and sixpence for each black and white drawing inside the paper, she felt rich. She was

invited by the Medici Society to design Christmas and birthday cards and soon commissions from other sources followed, including the *Sunday Despatch*, *Good Housekeeping*, the Epworth Press and a delightful series of fairyland postcards from CW Faulkner, published in 1931.

Jennifer began war service at the Ministry of Labour, then moved to the BBC, where she worked as a transmission engineer. She enjoyed working on the night shift, as it enabled her to illustrate books by day. By this time, she was working for Evans Bros, publishers of popular children's books, illustrating stories about woodland animals for the very young. Titles included: *Belinda Bunny* by Deidre O'Brien (1944), *The Teddy Bear who Lost his Squeak* by Deidre O'Brien (1945), *Little Teddy Stories* by Margaret Rhodes and *Two Little Bunnikins* by Margaret Rhodes (1949). She also wrote and illustrated *The Kind Hearted Duckling* for the National Magazine Company.

In 1948, she married an army officer, Brigadier JH Nash and withdrew from commercial illustration. Nowadays, she prefers to concentrate on patchwork and batique, two pursuits at which she excels.

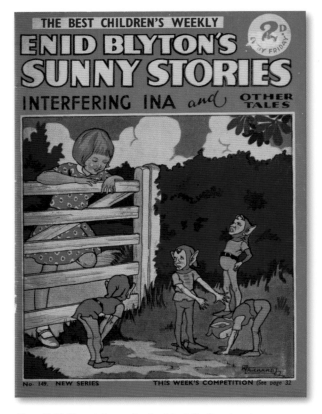

*Above:* Enid Blyton's Sunny Stories. No. 149. *Cover by Jennifer Rickard. [November 1939]. Below:* The Kind Hearted Duckling, *pub. National Magazine Co. [c.1946]*

*Artist: Jennifer Rickard*
*Pub: CW Faulkner.*
*Series 2010*
*[1931]*

Will it hold?

The Warrior Bold

The Dragon

Out of Reach

An Interrupted Tea

Caught

# Freda Mabel Rose (1909-1987)

*Freda Mabel Rose. [c.1940]*

Freda Mabel Rose painted an indelible picture of happy childhood, with the accent on the brighter side of life and hope of an optimistic future. Storm clouds are always way over the horizon. Those were the pictures she enjoyed – images that reflected her own desires. She loved simple pleasures and the knowledge that those around her were happy and being fairly treated.

Freda was born in Thornton Heath, south London and spent her childhood in Streatham with her parents, who were both school teachers, and her younger brother, Raymond. Within a secure home, she soon learned about caring for the needs of others – a feature of her personality that was always to the fore throughout her life, particularly in her vigorous campaigning for children and defenceless animals.

As a child, drawing and painting was her passion. She fitted out a studio in the house and persuaded her parents to allow her to attend art school in south London. She did not waste the opportunity and worked hard to make the most of her artistic talent. On leaving, she was rewarded with the offer of a job at the studio of Chad Valley in Birmingham. In the late twenties, the company was one of Britain's most successful manufacturers of children's toys. Freda joined a team of artists designing and illustrating toy boxes and games. This

experience gave her the chance to discover the value of bold design and bright, striking colours.

Her uncompromising and forthright personality made it difficult to come to terms with the constraints of employment. So, with some valuable experience under her belt, she left to make her own way in the world and to gain the independence, if not the security, she needed.

Before the war she was commissioned by a number of companies including toy makers Unity in Southport and William Walker in Otley, for whom she contributed to *Tip Top Annuals* for several years.

Her career as a postcard illustrator began at J Salmon of Sevenoaks in 1935. She designed and provided the captions for some delightful postcard series, including those depicting happy animal families, fairyland scenes and childlike quips in the style of Mabel Lucie Attwell. Her major influences seem to be Attwell, Donald McGill and Agnes Richardson, all very

*The family home, 50 Ellison Road, Streatham. [c.1915]*

popular illustrators of the day. Just before the war she began to work regularly for J Arthur Dixon, the Isle of Wight publisher, and became one of the company's most successful illustrators of postcards and booklets for young children. The Dixon catalogue for 1947 proudly presents her thus: *"Freda Baker, our artist has caught the trick of drawing happy looking children and these four designs are a fair example of the quality of her work."*

Captions from this Dixon series such as *"I'se going to bed to dream of you"* and *"There isn't a word (I've looked right frough) that says how much I'm in love with you,"* reflect Freda Mabel Rose's intense sense of care for people. These sentiments along with her deft drawing skills, colour sense and composition, captured effectively the hearts of the very young during the years before and after World War II.

An imperfect marriage in 1938 to Gordon Baker, an army officer, did not last, but provided her with two children. During the war times were hard for Freda, with little call for artwork. But she was nothing if not resourceful and took her children to the Sussex home of Sir Eric Miller, the theatrical impressario, where she worked as his cook and housekeeper. In 1948 the family moved to Costessey near Norwich and it was there, because of her love of animals, she brought up her two children in a home full of pets. In fact, whenever she heard of a sick animal or a

creature in need of care and attention, she would give it refuge. As her reputation spread, people would bring all manner of animals to her for shelter – cats, dogs, rabbits, goats, pigs, chickens, geese, ducks and budgerigars.

Freda was loved and respected locally, for her involvement with charities. She became a devoted supporter of Animal Rescue, Swan Rescue, the RSPCA, the NSPCC and the Children's Country Holiday Fund. She fostered children along with her own and even had time to carry out local *Meals On Wheels* duties to help the sick and elderly. She followed in her parents footsteps and became a supply teacher in schools around Norwich. She was a gifted pianist and violinist and used these talents to the benefit of the local community. A familiar personality locally and loved by many, some may have regarded her as eccentric and unconventional, but she played by her own rules to achieve her worthy objectives.

*Crochet Knitting Outfit, produced by Chad Valley Ltd. [1928]*

*Top row:*
*Artist: Freda Mabel Rose*
*Pub: Salmon*
*Series 4544*
*Nos. 4544/4548/4549*
*[3 of 6]*
*[1936]*

*Below left:*
*Artist: Freda Mabel Rose*
*Pub: Anon*
*Mabel Rose Series*
*No. 43*
*[c.1938]*

*Below centre:*
*Artist: Freda Mabel Rose*
*Pub: Anon*
*Mabel Rose Series*
*[c.1938]*

*Below right:*
*Artist: Freda Mabel Rose*
*Pub: Anon*
*Mabel Rose Series*
*[c.1938]*

FINKS I COULD GET MARRIED NOW.

WHEN I'SE GOOD NOBODY SEES
WHEN I'SE NAUGHTY EVERYONE'S LOOKING

WHAT WOULD THE MEN DO WIVOUT US?

# Harry Rountree (1878-1950)

*Harry Rountree sketching in* The Sloop. *[1948]*

Harry Rountree liked to tell everyone that he started his professional career in his native New Zealand as a lithographer and designer of jam jar labels. However, it is unlikely that label design commanded his attention for long and realising that opportunities for an aspiring young illustrator would be limited in his home country, he set off for England in 1901.

He was drawn to England partly on account of his interest in the work of Tom Browne, Dudley Hardy, John Hassall, Phil May and others members of the London Sketch Club. The story goes that on arrival in England the editor to whom he had been given an introduction advised him to invest his savings in a ticket home. Rowntree's although his work was good, the editer had other artists on his books whose work was better.

Harry decided to ignore the editor's advice and stay in London. Best known for his animal drawings, he claimed to have stumbled on the idea of drawing them quite by chance. He had never attempted drawing them in New Zealand, but did remember spending endless hours as a youngster watching animals and birds in the rural grasslands, trying to work out how they managed to communicate with one another.

He spent a great deal of time studying the originals of contemporary illustrators

and returning home to attempt to emulate them. Finally, he enrolled at a London art school and although he was not an inspired student he worked hard. He drew for the press in his spare time and hawked his work round editors hoping to sell his ideas – a process which left him with a large quantity of drawings on his hands.

Eventually and by chance he contacted SH Hamer, editor of *Little Folks* and together they devised a book dealing with funny animals and their antics. Harry discovered he had an aptitude for drawing these better than anything else and this encouraged him to put renewed energy into his work. He visited London Zoo regularly and studied his animal subjects with care and diligence.

In 1904 he joined the London Sketch Club, an organisation whose membership did so much to release commercial art from the strictures of the Victorians. Humour played a leading part in the club's philosophy so Rountree fitted in like a hand in a glove. By now he had earned a reputaton as one of London's most talented book illustrators. He had developed a unique brand of animal humour that is evident in his postcard illustrations for CW Faulkner, Vivian Mansell and the British Showcard and Poster Company. He did not resort to ribald caricatures like a

*Harry Rountree in his Bohemian Den. [1948]*

number of his contemporaries, nor did he attempt to humanise his animal subjects, but his deft observations and amusing quips were particularly effective on a medium that demands an instant reaction.

His fluent artistic style combined with his cheerful humour endeared him to young people, proven by his regular contributions to *Little Folks* for a period in excess of twenty years. Volume 94 of 1921 paid tribute to their most senior illustrator: *"Harry Rountree – A Little Folks veteran. You will see some of his queer animals in the section for Very Little Folks: his wonderful colours and quaint, frolicsome animals have brightened up the covers and the inside pages of our magazine for years and years. I have told him to carry on until the centenary."*

*Whist score card. Ogden's Robin cigarettes [nd]*

Playing golf was Harry Rountree's way of unwinding. He was a scratch player and found the game relaxing after hours crouching over the drawing board in his 'Bohemian Den'. When he retired to St Ives, Cornwall he spent many pleasant evenings in *The Sloop* sketching the locals and amusing them with his humorous stories. He died in St Ives, impecunious but happy.

*I may be wicked, but I am beautiful*

It's awfully cold here

The Weather is perfect

"MEASURE FOR MEASURE"

I am in a great hurry

I'm feeling a bit off color

RUNNING

# Hilda Dix Sandford (1875-1946)

*Hilda Dix Sandford at Hendon. [1923]*

Hilda Rose Dix was born in Bristol in 1875, the fifth of eight children, to William Chatterton Dix (1837-1898) and his wife Juliet. William worked as a clerk at the Post Office in Bristol and later as an insurance company manager. He was a devout churchman with a gift for hymn writing. He wrote popular hymns of the day, many of which appeared in *Hymns of Love and Joy* [1861] and *Altar Songs, Verses on the Holy Eucharist* [1878]. Many, like *As with Gladness Men of Old* are still popular today.

As a young girl, Hilda was encouraged in art. She enjoyed competitions and was successful in two of *The Studio* design competitions she entered. She won an Honourable Mention in 1895, aged 19, for a pen-and-ink drawing of a group of figures and later, in 1904 she was given a similar award for a nursery rhyme illustration entered under her married name, Hilda Sandford.

Hilda's father died in 1898, the year she married John Sandford, a mechanical engineer from Torrington in Devon. His father was known as *the Iron Master of Australia*, having established an important iron foundry and coal mine in Esbank, New South Wales. Shortly after the wedding, the couple spent three years with his parents in Australia. The journey, which took weeks by sea and rail, was an exciting adventure for Hilda, who had never been abroad before. After leaving the train at the railhead, the couple still had a considerable distance to travel by covered wagon drawn by bullocks, through the bush to their destination.

The journey through the outback left an indelible impression on Hilda and provided her with a bulging sketchbook, full of ideas for future projects. As they passed through small villages along the way, Hilda drew the happy and animated aboriginal children at play.

Piccaninnies, as black children were referred to in those days, were a highly popular theme amongst the British public. Worldwide travel was reserved only for the very few and people, many of whom had never seen a black child, were fascinated by these jolly children.

Hilda could hardly wait to return to England to start work on the sketches she had made. As soon as they arrived back in 1903, she approached Raphael Tuck and her ideas were well received. Tuck published many series of her popular *Happy Little Coons*, which sold in their thousands.

Boys and girls at play, black or white, was Hilda Dix Sandford's abiding theme, perhaps some compensation for having none of her own. Clever composition, deft interplay of rich colours and the ability to capture the telling nuances in childhood expression, give her pictures a great sense of movement and vitality. Her images of Santas and happy children at Christmastime rank with the very best.

She worked almost exclusively on postcards and greetings cards for Tuck from 1904 until 1910, while the craze was at its peak. She ended her career during World War I and moved to Sheffield where she and her husband lived through the nineteen twenties. They returned to Winscombe in the West Country, where she wrote, produced and acted in local amateur dramatics.

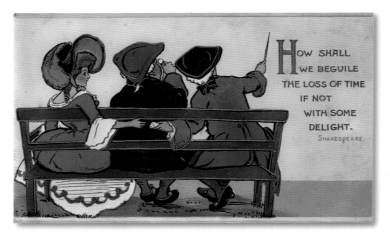

*Two folded greetings cards by Raphael Tuck. [1904/5]*

LEFT HAND PAGE

Below
Artist: Hilda Dix Sandford
Pub: Raphael Tuck
Oilette Series 9227
Happy Little Coons III
Packet
[1905]

RIGHT HAND PAGE

Above left:
Artist: Hilda Dix Sandford
Pub: Raphael Tuck
Art Series 6891
Happy Little Coons
[1 of 6]
[1904]

Centre left:
Artist: Hilda Dix Sandford
Pub: Raphael Tuck
Oilette Series 9102
Boys and Girls Come
Out To Play
[1 of 6]
[1905]

Below left:
Artist: Hilda Dix Sandford
Pub: Raphael Tuck
Oilette Series 9227
Happy Little Coons III
[1 of 6]
[1905]

Above right:
Artist: Hilda Dix Sandford
Pub: Raphael Tuck
Juvenile Series 6082
[1 of 6]
[1904]

Centre right:
Artist: Hilda Dix Sandford
Pub: Raphael Tuck
Oilette Series 9220
Girls and Boys
[1 of 6]
[1905]

Below right:
Artist: Hilda Dix Sandford
Pub: Raphael Tuck
Oilette Series 9220
Christmas 8247
[c.1906]

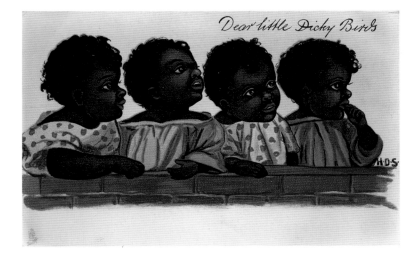

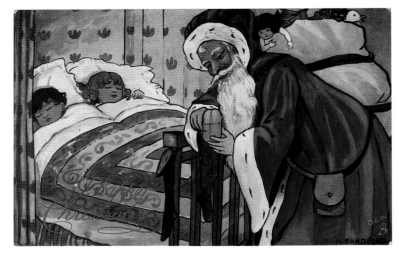

# CE Shand (1898-1979)

Cecily Elmslie Shand was born in Newcastle-on-Tyne in August 1898, the only girl in a family of four children. Her father, William, was an invalid and her mother, Marian, managed a small family hotel in Osborne Road. Other members of this close knit family lived nearby, including two artistic aunts – Christiana (known as Christine), her sister Helen who was a pianist and tutor and their brother Hinton, an engineer.

When Cecily was seven or eight years old, her uncle Hinton moved away from the area and her aunts Christine and Helen moved into her home. It was then that Cecily was introduced to painting and drawing.

Christine was an artist and art teacher of some stature and well connected in the art world. She was also a member of the Bewick Club, which was established in the 1880s by a group of northern artists to: *"promote a taste for Art, encourage contemporary Art, further the diffusion of artistic and aesthetic knowledge, to aid study and the advancement of Art in all its applications."*

Hall's *Artists of Northumberland* describes Christine thus: *"A landscape portrait and flower painter in oil and watercolour. Practised at Newcastle in the late 19th and early 20th centuries. She first appears to have exhibited her work at the"* Gateshead Fine Art & Industrial Exhibition, *"1883, showing a charcoal drawing: Landscape – Arran. In the following year she commenced exhibiting her work at the Bewick Club, Newcastle, showing two landscapes and two portraits, between that year (1884), and 1903, continuing to exhibit at the Club, and sending three works to the Royal Academy, three works to the Society of Women Artists' exhibitions, and various works to provincial exhibitions. She later exhibited her work exclusively at the Bewick Club, and from their inception in 1904, the Artists of the Northern Counties exhibitions at the Laing Art Gallery, Newcastle. She was a regular exhibitor at the latter until 1909."*

Cicely's aunts probably had a strong influence on her early life, having lived

*Cecily on her wedding day. [1917]*

close to her from the time of her birth. At the time they were living in Cecily's home, Christine was at the height of her career, exhibiting at the the Royal Academy, so art and drawing must have surrounded Cicely as a young girl. Art would have been a prime topic of conversation in the Shand household. Both aunts were teachers and by all accounts Christine was bossy and overbearing. In those circumstances, (and remembering the aspirations of the Bewick Club), it would have been unnatural if Christine had not encouraged Cicely to take an artistic path in life, if only to continue the family tradition in art.

Cecily's childhood was so stressful and frustrating, having to cope with an invalid father, a busy mother, teasing brothers and domineering aunts, that she seldom spoke to anybody about it in later life. She was educated privately in Newcastle and ended her studies in Paris while in her teens.

Cecily was only eighteen when she met her husband Cecil Sheppard, a naval officer twice her age. Although so young, she regarded marriage to Cecil as an opportunity to begin a new life.

During the early twenties, while he was away, she used to amuse herself drawing and painting delicately conceived figures in an attractive, modish style. Although she had no intention of making a career in art, she offered the paintings to The British Art Company, who accepted and published about sixty designs between 1922 and 1926.

The British Art Company was established just before WWI by a consortium of seven, mainly London based, art dealers, to *"carry on a business of fine art publishers and dealers, wholesale and retail dealers in works of art, prints and engravings, ancient and modern paintings, drawings etc., printers, stationers, colour process and halftone engravers, lithographers, photographic printers, etc."* Cecily may have been introduced to them by her aunt Christine. The company traded through the inter-war years and was wound up in 1939.

A few of her designs can be found on greetings cards for Scottish publishers Miller & Lang. These may have been sold on by the British Art Company.

Cecily was always uneasy and ambivalent about pursuing painting as a career. She had found a loving relationship and was determined to make a success of it. Cecil too, decided to resign from the Royal Navy, when confronted with the prospect of a two to three year tour of duty in the Far East. Instead the couple opened a private hotel at Westcliff, Bournemouth and enjoyed a happy life and successful business there until they retired in 1938.

She never mentioned her artistic endeavours to her family or friends, in the same way that she had been secretive about her early years. Perhaps she feared ridicule from her family, as she appeared to be less successful than Christine, or disapproval from her peers who still frowned on professional women artists.

*Artist: CE Shand*
*Pub: British Art Company*
*Unnumbered series*
*[c.1924]*

*Rival Suitors.*

*Sitting out.*

*His first proposal.*

*Fine Feathers.*

*Flowers of the East.*

*Winter.*

# May Smith (b.1904)

Winifred May Smith, precociously gifted, won a scholarship to Manchester High School for Girls in 1916. There, she benefitted from the influence of an inspiring art teacher, Hannah Ritchie, who had studied art at the Acadamie de la Grande Chaumière, Paris, with Frances Hopkins, later a member of the Newlyn Group. She was full of stimulating ideas and her teaching is said to have been 'in advance of it's time'. She read stories and poems that the girls could illustrate and opened their eyes to modern art, enabling them to look at the world from a new perspective. A year or two earlier, she had been an inspiration to Kathleen Hale (1899-1999), famous as the creator of *Orlando, the Marmalade Cat*.

May was born in Manchester, the only child of Sydney Smith, an engineer, and his wife Elizabeth. May remembers her mother as being 'very pretty', but she was also a firm disciplinarian. This might have had an

effect on shaping May's character, for she became an independent spirit and quite a bohemian. Her school reports reveal her excellence at art subjects and she showed determination to succeed as a designer and illustrator while still a young girl.

May's excellent grades in art resulted in a scholarship to Manchester School of Art in 1920, a college with a fine heritage in the applied arts, borne out of its association in the eighteen nineties with the Arts and Crafts movement. Many prominent people have been associated with the art school, including Walter Crane, LS Lowry and Sylvia Pankhurst, a former student and an inspiring beacon for any aspiring young female artist.

May chose to combine studies in fashion design and commercial art. She developed a drawing style of stark simplicity, influenced by a number of *Art Deco* illustrators of the day. She became a marvellous exponent in the use of black and white, bold colours and powerful patterns. Her strong sense of design and spatial awareness made her pictures look strikingly modern, at a time when many illustrators tended to over-sentimentalise their work. In 1924, she followed the footsteps of her former art teacher Hannah Ritchie and spent time in Paris before arriving in London, where she caught the

*May at Manchester High School for Girls, seated left. [1918]*

*Cover illustration for* The Man Who Caught the Wind, *Stories from the Children's Hour. [1936]*

eye of publishers thirsting for new ideas and modish styles.

Her early work includes greetings cards and postcards for The Medici Society and Valentines. She worked extensively for Humphrey Milford and contributed to many of their annuals for young children. She contributed to *Joy Street* for Blackwells, conceived a cartoon strip for the *Radio Times* called *Nat and Reg The Studio Hounds* and illustrated several books, perhaps the best of which was *The Man who Caught the Wind: Stories from the Children's Hour* by Margaret Gibbs and published by Chapman & Hall in 1936. In this book her full range of talents are on show, not least her ability

to devise striking and memorable patterns, so typical of the *Art Deco* movement.

In 1929, May married Maurice Bethell Jones, a colourful advertising agency copywriter, but continued to illustrate under her maiden name throughout the following decade. The couple lived in Skermet and in Turvil, Buckinghamshire, working tirelessly for the local Labour party, until the outbreak of war disrupted their lives. He joined the army and she enlisted in the WRNS, never to work as a professional illustrator again. They divorced in the late forties and May moved to a Puncknowle, a Dorset village close to the coast, where she has lived ever since.

*Above left to right:*
*Artist: May Smith*
*Pub: Valentine*
*Valentine's Fine Art Postcards*
*Nos. 3339 / 3341*
*[1939]*

*Centre left to right:*
*Artist: May Smith*
*Pub: The Medici Society*
*Packet 51*
*[nd]*

*Below left:*
*Artist: May Smith*
*Pub: The Medici Society*
*Packet 46/6321*
*[nd]*

*Below right:*
*Artist: May Smith*
*Pub: The Medici Society*
*Packet 45/6322*
*[nd]*

# Millicent Sowerby (1878-1967)

*Millicent Sowerby in 1918*

Amy Millicent Sowerby was born at Heathfield House, Ravenhill, Gateshead, the fourth child of a family of six. Millicent's father, John George Sowerby (1850-1914), a grandson of 18th century naturalist and illustrator James Sowerby, was a director of the Ellison Glassworks in Gateshead, the family business and the largest producer of pressed glass in the world during the 1880s.

Ravenhill was a large household, with relatives and business guests staying there regularly and a complement of maids, cooks, butlers and, of course, nurses to attend to the children – a theme that Millicent often returned to in her nursery pictures.

John Sowerby, a keen amateur oarsman, was a fine pressed glassware designer, able to produce vases and figures identical to authentic Venetian glass. He was also a gifted painter. In 1879 he began to exhibit his work at the Royal Academy, showing some twenty pictures in all. He exhibited at the Royal Scottish Academy, the Royal Institute of Painters in Watercolours and other leading galleries and was also interested in book illustration. One of his works entitled *At Home*, [1881], features a poem entitled *Millicent*, dedicated to his favourite little daughter.

After the death of his father in 1879, the family moved to Benwell Tower,

Newcastle and on John's retirement in 1894 due to ill health, moved out of the city to Chollerton in the Tyne Valley. Then a series of moves occurred – Slaggyford, Carlisle, then to Boxted House, Colchester in 1900, Reigate in 1903 and on to Sutton Courtenay in 1904. The move south provided members of the family easier access to London galleries and publishers.

Millicent began to show talent for drawing and painting at an early age. Encouraged by her father, she began to paint landscapes in watercolour, many of which she exhibited at the Bruton Gallery and the Royal Institute of Painters in Watercolours in London in the years immediately following the family's move south at the turn of the century.

Reminiscing in a letter to a friend, she wrote: *"I was painting from earliest childhood and was lucky finding help and encouragement at home. I attended art classes in Newcastle for a few years, but living some distance in the country, it meant only two days a week, but I worked hard at home."*

Millicent derived her style from artists and illustrators whose work she admired – particularly Thomas Crane, a close friend of her father and a keen follower of the Pre-Raphaelites and the Arts and Crafts movement.

Her early book and postcard illustration reflects a strong Arts and Crafts influence. Architectural detail and costumes in particular, clearly display the neo-gothic style. Her favoured subjects were children in Tudor or Elizabethan attire, set within the grounds of large Tudor houses. Neither can Kate Greenaway's influence be disguised. It is interesting to observe that the olden day costumes worn by Sowerby's children in her early designs, correspond with Greenaway's liking for similar outfits, harking back to a simpler, less stressful age.

Although her first love was flower and landscape painting in oil and watercolour, she turned to children's illustration to earn her living, but through her life retained an abiding passion for visiting galleries.

LEFT HAND PAGE

*Above:*
*Artist: Millicent Sowerby*
*Pub: CW Faulkner*
*Series 568E*
*Happy Childhood*
*[1 of 6]*
*[1906]*

*Centre:*
*Artist: Millicent Sowerby*
*Pub: Meissner & Buch*
*Series 1427*
*[1 of 4]*
*[1906]*

*Below left:*
*Artist: Millicent Sowerby*
*Pub: Misch & Co.*
*Series 834*
*In Greenaway Times*
*[1 of 4]*
*[1905]*

RIGHT HAND PAGE

*Millicent with elder sisters,*
*Helen (left) and Githa (centre)*
*at Chollerton, Northumberland.*
*[1894]*

*From Richard Brave-Heart by Alice Massie.* Mrs Strang's Annual for Children. *[1915]*

as a medium for illustration, as it allowed her to apply miniaturist's skills to this small format. Her first few series of designs for CW Faulkner, Misch & Co. and Meissner & Buch all had a distinct mediaeval flavour.

*Happy Childwood,* here first series for CW Faulkner, depicting Shakespearean scenes (series 568) attracted comment from the *Stationery Trades Journal: "One of the daintiest sets which has ever been published is that shown by CW Faulkner & Co this month, number 568 by M Sowerby are printed in chromolithography in tints and colours which remind us of the favourite Kate Greenaway colour schemes."*

Coincidentally, about the same time Misch & Co. published two more delightful series of postcards entitled *Greenaway Girls* and *In Greenaway Times.*

A major milestone in the careers of Millicent and Githa was their association in 1910 with the children's publishers Henry Frowde and Hodder & Stoughton, following a period of writing and illustrating for Chatto & Windus and JM Dent. They came to the publisher's attention when living at Abingdon, north Berkshire, through a link they had with printers Henry Stone of Banbury.

Her first book for Henry Frowde was *Little Stories for Little People* [1910] for which

LORDS · OF · THE · SEA ·
Anyone wanting to tackle our fleet?
Come if you dare, you will quickly retreat!
Ready and steady and merry are we,
Kings of the Castle and Lords of the Sea!

In another letter, she reflects: *"Being very fond of children, I turned naturally to painting them. It has always been the beautiful in life that has attracted me, not the humorous or grotesque. I love flowers and bright colours and I generally use these in the backgrounds of my paintings of children."*

In 1905, fifty years after *Alice's Adventures in Wonderland* was published, the copyright expired, enabling any artist to reinterpret the illustrations. Millicent Sowerby's version published by Chatto & Windus in 1907, containing colour plates, is believed to be the first post-Tenniel edition to be published.

Millicent and Katherine Githa (1877-1970), an older sister and an aspiring writer, joined forces. Although her own ambition was to become a novelist, Githa collaborated with Millicent at the start of their careers to create many enchanting children's books. Moreover, their father, a thoroughly congenial character, spent more than his fair share of the family's money on high living. Fortunately, the sisters managed to augment the family income in a successful partnership that continued for twenty years.

Millicent enjoyed painting miniature portraits and was attracted to the postcard

*Millicent with friends. [c.1900]*

A · FLIGHT · OF · ROSE-LEAVES
Oh, may your hours like rose-leaves take their flight,
All sweet, all beautiful, all calm and bright.

LEFT HAND PAGE

*Above:*
*Artist: Millicent Sowerby*
*Pub: Henry Frowde*
*Postcards for the Little Ones*
*Little Patriots*
*[1 of 6]*
*[1917]*

*Below:*
*Artist: Millicent Sowerby*
*Pub: Henry Frowde*
*Postcards for the Little Ones*
*Pleasant Days*
*[1 of 6]*
*[1915]*

RIGHT HAND PAGE

*Left hand column:*
*Artist: Millicent Sowerby*
*Pub: Henry Frowde*
*Postcards for the Little Ones*
*Playtime*
*[3 of 6]*
*[1917]*

*Right hand column:*
*Artist: Millicent Sowerby*
*Pub: Humphrey Milford*
*Postcards for the Little Ones*
*Sky Fairies*
*[3 of 6]*
*[1923]*

WITH·BAT·&·BALL
To bat before a wicket is always jolly fun,
Even if it isn't Cricket, but only tip-and-run!

WHEN FAIRIES HAVE A FROLIC AMONG FLOWER BEDS IN THE SKIES,—
THE SCATTERED PETALS FALL TO EARTH AND CHANGE TO BUTTERFLIES.

A TUG OF WAR
In Tug-of-War, I must confess, unless you're wondrous wise, you
Can never guess how it will end,—that always will surprise you!

WHEN MR. DUSTMAN SCATTERS DUST IN EVERY SLEEPY EYE—
THE TWILIGHT FAIRIES FETCH THE STARS, AND STICK THEM IN THE SKY.

SEE·SAW
Some folks play in meadows, some folks play in towns,—
But everyone plays See-saw, for life's all ups and downs!

ON APRIL DAYS I'D LIKE TO HAVE A FAIRY TELESCOPE—
TO SEE SKY FAIRIES SKIPPING WITH A RAINBOW FOR A ROPE.

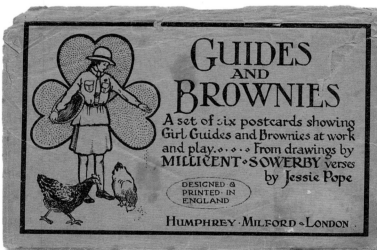

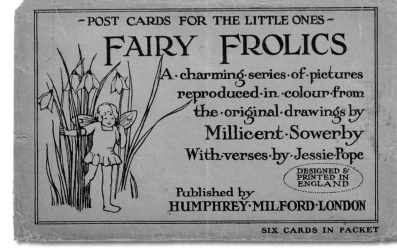

'PEACOCK' & CATERPILLAR

"DID EVER YOU SEE SUCH BEAUTIFUL THINGS
AS THE PEACOCK'S EYES ON MY VELVETY WINGS?
IF YOU WERE LIKE ME, I'M CERTAIN THAT YOU
WOULD BE 'VAIN AS A PEACOCK BUTTERFLY,' TOO!"

WEARING APRONS NEAT AND WHITE —
MAKING PASTRY FIRM AND LIGHT —
SOUP AND CAKES AND PUDDINGS, — LOOK
WE CAN SHOW YOU HOW TO COOK.

THIS CLEVER ELF KNOWS HOW TO BEND
THE FLOWER TOWARDS HIS THIRSTY FRIEND.
HE SCATTERS DROPS OF DEW TO DRINK.
ITS VERY KIND OF HIM, I THINK. —
J.P.

LITTLE · JACK · HORNER.
LITTLE · JACK · HORNER · SAT · IN · A · CORNER.
EATING · HIS · CHRISTMAS · PIE.

Githa and Millicent were paid £35 each.

Millicent was to become their leading illustrator of books for the very young. By now she was 33 years old and independent, with several years of commercial experience behind her. Gone were her Pre-Raphaelite leanings. Now she was developing her own unmistakable style, in keeping with a changing brief from her publishers.

By 1915 she earned £150 per annum from Henry Frowde, rising to £200 in 1920, £300 in 1921, when she reached her peak of popularity, then back to £250 by 1922. A short note to the publisher in 1921 to acknowledge a kindness, demonstrates her gentle, but underlying firmness rather well:
*"7 Queen Anne Street,*

*Dear Mr Le Strange,*

*Thank you so much for your letter. I am so glad to see you are raising my retaining fee to £300 per annum. I shall be very pleased to agree to this. Many thanks for suggesting my lunching with you to talk over matters: I should have been delighted, only just at present I do*

*Millicent (left) in a family group. [c.1925]*

*not feel quite up to it: I am so sorry. As an alternative, I wonder if you could possibly meet me at my sister's flat, 143 Colherne Court Mansions, S. Kensington. Perhaps you could come to tea here, or I could meet you there any time that would be most convenient to you. Wednesday is the only day I am engaged. Kind regards etc."*

Typical are her designs for the Milford series of *Postcards for the Little Ones,* where one observes happy little people in carefree mood dressed in the unchanging basics of children's fashions through the twenties and early thirties – sun hats, bar-shoes, sailor suits and smocked dresses. Hers was a simple style of painting, naturally appealing to the youngest readers. Her wholesome children with rosebud lips, full of jollity, sometimes mischievous but never vindictive, epitomised the children that doting aunts always imagine their nieces and nephews to be.

This postcard series began in wartime and enabled families separated during the war to keep in touch. So, it is not surprising that the early series illustrated by Millicent had a patriotic flavour. Titles, such as: *Sons of the Empire,* depicting courageous little boys in the uniforms of our allies, *Little Patriots,* showing womenfolk paying attention to the brave ones in uniform, *Little Folk of Many Lands*

and *Britain and her Friends* illustrating children of the allied nations. During wartime everyone was encouraged to contribute to the war effort. These early themes gave Millicent the opportunity to do so and take patriotism into the nursery in her inimitably gentle fashion. So popular were her postcards, many of them were reprinted again and again until the outbreak of World War II. Her illustrations for two series – *Pretty Wings* and the *Fairy Frolic Series* were combined and used as illustrations for the *Fairy Frolic Playbook* a board book for the very young.

Millicent Sowerby was small in stature and always considered frail, although seldom ill. In spite of her intense love of children, she never married. Towards the end of her life, known as Aunt Mill to her family, she continued to work happily in her attic studio in Bina Gardens, Chelsea. Her style set the tone for children's illustration in the twenties and she will be remembered as one of the best loved illustrators for young children of her day.

# Lorna Steele (1902-1990)

Lorna Ruth Steele was born in Muswell Hill, London and moved to Mill Hill while still a young child. Her father, Edgar, was a label maker, who worked with his father and later, his son, for the British Museum, labelling and registering treasures and artefacts as they were acquired.

Lorna's artistic flair came to the fore while she was a pupil at Highgate Girl's School, but it was her uncle Frank Jennens (1893-1957), an accomplished illustrator, who gave her the motivation she needed.

Frank was trained as a portrait painter at the Slade School of Fine Art, but turned to the Amalgamated Press for regular employment. For many years he drew black and white illustrations every week for the *Sunbeam* and *Tiny Tots*. He also contributed to a number of other popular books and annuals including: *The Joy Book Children's Annual*, 1923/1925, *Sunbeam Annual* 1933/1937/1938/1939, *Rainbow Annual* 1927/1928, *Bruin Boys Annual* 1928, *Tiny Tots* 1931, *Fun & Frolic Stories* and *Anytime Tales* for Bruce Publishing

and *Friendly Stories for the Very Young* for Hampstead Books 1957, his last book.

He lived in Leeds for a while where he worked as an actor. He appeared in productions at the *Little Theatre* and also appeared at the *Theatre Royal* Margate before World War II.

Lorna studied illustration at Hornsey School of Art between 1920 and 1923 and on leaving college, set up *The Fountain Studio* with her friend Clarissa Rose, at 7 Red Lion Square in Bloomsbury, London, close to many prominent publishers. Clarissa's mother acted as their representative and the contacts she made gave the girls many opportunities to get work.

The girls' commitment and positive attitude to their work, attracted the interest of many publishers, including the Epworth Press, Amalgamated Press and Evans Brothers for whom she mainly contributed stories and pictures for popular editions and children's annuals. In 1944 she wrote and illustrated *The Adventures of Andy and Ann* for Partridge.

One of her most successful associations was with J Salmon for whom she worked between 1944 and 1960. She illustrated greetings cards and postcards and wrote and designed charming children's stories for the very young. She also illustrated greetings cards for the *Society for the Promotion of*

*Frank Jennens. [c.1928]*

*Christian Knowledge*. She held a deep regard for the Church nurtured since childhood, for her father was a church organist and her mother Ruth was a deacon.

Such was her love of children, that shortly after leaving art school, she set up and supervised a drawing class for young people in her home neighbourhood. Sadly her own marriage to Philip Thomas, a Devonshire farmer and bee-keeper in 1943, was childless.

*Greetings card, pub. SPCK. [nd]*

The little people peeped out at Golly, and he wished he were at home, and he ran to hide—

The Three Little Elves jumped out of the flower-pot and played "Catch me if you can!"

*From* Three Little Elves, *published by J Salmon. [1944]*

*Left hand column:*
*Artist: Lorna Steele*
*Pub: J Salmon*
*Peeps at Pixies*
*Series 4964*
*Nos. 4964/4967*
*[1944]*

*Centre column:*
*Artist: Lorna Steele*
*Pub: J Salmon*
*Series 5012*
*Nos. 5012/5017*
*[1947]*

*Right hand column:*
*Artist: Lorna Steele*
*Pub: J Salmon*
*Series 5094*
*Nos. 5097/5099*
*[1949]*

# Margaret Winifred Tarrant (1888-1959)

*Margaret Tarrant in 1918, aged 29*

Margaret Winifred Tarrant was born in Battersea, the only child of artist Percy Tarrant. The Tarrants lived for a while in Margate and then in Clapham where Margaret attended the local high school. She started to train as an art teacher at Clapham School of Art, but soon realised she lacked the confidence to teach. So her father, himself a noted landscape artist and figure painter, guided her into his profession as an illustrator.

He was a successful magazine illustrator, and contributed to *The Illustrated London News,* Cassell's *Family Magazine* and the *Girls' Own Paper* and also greetings cards and books. As a child Margaret liked to play at 'art shows', pinning her drawings in an exhibition tent made from a clothes horse and inviting her parents in to view her work.

A year after the family had moved to Gomshall in Surrey in 1907, she received her first major commission – to illustrate a new edition of Charles Kingsley's *Water Babies* for JM Dent. Buoyed with success, she was soon inundated with work. In 1909, she illustrated a delightful series of six flower fairy postcards for CW Faulkner and a book entitled *Lucy-Mary, or the Cobweb Cloak* for Blackie, followed by four books for George Allen in 1910. The Faulkner flower fairies, series 923, were Margaret's

only commission from that publisher. The cards: *Dear Pansy, Fairy Blackberry, Lady Snapdragon, Little Snowdrop, Poppy* and *Sweet Clover,* were created when she was only twenty years old and predate her well-known flower fairies published by Medici and the famous *Flower Fairy Books* of her close friend Cicily Mary Barker by some fifteen years, yet may have provided the inspiration for them.

In the decade to follow she developed her illustrative talents, working extensively for Ward Lock and Harrap on many books. It was while working with Harrap that she began a fruitful working relationship with writer, Marion St John Webb. Margaret illustrated Mrs Webb's first book *The Littlest One* for Harrap in 1914 and went on to complete around twenty titles together – four for Harrap, two for The Medici Society and the rest for The Modern Art Society.

In 1920 she began a relationship with The Medici Society which was to continue for the whole of her working life. It came at a time when she had begun to take further courses of study at Heatherleys art school in London. Working for Medici gave her a wider variety of illustrative possibilities – books, calendars, prints and postcards – and gave her wide exposure.

*Marion St John Webb with whom Margaret enjoyed a working relationship into the late twenties.*

Her many religious paintings, fairy paintings and flower studies were all reproduced on postcards and were adored throughout the twenties and thirties.

It had been her deep sense of religion that had attracted her to The Medici Society and the opportunities she had there to apply her illustrative skills to the subjects she loved painting most of all.

*March Sunshine, greetings card 21, painted by Margaret Tarrant, published by The Medici Society. Inside she writes: 'The view from my Garden' at Troon, Gomshall Surrey. [nd]*

*Left top & bottom:*
*Artist: Margaret Tarrant*
*Pub: CW Faulkner*
*Series 923*
*[2 of 6]*
*[1909]*

*Centre top & bottom:*
*Artist: Margaret Tarrant*
*Pub: The Medici Society*
*The Fairies in our Garden*
*[2 of 6]*
*[1925]*

*Right top & bottom:*
*Artist: Margaret Tarrant*
*Pub: Harrap*
*From A Picture Birthday Book*
 *for Boys and Girls*
*[1915]*

Dear Pansy

THE LARKSPUR FAIRY

APRIL
The very rainbow showers
Have turned to blossoms
where they fell
And sown the earth with flowers

Lady Snapdragon

THE SNAPDRAGON FAIRIES

OCTOBER
Red leaves slip down from maples high
And touch my cheek as they flit by

*A hand drawn postcard sent to her friend Cicely Mary Barker at 23 The Waldrons by Margaret Tarrant in August 1942*

Her pictures of a child praying, of Christ or the Madonna, often surrounded by children or animals, reflected her own humility and simplicity, and were to be found in hundreds of nurseries, school rooms and children's corners in parish churches throughout the land. Her gnomes and fairies and animals in the role of children achieved, perhaps, an even greater popularity. Probably it was the painting of wild flowers and scenes in the Surrey countryside that gave her the greatest pleasure. For her, knapweed in flower or a bright red toadstool was a real joy and she took great pains to get the details correct in her pictures. She illustrated numerous children's stories, rhyme books and readers, her work being remembered for its soft colour and deft draughtsmanship.

While working on a series of pictures for a flower fairy alphabet, she chanced to meet Cicely Mary Barker who was working, quite independently, on designs for a similar theme. A life long friendship developed between the two women who shared a love of the countryside, a deep love of children and similar yet distinctive

artistic talents. As the two artists could be described as soul mates, it is not surprising that their choice of subject matter should correspond. Both have enjoyed tremendous popularity and are best known for their paintings of fairy scenes and flower fairies. As fairy artists they have flourished, while concentrating on the sentimental and gentle aspects of fairyland to please rather than frighten their young audiences.

It was when she moved to Peaslake, Surrey following the death of her parents in 1934, that Margaret Tarrant first met fellow Medici illustrator Molly Brett. They formed an enduring relationship which lasted many years. When poor health and failing eye sight forced her to leave her home in 1958, she joined Molly Brett in Cornwall until her death in in 1959.

*Greetings cards published by the Medici Society. Above: Gee Up! No. DO 2/2917 [nd] Below: The Little Lamb. No. T 6/3177 [nd]*

*Margaret Tarrant was a devout and committed Christian. The clarity and confidence displayed in her religious paintings, convinced many young people of the beauty and truth in following Christ. Her prints and pictures could be found in schools and Sunday schools up and down the country during the twenties and thirties. They provided solace and support for millions of people through the dark years of the depression.*

WINDFLOWERS
*by*
*Margaret W. Tarrant*

*Four corners to my bed, Four angels round my head, One to watch and two to pray, One to keep all fear away.*

*Left:*
*Greetings card*
*Artist: Margaret Tarrant*
*Pub: The Medici Society*
*No. T6/3669*
*[nd]*

*Below left:*
*Artist: Margaret Tarrant*
*Pub: The Medici Society*
*Packet 1*
*The Devotional Series*
*Windflowers*
*[nd]*

*Below right:*
*Artist: Margaret Tarrant*
*Pub: The Medici Society*
*The Old, Old Rhymes*
*Four Corners to my Bed*
*[nd]*

# Margaret Tempest (1892-1982)

Top:
*Artist: Margaret Tempest*
*Pub: The Medici Society*
*Packet 77/5132*
*The Hurdy Gurdy*
*[nd]*

Centre:
*Artist: Margaret Tempest*
*Pub: The Medici Society*
*Packet 52/6484*
*The Bicycle Ride*
*[nd]*

Bottom:
*Artist: Margaret Tempest*
*Pub: The Medici Society*
*Packet 86/6334*
*Gruel*
*[nd]*

Margaret Mary Tempest was born in Ipswich in 1892. As a girl she remembers spending most of her time lying on the floor drawing, while recovering from an illness that prevented her from remaining at school, so she enjoyed being educated at home with a friend. She loved reading the stories of Mrs Ewing and her favourite picture books were those illustrated by Kate Greenaway and Arthur Rackham.

Margaret enjoyed a privileged life in a fine home with two brothers. The family lived in a prosperous part of Ipswich and her father Charles was a pillar of local society, a stockbroker, Justice of the Peace and Mayor of Ipswich.

When she was 15 she started drawing classes at Ipswich Art School before going on to Heatherley's in Westminster and the Chelsea School of Art. In 1919 she joined a group of artist friends, including a Mrs Goode, from whom she drew a great deal of inspiration. They rented a studio in the loft of a barn of a Chelsea farmhouse and called themselves the *Chelsea Illustrators*. Margaret Tempest was the honorary secretary until it disbanded in 1939 at the outbreak of the war.

It was while she was taking the group's work round to publishers that Heinemann offered her the chance to illustrate Alison Uttley's first *Little Grey Rabbit* story. In *The Hare, the Squirrel and the Little Grey Rabbit*, Margaret Tempest first portrayed

the three animals and their friends with the charm and imaginative detail that has delighted children ever since. She was particularly concerned with the design of the books and it was her idea to surround the pictures with the coloured borders that make all the books so distinctive. Artist and author worked closely together. Margaret Tempest contributed to thirty four books in the series, for which sales have run into many millions.

Between 1919 and 1939, she lived in London during the week. As well as commissioned work, she taught drawing to a number of the aristocratic households of London, including the Elphinstones, cousins of the Queen. Most of her pupils led such a cloistered life that years later one of them told her that when she arrived for their lessons it was like a visit from Father Christmas! She loved to return to Ipswich at the weekends, in particular to the banks of the River Orwell, where she and her brother, both keen sailors, spent much of their time. She was a member of the Harwich Royal Yacht Club and the Ipswich Art Club for many years.

Although a few illustrations from the *Little Grey Rabbit* books were published as Christmas cards, they were never used on the postcards which have remained popular ever since The Medici Society started publishing them in 1936. Although the animal characters closely resemble the characters in the books, the designs for the books were specially created.

Margaret Tempest illustrated many books for children, some of which she wrote herself, including the tales of *Pinkie Mouse and the Curly Cobbler* books.

The writer of her obituary in *The Times* observed: *"The long-lived and productive artist's distinctive blend of nursery charm and cosiness made her work popular with several generations of children. She admired from childhood the illustrations of Kate Greenaway and Arthur Rackham, though her own pictures were more simple, with warm colours and clear lines that ensured their attraction for the very young".*

# GH Thompson (1853-1953)

*Portrait GH Thompson in 1910*

George Henry Thompson was born in Southampton of Irish parents on Christmas Eve 1853. George, his father, was a map engraver, who introduced his son to the printed image and encouraged him to become an artist.

As a yong man, George Henry became a painter of landscapes and seascapes, often chronicling his local neighbourhood. He studied painting in Belgium and on his return, one of his pictures, *Sunrise – The Arundel Tower, Southampton*, was accepted by the Royal Academy for the summer exhibition of 1885. It was typical of his paintings – an accurate and detailed rendering of a rural corner of Southampton. Two figures in the picture are positioned in the middle distance, almost as if he was keeping them at arms length.

Another picture, *Elling, near Southampton, Low Tide*, documents ships moored in the estuary, waiting for the tide to turn. Thompson successfully evokes a sense of stillness and rural tranquility in his pictures accentuated by relegating the figures in the picture to mere pinpricks in the distance,

suggesting either an unease with people or a lack of confidence in his ability to draw them.

In 1890 he married Lady Katherine Annesley, sister of the 7th Earl Annesley and they had a son Harold, who was killed on naval service in 1936. The Annesleys were an adventuring family, with a strong army tradition, who travelled and fought bravely in battles on many continents. Something of this spirit must have existed in Lady Katherine which may have attracted her future husband. For GH Thompson, (he never used his christian names professionally), the thought of buccaneering around the globe could have been a romantic dream, something quite new to him. Thompson loved the outdoor life and travelling. Even in his eighties, he travelled abroad to various parts of the world, including Belgium, Italy, Yugoslavia and Malta, where he spent two years. He enjoyed walks in the countryside or along the seashore, seeking inspiration and new scenes to paint.

Like Louis Wain, GH Thompson had an uncanny talent for expressing human characteristics through animals. With the use of subtle expression and innuendo he created the most hilarious of animal characters. He delighted giving the most grotesque creatures human characteristics. All the time one senses he enjoyed parodying people and had great fun lampooning his relatives and other folk he knew. In striking contrast to his empty landscapes, his highly colourful animal scenes are filled with movement and animal capers commanding attention. The accomplished serene landscape backgrounds to the pictures pass unnoticed or are obstructed by a babel of animal antics.

Using this extraordinary talent, he created his greatest success *The Animals,* a series of books published during Edwardian times by Ernest Nister, with narrative verses by Clifton Bingham (1853-1913).

Like Thompson, Clifton Bingham was Irish, the son of a bookseller. It is possible

RIGHT HAND PAGE

*Left hand column:*
*Artist: GH Thompson*
*Pub: Ernest Nister*
*Series 181*
*The Animals' Rebellion*
*[3 of 6]*
*[1905]*

*Right hand column:*
*Artist: GH Thompson*
*Pub: Ernest Nister*
*Nos. 320/330*
*[1902]*

Sunrise – The Arundel Tower, oil on canvas. *[1883]*

The Animals' Rebellion, *published by Ernest Nister. [1905]*

there was a family link between the two men through Thompson's marriage, as the Binghams and the Annesleys are two closely connected Irish families. Although Bingham worked extensively for Ernest Nister, his primary talent was that of a lyricist. He wrote the words to hundreds of songs, perhaps the most familiar being *Love's Old Sweet Song (Just a Song at Twilight)*. However, there's no doubt that Clifton Bingham and GH Thompson made a fine artist and writing team.

When the *Animals' Trip to Sea* was published by Ernest Nister in Britain and E Dutton in the United States, it was greeted by the public and critics with acclaim. This was the heyday of dressed animals; Victorians found them highly amusing; circuses and peepshows were all the rage and Louis Wain's cats were already very popular.

*"The most fascinating thing of the kind we ever saw"; "The cleverest thing we have seen for many moons in the shape of a picture book for children"; "Cannot fail to elicit shouts of laughter from the observing little ones"*. These press comments continued when *The Animals' Picnic* was published shortly afterwards: *"The illustrations should bring a smile to the most sedate countenance"*, and *"Absolutely brimming over with wit and humour"*.

In 1905 Ernest Nister followed up the success of the first three Animals books, *The Animals Trip to Sea, The Animals' Picnic* and *the Animals' Rebellion* by issuing the colour plates from the books in three equally popular series of six postcards (series 179-181 respectively). A further series of four postcards was published by TSN in France at the same time.

GH Thompson, 'Uncle Tompo' to his relatives, illustrated other equally hilarious animal postcards for Ernest Nister during the early nineteen hundreds, then after World War I little was heard of him. He lived in Hythe, Kent, for the last twenty four years of his life and died there one month short of his hundredth birthday.

# Mary Tourtel (1874-1948)

*Mary (right) and her family. [c.1895]*

Mary Caldwell was born in Canterbury in 1874 to Samuel Austen Caldwell and his wife Sarah. Her artistic leanings were fuelled by her father, a stone mason, who also designed and restored stained glass for Canterbury Cathedral. One of her brothers, Samuel, followed in his father's footsteps and continued to maintain the glass in the cathedral for fifty years. Mary's eldest brother Edmund, was a book illustrator and animal painter who exhibited at the Royal Academy.

Mary studied art at The Sidney Cooper School of Art in Canterbury from 1890, where she became an outstanding student under the tutelige of Thomas Sidney Cooper (1803-1902), a most accomplished painter of cattle. She won a National Bronze Medal in 1891, a National Book Prize in 1893 and a number of other major national awards, including The Rosa Bonheur prize and an Owen Jones Medal for tapestry competing with over 10,000 students. She continued her studies at the

Royal College of Art between 1897 and 1900, where she first met her husband, an aspiring poet who was searching for an artist to illustrate his poetry.

Mary won her first book commission in 1901 – *A Horse Book* (number 10 in the *Dumpy Books* series) published by Grant Richards, followed by *The Three Little Foxes* in 1903. Others commissions followed, but in 1904 she illustrated eight sets of six nursery rhyme postcards published by the Living Picture Company of Leicester –

the publisher's trade mark appearing on only three of the eight series envelopes. The series were as follows:

1 *Curly Locks/Jack & Jill*
2 *The Knave of Hearts*
3 *There was a Little Man/Ride a Cock Horse*
4 *Hey Diddle Diddle/Little Miss Muffit*
5 *Where are You Going to My Pretty Maid?*
6 *Little Bo-Peep*
7 *Sing a Song of Sixpence*
8 *Simple Simon*

*Left hand column:*
*Artist: Mary Tourtel*
*Pub: The Living Picture Co.*
*Nursery Rhymes*
*Series 1*
*Curly Locks/Jack & Jill*
*[Packet and 2 of 6]*
*[1904]*

*Right hand column:*
*Artist: Mary Tourtel*
*Pub: The Living Picture Co.*
*Nursery Rhymes*
*Series 2*
*The Knave of Hearts*
*[Packet and 2 of 6]*
*[1904]*

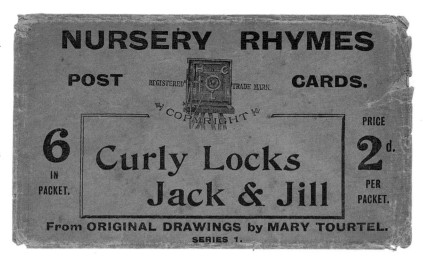

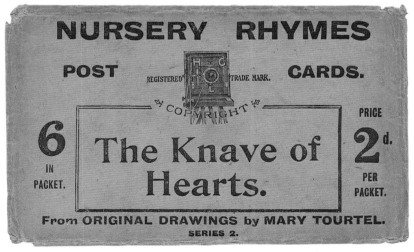

In 1920, Herbert Tourtel who was a senior executive at the *Daily Express* responded to editorial concerns about rival papers' success with children's cartoons. Mary, having built an artistic reputation had already contributed *In Bobtail Land* and *Animals at Work* to the paper the previous year, and she seemed to be the obvious choice, combining with Herbert who would provide the words.

And so the little bear in a yellow scarf, red sweater, check trousers and sturdy shoes appeared in the *Daily Express* on 8 November 1920. Unaware of his potential, the editorial team had launched the best known and best loved children's newspaper animal character that this country has ever produced and he and his chums are still as popular today as they ever were.

Rupert became a firm favourite and annuals and other Rupert merchandising followed, but curiously no Rupert

postcards were published in the UK before World War II. However, Rupert has always had a strong following in Holland and at least three series were published there during the nineteen thirties.

After her husband's death in 1931, Mary Tourtel's commitment to Rupert waned. She found it hard to continually meet the demanding deadlines and it was agreed to hand over the task of illustrating Rupert to a successor.

Alfred Bestall (1892-1986), the son of a Methodist minister, had studied art at Birmingham School of Art. It was Bestall who consolidated and enhanced Rupert's appeal over the next thirty years. *"I was always conscious of the responsibility I had when chronicling Rupert's adventures.*

*The thought of Rupert being in people's homes and in so many children's heads was a perpetual anxiety to me."*

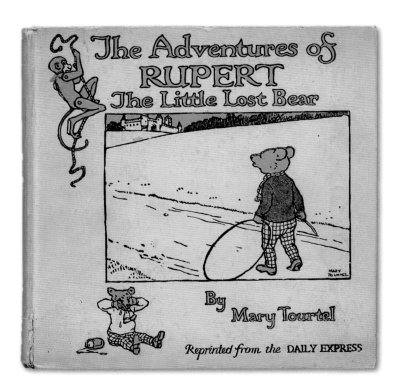

The Adventures of Rupert The Little Lost Bear, *published by Thomas Nelson. [Nov. 1921].*
*The first Rupert Book, a compilation of the first Rupert story to appear in the* Daily Express *in thirty six daily episodes from 8 November 1920.*

Bij het nijlpaard heeft Bruintje het wel naar de zin,
Een wandelende theepot schenkt thee voor hem in.

Als vader Snuit hun avonturen hoort,
Is hij op Fred en Bruin een oogenblik verstoord.

# Florence Upton (1873-1922)

LEFT HAND PAGE

*Above:*
*Artist: Mary Tourtel*
*Pub: Anon (Dutch)*
*No. 409*
*[c.1934]*

*Centre:*
*Artist: Mary Tourtel*
*Pub: NV Algemeen Handelsblad*
*Series 1 No.2*
*[c.1935]*

*Below:*
*Artist: Mary Tourtel*
*Pub: EH & Co*
*No. C5*
*[c.1934]*

RIGHT HAND PAGE

*Artist: Florence Upton*
*Pub: Raphael Tuck*
*Golliwogg Art Series*
*Series 1282*
*From* The Adventures
  of Two Dutch Dolls
  and a Golliwogg (1895)
*[3 of 6]*
*[1903]*

Born in New York of English parents, Florence Kate Upton grew up with two sisters and a brother. Her father was a sensitive artist who loved literature and her mother was a singer. They were not a rich family, but lived happily until her father died suddenly in 1889. His death forced her to leave school, but by that time Florence was already showing signs of considerable artistic talent. She loathed New York and longed to return to England. *"I miss the patina of age on London's buildings and need the influence of historical association."*

When Florence and her sisters were little girls, someone had given them a black doll to which they had grown very

*From* Pax and Carlino. *Pen and ink. [1894]*

attached. Wherever they went the doll went too – including trips to England, when they visited family members in Hampstead. Alas, the doll was left behind one year when they returned to America and eventually forgotten.

When Florence and her mother visited England in 1893, she was intent on earning money to help the family and assist with her brother Desmond's architectural training.

Six unremarkable watercolours in monochrome appeared in *Pax and Carlino*, from the *Children's Library* series, published by Unwin in 1894 – her first attempt at book illustration. Yet, she was determined to devise her own book for children and found some Dutch dolls to use as models. She started sketching them but found it impossible to create a good story without a central character. The whole idea could have fallen flat, but for her grandmother who rummaged around and found the forgotten doll from her childhood days. In an instant she had the hero she was looking for. Fascinated by its benign expression she hit on the name *Golliwogg*. Bertha, her mother, entered into the spirit of the romantic scheme and wrote the stories. The *Golliwogg* series was born.

When *The Adventures of Two Dutch Dolls and a Golliwogg* was published in 1895, the book became an instant success. The striking Golliwogg, in his blue jacket, red trousers and bow tie became a favourite character and over the next ten years a series of thirteen books ensued. Upton's robust style and full page colour plates provided a refreshing contrast from the precious, genteel Victorian books that preceded them. Sadly Florence, like many artists before and since, lacked business acumen and failed to patent her creation. Buoyed with the success of the *Golliwogg*, she tried to invent other characters, such as those in the *Vege-men's Revenge*, from 1897. This is the story of a girl gathering vegetables, who is captured and paraded in front of the King of the Vege-men and

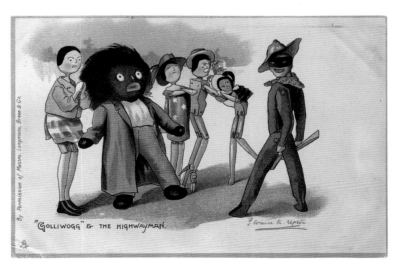

threatened with being boiled in a pot, only to wake up and discover it was all a dream. It was a poor and unsuccessful copy of *Alice in Wonderland* and Florence chose to continue with the series of the popular Golliwogg.

In 1903, Raphael Tuck issued the Golliwogg book illustrations as colourful folded greetings cards and picture postcards – around fifteen sets of six designs with blue, green, red/black or green/black borders. These cards were also issued with overprinted Christmas and New Year greetings.

Although she received royalties for her books, she never benefited from the toys or the quantities of nurseryware which were marketed on the back of the books' success.

In the early 1900's, Florence worked as a portrait painter in a Paris studio. She travelled widely and studied in Holland, later returning to London. During her career as a painter, she exhibited in

America, at the Royal Academy, the Salon de Paris and other continental exhibitions.

In an attempt to help the war effort during the World War I, she sent her collection of manuscripts to Christies for auction, along with the *Golliwogg* and Dutch dolls. The 450 guineas raised, paid for a Red Cross ambulance affectionately named *Golliwogg*. The purchaser presented the characters to the Prime Minister's country residence at Chequers where they resided in the Long Gallery for many years.

Although it had been her ambition to succeed as a portrait painter, Florence Upton's name will always be synonymous with the *Golliwogg* and for the fun and excitement he generated amongst children – a fact recorded on her gravestone in Hampstead Cemetery. However, *Golliwogg* didn't go uncriticised. A critic remarked *"I can't think why anything so hideous should fascinate children"*. But it did.

*From* The Vege-men's Revenge, *published by Longmans, Green & Co. [1897]*

*LEFT HAND PAGE*

*Above & centre:*
*Artist: Florence Upton*
*Pub: Raphael Tuck*
*Golliwogg Postcard Series*
*Series 6065*
*From* The Golliwogg's
  Bicycle Club *(1896)*
*[1904]*

*Below::*
*Artist: Florence Upton*
*Pub: Raphael Tuck*
*Golliwogg Postcard*
*Series 6065*
*From* The Golliwogg
  at the Seaside *(1898)*
*[1904]*

*RIGHT HAND PAGE*

*Left hand column:*
*Artist: Florence Upton*
*Pub: Raphael Tuck*
*Golliwogg Postcard*
*Series 6066*
*From* Golliwogg's Polar
  Adventures *(1900)*
*[3 of 6]*
*[1904]*

*Right hand column:*
*Artist: Florence Upton*
*Pub: Raphael Tuck*
*Golliwogg Postcard*
*Series 6067*
*From* The Golliwogg
  at the Seaside *(1898)*
*[3 of 6]*
*[1904]*

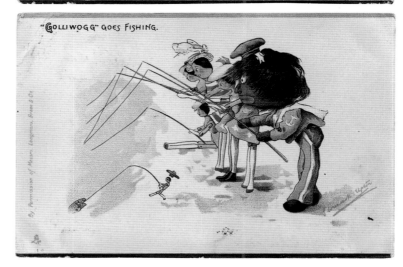

# Louis Wain (1860-1939)

Picture postcards were the ideal medium for the art of Louis Wain. His pictures were so strong, expressive and funny, they spoke for themselves, supporting words or stories were somehow superfluous. At the time Louis Wain was at his peak, millions of postcards were being sent daily – a fast and effective means of communication. What better than to send a Louis Wain postcard to a friend who needed cheering up.

Even from an early age, Wain was regarded as an eccentric. He was born in Clerkenwell, the eldest child of William Matthew Wain, a textile traveller and Felicia, a designer of carpets and church fabrics. He had five sisters. He suffered from vivid dreams and cocooned himself in a fantasy world. His schoolfellows regarded him as an outsider, obsessed by what was going on in his own intense private world.

Wain had a troubled youth. His father died when he was 17, thrusting him into the role of family breadwinner. His youngest sister suffered from the delusion that she had leprosy and that her teeth were falling out and eventually died in a lunatic asylum in 1913. His wife, ten years his senior, whom he loved dearly, was diagnosed with breast cancer soon after their marriage in 1882 and died in her early thirties.

Wain had always loved animals and at

first saw himself as an animal artist who painted any animal but cats, but when his dying wife persuaded the editor of the *Illustrated London News* to publish his drawings of Peter, the Wains' pet black and white cat, a new phase in Louis Wain's career began. Gradually, Wain's uncanny knack of giving cats human expressions and characteristics, was drawn from the depths of his childhood fantasies. As his confidence grew, his catty ideas became more extreme and funnier and his fame and popularity spread like wild fire.

He became a crusader for cats and was elected president of the *National Cat Club*, a position that provided him with plenty of opportunities to pontificate on behalf of cats and expound his own homespun theories about cat behaviour. His own words describe how cats were regarded before his pictures of feline antics caught the public's imagination: *"When I was young, no man would have dared acknowledge himself a cat enthusiast…the man who would take an interest in the cat movement was looked upon as effeminate – now even MPs can do so without danger of being laughed at."*

Louis Wain first worked for Raphael Tuck, perhaps his most important publishing outlet, from around 1900 and designed and illustrated some seventy series of postcards, along with painting books, annuals, story books and many other printed novelties, over a twenty year period. But as his popularity grew, just about every postcard publisher in the land seemed to be in need of his services.

Things went well for a while, but alas, his shy disposition and lack of business acumen eventually took its toll. He was exploited and denied the returns he should have gained from his extraordinary and unique talent. Soon there was a surfeit of Louis Wain drawings available, from which publishers drew, reusing his drawings again and again without paying him. New commissions waned with the onset of war and hard times were just around the corner. Opportunities to move into

LEFT HAND PAGE

*Left hand column:*
*Artist: Louis Wain*
*Pub: Raphael Tuck*
*Series 8123*
*Christmas Postcard*
*[2 of 6]*
*[1904]*

*Right hand column:*
*Artist: Louis Wain*
*Pub: Alphalsa*
*Series 895*
*[2 of 6]*
*[nd]*

RIGHT HAND PAGE

*Top row:*
*Artist: Louis Wain*
*Pub: CW Faulkner*
*Series 454A/F*
*[2 of 6]*
*[1904]*

*Bottom row:*
*Pub: Raphael Tuck*
*Series 8126*
*Christmas Postcard*
*[3 of 6]*
*[1904]*

The swing

I sent a letter to my love

THE "LOUIS WAIN" SERIES.

PUSS IN BOOTS.

*Christmas Greetings.*

THE "LOUIS WAIN" SERIES.

JACK THE GIANT-KILLER.

*A Merry Christmas to You.*

THE "LOUIS WAIN" SERIES.

JACK AND JILL.

*Christmas Greetings.*

animated cartoon films became an exciting option, but he was intimidated by the thought of having to master the new technology.

His sister Caroline had made most of the family decisions after their mother died in 1910. Her death in 1917 through influenza, had a profound effect on him.

He became suspicious of everyone around him, triggering schizophrenia, which led to his committal to Springfield Hospital in Tooting.

During the later stages of his career, Wain produced a series of 'schizophrenic' cats. He experimented with vivid abstract patterning, often rendering his cats almost

unrecognisable. It was as if strong electric currents were running through the cats' fur – a theory he had espoused years earlier in connection with cats being able to travel long distances back to their home.

This is a phase of his work which is a refreshing and exciting departure from what was by comparison, his more

subjective renderings of animal fun and antics, so familiar to us on his postcards. His popular style had by then attracted many imitators, but his abstract cats, whether inspired by schizophrenia or not, demonstrate a lifetime's in-depth devotion to the creatures he loved, that no other animal artist has transcended.

# Ellen Welby (1851-1936)

*Ellen Welby in the 1920's*

Ellen Ann Welby and her sister Rose Ethel (1855-1948) were two of nine children born to William, High Baliff to the County Court of Canterbury and his wife Anne. The sisters shared their father's passion for the arts and his friendship with Sidney Cooper, the animal painter, from whom they may have received tuition.

Ellen became an accomplished painter in oils and watercolours and is described as a 'painter of genre and flower subjects'. She was also an accomplished painter of ceramics, for which she won a gold medal in an international competition in 1886.

The sisters moved to London and lived at various addresses in the West End until their father's death in 1903. They exhibited pictures between 1883 and 1925, at leading galleries including the Royal Academy and the Royal Institute and were members of the Society of Women Artists.

In 1888, Ellen joined the staff of Raphael Tuck's *London Studios* as an artist and illustrated greetings cards, postcards and books, including titles: *By the Light of the Nursery Lamp* and *Told by the Waterlilies.* She also contributed illustrations to many other Tuck books including *Her One Ambition* and *Little Nightcaps.* As with the work of many of her contemporaries, it is not unusual to find her pictures reproduced in books as well as on postcards.

# Dorothy Wheeler (1891-1966)

*LEFT HAND PAGE*

*Left hand column:*
*Artist: Ellen Welby*
*Pub: Raphael Tuck*
*Series 124*
*Happy Childhood*
*[2 of 6]*
*[1901]*

*Right hand column:*
*Artist: Ellen Welby*
*Pub: Raphael Tuck*
*Series 99*
*Birds and Blossoms*
*[3 of 6]*
*[1901]*

*Dorothy Wheeler in 1948.*

Dorothy Marion Wheeler was born in Plumstead, Kent in August 1891 to Harry, a bank clerk and his wife Bertha. Dorothy's generation were artistic. Her sister Millicent studied at the Slade School of Fine Art and her cousin Charles was President of the Australian Royal Academy.

In 1910, as a student at the Blackheath School of Art, south London, she won a Commendation in the Board of Education National Competition for book illustration and another for colour prints.

Dorothy became a fine watercolourist – a landscape and figure painter and an illustrator of children's books. She exhibited regularly at the Royal Academy and the Society of Women Artists.

Shortly after leaving art school, she joined The Carlton Studio in London as a general artist. It was from here that she illustrated her first and most enduring book, *English Nursery Rhymes*, with music, published by A&C Black in 1916. It was a classic of its kind. The book contains thirty exquisite illustrations of traditional rhymes painted in a timeless style and proved to be so popular that it was reprinted three times in five years. *The Bookman* is generous in its praise for her work: *"...beautiful and appropriate illustrations. For colour and design these pictures are delightful – each one so perfect that one wants to take it out and frame it..."*

In 1926 A&C Black reproduced a selection of the illustrations as five sets of six cards in their *Black's Beautiful Postcards* series. Series 43 *English Nursery Rhymes* was reproduced without music; series 44, 44a, 45 and 45a were reproduced with music at the foot of each card. These remained in print

*Humpty Dumpty, from* English Nursery Rhymes

*Pussy cat, pussy cat, from* English Nursery Rhymes

for many years. She illustrated a few series for other publishers, including *Woodland Secrets* and *Fairy Secrets* for Bamforth (c.1938), *A Day at the Fair* and *Snow Babies* for Humphrey Milford (1930) and one series for J Salmon of Sevenoaks (1938).

Dorothy Wheeler illustrated many of the Enid Blyton stories, including the memorable *Josie, Click and Bun* that appeared in *Enid Blyton's Sunny Stories* for many years.

Sadly, she never maintained her early promise, although her illustrations remained popular with young children. Her work, became stylised and took on an appearance of almost geometric simplicity, in fact she based a lot of her work on the patterns seen in soap bubbles and designed a special machine to make the bubbles for her to study in detail.

She specialised in the comic strip format, with frame-by-frame pictures, accompanied by text. Like many of her peers working as full-time illustrators, she worked tirelessly on magazines and books at the popular end of the market, producing black & white text illustrations for forgettable titles.

Dorothy never married. She lived in Esher, Surrey during the nineteen twenties and in Lee, south London, in the thirties before moving to Newton Abbot, Devon where she spent the remainder of her life with her cousin Edith Wheeler, the headmistress of a local girls' grammer school. Both ladies played an active role in the Newton Abbot Repertory Company, Dorothy acting as wardrobe mistress.

Right up until the end she continued to do drawings for a *News Chronicle* cartoon strip and in their obituary notice in March 1966, *The Mid Devon Advertiser* remembered her: *"...Being by nature a very quiet and retiring person it may not have been fully realised the amount of work and care that Dorothy Wheeler gave to keeping the wardrobe and properties in immaculate condition....Miss Wheeler was also a talented and charming book illustrator and commercial artist. She was responsible for illustrating many children's books including early Enid Blyton. The Rep has also benefitted from theatrical productions of many kinds, fitted out with care, thought and competence by the wardrobe mistress,* [Dorothy] *the hiring fees adding to the company's finances. This gentle unassuming member of the Rep will be greatly missed and very hard to replace."*

*Frieze from the endpapers of* English Nursery Rhymes [1916]

WOODLAND FRIENDS.  Dorothy Wheeler.

THE DRAGON-FLY.  Dorothy Wheeler.

Birthday Remembrance.

THE DUET.  Dorothy Wheeler.

THE PICNIC.  Dorothy Wheeler.

Here is a bit of news for you about a new
Enid Blyton book.
The stories and pictures of TUMPY and his
marvellous CARAVAN are being put into a
lovely book; so look out for it in November. It
is called MR. TUMPY AND HIS CARAVAN
and is published by Sidgwick & Jackson. Price
5/-. You can get it from any bookshop.

# Flora White (1878-1953)

Jabez White was a wood carver. He lived with his wife and family. at 70 West Street, Brighton from where they ran the family business. The property is to be demolished, but if you look skywards you will see a sign set into the concrete rendering of the building: *White's Library & Carving Works.*

*70 West Street, Brighton. [1999]*

Jabez had run his stationers and wood carving shop from the West Street premises since 1860. Prior to that his mother had carried out her millinery business from that address. By 1870, the shop was ideally situated, amongst hotels and restaurants, to sell souvenirs to the growing tourist trade that Brighton was attracting.

It was in Florence, Italy, where Jabez met Adèle Naldini, his wife to be, while studying wood carving. They married and returned to look after the stationers shop and start a family.

Jabez was so fascinated by Greek mythology, that he named all of his five daughters after Greek goddesses – Hebe Minerva, Flora Juno, Zoë Diana, Adelina Ios, and Effe Rosina.

All the girls were interesting, artistic, well spoken, well read and they all had individual characteristics. Their proud father took a keen interest in their development and used to coach them and take them for walks around Brighton and up onto the Sussex Downs.

Hebe the eldest daughter helped her father in the shop and was, by all accounts, the best educated. She became a historian

and writer and was at the forefront of the suffragette movement, co-ordinating the organisation's activities around the world.

Effe was captivated by the stage. She married an actor, Edgar K Bruce and played small parts in theatrical productions, using the stage name Rosina Hicks.

Flora was regarded as the odd member of the family. A bohemian by nature, she dressed unconventionally and did things that young ladies of the day weren't supposed to do. She was different to the other girls – she expressed herself through pictures rather than words and when she was twenty attended painting classes at Brighton School of Art.

After her father died in 1901, her mother remarried a much younger Italian man, who lived in England, but he died soon after the marriage. It was left to the women in the family to keep the shop running and it was when the shop was finally disposed of in 1915 that Flora was able to embark on her career as a commercial artist

During World War I, Flora was in love with a soldier who, we believe may have been killed. She never saw him again and this left a tragic mark on her for the rest of her life. Nobody knows if this is why she cut herself off, but she withdrew to Burgess Hill, Sussex and had little contact with the rest of her family thereafter.

Postcard illustration was frowned upon in certain quarters of the artistic fraternity in those days – book illustration was the thing to do. Perhaps this is another of those contrary facets to Flora White's nature. She explained why she enjoyed postcard illustration: *"I work very quickly, I have a great deal of freedom of choice in my subject matter, complete the artwork and receive payment. There's too much fuss with books."* Flora illustrated very few books, the most notable of which was *Peter Pan's ABC*, published by Henry Frowde and Hodder & Stoughton in 1916.

Flora's earliest postcards were for E Mack around 1916, whose relationship

*Dean's Catalogue for 1929. [1928]*

*Flora White at Hastings. [1939]*

with publishers J Salmon of Sevenoaks was close. Soon, her card designs were to be published by Salmon, for whom she worked on a continuous basis until 1935. Her busiest years were between 1917 and 1920, when she was producing an average of seven sets a year for Salmon alone. She also illustrated a considerable number of postcards for Photochrom during the same period. She loved to illustrate the popular nursery themes – nursery rhymes and tales, (Salmon published her rhymes and tales in booklet form also), fairyland, games, patriotic, Christmastime and many more.

JACK and Jill went up the hill
To fetch a pail of water ;
Jack fell down and broke his crown,
And Jill came tumbling after.

LITTLE TOM TUCKER.

Little Tom Tucker, | How shall he cut it,
Sang for his supper ; | Without e'er a knife?
What shall he eat ? | How shall he marry
White bread and butter. | Without e'er a wife?

DICK·WHITTINGTON·

SIMPLE Simon met a pie-man,
Going to the fair ;
Said Simple Simon to the pie-man,
" Let me taste your ware."

TOM·TOM·THE·PIPERS·SON.

Tom, Tom, the piper's son, ——
Learned to play when he was young,
But all the tunes that he could play
Was " Over the hills and far away.

FROG : PRINCE

*Left hand column:*
*Artist: Flora White*
*Pub: J Salmon*
*Series 1844*
*Nos. 1847/1849*
*[2 of 6]*
*[1920]*

*Centre column:*
*Artist: Flora White*
*Pub: J Salmon*
*Series 1317*
*Nos. 1317/1318*
*[2 of 6]*
*[1917]*

*Right hand column:*
*Artist: Flora White*
*Pub: J Salmon*
*Series 1467*
*Nos. 1467/1468*
*[2 of 6]*
*[1919]*

*Left hand column:*
*Artist: Flora White*
*Pub: Photochrom*
*Celesque Series*
*Nos. 1534/1535*
*[2 of 6]*
*[c.1922]*

*Centre column:*
*Artist: Flora White*
*Pub: J Salmon*
*Series 1202*
*Nos. 1204/1213*
*[2 of 12]*
*[1917]*

*Above right:*
*Artist: Flora White*
*Pub: J Salmon*
*Series 4339*
*Nos. 4342*
*[1 of 6]*
*[1933]*

*Below right:*
*Artist: Flora White*
*Pub: J Salmon*
*Series 3332*
*Nos. 3337*
*[1 of 6]*
*[1928]*

A SONG OF THE SEA.

# Henriette Willebeek le Mair (1889-1966)

*Henriette Willebeek le Mair. [c.1930]*

Born in Rotterdam, Henriette Willebeek le Mair was the daughter of a wealthy corn merchant, whose hobbies included travel, collecting art and sketching. At home Henriette lived in a pervading atmosphere of culture and refinement. Her childhood days were spent in a well appointed nursery amid surroundings from which inspired her to create motifs for the interiors and scenes in her own illustrations.

Her first book, illustrated when she was only fifteen, entitled *Premières Rondes Enfantines*, was published in France by Sandoz, Jobin et Cie. At the same time a German version was published entitled *Für Unsere Kleinen*. At that time she was greatly in awe of the French illustrator Henri Boutet de Monvel and she was keen to take lessons from him. But when they met he advised against it, suggesting that she should develop her own style of drawing.

In her early twenties, she ran a school for about a dozen young pupils whom she taught at her home. This experience doubtless provided material for the closely observed and precisely drawn graceful little figures which she portrayed later on in her career. It is said that she would soak the children with water, making their clothes cling to their bodies so that she could observe their form more accurately. She was fastidious to a fault with her drawing. She would carry out countless sketches before her pictures were finally executed. In her composition *Oranges and Lemons*, she went to great lengths to ensure that the background – a London skyline – was correct in every detail.

By 1911, Willy Strecker, managing director of the music publisher Augener in London, had recognised her talent. He was attracted by three features of her work:

first, the design and composition of her drawings and the feeling she had for borders and decoration; second, the exquisite quality of her line which, for all its extreme delicacy, never betrays a hint of uncertainty, and third, the wonderful portrayal of carefree children immersed in a world of toys and make believe.

Strecker commissioned her to illustrate a series of nursery books created over a six year period from 1911 to 1917. These were to be the cream of her career:

1. Our Old Nursery Rhymes [1911]
2. Little Songs of Long Ago [1912]
3. Schumann Album of Children's Pieces [1913]
4. The Children's Corner [1914]
5. Little People [1915]
6. Old Dutch Nursery Rhymes [1917]

Items 1, 2, 3, 4, and 6 were published with rhymes set to music.

The sixth of the titles, Old Dutch Nursery Rhymes of 1917, was perhaps her pièce de resistance. Nothing she attempted afterwards captured the quality and originality of this wonderful volume.

The press preview enthused over the quality of the illustrations, in particular: "The Marionettes shows her exquisite sense of design. The directional pull of the lines in the striped curtains, chequered floor and puppet strings is a perfect balance, with the pure colour highlighting the symmetry and grace of the composition."

Alongside these books, in 1913, Augener issued a series of four postcard size Little Rhyme Books along with nine sets of postcards, thus utilising the same colour printing blocks for both. Each rhyme book contained twelve rhymes and pictures. When Old Dutch Nursery Rhymes was published in 1917, two more rhyme books were added, making six in all, each containing ten rhymes and pictures. Two further series of postcards were also issued, Old Dutch Nursery Rhymes and English and Dutch Rhymes. The first four series of postcards were issued in 1913, the first printings of which include a copyright clause up the right hand side of the face of the card. Postcards from series 1 to 9, with a reference to 'David McKay, Philadelphia' on the reverse are not first printings as an association was not formed with that firm until 1917.

Marriage in 1920 to Baron van Tuyll van Serooskerken brought a profound change in Henriette's life. Her husband was a Sufi and she joined the movement soon after their marriage, taking the Sufi name Saida. She became more and more involved in eastern cultures and religions and travelled abroad with her husband. Only three books of note were published during her lifetime after 1920: A Gallery of Children (1925), A Child's Garden of Verses (1926) and Jataka Tales (1939).

Oranges and Lemons.

The North Wind doth blow.

| Willibeek Children's Postcards. 11 sets of 12 postcards | |
|---|---|
| Postcard series title | Book titles from which postcard series are drawn |
| 1  Our Old Nursery Rhymes | Our Old Nursery Rhymes |
| 2  Little Songs of Long Ago | Little Songs of Long Ago |
| 3  Old Rhymes with New Pictures | Our Old Nursery Rhymes |
| 4  Small Rhymes for Small People | Little Songs of Long Ago |
| 5  More Old Nursery Rhymes | Our Old Nursery Rhymes / Little Songs of Long Ago |
| 6  The Children's Corner | The Children's Corner |
| 7  Children's Pieces of Schumann | Schumann Album of Children's Pieces for Piano |
| 8  Games and Pastimes | The Little Rhyme Books / The Children's Corner  Little People / Little Songs of Long Ago |
| 9  Little People | Little People |
| 10  Old Dutch Nursery Rhymes | Old Dutch Nursery Rhymes |
| 11  English and Dutch Rhymes | Little Songs of Long Ago / Old Dutch Nursery Rhymes,  Little People / Baby's Diary |

The merry peasant.          Fröhlicher Landmann.

N. Willebeek Le Mair.                    Johnny's breakfast.

H. Willebeek Le Mair.                    Poor Baby.

H. Willebeek Le Mair.          De marionetten. — The Marionettes.

Henriette had made contact with an American named Mildred Massey, during the early twenties and through her, won a lucrative contract to create a series of advertisements for Colgate Fab baby soap. The ads ran in a number of ladies' fashion magazines in 1923, but proved to be unsuccessful and the campaign was 'pulled' before completion. However, publishers Stanley Paul, were so impressed by the quality of the twelve images, that they took the unusual step of commissioning AA Milne to write the book, *A Gallery of Children*, around these pictures.

When her husband became the national representative for the Sufi movement in the Netherlands, her artwork changed in style and character, focusing on eastern cultures and religions. During the nineteen thirties she produced material for two books – *The Flower Garden of Inayat Khan* and *Birth Stories of the Prophets,* neither of which were published until 1978.

Throughout her life, Henriette enjoyed the material advantages of a fine home and a wealthy family, but she always worked extremely hard and made the most of her many talents. She was a keen sportswoman, a linguist and a gifted musician who was especially fond of dancing. In later life she became devoted to religion and helping the poor. Her contribution to children's illustration was amongst the most poignant

and delicate of the twentieth century. Indeed, Arthur Reddie, a correspondent, writing about Henriette in the 15 August issue of *The Studio* said of her: "*Since the days of Kate Greenaway, I know of no one who has caught the pure spirit of childhood as Miss le Mair.*"

ASSELT (L.) KINDERKAPEL. SCHILDERINGEN VAN MEJ. H. WILLEBEEK LE MAIR.
Foto Mathieu Koch, Roermond.

# Madge Williams (1902-1986)

LEFT HAND PAGE

*Above left:*
*Artist: Henriette Willebeek le Mair*
*Pub: Augener*
*The Children's Corner*
*(book published 1914)*
*Series 6*
*[1 of 12]*
*[c.1915]*

*Centre left:*
*Artist: Henriette Willebeek le Mair*
*Pub: Augener*
*Little People*
*(book published 1915)*
*Series 9*
*[1 of 12]*
*[c.1915]*

*Below left:*
*Artist: Henriette Willebeek le Mair*
*Pub: Augener*
*Old Dutch Nursery Rhymes*
*(book published 1917)*
*Series 10*
*[1 of 12]*
*[c.1920]*

*Above right:*
*Artist: Henriette Willebeek le Mair*
*Pub: Anon*
*Series: Voor het Kind*
*[1936]*
*This is a reproduction of a*
*design that first appeared in the*
*December 1925 issue of* The
Ladies Home Journal

*Below right:*
*The children's chapel at Asselt,*
*Netherlands showing a mural by*
*Henriette Willebeek le Mair*
*[1 of 6]*
*[c.1935]*

Before moving to Holton Rectory, near Halesworth in Suffolk, David Williams and his wife Marjorie, an aunt of TV actor Hugh Moxey, had lived in Bristol where Madge and her sister Barbara were born. Madge and Barbara were both encouraged in the arts. Barbara played the piano while Madge, who always had a natural talent for drawing and painting and loved fashion drawing, attended art school in London.

On leaving college Madge settled into a career as a commercial artist. She found opportunities to contribute to a few children's annuals, but became a prolific illustrator of children's postcards which provided her main source of income.

She combined her love of children with her ready wit and creative imagination to bring innocent fun and enjoyment to the nurseries of the twenties, thirties and beyond, with her scenes from fairyland and kiddies at play.

Madge first approached J Salmon in 1926 and worked with them on a regular basis until 1956, having designed around forty postcard series and greetings cards. Her designs were also published by the Art & Humour Company, ETW Dennis, Inter Art and Raphael Tuck, for whom she illustrated cards in the *Pinch & Squeak Series* and the post-World War II *Madge Williams Fairy Series*. She was popular because her illustrations depicted happy childhood.

*Above: Holton Rectory. Below left: Madge in 1927. Below right: Madge and Barbara [c.1922]*

To Greet Your Birthday.

I know something and I'll tell:
If you will promise true:
To love me on Your Birthday,
As you know that I love you!

Dignity
and
Impudence

"PLEASE, 'JU KNOW ANYBODY WHO'S LOST
A BOY AN' A DOG?"

'A FALSE ALARM.

There's plenty of excitement
at St. Leonards-on-Sea.

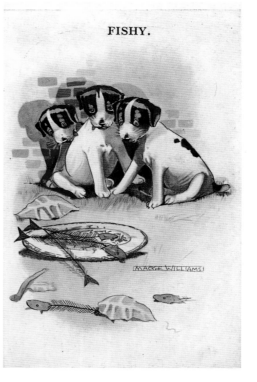

FISHY.

HERE WE ARE—ENJOYING OURSELVES !

"JUS' STEALING A MOMENT TO SEND THIS CARD."

WISH YOU WERE COMING TOO !

"IF EVER A MAN SUFFERED."

WE'RE OFF FOR OUR HOLIDAYS !

"BEWARE OF PICK-PACKETS!"

# Alan Wright (1864-1959)

As a boy, Alan Wright was surrounded by books. His father William was a publisher, printer and bookseller, in the High Street, Newmarket. By the time Alan reached his teens, his eldest brother Arthur, heir to the family business, was already working with his father. Alan, the third of five children, three boys and two girls, was sent at the age of twelve to Trent College, a boarding school in Long Eaton, near Nottingham. The school, which was founded for the benefit of 'lower middle class tradespeople', housed about one hundred boys from all parts of the country and a few from overseas. In later years, Alan spoke little of his school days, but shared vivid memories of spending many of his summer holidays with friends, quite possibly school friends, in Dorset's Blackdown Hills. His love of the countryside and keen observation in this remote rural setting would prove to be the key to his future – his love of nature and animals living in the wild.

On leaving school in 1882, Alan found lodgings in Hamilton Gardens, London NW and enrolled at the St John's Wood School of Art to improve his drawing and painting skills. On completion of the three year course, he began to look for work as a freelance magazine and newspaper illustrator. During this period he met and befriended Gleeson White, who was to

*From* The Wallypug Birthday Book. *[1904]*

*I Saw a Ship from* Buttercups and Daisies, *published by Henry Frowde and Hodder & Stoughton. [c.1909]*

become the first editor of *The Studio* magazine in 1895 and author of notable books and articles on design. They became good friends and shared accommodation in Sterndale Road, Ealing in the late eighteen eighties. They also shared the same dry sense of humour.

At this time Alan was unsure where his future lay. Between 1888 and 1891 he exhibited paintings and design at the Royal Academy, encouraged by White. By the early nineties, he was building a reputation by contributing drawings to a number of popular magazines and periodicals, including: *The Dome, The Girl's Own Paper, The Idler, Pall Mall, Parade, The Strand, Sunday Pictorial,* and *the Windmill.*

On a visit to Christchurch, Hants,

Gleeson White introduced him to Frederick Rolfe, the self-styled Baron Corvo. The celebrated, but highly eccentric painter and critic invited Alan to illustrate an article he had written for *Wide World Magazine.* He agreed to do so, but the story by the high profile Corvo received a very bad press and temporarily dented Wright's reputation.

He had already completed a number of

book projects, but a turning point in his career arrived when he took over from Harry Furniss in 1898, as illustrator of *Wallypug*, a zany series of books by GE Farrow, about a king who was ruled by his subjects. Wright had developed a humorous style, reminiscent of John Tenniel and eminently suited to illustrating the grotesque characters the subject matter demanded.

By 1905 he was finding it difficult to attract work. The dawn of the Edwardian era heralded rapid change. New styles of illustration were in demand. The camera had taken over from those magazine illustrators, like Wright, whose job it was to literally record events and he felt that his work was becoming distinctly dated.

He formed a close friendship with painter George Vernon Stokes (1873-1954) and his cousin Cynthia Harnett, which was to endure throughout their lives. By 1910, he was sharing a studio with Stokes in West Kensington and they worked together on books, including *The Christmas Book of Carols and Songs*. Stokes encouraged Alan Wright to work in watercolours which helped him develop a less formal, freer style more conducive to his animal paintings. This was further enhanced when he met Anne Anderson at publishers Henry Frowde and Hodder & Stoughton where they were both working on projects. He had a great admiration for her fresh approach to illustration and her lyrical style.

The couple married in June 1912 and moved into the three room cottage where she was already living – *Little Audrey*, Burghfield Common, near Reading. Alan was forty eight and Anne, whom he called Nancy, was thirty eight. Their guests enjoyed a wedding breakfast in the summer sunshine at Pinchcut, part of the common near the cottage and each year the couple walked up there to celebrate their anniversary.

Alan and Nancy were well suited. He was a short man, about five foot six inches tall, laconic and unambitious in material

terms. He worked hard in spasms, while she was retiring, industrious and like her husband, spurned materialism.

The couple remained at the cottage and added two rooms and extended the studio, but they lived modestly and were ecologically conscious, trying to be as self-sufficient as possible. He loved to tend his kitchen garden and to rearrange the roof tiles whenever necessary, while Nancy worked in the studio. Both enjoyed etching and landscape painting and were members of the Reading Fine Art Society during the nineteen thirties.

Their artistic styles complemented one another, enabling them to collaborate on a good many books together. Whenever Nancy needed birds or animals in her compositions, Alan would provide them.

*Mrs Bunnykin's Busy Day* and *The Tale of a Trail of a Snail* were published by Jarrolds in 1919. Who could be disparaging about these lovable and docile dressed animals, going about their daily lives unthreatened by their deadliest enemies – people? The books which show clearly Alan's love of drawing animals, were also published as postcards by the Regent Publishing Co. in 1920. Illustrations from *Mrs Bunnykin's Busy Day* formed Regent series 1010 and 1011 and those from *The Tale of a Trail of a Snail* were issued as Regent nos. 1042-1051. Cards from *Mrs Bunnykin's Busy Day* were later given individual numbers.

Alan Wright, always practical and down to earth, attributed the the success of his marriage to Anne Anderson to be *"due in part to the need to work hard and earn a decent income."* He breezed through his long life imbuing those with whom he came into contact with a true sense of well-being. He treated the prospect of his eventual departure with the same degree of humour and resignation by providing his biographer with his own comforting epitaph:

*"Here lies the body of old AW,*
*Who never more in this life will trouble you,*
*He's gone at last to his long delight,*
*A dreamless sleep in an endless night."*

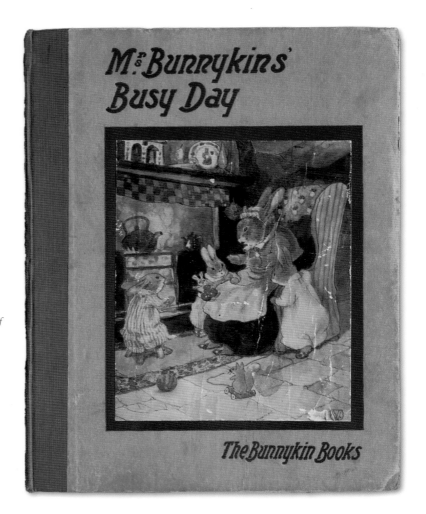

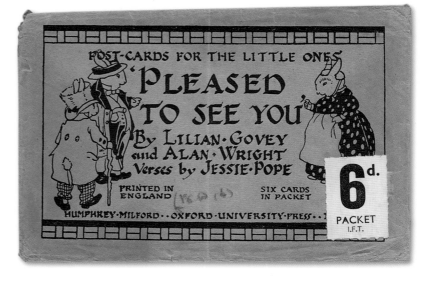

*LEFT HAND PAGE*

*Below:*
*Pub: Humphrey Milford*
*Postcards for the Little Ones*
*Pleased to See You packet*
*[1930]*

*RIGHT HAND PAGE*

*Top row:*
*Artist: Alan Wright*
*Pub: Regent Publishing*
*No. 1010*
*From Mrs Bunnykin's Busy Day*
*[1920]*

*Bottom row:*
*Artist: Alan Wright★*
*Pub: Humphrey Milford*
*Pleased to See You*
*Postcards for the Little Ones*
*[3 of 6]*
*[1930]*
*★3 of the series by Alan Wright,*
*3 by Lilian Govey*

The Bunnykins keep their chimneys swept clean.
Keep your heart open, your thoughts bright and keen.
S.H.

The Bunnykins play a hide-a-seek game.
When lessons are finished you do the same.
S.H.

The Bunnykins dance to the gay little tune.
We hope you will dance out our way quite soon.
S.H.

The Bobtails every year invite
Their friends to tea on ~ ~
~ ~ Christmas night.
That's why the family are dressed,
Even the babies, in their best.
J.P.

"Come in, come in!" cried Mrs Bun.
"We weren't expecting anyone.
But Flipperty just said to me
He wished some friends would
come to tea".
J.P.

Said Mummy Bun, "we make no fuss
When folks drop in to dine with us".
Said Hedgehog, "After this huge dinner
I shan't be feeling any thinner!"
J.P.

# Book and postcard listings by artist

This listing is by no means definitive. It attempts to indicate the range and diversity of the respective artists.

**Publisher's abbreviations**
E&S – Eyre & Spottiswoode
HF/H&S – Henry Frowde and Hodder & Stoughton
H&S – Hodder & Stoughton
RTS – The Religious Tract Society
SPCK – The Society fot the Promotion of Christian Knowledge

**Postcard listings**
The postcards listed are those that have been illustrated with children and young people in mind. For instance, Cecil Aldin, illustrated humorous postcards, many of which focused on country life and hunting. These have not been included.

Please note that titles in **'Bold'** represent known series titles (or in some cases individual card names). 'Roman' indicates descriptions of card themes where the series title is unknown.

Additional or corrected information that readers can provide for future editions of this book would be gratefully received – Email: copecomms@demon.co.uk

In compiling a list such as this, one has to recognise publishers' inconsistencies in series numbering. As a general rule, publishers issued postcards in packets containing six designs. Consistent in this regard were AM Davis, CW Faulkner, Humphrey Milford, Raphael Tuck (Art & Oilette series) and Vivian Mansell. However, there were many exceptions. Raphael Tuck often issued Christmas and other greetings series with three of each of two designs in a packet of six postcards, while other publishers, ETW Dennis, Photochrom, J Salmon and Valentine issued individual postcards or cards in groups of two or three. The EW Savory Clifton Series were presented in sets of four. So, as complete publishers records no longer exist, accurate information is difficult to formulate.

## Cecil Aldin (1870-1935)

***Postcards illustrated include***
***Hills & Co***
**For the Empire Series 5092 Jack & Jill [1903]**
**For the Empire Series 5093 Ride a Cock Horse [1903]**
**For the Empire Series 5094 Jack Sprat [1903]**
**For the Empire Series 5095 Christmas is Coming [1903]**
**For the Empire Series 5096 Tom, Tom, the Piper's Son [1903]**
**For the Empire Series 5097 Hark! Hark! the Dogs... [1903]**

***Children's books illustrated include***
*A Conceited Puppy* / Emanuel (Dutton NY 1905)
*A Dog Day* / Emanuel (Heinemann 1902)
*Animal Revels* / Byron (HF/H&S 1916)
*An Old Fashioned Christmas Day* (H&S 1910)
*Bunnyborough* (Milford 1919)
*By the Sea* / Mrs Strang [ed] (HF/H&S (c.1912)
*Cecil Aldin's Farm Book* [Rag book No. 217] (Dean 1920)
*Cecil Aldin's Happy Family No 1 (Hungry Peter)* (HF/H&S 1912)
*Cecil Aldin's Happy Family No 2 (Rufus)* (HF/H&S 1912)
*Cecil Aldin's Merry Party* (HF/H&S 1913)
*Dogs of Character* (E&S 1927)
*Farm Babies* (HF/H&S c.1912)
*Field Babies* (HF/H&S c.1912)
*Jack and Jill* / Byron (HF/H&S 1914)
*Jerry: the Story of an Exmoor Pony* / Helme/Paul (E&S nd)
*Mac: The Adventures of a Scotch Terrier* (HF/H&S c.1916)
*Merry & Bright* (HF/H&S nd)
*Moufflou* / Ouida (Jack c.1910)
*Mrs Tickler's Caravan* (E&S 1931)
*My Dog* / Maeterlinck (Allen 1913)
*My Pets* (Milford 1924)
*Nature Tales from Many Lands* (Collins c.1913)
*Pickles, A Puppy Dog's Tail* (HF/H&S 1909)
*Portraits at the Zoo* (HF/H&S 1915)
*Puppy Dog Frolics* (Collins c.1929)
*Puppy Tails* / Waylett (Lawrence & Jellicoe 1910)
*Pussy and Her Ways* (HF/H&S c.1910)
*Rags, His Adventures* / Byron (HF/H&S 1911)
*Rough and Tumble* (HF/H&S 1916)
*Stories from Puppyland* / Sutton Smith (Donohoe 1904)
*Ten Little Puppy Dogs* (Sands c.1902)
*The Animal's Picnic* [Rag Book No. 270] (Dean 1929)
*The Black Puppy Book* (HF/H&S 1908)
*The Bunch Book* / Douglas (E&S 1932)
*The Doggie Book* / Waylett (SPCK nd)
*The Dog Who Wasn't What He Thought He Was* / Emanuel (Tuck 1914)
*The Great Adventure* (Milford 1921)
*The Joker and Jerry Again* / Helme (E&S 1932)
*The Merry Puppy Book* (HF/H&S 1916)
*The Red Puppy Book* (H&S 1910)
*The Twins* (HF/H&S nd)
*The Water Babies* / Kingsley/Steedman [ed] (Nelson nd)
*The Young Folks Birthday Book* (Hills c.1900)
*Us* (Milford 1922)
*Who's Who in the Zoo* / Morton (E&S 1935)
*Willie Winkie's Animal Book* (Collins 1927)
*Zoo Babies* (HF/H&S 1913)
***'Cecil Aldin Letter Books'***
*Black Billy* (Milford c.1920)
*Cock-o-lorum* (Milford c.1920)
*Pale Peter* (Milford c.1920)
*Puss Puss* (Milford c.1920)
*Ugly Duckling* (Milford c.1920)
*White Rabbit* (Milford c.1920)
***'Cecil Aldin's Painting Books'***
*The Baby Book* (Lawrence & Jellicoe c.1915)
*The Doggy Book* (Lawrence & Jellicoe c.1915)
***'Cecil Aldin's Puppy Books'***
*Black Puppy Book* (HF/H&S nd)
*Bobtail Puppy Book* (HF/H&S nd)
*Farmyard Puppy Book* (HF/H&S nd)
*Mongrel Puppy Book* (HF/H&S nd)
*Red Puppy Book* (HF/H&S nd)
*The White Kitten Book* (H&S nd)
*White Puppy Book* (HF/H&S 1909)
***'Cecil Aldin Shilling Series'***
*Forager, his Adventures* / Byron (HF/H&S c.1911)
*Forager's Hunt Breakfast* (HF/H&S nd)
*Humpty and Dumpty* (HF/H&S nd)
*Humpty and Dumpty's Fancy Dress Ball* (HF/H&S nd)
*Hungry Peter* (HF/H&S nd)
*Master Quack* (HF/H&S nd)
*Master Quack Gives a Water Picnic* (HF/H&S nd)
*Peter's Dinner Party* (HF/H&S nd)
*Rags* (HF/H&S nd)
*Garden Party* (HF/H&S nd)
*Rufus* (HF/H&S nd)
*Tabitha's Tea Party* (HF/H&S nd)
***Books illustrated with others include***
*Children's Playhour Book* 1929 (Longmans Green 1929)
*Princes and Fairies* / Mead (Nisbet 1930)
*Starlight Tales* (Cassell c.1910)
*The Mammoth Wonder Book for Children* (Odhams 1935)
*The Story Wonder Book* (Ward Lock 1937)
*This Train for Storyland* (Cassell c.1915)
*This Way for Fun* (Cassell c.1920)
*Tiny Tots – A Picture Story Book for Little People* / Blyton (Cassell 1925)
*Tub Tales* (Dean c.1928)
*Wonder Book* 1923/24 (Ward Lock 1923)
***Annuals illustrated with others include***
*Blackie's Children's Annual; Bo-Peep Annual for 1924; Cassell's Children's Annual; Cassell's Family Magazine; Little Folks; Partridge's Children's Annual; Tiger Tim's Annual; The Tiny Folks' Annual; Tiny Tots; Wilfred's Annual*

## Anne Anderson (1874-1930)

***Postcards illustrated include***
***ETW Dennis***
**4328-4330** (Nursery rhymes) **[1912]**
***CW Faulkner***
**Series 1082** (Popular sayings) **[1910]**
***EW Savory***
**(4 designs per series)**
**Clifton Series 518** (Spring/summer/autumn/winter) **[1917]**
**Clifton Series 524** (Nursery rhymes) **[1917]**
**Clifton Series 622** (Elves & fairies) **[1917]**
**Clifton Series 623** (Fairy wishes) **[1917]**
**Clifton Series 624** (Keeping in touch) **[1917]**
**Clifton Series 634** (Nursery rhymes) **[1917]**
**Clifton Series 635** (Proverbs) **[1917]**
**Clifton Series 639** (Proverbs) **[1917]**
**Clifton Series 645** (Baby proverbs) **[1917]**
**Clifton Series 690** (Come for a day...) **[1918]**
**Clifton Series 684** (Nursery rhymes) **[1918]**
**Clifton Series 689** (Just a line...) **[1918]**
**Clifton Series 688** (Kind thoughts) **[1918]**
**Clifton Series 749** (Girl in red cloak) **[1919]**
**Clifton Series 778** (Friendly greeting) **[1919]**

***Books illustrated include***
*Aladdin & the Wonderful Lamp* (Nelson c.1919)
*Ali Baba and the Forty Thieves* (Nelson c.1920)
*All About Old Goody Goose* (Dean c.1915)
*Andersen's Fairy Stories* (Collins 1926)
*Aucassin and Nicolette* / Child (intr.) (A&C Black 1911)
*Baby's Record* (Harrap 1920)
*Big Cosy Chair Stories* / Morrison (Collins 1924)
*Cosy Comfy Book* / Talbot (Collins 1920)
*Cosy Time Tales* / Joan (Nelson 1922)
*Fairy Tales of Grimm and Andersen* (Collins nd)
*Favourite Fairy Tales* (Nelson c.1920)
*Fireside Stories* / Barnes (Blackie 1922)
*Grimm's Fairy Tales* (Collins 1922)
*Hans Andersen's Fairy Tales* (Collins 1924)
*Heidi* / Spyri (Harrap 1924)
*Hop o'My Thumb* (Nelson nd)
*Humpy and Grumpy* (HF/H&S c.1916)
*Lie-Down Stories* / Joan (Blackie nd)
*Little Dwarf Nose & the Magic Whistle* (Harrap 1916)
*Merry Folk* (Collins 1930)
*Mr Pickles & the Party* / Heward (Warne 1926)
*Mr Why and Mr What, Old Nature Tales* (Nelson nd)
*Nursery Rhymes* (Nelson nd)
*Old English Nursery Songs* (Harrap 1915)
*Old French Nursery Songs* / Mansion (arr) (Harrap c.1915)
*Old French Songs for the Nursery* (Harrap 1917)
*Old Mother Goose Nursery Rhyme Book* (Nelson c.1926)
*Old, Old Fairy Tales* (Nelson c.1920)
*Over the Treetops* / Macnair (Dean 1920)
*Peggy from Kerry* / Meade (Chambers 1912)
*RIP* / Garrett (Milford 1919)
*Stirabout Stories* / Barnes (Blackie (c.1930)
*Tales for Teeny Wee* / Joan (Milford 1925)
*Tales that History Tells (Book 1)* / Smith (Great Education Co. 1950)
*The Anne Anderson Fairy Tale Book* (Nelson 1923)
*The Anne Anderson Picture Book* (Collins 1927)
*The Betty Book* (Nelson 1917)
*The Dandy-Andy Book* (Nelson nd)
*The Dickie Birdie Book* (Nelson 1916)
*The Fairy Tale Omnibus* (Collins nd)
*The Funny Bunny ABC* (painting book) (Nelson 1912)
*The Gateway to Chaucer* / Underdown (Nelson 1912)
*The Gillyflower Garden Book* (Nelson 1920)
*The Green Book* (HF/H&S nd)
*The House Above the Trees* / Cook Eliot (Butterworth nd)
*The Jackie Jackdaw Book* (Nelson 1916)
*The Jacky Horner ABC* (Dean nd)
*The Jolly Book* (Nelson 1921)
*The Little Busy Bee Book* (Nelson c.1917)
*The Lord's Prayer* [Rag Book No. 191] (Dean 1916)
*The Maisie-Daisie Book* (Nelson c.1913)
*The May Queen* / Mrs Strang [ed] (Milford nd)
*The Old English Nursery Songs* (Harrap c.1920)
*The Old Mother Goose* (Nelson nd)
*The Posie Poetry Book* (Nelson nd)
*The Purple Book* (HF/H&S c.1915)
*The Rosie-Posie Book* (Nelson c.1920)
*The Sleepy Song Book* (Harrap 1917)
*The Water Babies* / Kingsley (Jack 1924)
*Turkish Delight* (Milford c.1920)
*Wanda & the Garden of the Red House* / Garrett (Milford 1924)
***Books illustrated with Alan Wright include***
*The Busy Bunny* (Nelson nd)
*The Cuddly Kitten and the Busy Bunny* (Nelson 1926)
*The Cuddly-Kitty Book* [Nursery Zoo Ser.] Nelson nd (c.1922)
*Sing Song Stories* / Herbertson (Milford 1922)
*Tales for Teeny Wee* / Joan (Milford [nd)
*The Daring Duckie Book* (Nelson c.1915)
*The Full-of-Fun Picture Book* (Ward Lock nd)
*The Isle of Wirrawoo* / Purse (Milford c.1922)
*The Nursery Zoo* (Nelson nd)
*The Naughty Neddie Book* (Nelson nd)
*The Patsy Book* (Nelson 1919)
*The Podgy Puppy Book* (Nelson 1927)
*Two Bold Sportsmen* (Nelson 1918)
*Two Tiny Tomboys* (Nelson nd)
***Books illustrated with others include***
*A Book of Elves and Fairies* (Collins nd)
*The Big Book of Pictures and Stories* (Blackie nd)
*Boys and Girls Story Book* (Blackie nd)
*Boys and Girls Wonder Book 1927* (Ward Lock c.1927)
*Brighteyes Merry Book* (Coker c.1922)
*Children's Golden Treasure Book* (Odhams nd)
*Children's Playhour Book 1929* (Longmans Green 1929)
*Fairy Stories for Tiny Folk* [with Lilian Govey] (Milford 1930)
*Hush-a-bye Stories* (Collins nd)
*Listen-To-Me Land* (Collins c.1915)
*Playtime Reading with Mother* (Harrap nd)
*Santa Claus Picture Book* (Collins c.1930)
*Selfridge's Childrens's Story Book* (Selfridge's c.1920)
*The Big Christmas Wonder Book* (Odhams (1917)
*The Big Christmas Wonder Book* (Odhams 1936)
*The Blackbird Story Book* (Blackie nd)
*The Children's Play Hour Book* / Southwold (Longmans Green 1928)
*The Children's Wonder Book* (Collins nd)
*The Chummy Book* (Nelson 1919)
*The Cosy Corner Book* (Collins 1943)
*The Fairy Tale Book* (Nelson nd)
*Tub Time Tales* (Blackie 1919)
***Annuals illustrated with others include***
*Blackie's Children's Annual; Blackie's Little One's Annual; Cassell's Children's Annual; Collins' Children's Annual; Collins' Fairy Folks' Annual; Mrs Strang's Annual for Children; Pip and Squeak Annual; Playbox Annual*

## Florence Mary Anderson (1893-1972)

***Postcards illustrated include***
***Vivian Mansell***
**Series 2115** (Fairyland) **[1920]**
***Little Folks***
**Unnumbered promotional postcards**

***Books illustrated include***
*Adventures in Magic Land* / Black (Harrap 1917)
*Adventures of Dolly Dingle* / Wynne (Jarrolds 1920)
*A Thrilling Term at Janeways* / Brent Dyer (Nelson c.1938)
*A Treasury of Flower Stories* (Harrap nd)
*Castaway Island* / Newbery (Harrap nd)
*China Clay* / Blakemore (Heffer 1922)
*Come Christmas* / Farjeon (Collins 1927)
*Mumbudget* / Simpson (Heinemann 1928)
*My Fairyland* / Malcolm (Harrap 1916)
*Nutcracker and Mouse King* / Browne (Harrap 1916)
*Secrets of the Flowers* / Coker (Jarrolds c.1920)

The Black Princess / Chrysanthème (Simpkin Marshall 1916)
The Cradle Ship / Howes (Cassell 1916)
The Dream Pedlar / Sackville (Simpkin Marshall 1914)
The Magic Kiss / Chaundler (Cassell 1916)
The Magic Whistle / Browne (Harrap 1920)
The Password to Fairyland / Southwart (Simpkin Marshall c.1920)
The Rainbow Twins (Johnson 1919)
The Singing Fish / Hawes (Cassell 1921)
The Travelling Companions / Sackville (Simpkin Marshall 1915)
The Treasure of the Towers (RTS 1926)
Tribute (Pelican Press 1925)
Valentine and Orson / Littlewood (Simpkin Marshall 1919)
Woodcuts and Verses (British Museum, Dept of Prints 1922)
**Books illustrated with others include**
Children's Playhour Book (Longmans Green 1929)
Princes and Fairies [et al] / Mead (Nisbet 1930)
Starlight Tales (Cassell c.1910)
This Train for Storyland (Cassell c.1915)
This Way for Fun (Cassell c.1920)
**Annuals illustrated with others include**
Blackie's Children's Annual; Bo-Peep Annual; Cassell's Children's Annual; Cassell's Family Magazine; Little Folks; Partridge's Children's Annual; Tiny Tots

## Ellen Jessie Andrews (1858-1907)

**Postcards illustrated include**
Stroefer (TSN)
   Serie XXXIX (10 or 12 designs) Mädchen [1901]
Raphael Tuck
   Art Series 1156 Ping Pong in Fairyland [1902]
   Art Series 1629 [1904]
   Art Series 6686 My Motor [1907]
   Art Series 6731 Little Motorists [1907]
   Art Series 6884 Outdoor Games [1907]
   Art Series 6890 [1907]
   Art Series 6948 Flower Maidens [1907]
   Christmas Series 1815 Fairy Tales [1902]
   Christmas Series 8010 [1904]
   Christmas Series 8016 [1904]
   Christmas Series 8020 [1904]
   Christmas Series 8030 [1904]
   Christmas Series 8036 [1904]
   Christmas Series 8037 [1904]
   Christmas Series 8057 [1904]
   Christmas Series 8420 [1906]
   Christmas Series 8431 [1906]
   Christmas Series 8442 [1906]
   Christmas Series 8447 [1906]
   Birthday Series 2004 [1902]
Anonymous publisher
   Unnumbered series
   6 designs similar to Tuck Flower Maidens

**Books illustrated include**
Butterfly Valley [et al] [Children's Gem Library] / (Tuck nd)
Favourite Fairy Stories [et al] (Tuck nd)
Little Snow White and Other Stories [et al] (Tuck nd)
Old Fairy Tales [et al] / Vredenburg (Tuck nd)
Old Time Stories [et al] / [Golden Gift Series] Vredenburg (Tuck nd)
Playtime Hours [et al] (Tuck nd)

## Honor Appleton (1879-1951)

**Postcards illustrated include**
Wells Gardner Darton
   Series of 6 postcards promoting The Children's Poets
   [c.1912] 2 of which are by Honor Appleton

**Books illustrated include**
A Christmas Carol / Cradock (Simpkin, Marshall 1914)
A First Peter Pan / Barrie (Brockhampton 1962)
A Short Robinson Crusoe (Harrap nd)

A Treasury of Tales for Little Folks [with Nora Fry] (Harrap 1927)
Babies Three (Nelson 1921)
Betty and the Boys / Russell (Jack c.1917)
Betty's Diary / Russell (Blackie 1914)
Big Book of Pictures and Stories [et al] (Blackie nd)
Blackie's Christmas Diary 1920 / Holmes (Blackie 1919)
Book of Tales for Little Folks [with Nora Fry] (Harrap 1936)
Brother Rabbit [with Patten Wilson/W Pogany] (Harrap 1926)
Children in Verse (Duckworth 1913)
Children's Diary for 1920 (Blackie 1920)
Dumpy Proverbs [a Dumpy book] (Grant Richards 1902)
Epaminondas & Other Stories / Bryant (Harrap 1926)
Fairy Tales / Perrault (Simpkin Marshall nd)
Fairy Tales by Hans Christian Andersen (Nelson 1920)
Heather the Second / Wynne (Nelson 1938)
How I Tamed the Wild Squirrels / Tyrell (Nelson 1914)
Lots of Pictures [et al] (Blackie c.1930)
Marjory's White Rat / Leslie (Blackie 1926)
Me and My Pussies (Nelson 1924)
More About the Squirrels / Tyrrell (Nelson 1916)
More Fairy Tales [Nora Fry/Vernon Soper] (Harrap nd)
Nannie's Treasure Box / Barnes (Blackie nd)
Our Nursery Rhyme Book / Littlewood [ed] (Herbert & Daniel nd)
Pamela's Teddy Bear [The Enchantment Series] / Cradock (Jack 1927)
Pamela's Teddy Bears / Cradock (Nelson nd)
Peggy and Joan / Cradock (Blackie 1922)
Peggy's Twins / Cradock (SPCK 1920)
Perrault's Fairy Tales / Littlewood [ed] (Herbert & Daniel 1911)
Saint George of England / Hood (Harrap 1919)
Snuffles for Short / Chaundler (Nisbet 1921)
Songs of Innocence / Blake (Herbert & Daniel 1911)
Sylvia Finds a Fairy / Rudolf (SPCK 1923)
The Bad Mrs Ginger [a Dumpy Book] (Grant Richards 1903)
The Best Teddy Bear in the World / Cradock (Nelson 1926)
The Big Book of Josephine / Cradock (Blackie 1919)
The Big Book of Pictures and Stories (Blackie 1920)
The Bonny Book of Josephine [collection] / Cradock (Blackie 1926)
The Book of Animal Tales / Southwold (Harrap 1929)
The Book of English Verse (Harrap nd)
The Bower Book / Littlewood [ed] (O'Connor 1922)
The Bowl of Mist / Marzials (Harrap 1928)
The Child of the Sea / Littlewood (Simpkin Marshall 1915)
The Children of the New Forest / Marryat (Harrap c.1934)
The Children's Alice / Lee (adapt) (Harrap 1949)
The Children's Aladdin (Harrap 1938)
The Children's Black Beauty / Harris (Harrap 1941)
The Children's Book of Heroes (Harrap nd)
The Children's Book of Saints (Harrap nd)
The Children's Brer Rabbit (Harrap 1941)
The Children's First English Fairy Book (Harrap 1953)
The Children's Greek Stories (Harrap nd)
The Children's Hereward / Lee (adapt) (Harrap 1936)
The Children's Hiawatha / Lee (adapt) (Harrap nd)
The Children's Jackanapes (Harrap nd)
The Children's Norse Tales (Harrap nd)
The Children's Joan of Arc (Harrap nd)
The Children's King Arthur (Harrap 1941)
The Children's Swiss Family Robinson (Harrap nd)
The Children's Uncle Remus (Harrap 1946)
The Fairy Book (Nelson nd)
The Forest Children / Joan (Nelson 1927)
The Gingerbread Man / Bryant (Harrap 1926)
The House of Fancy / Cradock (O'Connor 1922)
The Josephine Dolly Book (3 bks) / Cradock (Blackie c.1929)
The Merry Laughter Book [et al] (Blackie c.1924)
The Nabob's Garden / Bennett (Nelson nd)
The Secret Passage / Russell (Jack/Nelson 1917)
The Snow Queen / Andersen (Nelson c.1920)
The Thirteenth Orphan / Chaundler (Nisbet 1920)
The Twins of Tumbledoundreary / Horsfall (Duckworth 1912)
The Worlds Best Stories for Children (Jack/Nelson c.1920)
Treasury of Verse for School & Home (Harrap nd)
Under Sevenshields Castle / Scott-Hopper (Harrap 1919)
Wanted, a Mother (Jack 1920)
Where the Dolls Lived / Cradock (SPCK 1919)
Where the Rainbow Ends / Mills (Harrap nd)

### The Josephine Books
Josephine and her Dolls / Cradock (Blackie 1915)
Josephine's Birthday / Cradock (Blackie 1920)
Josephine is Busy / Cradock (Blackie 1918)
Josephine's Christmas Party / Cradock (Blackie 1927)
Josephine Goes Shopping / Cradock (Blackie 1926)
Josephine Goes Travelling / Cradock (Blackie 1940)
Josephine's Happy Family / Cradock (Blackie 1917)
Josephine, John and the Puppy / Cradock (Blackie 1920)
Josephine Keeps House / Cradock (Blackie 1931)
Josephine Keeps School / Cradock (Blackie 1925)
Josephine's Pantomime / Cradock (Blackie 1939)
**Annuals and periodicals illustrated with others**
Blackie's Annual; Pictorial Educational Quarterly

## Mabel Lucie Attwell (1879-1964)

*For books and postcards illustrated see*
*The Collectable World of Mabel Lucie Attwell*
*by John Henty, published by Richard Dennis 1999*

## Margaret Banks (1899-1988)

**Postcards illustrated include**
Raphael Tuck
   Oilette Series 3381 Dressing Dolls [1922]
   Oilette Series 3394 Mechanical Dolls Series I [1922]

**Books illustrated include**
Bo-Peep's Bumper Book 1934 [et al] (1934)
Our Toys [Rag book No. 311] (Dean 1934)
The Last Word (Sidgwick & Jackson 1964)

## Sybil Barham (1877-1950)

**Postcards illustrated include**
CW Faulkner
   Series 502 The New Moon [1905]
   Series 582 (Shakespearean interpretations) [1905]
   Series 701 (Girls and flowers) [1907]
   Series 875 Beautiful Spring [1908]
   Series 964 Songs of Innocence [1911]
   Series 1190 Lantern Light [1911] [Munk 735]
   Series 1217 Peter Pan [1912]
   Series 1218 Where the Rainbow Ends [Mavis Yorke] [1912]
   Series 1219 Memories of Pavlova [1912]
   Series 1268 The Chinese Lantern [1912]
   Series 1345 (Shakespearean interpretations) [1913]
   Series 1347 Where Pan Pipes [1913]
   Series 1551 (Owen Meredith interpretations) [1915]
   Series 1581 (Shakespearean interpretations) [1916]
   Series 1648 (Spiritual interpretations) [1918]
   Series 1730 (Literary interpretations) [1921]
   Series 1731 The Pied Piper of Hamelin [1921]
   Series 1785 (Literary interpretations) [1923]
   Series 1792 (Traditional dances) [1923]
   Series 1793 (From a Child's Garden of Verses) [1923]
   Series 1814 (Nursery rhymes) [1924]
   Series 1856 (Children, flowers, etc.) [1925]
   Series 1859 Flower Fairies [1925]
   Series 1878 (Shakespearean interpretations) [1925]
Reinthal & Newman
   Unnumbered series (Childhood days) [c.1912]

**Books illustrated include**
Peter Pan Postcard Painting Book (CW Faulkner c.1920)
Stories from Browning / Turnbull (Harrap 1914)
The Elf of the Orchard [with E Peacock] / Moss (Darton nd)
The Story of Angelina Wacks / Clayton Palmer (Darton 1913)

## Cicely Mary Barker (1895-1973)

**Postcards illustrated include**
CW Faulkner
   Series 1644 Shakespeare's Boy Characters [1917]
   Series 1704 Shakespeare's Girl Characters [1920]
Harvey Fine Art
   Elves & Fairies [1918]
J Salmon
   Series 921-926 Picturesque Children of the Allies [1915]
   Series 2475-2481 Seaside Holiday [1918]
**Books illustrated include**
A Child's Garden of Verses (Blackie 1944)
A Flower Fairy Alphabet (Blackie 1934)
A Little Book of Rhymes New and Old (Blackie 1937)
Autumn Songs with Music (Blackie 1927)
Bluebell Story Book (Blackie 1924)
Fairies of the Flowers and Trees (Blackie 1950)
Fairies of the Trees (Blackie 1940)
Flower Fairies of the Autumn (Blackie 1926)
Flower Fairies of the Garden (Blackie 1944)
Flower Fairies of the Spring (Blackie 1923)
Flower Fairies of the Summer (Blackie 1925)
Flower Fairies of the Wayside (Blackie 1948)
Flower Songs of the Season / Linnell (music) (Blackie c.1932)
Groundsel and Necklaces (Blackie 1946)
He Leadeth Me / D Barker (Blackie 1936)
Old Rhymes for All Times (Blackie 1928)
Our Darling's First Book (Blackie 1929)
Red Clover (Blackie 1924)
Rhymes New and Old (Blackie 1933)
Spring Songs with Music (Blackie 1923)
Summer Songs with Music (Blackie 1926)
The Book of the Flower Fairies (Spring/Summer/Autumn) (Blackie 1927)
The Children's Book of Hymns (Blackie 1929)
The Flower Fairy Picture Book (Blackie 1955)
The Little Picture Hymn Book (Blackie 1933)
The Lord of the Rushie River (Blackie 1938)
**Books illustrated with others include**
Child Thoughts in Picture and Verse / Westcott (Blackie nd)
Lots of Pictures (Blackie c.1930)
My Lovely Big Book (Blackie c.1930)
Our Nursery Book (Blackie c.1926)
The Blackbird Story Book (Blackie nd)
The Foxglove Story Book (Blackie nd)
The Sweetbriar Story Book (Blackie c.1923)
**Annuals illustrated with others include**
Blackie's Children's Annual

## Doris Bowden (1900-1943)

**Postcards illustrated include**
CW Faulkner
   Series 1811 Little Folk Lands [1924]
   Series 1812 (Children at play) [1924]
Hills & Co.
   (Easter series) [nd]

**Books illustrated include**
Fairies and Chimneys / Rose Fyleman (nd)
**Annuals illustrated with others include**
Leading Strings (Wells Gardner & Darton c.1926)

## Ada Leonora Bowley (1866-1954)

**Postcards illustrated include**
Raphael Tuck
   Oilette Series C218 Christmas postcard [c.1907]
   Oilette Series C219 Christmas postcard [c.1907]
   Oilette Series C1282 Christmas postcard [nd]
   Oilette Series C1757 Christmas postcard [c.1909]
   Oilette Series C1758 Christmas postcard [c.1909]
   Oilette Series C2098 Christmas postcard [c.1914]
   Oilette Series C2099 Christmas postcard [c.1914]

**Oilette Series 3004 Birthday postcard [with MB][c.1923]**
**Oilette Series 3005 Birthday postcard [c.1923]**
**Oilette Series 3006 Birthday postcard [with MB][c.1923]**
**Oilette Series 3382 Dressing Dolls II [1922]**
**Oilette Series 3383 Dressing Dolls III [1922]**
**Oilette Series 3386 The Fairyland Panorama Series [1922]**
**Oilette Series 3399 Father Tuck's Toy Rockers [1923]**
**Oilette Series 3403 Merry Little Men [c.1923]**
**Oilette Series 3405 Swinging Dolls [c.1923]**
**Oilette Series C3781 Christmas postcard [c.1911]**
**Oilette Series C3782 Christmas postcard [c.1911]**
**Oilette Series C5005 Christmas postcard [c.1920]**
**Oilette Series C5095 Christmas postcard [c.1921]**
**Oilette Series C5645 Christmas postcard [c.1922]**
**Oilette Series C6037 Christmas postcard [c.1919]**
**Oilette Series C7160 Christmas postcard [c.1912]**
**Oilette Series C7161 Christmas postcard [c.1912]**
**Oilette Series C8437 Christmas postcard [1906]**
**Oilette Series C8449 Christmas postcard [1906]**
**Oilette Series 9603 The Brownie Family [1907]**
***Valentine***
**Artotype series (Christmas postcard) [c.1910]**

***Books illustrated include***
*Alice in Wonderland* [Golden Treasury Series] / Carroll (Tuck 1921)
*Alice in Wonderland* [The Storyland Treasury Series] (Tuck 1921)
*Alice in Wonderland* [et al] [Modern Lib. for Boys & Girls] (Tuck nd)
*Alice in Wonderland* (painting book) (Tuck 1925)
*Country Pleasures Told in Rhyme...*[Woolly Woolly Ser.] (Tuck nd)
*Fairy Tale Adventures* [with Molly Benatar] (Tuck nd)
*Fantasies* [with May Bowley] / Nembhard (Allen 1896)
*Father Tuck's Alice in Wonderland Panorama* (Tuck nd)
*Father Tuck's Little Playmates at Work* (movable) / Bingham (Tuck nd)
*Father Tuck's Toy Rockers Modelling Book* [No.9762] (Tuck c.1905)
*Father Tuck's Peep-show Pictures of Fairy Tales* [No.9760] (Tuck c.1905)
*Favourite Fairy Stories* [et al] Tuck / Vredenburg [ed] (1920)
*From Fairyland* [et al] (Tuck 1915)
*Good Time Stories* [et al] (Tuck c.1910)
*Long Ago Fairy Tales* [et al] (Tuck nd)
*Moonlight Manor* / Scrymgeour (Valentine c.1907)
*My Playtime Book* [et al] / Vredenburg [ed] (Tuck nd)
*Nancy the Naughty* / Lea (Partridge 1920)
*Old Fairy Tales* (cover Agnes Richardson) /Vredenburg (Tuck nd)
*Tales that are True for Brown Eyes and Blue* [et al] / Nesbit (Tuck nd)
*The Children's Playmate* [et al] Tuck nd)
*Playtime Hours, Favourite Fairy Stories* [et al] (Tuck nd)
***Annuals illustrated with others include***
*The Infant's Magazine; The Rosebud Annual; Tub Tales Wonder Book; A Picture Annual for Boys and Girls; Father Tuck's Annual; Little Folks; Partridge's Children's Annual*

## Sophia May Bowley (1864-1960)

***Postcards illustrated include***
***J Salmon***
**Series** (British birds) **3835-3840 [1927]**
***Raphael Tuck***
**Christmas Series C165 postcard [1907]**
**Oilette Series C3000 Christmas postcard [c.1923]**
**Oilette Series C3001 Christmas postcard [c.1923]**
**Oilette Series C3004 Christmas postcard [c.1923]**
**Oilette Series 3004 Birthday postcard [with ALB] [c.1923]**
**Oilette Series 3006 Birthday postcard [with ALB] [c.1923]**
**Oilette Series 3375 Birds on the Wing I [1922]**
**Oilette Series 3375 Birds on the Wing II [1922]**
**Oilette Series E3657 Easter postcard [c.1912]**
**Oilette Series E3658 Easter postcard [c.1912]**
**Oilette Series C6038 Christmas postcard [c.1919]**
***Valentine***
**Series** (Studies of Children) **[c.1904]**
**Series Old English Songs [c.1905]**
**Series** (Proverbs) **[c.1905]**
**Series** (Days of the week) **[c.1905]**
**Series** (Fairy tales) **[nd]**

***Books illustrated include***
*Betsy Brian's Needle...* [et al] [Children's Gem Lib.] / Hoyer (Tuck nd)
*Butterfly Valley* [et al] [Children's Gem Library] / Thwaites (Tuck nd)
*Cat's Cradle* [et al] [Children's Gem Library] / Marshall (Tuck nd)
*Children's Stories from English History* / Nesbit/Ashley (Tuck c.1914)
*Country Pleasures Told in Rhyme* ...[Woolly Woolly Ser.] (Tuck nd)
*Effie's Little Mother* [et al] [Children's Gem Library] (Tuck nd)
*Fairy Tale Adventures* [with Molly Benatar] (Tuck c.1920)
*Fantasies* [with AL Bowley] / Nembhard (Allen 1896)
*Favourite Fairy Stories* [et al] / Vredenburg [ed] (Tuck nd)
*Favourite Fairy Tales* [et al] (Tuck 1908)
*Holiday Times* [with A Richardson] / Vredenburg [ed] (Tuck nd)
*My Sunshine Book* [et al] [Golden Gift Ser.] / Labrousse (Tuck nd)
*Old Fairy Tales* [with Agnes Richardson] / Vredenburg [ed] (Tuck nd)
*Playtime Stories* [et al] (Tuck nd)
*Royal Children of English History [et al]* (Tuck 1897)
*Sunny Tales* [et al] [Golden Gift Ser. 4640] / Hopper (Tuck nd)
*Tales from Tennyson* / Chesson (Tuck nd)
*Tales that are True for Brown Eyes and Blue* [et al] / Nesbit (Tuck 1894)
*The Children's Shakespeare* [et al] / Nesbit (Tuck 1897)
*The Children's Song Book* [et al] (Anderson c.1905)
*The Happy Home ABC* (Tuck nd)
*The Rainbow Queen...* [et al] [Children's Gem Library] (Tuck 1905)
*The Ruby Fairy Book* [et al] / Vredenburg [ed] (Tuck nd)
*Tick Tock: Tales of the Clock* [et al] / Nesbit (Tuck 1895)
*Tubbie & Toddie in the Country* (Dean 1922)
*With Father Tuck in Fairyland* [panorama] (Tuck nd)
*With Father Tuck in Playtime* [Mechanical Ser.] / Bingham (Tuck nd)
*Woodland Stories Told in Rhyme...*[Woolly Woolly Ser.] (Tuck nd)
***Contributions written and illustrated with others include***
*Blackie's Children's Annual; Fairy Flights; Father Christmas, The Children's Annual; Father Tuck's Annual; Lady's Pictorial; Little Folks; Nister's Holiday Annual; Partridge's Children's Annual; St Nicholas; Sylvia's Journal; The Gentlewoman; The Ladies' Field Supplement; Ladies' Pictorial; Lady's Realm; The Queen; The Tatler*

## Molly Brett (1902-1990)

***Postcards illustrated include***
***CW Faulkner***
**Series 1983** (Fairies & animals) **[c.1935]**
**Series 1984** (Fairies & flowers) **[c.1935]**
**Series 1999 Fairy Games [c.1938]**
**Series 2027 Pixie Playthings [c.1938]**
***The Medici Society***
**Pkt 139 Swing High, Swing Low [c.1950]**
**Pkt 140 Fun by the Sea [c.1950]**
**Pkt 141 Playtime [c.1950]**
**Pkt 142 Any Luck, Pussy? [c.1950]**
**Pkt 143 Scottie's See Saw [c.1950]**
**Pkt 144 Schoolmaster [c.1950]**
**Pkt 145 Rock-a-Bye Baby [c.1950]**
**Pkt 146 Little Miss Muffett [c.1950]**
**Pkt 147 Jack and Jill [c.1950]**
**Pkt 148 There Was an Old Woman [c.1950]**
**Pkt 154 Little Polly Flinders [c.1950]**
**Pkt 155 Simple Simon Met a Pieman [c.1950]**
**Pkt 158 Humpty Dumpty [c.1950]**
**Pkt 159 Mary, Mary Quite Contrary [c.1950]**
**Pkt 166 Aesop's Fables. Town Mouse & Country Mouse [c.1950]**
**Pkt 167 Aesop's Fables. Dog in the Manger [c.1951]**
**Pkt 168 Aesop's Fables. Hare and the Tortoise [c.1951]**
**Pkt 169 Aesop's Fables. Fox and the Grapes [c.1951]**
**Pkt 170 Polly Put the Kettle On [c.1951]**
**Pkt 175 Old King Cole [c.1951]**
**Pkt 176 Wee Willie Winkie [c.1952]**
**Pkt 177 See Saw Margery Daw [c.1952]**
**Pkt 178 Little Jack Horner [c.1952]**
**Pkt 179 Where are you going to... [c.1950]**
**Pkt 185 Pat-a-Cake, Pat-a-Cake [c.1953]**
**Pkt 187 When Scottie Plays [c.1953]**
**Pkt 188 The Daisy Chain [c.1953]**
**Pkt 200 Sing a Song of Sixpence [c.1953]**
**Pkt 201 Harvest Picnic [c.1953]**
**Pkt 217 Fun on the Farm [c.1954]**
**Pkt 226 Time for School [c.1954]**
**Pkt 233 Bedtime Story [c.1954]**
**Pkt 245 Primrose Procession [c.1954]**
**Pkt 250 Kitten's Camp [c.1954]**
**Pkt 283 Bonfire Night [c.1955]**
**Pkt 288 Have You Heard the Cuckoo? [c.1955]**
**Pkt 289 He Giveth His Beloved Sleep [c.1955]**
**Pkt 292 The Rescue [c.1955]**
**Pkt 297 Catching the Train [c.1955]**
**Pkt 298 Musical Chairs [c.1955]**
**Pkt 301 The Farmyard Circus [c.1955]**
**Pkt 311 A Splash in a Puddle [c.1955]**
**Pkt 319 Teddy and His Car [c.1955]**
**Pkt 320 Goldcrests [c.1955]**
**Pkt 325 Teddy's Tractor [c.1955]**
**Pkt 326 Goldcrest on Jessamine [c.1955]**
**Pkt 340 A Swing for Teddy [c.1955]**
**Pkt 353 Caught a Tadpole Teddy? [c.1955]**
**Pkt 367 A Day by the Sea [c.1955]**
**Pkt 416 Rabbit, Robin, Mouse and Wren [c.1956]**
**Pkt 423 Conversation Piece [c.1956]**
**Pkt 464 Caught Napping [c.1957]**
**Unnumbered series The Gnome Series [nd]**
**Unnumbered card All the Fun of the Fair [nd]**
**Large format postcards 5 7/8 x 4 1/8**
**1045 A Lesson for the River Folk [nd]**

***Books illustrated include***
*A Surprise for Dumpy* (Medici 1964)
*Clicky and Father Christmas* / Blyton (Brockhampton 1956)
*Clicky and the Flying Horse* / Blyton (Brockhampton 1957)
*Clicky Gets Into Trouble* [strip book] / Blyton (Brockhampton 1958)
*Drummer Boy Duckling* (Partridge nd)
*Flip Flop's Secret* (Medici 1970)
*Happy Holiday Clicky* [strip book] / Blyton (Brockhampton 1961)
*Hello, Little Twins* / Blyton (Brockhampton 1951)
*Jiggy's Treasure Hunt* (Medici 1973)
*Jolly Story Book* (Children's Press nd)
*Master Bunny the Baker's Boy* / Winn (Brockhampton nd)
*Master Bunny has a Birthday* / Winn (Brockhampton nd)
*Master Bunny at the Seaside* / Winn (Brockhampton nd)
*Midget and the Pet Shop* (Medici 1975)
*Mother Goose* (Love 1948)
*Paddy Gets into Mischief* (Medici 1972)
*Mr Turkey Runs Away* (Brockhampton nd)
*Play Hours* [with Gordon Robinson] (Blackie nd)
*Plush and Tatty on the Beach* (Medici nd)
*Robin Finds Christmas* (Medici 1961)
*Teddy Flies Away* (Medici 1972)
*Teddy's Tent* (Medici nd)
*The Bed that Knew How to Fly* / Maitland-Nimmo (Warne 1963)
*The Forgotten Bear* (Medici c.1968)
*The Golliwog Grumbled* / Blyton (H&S nd)
*The Hare in a Hurry* (Medici 1975)
*The Japanese Garden* (Warne nd)
*The Jingle Book* [Silver Torch Series 13] / Derwent (Collins nd)
*The Jumble Bears* (Medici 1977)
*The Little Garden* (Warne 1936)
*The Mad Teapot* / Blyton (Brockhampton 1952)
*The Magic Spectacles and Other Tales* (Medici 1969)
*The Molly Brett Picture Book* (Medici 1979)
*The Party that Grew* (Medici 1976)
*The Proud Golliwog* [Little book no 3] / Blyton (Brockhampton nd)
*The Mammoth Wonder Book for Children* [et al] (Odhams 1935)
*The Rainbow Readers. (book one)* (Collins nd)
*The Story of a Toy Car* (Warne nd)
*The Untidy Little Hedgehog* (Medici 1966)
*Through the Magic Mirror* / Scarr (Warne 1940)
*Tom Tit Moves House* (Medici 1962)
*Town Mouse, Country Mouse* (Scholastic nd)
*Two in a Tent* (Medici 1969)
*Visitors in the Night* [Little book No.14] / Blyton (Brockhampton nd)
*What a Surprise* / Blyton (H&S 1954)
***Annuals illustrated with others include***
*Leading Strings; The Baby's Annual; Puck Annual; The Prize; Tiny Tots*

## Barbara Briggs (1887-1976)

***Postcards illustrated include***
***Humphrey Milford***
***Postcards for the Little Ones Series***
**Our Dogs** (Dogs) **[1917]**
**Our Terriers** (Terriers) **[1917]**
**The Busy Bees** (Children at play) **[1917]**
***EW Savory***
**Clifton Series 504** (Dogs) **[1917]**
**Clifton Series 637** (Dogs) **[1917]**
**Clifton Series 638** (Dogs) **[1917]**
**Clifton Series 652** (Dogs Xmas series) **[1917]**

***Books illustrated include***
*All about Pets* [with Saville Lumley] / Gash (Harrap 1920)
*Animals of the Bible* / Helme (RTS 1927)
*Barbara Briggs' Painting Book* [Little Dots Picture Book] (RTS 1930)
*British Birds* (Lutterworth 1937)
*British Trees* (Lutterworth 1932)
*Down the Stream* / Helme (Great Thoughts 1929)
*Feathered Friends of Field & Forest* / Helme (RTS 1928)
*Feathered Friends of Stream & Shore* / Helme (RTS 1929)
*Flowers & Plants of New South Wales and Southern Queensland* (Reed nd)
*Four Footed Helpers* / Helme (RTS 1926)
*Friends of Field & Forest* / Helme (RTS 1926)
*Licorice* (Aladdin 1949)
*Logging, the Story of an Industry* / Taylor (Lane Book Co 1962)
*Our Friendly Trees* (Lutterworth 1933)
*Playmates* [Little Dots Picture Book] (RTS nd)
*Some Other Friendly Trees* (Lutterworth 1934)
*The Biggest Whitest Egg* (Golden Gate Junior Books 1966)
*The Book of Birds & Beasties* / Helme (RTS 1927)
*Trees of Britain, Their Form & Character* (Lutterworth 1936)
*The Otter Twins* (McKay c.1959)
*Tobias* (Knopf 1946)
*Zoo Friends* (RTS nd)

## Ethel Constance Brisley (1886-1961)

***Postcards illustrated include***
***Carlton Publishing***
**Series 686** (Portraits of young children) **[nd]**
**Series 736** (Portraits of young girls in hats) **[nd]**
***A Vivian Mansell***
**Series 1005** (Portraits of girls in hats) **[1916]**
**Series 1015** (Portraits with flowers) **[1916]**
**Series 1090** (Children dressing up) **[1918]**
**Series 1106** (Portraits of girls in hats) **[1918]**
**Series 1126** (Portraits of girls in summer hats) **[1919]**
**Series 1127** (Portraits of ladies in hats) **[1919]**

***Books illustrated include***
*Tell me a Tale* [with N Brisley] / Clark (Univ. of London Press 1938)
*Uncle Sandy's Holiday* / Garratt (Harrap 1941)

## Joyce Lankester Brisley (1896-1978)

***Postcards illustrated include***
***Vivian Mansell***
**Series 1156** (Children/hairstyles) **[1920]**

***Books illustrated include***
*Adventures of a Teddy Bear* / Kitchen (Harrap nd)
*Another Bunchy Book* (Harrap 1951)
*Bunchy* (Harrap 1937)
*Further Doings of Milly-Molly-Mandy* (Harrap 1932)
*Jane's First Term* / Catty (Harrap 1949)
*Lambs-tails and Suchlike Verses and Sketches* (Harrap 1930)
*Marigold in Godmother's House* (Harrap 1934)
*Milly-Molly-Mandy & Billy Blunt* (Harrap 1967)
*Milly-Molly-Mandy & Co.* (Harrap 1955)
*Milly-Molly-Mandy Again* (Harrap 1948)

*Milly-Molly-Mandy Stories* (Harrap 1928)
*More Adventures of a Teddy Bear* / Cradock (Harrap 1942)
*More of Milly-Molly-Mandy* (Harrap 1929)
*My Bible Book* (Harrap nd)
*Pretender's Island* / Williams (Knopf 1942)
*Teddy Bear's Farm* / Cradock (Harrap 1956)
*The Dawn Shops and Other Stories* (Harrap 1933)
*The Adventures of Purl and Plain* (Harrap 1941)
*The Dawn Shops and Other Stories* (Harrap 1933)
*The Joyce Lankaster Brisley Book* / Waters (Harrap 1981)
*The May Queen* / Mrs Strang [ed] (Milford nd)
*The Milly-Molly-Mandy Omnibus* (3 books in one) (Harrap 1972)
*The Story of Jane* / Catty (Harrap 1933)
*Three Little Milly-Molly-Mandy Plays* (Harrap 1938)
*Wide, Wide World* / Wetherell (Univ. of London Press 1950)

***Books illustrated with others include***
*Boys and Girls' Wonder Book 1927* (Ward Lock 1926)
*Golden Journeys – Story and Study* (McDougalls Educ. Co. 1933)
*The Wonder Book for Children* (Odhams nd)

***Annuals and periodicals illustrated with others include***
*Blackie's Children's Annual; Christian Science Monitor; Home Chat; Partridge's Children's Annual; Pip and Squeak Annual; Wilfred's Annual*

## Nina Kennard Brisley (1897-1978)

***Postcards illustrated include***
***A Vivian Mansell***
**Series 1016** (Playtime) **[1916]**
**Series 1024** (Boy soldiers & sailors) **[1916]**
**Series 1034** (Games & adventures) **[1917]**
**Series 1035** (Children & animals) **[1917]**
**Series 1036** (At the zoo) **[1917]**
**Series 1037** (Childhood games) **[1917]**
**Series 1057** (At the seaside) **[1917]**
**Series 1058** (Children with toys) **[1917]**
**Series 1059** (Fairies & goblins) **[1917]**
**Series 1064** (Dressing up) **[1917]**
**Series 1066** (In the garden) **[1917]**
**Series 1069** (Children & their dogs) **[1918]**
**Series 1073** (Little mothers) **[1918]**
**Series 1074** (Talking to the birds) **[1918]**
**Series 1103** (Adventures with animals) **[1919]**
**Series 1113** (Toys & games) **[1919]**
**Series 1125** (At the seaside) **[1919]**
**Series 1141** (Sports & games) **[1919]**
**Series 1144** (In my window) **[1919]**
**Series 1168** (Girls & flowers) **[1921]**
**Series 1185** (At the seaside) **[1922]**
**Series 1196** (Games & pastimes) **[1922]**
**Series 2107** (Girls with toys) **[1925]**

***Books illustrated include***
*A Head Girl's Difficulties* / Brent-Dyer (Chambers 1923)
*Blue Roan: A Dog Tale* / Gass (Univ. of London Press 1942)
*Deb at School* / Oxenham (Chambers 1929)
*Deb of Sea House* / Oxenham (Chambers 1931)
*Dobbin and the Silver Shoes* / Clark (Hazell, Watson & Viney 1937)
*Eustacia goes to the Chalet School* (Chambers nd)
*Fairies and Giants* / Masters (Grant Educ. Co. nd)
*Heather leaves School* / Brent-Dyer (Chambers nd)
*Jo of the Chalet School* / Brent-Dyer (Chambers 1926)
*Jo Returns to the Chalet School* / Brent-Dyer (Chambers [1936])
*Kenya Kiddies* / Baldwin (Chambers 1926)
*Lavender Laughs in the Chalet School* / Brent-Dyer (Chambers nd)
*More Stories and How to Tell Them* / Clark (Univ. of Ldn Press 1928)
*Peggy of the Chalet School* / Brent-Dyer (Chambers nd)
*Sunshine Tales for Rainy Days* / Clark (Univ. of London Press 1948)
*Tales for Jack and Jane* / Clark (Univ. of London Press 1936)
*The Cat that Climbed the Christmas Tree* (Univ. of Ldn. Press 1951)
*The Chalet Girls in Camp* / Brent-Dyer (Chambers 1932)
*The Chalet School and Jo* / Brent-Dyer (Chambers 1931)
*The Chalet School Goes to It* / Brent-Dyer (Chambers nd)
*The Exploits of the Chalet Girls* / Brent-Dyer (Chambers 1933)
*The Farmer and the Fairy* / Clark (Univ. of London Press 1937)
*The Head Girl of the Chalet School* / Brent-Dyer (Chambers 1928)
*The Lost Staircase* / Brent-Dyer (Chambers 1946)
*The Maids of La Rochelle* / Brent-Dyer (Chambers 1924)
*The New Chalet School* / Brent-Dyer (Chambers 1938)
*The Princess of the Chalet School* / Brent-Dyer (Chambers 1927)
*The Rivals of the Chalet School* / Brent-Dyer (Chambers 1929)
*The School at the Chalet* / Brent-Dyer (Chambers 1925)
*The School in the Wilds* / Baldwin (Chambers 1925)
*The Secret of the Beeches* / Norman (Univ. of London Press 1950)
*The Squire's Young Folk* / Stokes (Partridge c.1920)
*The Tale that Had no Ending* / Clark (Univ. of London Press 1929)
*The Talkative Sparrow* / Clark (Univ. of London Press nd)
*Twenty Tales for Telling* / Clark (Univ. of London Press 1933)
*Twilight and Fireside* / Clark (Univ. of London Press 1942)

***Books illustrated with Margaret Tarrant include***
*Telling the Time* / Golding (Tiger Books 1988)
*The Animal ABC* / Golding (Ward Lock nd)
*The Book of Games* / Hayes (Ward Lock 1920)
*The Book of the Clock* (Ward Lock 1920)

***Books illustrated with others include***
*Favourite Fairy Tales* (Ward Lock 1922)
*Favourite Fairy Stories* (Ward Lock 1923)
*Old Fairy Tales* (Ward Lock 1923)
*Our Darlings Play Book* (Milford nd)
*SPCK Giant Picture Books* (SPCK 1950)
*Tell me a Tale* [with E Brisley] / Clark (Univ. of London Press 1938)
*The First War-time Christmas Book* (Univ London Press 1939)
*The Foxglove Story Book* (Blackie nd)
*The Story Wonder Book* (Ward Lock nd)

***Annuals and periodicals illustrated with others include***
*Blackie's Children's Annual; Christian Science Monitor; Home Chat; Partridge's Children's Annual; Pip and Squeak Annual; Tiny Folks' Annual; Wilfred's Annual; The Wonder Book*

## Randolph Caldecott (1846-1886)

**Postcards illustrated**
**See page 105**

***Books illustrated include***
*A Sketchbook* (Routledge c.1880)
*Baron Bruno & Other Fairy Stories* (Macmillan 1875)
*Bracebridge Hall* (Macmillan 1877)
*Breton Folk* (Sampson Low 1880)
*Complete Collection of RC's Contributions to the Graphic* (Routledge 1888)
*Daddy Darwin's Dovecote* / Ewing (SPCK 1884)
*Flint – Historic Notices* / Taylor (Eliot & Stock 1883)
*Gleanings from the Graphic* (Routledge 1889)
*Graphic Pictures* (Routledge 1883)
*Jackanapes* / Ewing (SPCK nd)
*Jack and the Beanstalk* / H Tennyson (Macmillan 1886)
*Juliana Horatia Ewing and her Books* / Gatty (SPCK 1885)
*Last Graphic Pictures* (Routledge 1888)
*Lob Lie-by-the-Fire* / Ewing (SPCK nd)
*More Graphic Pictures* (Routledge 1887)
*North Italian Folk* / Comyns Carr (Chatto & Windus 1878)
*Old Christmas* / Irving (MacMillan 1876)
*Randolph Caldecott's Sketches* (Sampson Low 1890)
*Randolph Caldecott's Painting Book* (Warne c.1905)
*Some of Aesop's Fables with Modern Instances* / (Macmillan 1883)
*The Harz Mountains* / Blackburn (Sampson Low 1873)
*The Hey-Diddle-Diddle Picture Book* (Routledge nd)
*The Panjandrum Picture Book* (Routledge nd)
*The Owls of Olynn Belfry* (Field & Tuer nd)
*What the Blackbird Said* / Locker (Routledge 1881)
*Randolph Caldecott, a Personal Memoir..* .(Sampson Low 1886)

***'R Caldecott's Picture Books'***
*A Frog He Would a-Wooing Go* (Routledge 1883)
*Come Lasses and Lads* (Routledge 1884)
*Hey Diddle Diddle and Baby Bunting* (Routledge 1881)
*Mrs Mary Blaize* (Routledge 1885)
*Ride a Cock Horse.../ A Farmer went Trotting...* (Routledge 1884)
*Sing a Song for Sixpence* (Routledge 1880)
*The Babes in the Wood* (Routledge 1879)
*The Diverting History of John Gilpin* (Routledge 1878)
*The Farmer's Boy* (Routledge 1881)
*The Fox jumps over the Parson's Gate* (Routledge1883)
*The Great Panjandrum Himself* (Routledge 1885)
*The House That Jack Built* (Routledge 1878)
*The Mad Dog* (Routledge 1879)
*The Milkmaid* (Routledge 1880)
*The Queen of Hearts* (Routledge 1881)
*The Three Jovial Huntsman* (Routledge 1880)

***Annuals and periodicals illustrated with others include***
*Aunt Judy's Annual; The Graphic; The Illustrated London News; The Imprint*

## Dorothy Carleton Smyth (1880-1933)

***Postcards illustrated include***
***Valentine***
**Nursery Rhymes [1904]**

## René Cloke (1904-1995)

***Postcards illustrated include***
***Carwal Publications***
**Single card** (Angels and crypt) **Greetings for Your Birthday [nd]**
***CW Faulkner***
**Series 1002** (Fairies and birds) **[1937]**
**Series 2019** (Flower fairies) **[1937]**
**Series 2041** (Flower fairies) **[1937]**
**Series 2047** (Flower fairies) **[1937]**
***J Salmon***
**Series 4624-4629** (Boys and girls in the country) **[1935]**
**Series 5388-5393** (Woodland animals) **[1959]**
***Valentine***
**Series 340-343 René Cloke Postcards [1951]**
**Series 393-394 René Cloke Postcards [1951]**
**Series 727-732 Birthday Postcards (Years 1-6) [c.1954]**
**Series 1183-1188 René Cloke Postcards [1948]**
**Series 1325-1330 René Cloke Postcards [1949]**
**Series 1492-1497 René Cloke Postcards [1950]**
**Series 1758-1763 René Cloke Postcards [1950]**
**Series 1847-1852 René Cloke Postcards [1951]**
**Series 3327-3332 René Cloke Postcards [1936]**
**Series 3533-3538 René Cloke Postcards [1936]**
**Series 3713-3718 René Cloke Postcards [1937]**
**Series 3930-3935 René Cloke Postcards [1938]**
**Series 4142-4147 René Cloke Postcards [1938]**
**Series 4385-4390 René Cloke Fairy Series [1938]**
**Series 4617-4622 René Cloke Postcards [1939]**
**Series 4724-4729 René Cloke Postcards [1939]**
**Series 5105-5110 René Cloke Fairy Series [c.1940]**
**Series 5372-5377 René Cloke Fairy Series [c.1940]**
**Series 5571-5575 René Cloke Fairy Series [c.1942]**
***Edward Ward***
**Truth in a Tale Series [c.1952]**
**Birds and Butterflies Series [c.1952]**

***Books illustrated up to 1970 include***
*Adventure in Acorn Wood* (Blackie 1962)
*Alice in Wonderland* / Carroll (Gawthorne 1943)
*Alice in Wonderland, The World's Greatest ...* (Educ. Book Co. c.1945)
*Alice Through the Looking Glass* / Carroll (Collins 1951)
*All Things Bright & Beautiful Painting Book 1* (Methodist Youth Dept. nd)
*Amelia Jane is Naughty Again* / Blyton (Beaver nd)
*Barnaby's Cuckoo Clock* (Wheaton 1958)
*Beauty and the Beast* (Ward nd)
*Before We Go to Bed* (Juvenile Prod. nd)
*Bingo and Carrot* (Radiant Way Reader) / Peattie (Chambers nd )
*Birds of the River* (Ward nd)
*Chickweed* (Ward 1947)
*Crossword Painting Book* (Religious Educ Press 1966)
*Dragonfly Storybook* (Exeter 1965)
*Enid Blyton's Pixieland Story Book* (Collins 1966)
*Fairyland Tales* [with Hilda Boswell] (Collins nd)
*Fairy Stories* (Ward Lock nd)
*Fairy Stories from Hans Anderson* (Ward 1947)
*Favourite Stories from Hans Anderson* (Ward [1947)
*Grimm's Fairy Tales* (Gawthorne 1947)
*Hans Anderson's Stories* (1935)
*Jacko & Jumbo* (Sandle Bros nd)
*Joybells Picture and Story Book* (Juvenile Prod. 1949)
*Little Boy Blue Nursery Rhymes & Fairy Tales* (Juvenile Prod. 1949)
*Little Darling Book* [4 parts] (Sandle Bros 1964)
*Little Folks' Book of Nursery Tales* (Warne 1963)
*Little Folks' First Book* / Burchell (Warne 1964)
*Little Folks' Second Book* / Burchell (Warne 1966)
*Little Red Riding Hood* [The Children's Pantomime] (Juv Prod. nd)
*Maidlin to the Rescue* / Oxenham (Chambers 1934)
*Merry's New Hat* (Wheaton 1958)
*Mr Never-Lost* (Chambers nd)
*Mr Never-Lost Goes On* / Turnbull (Chambers 1934)
*Mr Podge of Oaktree Lodge* (1943)
*Music in the Meadow and Other Verses* (Hamlyn 1968)
*My Story Book* (Purnell 1964)
*No Dogs Please* (Exeter 1967)
*Nursery Rhymes* (Purnell nd)
*Our Child Begins to Pray* / Awdry (Ward 1951)
*Pantomime Series* (Ward Lock nd)
*Parade* (Renwick c.1945)
*Pat-a-cake Nursery Rhymes* (nd)
*Pat the Pedlar* [Radiant Way Reader] / Peattie (Chambers nd)
*Paul Piglet Keeps Shop* (Blackie 1960)
*Pixieland Rhymes* (Collins nd)
*Pixieland Storybook* (Collins 1966)
*Popkyn the Pedlar* (Blackie 1960)
*Pop-up Picture Nursery Rhymes* (Juvenile Prod. nd)
*Red Riding Hood goes to the Teddy Bears Picnic* (Crowther 1943)
*Ride a Cock-Horse Nursery Rhymes* (Juvenile Prod. nd)
*Round the Year Story Book* (Gawthorne nd)
*Sing a Song of Sixpence Nursery Rhymes* (Juvenile Prod. nd)
*Snow White and the Seven Dwarfs* (Collins nd)
*Snowy for Sale* (Blackie 1961)
*Spirit Stories for Children* / Burton (Shere nd)
*Stony Stream* / Sully (Ward 1950)
*Stories Jesus Heard* / Krall [ed] (Religious Education Press 1945)
*Stories for Bedtime* (cover) [with Willy Schmerle] (Purnell 1953)
*The Brave Tin Soldier* / Andersen (Dean 1969)
*The Happy Seasons* [poems] (Hamlyn 1968)
*The Little Blue Engine that Wanted a Drink* (Juvenile Prod. c.1956)
*The Little Roundabout Horse* (Blackie nd)
*The Nightingale* / Andersen (Ward 1945)
*The Snow Queen* / Andersen (Dean 1968)
*The Three Golliwogs* / Blyton (Dean 1969)
*The Three Little Pigs* (Collins nd)
*The Twins go to Market* (Wheaton 1965)
*The Ugly Duckling by Hans Andersen* (Ward nd)
*Through the Looking Glass and What Alice Found There* (Gawthorne nd)
*Tippety is Snowed Up* (Blackie 1954)
*Uncle Remus* (Gawthorne c.1944)

***Books illustrated with others include***
*Kiddies Gift Book* (Renwick c.1945)
*New Story Budget for Little Folks* [et al] (Nelson nd)
*Punch and Judy Annual* (Juvenile Prod. nd)
*The Radiant Way* (Chambers 1933)
*The Treasure Hunt* [with Olive Duhy] (Gawthorne nd)

## Phyllis Cooper (1895-1988)

***Postcards illustrated include***
***Millar & Lang***
**National series (Identified numbers)**
**1003 1004 1011 1018 1037 1038 1039 1041 1052 1053 1067 1068 1069 1070 1071 1072 1073 1074 1075 1076 1077 1078 3591 3599 3602 3650 3651 3652 3951 4031 4033 4034 4035 4037 4262**
***Raphael Tuck***
**Oilette Series C2250 Happy Land Christmas (3 designs) [1923]**
**Oilette Series C2251 Happy Land Christmas (3 designs) [1923]**
**Valentine Postcard No. 100 (2 designs) [c.1925]**
**Valentine Postcard No. 101 (2 designs) [c.1925]**
**Oilette Happy Land Series I 3463 [1924]**
**Oilette Happy Land Series II 3464 [1924]**

Oilette Happy Land Series III 3480 [1925]
Oilette Happy Land Series IV 3481 [1925]
Oilette Happy Land Series V 3482 [1925]
Oilette Happy Land Series VI 3486 [1925]
Oilette Happy Land Series VII 3487 [1925]
Oilette Nursery Rhymes Series III 3488 [1925]
*Valentine (Identified numbers)*
101  102 [c.1927]
*Advertising postcards*
Ovaltine P114-P119 [c.1924]
Ovaltine P149-P154 [c.1925]

*Books illustrated include*
*Betty & Babs Painting Book* [No. 100C/1] (nd)
*Circus Painting Book* (Tuck nd)
*Dolly Town Tracing Book* [No. 501] (nd)
*Father Tuck's Annual for 1926* [et al] (Tuck 1925)
*Handy Andy* [No. 705] (nd)
*Here We Go Stories* [No. 605] (nd)
*Jack in the Box* [No. 555C] (nd)
*Kiddies Tracing Book* (Juvenile Prod. nd)
*My Lucky Day* [No. 212] (nd)
*My Toys Tracing Book* [No. 791] (nd)
*Naughty Elephant* [No. 772] (nd)
*Nursery Rhymes* [No. 1602A] (Juvenile Prod. nd)
*Our Tracing Book* [No. 507] (nd)
*Picture Tales* [No. 656] (nd)
*Pip Pip Painting Book* (nd)
*Playtime Tracing Book* [No. 500] (nd)
*Pretty Pets Painting Book* [No. 1555C/2] (nd)
*Rain Day Stories and Rhymes* [No. 606] (nd)
*Snow White* [No. 2700/A] (nd)
*Sweet Dreams* (nd)
*Tommy Tucker's Painting Book* [No. 91] (nd)
*Toys for Girls & Boys Painting...*[No. 16] (Renwick nd)
*When We Grow Up* [No. 773] (nd)

## Kate Cowderoy (1875-1972)

*Postcards illustrated include*
*Gottschalk, Dreyfus & Davis*
Star Series (Shakespearean scenes) [c.1904]
*W Hagelberg*
Christmas postcard – A handsome hostess... [nd]
*Raphael Tuck*
Art Series 6630 Merry Snowtime [1905] [Tuck France 958]
Christmas Series C126 [1907]
Christmas Series C141 [1907]

## Hilda Cowham (1873-1965)

*Postcards illustrated include*
*CW Faulkner*
Series 1601 Fairy Revels [1916]
Series 1618 Merry Moments [1916]
*Inter Art*
Series 438-443 Fairies Series [1913]
Series 498-503 Christmas Series [1913]
Series 599-601 Cowham Series [1914]
Series 4025-4030 Comique Series [1922]
*Raphael Tuck*
Series 1009 The Write Away Series [c.1903]
Series 1270 Humorous Popular Plays [c.1907]
Series 1322 Seaside Series I [c.1907]
Series 1323 Seaside Series II [c.1907]
Series 1394 Motor Ways [c.1907]
Series 6003 Our Party I [1904]
Series 6076 Our Party II [1905]
*Valentine*
Unnumbered Series [1913]
*Advertising postcards*
Co-operative Wholesale Society Series [nd]
Two Steeples Productions Series [nd]

*Books illustrated include*
*A Bunch of Cousins and the Barn Boys* / Meade (Chambers 1908)
*Blacklegs & Others* (Kegan Paul 1911)
*Curly Heads and Long Legs* / Floyd [et al] (Tuck 1914)
*Father Tuck's Postcard Painting Book* (Tuck c.1909)
*Fiddlesticks* (Pearson 1900)
*For Somebody's Baby* (Tuck 1923)
*Good Old Nursery Rhymes* (Gale & Polden c.1915)
*Kitty in Fairyland* (nd)
*Mother Goose's Rag Book* [Rag Book No. 201] Dean (1917)
*My Playmate* [Father Tuck's Fairy Mascot Series] (Tuck 1923)
*My Playtime Book* [et al] / Vredenburg (Tuck nd)
*My Sunshine Book* [et al] [Golden Gift Ser.] / Labrousse (Tuck nd)
*Our Generals* / Player (Tuck 1903)
*Ping Pong People* / Golesworthy (1905)
*Poor Uncle Harry* / Jacberns (Chambers 1910)
*Princess Nusrat* (Hutchinson 1922)
*Sunny Tales* [et al] [Golden Gift Ser.4640] / Hopper (Tuck nd)
*The Adventures of Willy and Nilly* / Morris (Bodley Head 1921)
*The Fairy Princess* (sheet music) (Larway 1921)
*The Hilda Cowham Post Card Painting Book* (Faulkner nd)
*The Little Girl's Sewing Book* / Klickmann (Girls' Own Paper 1916)
*The Magic Curtain & Other Children's Poems* / (Merton Press nd)
*The Mysterious Twins* / Girvin (Cassell 1910)
*The Pink Foxglove No 38* [Ring-o-Roses Series] (Cassell nd)
*The Record Term* / Jacberns (Chambers 1906)
*The Tale of the Birds No 43* [Ring-o-Roses Series] (Cassell nd)
*The Wimple Children* / Lea (Fisher Unwin nd)
*Vivian's Lesson* / Grierson (Chambers 1907)
*Willy Wimple's Adventures* / Lea (Fisher Unwin 1908)
*Willy Wimple and Ragged Robin* / Lea (Fisher Unwin c.1911)
*Books illustrated with others include*
*Big Book of Pictures and Stories* (Blackie nd)
*Country Days* (no 5252) (Tuck nd)
*Days of Delight* [with Janet Murray] [Golden Gift Series] (Tuck nd)
*Little Frolic* (Shaw c.1934)
*Little Frolic* (Juvenile Prod. 1939)
*Little Sunbeams* [Golden Gift Series] / Vredenburg [ed] (Tuck nd)
*Our Darling's Own Book* (Cassell 1912)
*Pages of Pleasure* (Tuck nd)
*Pleasure Pages* [with Attwell] / Nesbit/Gale (Tuck nd)
*Romps and Revels* (c.1939)
*Something to Tell You* / Vredenburg (Tuck nd)
*Starlight Tales* (Cassell c.1910)
*Sunny Stories* [with MLA] / Vredenburg [ed] (Tuck nd)
*The Adventures of Willy and Nilly* / Morris (Bodley Head 1921)
*The Children's Playmate* [et al] (Tuck nd)
*The Fairy Shoemaker* (Cassell c.1910)
*The Happy Book* (Tuck 1931)
*The Ruby Fairy Book* / Vredenburg [ed] (Tuck c.1901)
*Wonder Book. a Picture Annual for Boys and Girls* (Ward Lock 1906)
*Annuals and periodicals illustrated with others include*
*Blackie's Childrens' Annual; Bo-Peep Annual; Bo-Peep's Bumper Book; Cassell's Children's Annual; Darton's Leading Strings; Father Tuck's Annual; Joy Book Children's Annual; Little Folks' Annual; Little People's Annual; Moonshine; My Lovely Big Book; Pearson's Magazine; Pick-me-up; Playbox Annual; Playtime Annual; Puck Annual; Punch; Sunday at Home; The Girls' Realm Annual; The Graphic; The Joy Book; The Oojah Annual; The Queen; The Royal Magazine; The Sketch; The Sphere; The Tatler; Tiny Tots Annual*

## Rie Cramer (1887-1987)

*Postcards illustrated include*
*Drukkerij Benefelder*
Voor het Kind (For the children) [1936]
Christmas designs in a large series by many artists.
*W de Haan*
Series 129 Lentebloemen [c.1916]
Series 130 Bergerettes [c.1920]
Series 131 Vieilles Chansons [c.1920]
Series 132 Le Temps Jadis [c.1922]
Series 133 Noels de France [c.1922]
Series 134 (Months of the year) [c.1926]
Series 135 Rie Cramer's Nieuwe Rijmpjes [c.1926]

Series 136 Au Bon Vieux Temps [c.1926]
Series 137 Kinderdeuntjes uit Grootmoeders Tijd [c.1930]
Series 138 Oudt Nederlandsche Minneliedjes [c.1930]
Series 139 L'amour à Travers des Siecles [c.1930]
Series 141 (Children's day series) [c.1930]
Series 142 Versjes van Vroeger [c.1930]
Series 152 Onze Lievelingen [c.1930]
*Humphrey Milford*
*Postcards for the Little Ones Series*
Joyous Days [1930]
*Roukes & Erhart*
(New Year Series) [c.1935]
*Books published in English include*
*Andersen's Fairy Tales* [with Lilian Govey] (Milford 1921)
*Favourite Fairy Tales* / ed Osborne (Penn Publishing 1930)
*Favourite French Fairy Tales* / Douglas [ed] (Harrap 1921)
*Goldilocks and the Three Bears* (Blackie nd)
*Grimm's Fairy Tales* / ed Olcott ((Hampton 1922)
*Hans Andersen's Fairy Tales* (Milford 1921)
*In Holland There's a House* (Blackie nd)
*In the Garden* / Joan (Milford 1921)
*Little Dutchy* [with A Anderson]/ Ransome/de Jong (Harrap 1925)
*Little Mothers* / Joan (Milford 1921)
*Little Picture Rhymes* / Martens [ed] (Augener c.1924)
*Little Picture Songs* / Martens [ed] (Augener c.1924)
*Old Songs in French and English* (Penn Publishing 1923)
*Oriental Fairy Tales* (Duffield 1923)
*Spring Flowers* / Vogel (Black c.1925)
*Sunshine Stories* [with Cora Patterson] (nd)
*The Little Dutch Girl* (Blackie nd)
*The Little Mermaid* (Blackie nd)
*The Snow Queen* (Blackie nd)
*Thumbelina* (Blackie nd)
*Winter* (Augener nd)

## Muriel Dawson (1897-1974)

*Postcards illustrated include*
*The Medici Society*
Pkt 19 Happy Hours [c.1928]
The Things I Take to Bed; Dolly's Bath; Critical!;
Firelight Fancies; Goodnight Everybody; Sleepy Head.
(In 1936, Pkt 19 was changed to include 4 designs by Muriel Dawson: The First Aconite, The Fisherman, Tea Time, Welcome to Fairyland and 2 by Margaret Horder)
Pkt 310 Mary's Child [nd]
Pkt 290 Madonna of the Meadows [nd]
Pkt 293 Christ child & spotted deer [nd]
Pkt 309 The New Born King [nd]
Pkt 19 Happy Hours [nd]
Pkt 19 Happy Hours [nd]
Large format postcards $5^{7/8}$ x $4^{1/8}$
1052 Young Hopeful
1058 How Many Peas in a Pod?
1065 Happy Springtime
1070 Friendly Greetings
1075 The Goose Girl
1077 On the Seashore
1079 Rabbits
1095 Finding the Leveret
1100 See Saw
1101 The Blue Butterfly
1171 Sea Breezes
1172 Curiosity
1329 The Ox Knoweth His Master

*Books illustrated include*
*A Mother is Love* [with Muriel Wood] (Hallmark 1970)
*Another Lovely Book of Nursery Rhymes* (Tuck nd)
*Happy Days* (Tuck nd)
*My Book of Nursery Rhymes* (Tuck nd)
*Nursery Rhymes and Jingles* (Warne nd)
*The Childhood of Jesus* [with Claire Dawson] (Medici nd)
*Wonderful Days* / Latham (Cecil Palmer 1929)

## Marjorie Dexter (1903-1992)

*Postcards illustrated include*
*J Salmon*
Series 3141-3146 (Studies of girlhood) [1926]
Series 3765-3770 (Girls and their pets) [1926]
*Valentine*
Unnumbered Series (6 cards) [c.1925]
Unnumbered Card. Jolly Dutch Twins are We [c.1925]

## Linda Edgerton (1890-1983)

*Postcards illustrated include*
*A Vivian Mansell*
Series 1042 Nursery Rhymes [1917]
Series 1067 (Nursery rhymes) [1917]
Series 1072 (Nursery rhymes) [1917]
Series 1096 (Nursery rhymes) [1917]
Series 1107 (Nursery rhymes) [1918]
Series 1110 (Nursery rhyme characters) [1919]*
Series 1111 (Nursery rhyme characters) [1919]*
Series 1140 (At the station) [1919]
Series 1146 (Nursery rhymes) [1919]
Series 1155 (Christmas series) [1919]
Series 1157 (Fairy tales) [1920]
Series 1158 (Nursery rhymes) [1920]
Series 1159 (Nursery rhymes) [1920]
Series 1160 (Riddle rhymes) [1920]
Series 1163 (Elves and fairies) [1920]
Series 1167 (In the fields) [1921]
Series 1170 (Nursery rhymes) [1921]
Series 1171 (Do you collect...?) [1921]
Series 1175 (The town boy, country boy etc) [1921]
Series 1179 (Counties and nursery rhymes) [1921]
Series 1187 (Play time at home [press outs]) [1921]
Series 1188 (Nursery rhyme [press outs]) [1921]
Series 1191 (Lesson time, play time etc) [1921]
Series 1194 (Nursery rhymes) [press outs] [1921]
Series 1196 (Little Red Riding Hood) [press outs] [1921]
Series 2105 (Nursery rhymes) [1922]
Series 2106 (Nursery rhymes) [1922]
*Also with Christmas captions
*J Salmon*
Series 4116-4120 [1936]
Single card 1989 Playtime [c.1936]
(also with Dutch captions)
*EW Savory*
Clifton Series (4 designs per series)
Clifton Series 782 (Flower rhymes) [1919]
Clifton Series 783 (Little workers) [1919]
Clifton Series 807 (Nursery rhymes) [1919]
Clifton Series 810 (Rhymes) [1919]
Clifton Series 811 (In the fields and on the shore) [1919]
Clifton Series 815 (Little girl at the window) [1919]
Clifton Series 824 (Making things with vegetables) [1920]
Clifton Series 841 (Christmas games) [1920]

*Books illustrated include*
*Boy Blue and His Chum* [Playbook No 6040] (Tuck nd)
*London Cries Painting Book* [Little Artists Ser. 4070] (Tuck nd)
*Nursery Rhymes Painting Book* [Little Artists Ser. 4060] (Tuck nd)
*Peggy's Pig* (Tuck nd)
*Red Riding Hood's Cottage* [Playbook] (Tuck nd)
*Spring Summer Autumn Winter Painting Book* (Tuck nd)
*Ten Favourite Fairy Tales* [Playbook No 505] (Tuck nd)
*Ten Little Favourite Toys* [Playbook No 501] (Tuck nd)
*Ten Little Nursery Dolls* [Playbook No 500] (Tuck nd)
*'Colour Me and Cut Out Series'*
*Bobby's Book* (Mansell c.1920)
*Bo-peep and Boy-Blue* (Mansell c.1920)
*Colour Me and Cut Out* (Mansell c.1920)
*Mother Goose Book* (Mansell c.1920)
*Pat and Robin's ABC* (Mansell c.1920)
*The House that Jack Built* (Mansell c.1920)
*The Brownies' Circus Book* (Mansell c.1920)

## William Henry Ellam (1859-1935)

***Postcards illustrated include***
***ETW Dennis***
**Puzzle 'Em Message Card Series [1918]**
***E Mack***
***Toy Town Series***
**Series 025 The Toy Shop Pkt. [1920]**
**Series 040 Shadowgraph [1920]**
**Series 070 The Holiday Pkt. [1920]**
**Series 076 My Zoo [1920]**
**Series 082 Dolls Furniture Pkt. [1920]**
**Series 106 Famous Buildings Pkt. [1920]**
**Series 112 The Motor Pkt. [1920]**
**Series 118 Dolls Furniture II Pkt. [1920]**
**Series 124 Toy Town Cinema [1920]**
**Series 130 The Scout Pkt. [1920]**
***J Salmon***
***Miniature Models Series (6 designs)***
**Series 2435 Motor Cars [1923]**
**Series 2449 Farm Yard Postcards [1923]**
**Series 2587 Panorama Model P/Cs [1924]**
**Series 2931 Children's Circus [1925]**
***Raphael Tuck***
**Platform Series I 6809 [1910]**
**Platform Series II 6810 [1910]**
**Oilette Series 9562 Mixed Bathing [1908]**
**Oilette Series 9636 Mixed Bathing II [1909]**
**Oilette Series 9684 Trunks Full of Fun [1909]**
**Oilette Series 9793 Teddy Bears at the Seaside [1910]**
**Oilette Series 9935 Aeroplanes [1911]**
**Oilette Series 9980 Our Boy Scouts [1911]**
**Oilette Series 3404 Model Railway Engines [1923]**

***Books illustrated include***
*Trafalgar* (Castell Brothers 1905)
*Waterloo* (Castell Brothers 1905)

## Charles Folkard (1878-1963)

***Postcards illustrated include***
***A&C Black***
**Series 43 English Nursery Rhymes [1926]**
**Series 80 Alice in Wonderland [c.1928]**
**Series 91 Nursery Rhymes and Tales [1930]**
(4 designs by Charles Folkard, 2 by JH Hartley)
***Valentine***
**Fine Art Series (Teddy Tail) [1922]**

***Books illustrated include***
*Aesop's Fables* (Black 1912)
*A Fairy Ballet* [sheet music] (Murdoch & Co. nd)
*Alice's Adventures in Wonderland* / Carroll (Black 1929)
*Arabian Nights* (Black c.1916)
*Belgian Playmates* / Pollock (Gay & Hancock 1914)
*Flint Heart: a Fairy Story* (Elder 1910)
*Grimm's Fairy Tales* (Black 1911)
*How Lotys had Tea with a Lion* / Kirkman (Black 1921)
*How the Knot Came into Teddy's Tail* (Juvenile Prod. nd)
*Jolly Calle* / Nyblom (Dent 1913)
*Mother Goose's Nursery Rhymes* / Walter [ed] (Black 1922)
*Mother Goose's Nursery Tales* / Walter [ed] (Black c.1923)
*Nursery Rhymes* [with Dorothy Fitchew (de la More Press 1925)
*Nursery Rhyme Alphabet* (Black 1921)
*Ottoman Wonder Tales* / Garnett [ed] (Black 1915)
*Peggy the Pup* [Noah's Ark Cut Outs] / Fry (Allday 1921)
*Pinnochio: The Tale of a Puppet* / Collodi (Dent 1926)
*Rocking Horse Rhymes* (1932)
*Songs from Alice in Wonderland & Through the Looking Glass* (Black 1921)
*Swiss Family Robinson* / Wyss (Dent 1910)
*Tales for Children from Many Lands* [with M Chadburn] (Dent 1939)
*Tales of the Taunus Mountains* / Dehn (Blackwell 1937)
*Teddy Tail and the Magic Flowers* (Juvenile Prods. nd)
*Teddy Tail at the Seaside* (Black 1920)
*Teddy Tail of the 'Daily Mail' in Fairyland* (Black nd)
*Teddy Tail of the 'Daily Mail' in Nursery Rhyme Land* (Black 1915)
*Teddy Tail's Adventures in the A, B, Sea* (Black 1926)
*Teddy Tail's Alphabet* (Black 1921)
*Teddy Tail's Fairy Tales* (Black 1921)
*Teddy Tail in Toyland* (Black 1922)
*The Adventures of Teddy Tail of the 'Daily Mail'* (Black 1915)
*The Arabian Nights* / Barham (Black 1913)
*The Book of Nonsense* / Green (Dent 1956)
*The Children's Shakespeare* (Dent 1911)
*The Flint Heart* / Phillpotts (Dutton 1910)
*The Jackdaw of Rheims* (Gay & Hancock 1913)
*The King's Friend* (Church Newspaper Co. 1898)
*The Land of Nursery Rhyme* (Dent 1932)
*The Magic Egg* / Black (Black 1922)
*The Princess and the Goblin* / Macdonald (Dent nd)
*The Princess and Curdie* / MacDonald (Dent nd)
*The Seven Champions of Christendon* / Wynne (Jarrold 1920)
*The Swiss Family Robinson* (Dent 1926)
*The Troubles of a Gnome* / Gardner (Black 1928)
*The Young Discoverers* [et al] (Cassell nd)
*Twenty Folk and Fairy Tales from East to West* (Black 1939)
*Water Sprites* (sheet music) / W Carroll (Forsyth nd)
*Witches Hollow* / Brook (Black 1920)
***'Noah's Ark Cut Out Series'***
*The Story of Big Bill, a Brown Bear* / Fry (Allday 1921)
*The Story of Big Eye, a Barn Owl* / Fry (Allday 1921)
*The Story of the Frog* / Fry (Allday 1921)
*The Tale of Pengy, a Penguin* / Fry (Allday 1921)
*What Billy Bunny Told* / Fry (Allday 1921)
***Annuals illustrated with others include***
*Little Folks; Joy Street; Pip and Squeak Annual; Playbox Annual; Prattle's Annual; Printer's Pie; The Sphere; The Tatler; The Infant's Magazine; Bo-Peep; Cassell's Annual for Boys and Girls; Father Tuck's Annual*

## Maude Goodman (1853-1938)

***Postcards illustrated include***
***Raphael Tuck***
**Series 143 (Nos. 824-835) The Maud Goodman Series [1901]**
**Art Series 6615 Brown Eyes and Blue [1905]**
**Art Series 6746** (Genre studies) **[1905]**
**Art Series 6747** (Genre studies) **[1905]**
**Art Series 6748** (Genre studies) **[1905]**
**Oilette Series 8651 Thinking of Somebody [c.1906]**

***Books illustrated include***
*A Christmas Visit* / Scannell (Tuck c.1895)
*Flowers I Bring and Songs I Sing* [with Arthur Scanes] (Tuck 1890)
*Golden Days and Silver Eves* [with Arthur Scanes] (Tuck nd)
*Listen Long and Listen Well* [with Ellen Welby] / Nesbit (Tuck c.1893)
*Little Nightcaps* [et al] / Vredenburg [ed] (Tuck nd)
*Little Phoebe* (Castell 1889)
*Playtime Stories* [et al] (Tuck nd)
*Rosy Cheeks and Golden Ringlets* / Nesbit (Tuck c.1894)
*Tales that are True for Brown Eyes and Blue* / Nesbit [et al] (Tuck 1894)

## Lilian Govey (1886-1974)

***Postcards illustrated include***
***Humphrey Milford***
***Postcards for the Little Ones Series***
**The Mouseykins [1924]**
**The Little Mouse Family [1924]**
**Dreams and Fairies [1922]**
**A Day at the Zoo [1925]**
**Pleased to See You [1930]** (3 by Alan Wright)
**Nursery Rhymes from Animal Land [1930]**
***Wildt & Kray***
**Series 3809** (Patriotic) **[c.1915]**
**Series 3846** (Patriotic) **[c.1915]**
**Series 3910 [c.1915]**
**Series 3911** (Patriotic) **[c.1917]**
**Series 4021** (Christmas series) **[c.1918]**
**Series 4139** (Christmas series) **[c.1919]**

***Books illustrated include***
*Acorn Elf* [A Stick Book] (HF/H&S 1911)
*A Kind Little Kitten* (HF/H&S nd)
*A Little Book of Toys* [Little Big Book] / Hancock (Milford 1928)
*Birds, Beasts and Fishes* (HF/H&S nd)
*Bunny the Bold* [Dumpy Series] (HF/H&S c.1915)
*Cheeps the Chicken* [Dumpy Series] (HF/H&S c.1915)
*Felix Frog* [Heads and Tails Series] (HF/H&S c.1915)
*Geraldine* / Davidson (Nelson nd)
*Grandpa and the Tiger* / Heward (Harrap 1924)
*Grimm's Fairy Stories* / H Strang [ed] (Milford nd)
*Hazel and Willow* [A Pocketful of Rye Series] (HF/H&S 1914)
*How Bee Wee Built a House...* / Herbertson (Dean 1921)
*Jane the Determined* / Davidson (Nelson nd)
*Jewel Jam* [Ting-a-Ling Tales] (HF/H&S 1914)
*Judy, the Guide* / Brent-Dyer (Nelson nd)
*Kathleen's Adventure* [with HR Millar / Girvin (Milford 1926)
*Little Folks at the Farm* [Little Big Book] / Handcock (Milford 1928)
*New Book of the Fairies* / Harradon (Milford 1915)
*Nursery Rhymes with Sauc(e)y Endings* [advertising] (HP Sauce nd)
*Old Fairy Tales* (Nelson 1936)
*Peter Porker* [Heads and Tails Series] (HF/H&S c.1915)
*Piggy the Proud* [Dumpy Series] (HF/H&S c.1915)
*Pixie Brown* / Pitt-Taylor (Dean 1920)
*Strawberry Bay* [A Stick Book] (HF/H&S nd)
*Tales of Happy Common* / Herbertson (Dean 1920)
*Tales From Toyland* / Joan (Milford 1924)
*Teeny Weeny's Merry Book* (Milford 1932)
*The Book of Happy Gnomes* / Herbertson (Milford 1924)
*The Creepie Man* / Herbertson (Dean 1920)
*The Creepie Man's Poke Sack* / Herbertson (Dean 1921)
*The Dolly Book* / Herbertson (Dean 1920)
*The Happy Families* / Bradby (HF/H&S 1914)
*The Holiday Book* / Herbertson (Dean nd)
*The House that Jack Built* (HF/H&S 1916)
*The May Queen* / Mrs Strang [ed] (Milford nd)
*The Needle Witch's Pepper Pot* / Herbertson (Dean 1921)
*The Old Fairy Tales* (Nelson 1926)
*The Rose Book of the Fairies* (Milford nd)
*The Rose Fairy Book* / Mrs Strang [ed] (HF/H&S 1912)
*The Self-Willed Prince* / Paget (Wells, Gardner 1916)
*The Seven Little Spillikins* (Harrap 1926)
*The Wonderful Journey of Bee Wee...* / Herbertson (Dean 1921)
*There Was a Little Pig* [Strang's Penny Books] (Milford 1933)
*Toby and the Odd Beasts* / Syrett (Butterworth 1921)
***'Blinker Series'***
*Blinker the Bunny* (Milford c.1926)
*Flannelfeete the Wizard* (Milford c.1926)
*Mr & Mrs Mouseykins* (Milford c.1926)
*Three Little Geese* (Milford c.1926)
***'Stories from Elfland'***
*Golden Leaf* [Bk I] (Milford 1926)
*The Little Spinning Wheel* [Bk II] (Milford 1926)
*Little Green Shoes* [Bk III] (Milford 1926)
*Goblin Grey* [Bk IV] (Milford 1926)
*The Princess's Nightcap* [Bk V] (Milford 1926)
*Too-Tall the Giant* [Bk VI] (Milford 1926)
***Books illustrated with others include***
*Andersen's Fairy Tales* [with Rie Cramer] (Milford 1921)
*Chickabiddies' Play Book* (Milford nd)
*Fairy Stories for Tiny Folk* [with Anne Anderson] (Milford 1930)
*Happy Stories for Tiny Folk* [with Anne Anderson] (Milford 1930)
*Jolly Days Play Book* (Milford nd)
*Kathleen's Adventure* [with HR Millar] / Girvin (Milford 1926)
*Mick and Me* (cover) [et al] [Little Giant Books] (Milford 1926)
*Mrs Pretty Pussy's Play Book* (Milford nd)
*Starlight Tales* (Cassell nd)
*The Daisy Book* / Mrs Strang [ed] (HF/H&S nd)
*The Fairy Tale Book* (Nelson nd)
*The Hideaway Four* [with M Sowerby, A Wright et al] (Milford 1928)
*The Pageant of Flowers* [with H Miller] / Koebel (Butterworth 1922)
*Tiny Tots' Play Book* (Milford 1921)
***Annuals illustrated with others:***
*Cassell's Children's Annual; Little Folks; Mrs Strang's Annual for Baby; Mrs Strang's Annual for Children; Oxford Annual for Tiny Folks; Tiny Folks Annual; Mrs Strang's Play Books; The Jolly Book for Girls*

## Lilian Price Hacker (1897-1948)

***Postcards illustrated include***
***Liberty & Co***
**Susan [1912]**
(Republished by Milford [1923]

***Books illustrated include***
*Numbers of Things* (Milford 1921)
*Susan* (HF/H&S 1912)

## Evelyn Stuart Hardy (1866-1935)

***Postcards illustrated include***
***McDougall Educational Co.***
**The Circling Year (12 designs) [c.1903]**
***Ernest Nister***
**Series 41 Aesop's Fables [1902]**

***Books illustrated include***
*A Bunch of Cherries* / Meade (Nister 1898)
*Alice's Adventures in Wonderland* / Carroll (Shaw c.1918)
*A Young Crusader* / Braine (Nister 1900)
*At the Farm* (Nelson nd)
*Baby's Book of Pretty Pictures & Short Stories* [et al] (Nister nd)
*Bunnies, Birds and Blossoms* / Jewett (Nister nd)
*Favourite Fairy Tales* (Nister nd)
*Grimm's Fairy Tales* [et al] (Nister 1897)
*Honour Bright – the Story of the Days of King Charles* (Nister nd)
*Hop 'o My Thumb's Wanderings* [et al] (Nister 1897)
*Humpty Dumpty* (Nister c.1905)
*Jack and the Beanstalk* [with GH Thompson et al] (Nister 1895)
*Laugh and Play* (Nister c.1901)
*Little Bo Peep* (Nister c.1905)
*Little Miss Muffet* [No. 892] (Nister c.1906)
*Little Workers* / Lowe (Nister nd)
*Moo-Cow Tales* / Nesbit (Nister c.1905)
*Mother Goose and What Happened Next* / Smith (Nister 1910)
*Mother Goose's Nursery Rhymes* [et al] (Nister nd)
*My Own Pussy Cat Book* (Nister nd)
*Nursery Land Favourites* (Nister nd)
*Nursery Tales* [et al] (Nister 1903)
*Omar Khayyam* / Fitzgerald (Nister nd)
*Our Darlings Surprise Pictures* [et al] / Weatherley [ed] (Nister nd)
*Our Little Dots* [et al] (RTS 1898)
*Picture Companions* [et al] (Nister nd)
*Picture Palace in Story Town* [et al] (Nister nd)
*Pretty Pictures* [pop up] / Weedon (Nister nd)
*Push and Pull Pictures* [moveable No. 849] (Nister c.1901)
*Stories for All Times* (No. 3929) (Nister nd)
*Stories from the Book of Books* / C Shaw (Shaw 1915)
*Stories from Hans Andersen* (Nister nd)
*The Book of Gnomes* (No. 907) (Nister nd)
*The Diverting History of John Gilpin* / Cowper (Nister nd)
*The Land of Long Ago* [moveable] / Weedon (Nister nd)
*The Pigeon Tale* (Nister nd)
*The Story of Five Rebellious Dolls* / Nesbit (Nister 1904)
*The Three Bold Pirates* / Gask (Nister nd)
*True Stories About Dogs* [with Dorothy Hardy] / Gask (Harrap 1925)
***Annuals illustrated with others include***
*Little Folks' Annual; Nister's Holiday Annual; Our Darlings*

## Florence Hardy (1867-1957)

***Postcards illustrated include***
***ETW Dennis***
**No. 5930/5932** (Birthday series) **[c.1930]**
***CW Faulkner***
**Series 500** (Dutch children) **[1905] [Dondorf 143]**
**Series 501 Merry Little Folk [1906] [Dondorf 141]**
**Series 696 The New Pierrots II [1906]**
**Series 732 Childhood's Happy Time [1907]**
**Series 779** (Courtship) **[1907] [Munk 382]**
**Series 780** (Xmas snowscene) **[1907] [Dondorf 263]**

**Series 781** (Xmas snowscene) **[1907]** [Dondorf 266]
**Series 886** (Xmas snowscene) **[1908]** [Munk 410]
**Series 900** (Period costume) **[1908]** [Munk 451]
**Series 909** (Courtship) **[1908]** [Dondorf 336]
**Series 914** (Dancing) **[1909]**
**Series 958** (Xmas/Period costume) **[1909]** [Dondorf 391]
**Series 959** (Courtship) **[1909]** [Dondorf 405]
**Series 1050** (Pierrot and pierrette) **[1910]**
**Series 1081** (Courtship) **[1910]**
**Series 1083** (Xmas courtship) **[1910]**
**Series 1084** (Popular sayings) **[1910]**
**Series 1085** (Xmas snowscene) **[1910]**
**Series 1107** (Snowscene) **[1911]** [Dondorf 494]
**Series 1158** (Dutch courtship) **[1911]**
**Series 1166** (Pierrots and pierrettes) **[1911]**
**Series 1183** (Courtship) **[1913]**
**Series 1197** (Dutch courtship) **[1913]**
**Series 1238** (Dutch courtship) **[1913]**
**Series 1399** Pierrot's Courtship **[1914]** [Dondorf 608]
**Series 1407** (Courtship) **[1914]** [Dondorf 617]
**Series 1408** (Courtship) **[1914]**
**Series 1420** (Dutch courtship) **[1914]**
**Series 1506** (Patriotic) **[1915]**
**Series 1525** (Patriotic) **[with Ethel Parkinson] [1915]**
*Hildesheimer*
**12 designs** (Young girls) **[1902]**
**Meissner & Buch**
**Series 1814** (Period costume) **[1907]**
**Misch & Co**
**Series 951** On the Ice **[c.1906]**
**M Munk**
**Series 186 337 617**
*Raphael Tuck*
**Oilette Series 9694** Young Hearts **[1907]**
**Oilette Series E1159** Joyous Easter **[c.1907]**
*Advertising*
**Errington & Martin** (Christmas greeting) **[c.1902]**

**Books illustrated include**
*Fairy Stories for Young Folk* / Lady Kathleen [ed] (Aldine nd)
*Look Inside* [illustrated alphabet] / (Dean 1902)
*Magic Moments* [moveable] / Bingham (Nister 1896)
*Many Pictures for Little Treasures* [Golden Gift Series] [et al] (Tuck nd)
*Nurse Jane!* (Castell c.1905)
*Scout Quack* (Partridge 1920)
*Scout Quack and Dolly Dutch* / L Rossel (Partridge c.1920)
*Seven Jolly Fairy Tales* (Shoe Lane Publishing c.1925)
*Stories of Tuffy the Tree Elf* (Aldine 1925)
*The Blue Book* [The Rainbow Series] (HF/H&S c.1912)
*The Brown Book* [The Rainbow Series] (HF/H&S c.1912)
*The Children's Wonderland* [moveable] / Burnside (Nister 1900)
*The Little People's Painting Book* (Aldine 1920)
*The Mousie Minstrel and Dolly Dutch* (Partridge 1920)
*The Stick Book* (HF/H&S c.1912)
*The Wonders of the Secret Cavern* / (Drowley c.1895)
*The Yellow Book* [The Rainbow Series] (HF/H&S c.1912)
**Annuals illustrated with others include**
*Little Folks; Partridge's Children's Annual; Prattle's Annual;*
*The Joy Book*

## John Hassall (1868-1948)

**Postcards illustrated include**
*Davidson Brothers*
**Series 3507** Nursery Rhymes Illustrated **[c.1909]**
*CW Faulkner*
**Series 72** Fun and Frolic **[1901]**
**'Arry's 'Oliday, Country Pastimes, Cricket, Football, Guy Fawkes, Hockey, Kites, Seaside Frolics, Skating, The Army & Navy, The Rat Hunt, The Yule Log**
One of CW Faulkner's earliest 'Write-Away' series.
12 designs with undivided backs depicting boys' sports:
*Wrench*
**The Wrench Series** (Nursery Rhymes) **[c.1907]**

**Books illustrated include**
*Absurd Ditties* / Farrow (Routledge 1903)
*A Fairy Tale ABC* [Rag Book No. 234] (Dean 1923)
*Albert, 'Arold and Others* / Edgar (Francis Day & Hunter nd)
*Albert & Balbus & Samuel Small* / Edgar (Francis Day & Hunter nd)
*Barbara's Song Book* / Hartog (Allen 1900)
*Blackie's Green Picture Book of Nursery Rhymes* (Blackie 1920)
*Blackie's Popular Tales* (Blackie nd)
*Blackie's Popular Nursery Rhymes* (Blackie 1915)
*Christmas Day at Kirkby Cottage* / Trollope (Sampson Low nd)
*Dean's Patchpuz Book Number 9* [Cut out book] (Dean nd)
*Ding! Dong! Bell!* [Rag book No. 9] (Dean c.1903)
*Dodge's Red Picture-Book. Fairy Tales...* (Dodge Publ Co. nd)
*Fairy Tales* / Merrythought (Simpkin Marshall c.1920)
*Fairy Tales from Wonderland* (Blackie 1932)
*Granny's Book of Fairy Stories* (Blackie 1930)
*Grimm's Fairy Tales* (Gardner 1920)
*Gulliver's Travels* (Blackie 1910)
*Hansel and Gretel and Snow Drop* (Blackie nd)
*Hassall's Postcard Painting Book* (Dean & Son nd)
*Little Robin Hood* / Byron (HF/H&S 1908)
*Maroon Island* / Dell (Newnes nd)
*Mercury the Story Teller* (Campbell & Mord c.1914)
*Miss Manners* / Orr (Melrose 1909)
*Mother Goose's Nursery Rhymes* (Blackie 1908)
*My Very First Little Book of Other Countries* (Milford c.1918)
*Never* / Emanuel (Pitman 1907)
*Our Diary* (Nelson 1905)
*Peter Pan* / Barrie (Mills & Boon nd)
*Pug Peter King of Mouseland* [with H Rountree] (Cooke 1906)
*Puss in Boots* (Blackie nd)
*Regular Romps* (Nelson 1905)
*Robinson Crusoe* / Robarts [ed] (Blackie nd)
*Robinson Crusoe on his Island* (Blackie 1910)
*Round the World ABC* / Farrow (Nister nd)
*Six and Twenty Boys and Girls* / Bingham (Blackie nd)
*Sport and Play* / Shirley (Nelson 1914)
*Swiss Family Robinson* / Robarts [ed] (Blackie nd)
*The Chums* (Nelson 1906)
*The Dear Old Nursery Rhymes* (Blackie c.1906)
*The Doll's Diary* / Thomas (Grant Richards 1909)
*The Firelight Book of Nursery Rhymes* (Blackie nd)
*The Good Old Nursery Rhymes* (Blackie nd)
*The Hassall ABC* (Collins 1918)
*The John Hassall Lifestyle* (biography) / Cuppleditch (Dilke 1976)
*The Jolliest Holiday* (Nelson 1905)
*The Magic Shop* / Byron (Cooke c.1917)
*The Old Nursery Stories and Rhymes* (Blackie nd)
*The Pantomime ABC* (Sands & Co nd)
*The Sleeping Beauty* (Blackie nd)
*The Story of Roger in the Maze of Many Wonders* / Byron (HF/H&S nd)
*The Swiss Family Robinson* (Blackie nd)
*The Three Bears* (Blackie nd)
*The Zoo, A Scamper* / Emanuel (Rivers 1904)
*Tommy Lobb* / Emanuel (Chapman & Hall 1912)
*Ye Berlin Tapestrie* (Edmund Evans 1916)
**'John Hassall Books'**
*Aladdin* (Blackie 1915)
*Beauty and the Beast* (Blackie c.1914)
*Cinderella* (Blackie c.1914)
*Hey Diddle Diddle* (Blackie c.1914)
*Jack and Jill* (Blackie c.1914)
*John Gilpin* (Blackie c.1914)
*Little Bo-peep* (Blackie c.1914)
*Little Boy Blue* (Blackie c.1914)
*Peter Piper* (Blackie c.1914)
*Puss in Boots* (Blackie c.1914)
*Red Riding Hood* (Blackie c.1914)
*Sleeping Beauty* (Blackie c.1914)
**Books illustrated with others include**
*Auld Acquaintance* / Savory [arr] (Dent 1907)
*Big Book of Pictures and Stories* (Blackie nd)
*Little Stories for Little People* (Nelson 1916)
*La Reine des Abeilles* (Nelson, Paris nd)
*Mixed Pickles* [et al] / Waylett (Gale & Polden c.1917)
*My Lovely Big Book* (Blackie nd)

*Starlight Tales* (Cassell nd)
*The Odd Volume* (National Book Trade Provident Society 1917)
*This Train for Storyland* (Cassell nd)
*Two Well Worn Shoes* [with Cecil Aldin] (Sands 1899)
**Annuals illustrated with others include**
*Blackie's Childrens' Annual; Collins Childrens Annual;*
*Herbert Strang's Annual; Little Folks; The Happy Annual*

## Racey Helps (1913-1971)

**Postcards illustrated include**
*Medici Society*
**Pkt 190** Haymaking **[1953]**
**Pkt 192** Bedtime Story **[1953]**
**Pkt 197** The Balloon Race **[1953]**
**Pkt 220** Fun on Skis **[1953]**
**Pkt 221** Bunnies Picnic **[1953]**
**Pkt 227** Hot Chestnuts **[1953]**
**Pkt 236** The Waits **[1954]**
**Pkt 240** The New Car **[1954]**
**Pkt 254** The See Saw **[1954]**
**Pkt 257** The Tug of War **[1954]**
**Pkt 261** Catching the Post **[1954]**
**Pkt 263** Prize Day **[1954]**
**Pkt 273** The Cygnet **[1954]**
**Pkt 276** The Sale **[1954]**
**Pkt 277** A Trip Around the World **[1954]**
**Pkt 278** The Moon Rocket **[1954]**
**Pkt 285** Picking Blackberries **[1954]**
**Pkt 315** Making the Feathers Fly **[1955]**
**Pkt 349** A Visit to the Doctor **[1955]**
**Pkt 350** Ship Ahoy **[1955]**
**Pkt 351** The Traction Engine Race **[1955]**
**Pkt 362** The Wheelbarrow Race **[1955]**
**Pkt 364** A Sail Around the Bay **[1955]**
**Pkt 365** Boating on the River **[1955]**
**Pkt 371** Summer on the Lake **[1955]**
**Pkt 373** A Visit to the Cobbler **[1955]**
**Pkt 375** Woodland Gossips **[1955]**
**Pkt 379** The Photographers **[1955]**
**Pkt 388** The Astonished Angler **[1955]**
**Pkt 397** Letter for Mrs Squirrel **[1956]**
**Pkt 398** Teapot to Let **[1956]**
**Pkt 399** The Cornfield **[1956]**
**Pkt 400** The Bouquet **[1956]**
**Pkt 426** Somebody's Watching **[1956]**
**Pkt 435** The Proud Mother **[1956]**
**Pkt 452** The Sack Race **[1956]**
**Pkt 454** Sledging **[1956]**

**Books illustrated include**
*Barnaby Camps Out* (Collins 1947)
*Barnaby in Search of a House* (Collins 1948)
*Barnaby & the Scarecrow* (Collins 1955)
*Barnaby's Paint Book* (Collins nd)
*Barnaby's Spring Cleaning* (Collins 1956)
*Diggy Takes His Pick* (Medici 1964)
*Fairy Tales from Grimm* (cover) (Hamster nd)
*Footprints in the Snow* (Collins 1946)
*Guinea Pig Podge* (Medici 1971)
*Happy Animals' ABC* (Rand McNally 1966)
*Just Wilberforce* (Medici 1970)
*Kingcup Cottage* (Medici 1962)
*Little Dilly's Party* (James & Jon 1951)
*Littlemouse Crusoe* (Collins 1948)
*Little Tommy Purr* (Collins nd)
*Mr Roley to the Rescue* (Chilton nd)
*My Book of Kittens and Puppies* / Wallace (Haddock nd)
*My Friend Wilberforce* (Collins 1948)
*Nobody Loves Me, The Tale of a Dutch Doll* (Hutchinson 1950)
*Pinny Takes a Bath* (Chilton 1967)
*Pinny's Holiday* (Medici 1970)
*Prickly Pie* (Collins 1957)
*Selina the Circus Seal* (Chilton 1967)
*The Animals' Boat Ride* (Rand McNally 1966)

*The Animals of the Seashore* (Rand McNally 1966)
*The Blow-away Balloon* (Chilton 1967)
*The Clean Sweep* (Chilton 1967)
*The Tail of Hunky Dory* (Collins 1958)
*The Upside Down Medicine* (Collins 1946)
*Two from a Teapot* (Chilton 1966)
*Two's Company* (Collins 1955)

## Lydia Margaret Hine (1904-1964)

**Postcards illustrated include**
*British Art Company*
**Fairies and Pixies** (6 designs, 12 cards per packet) **[1924]**

## Eva Hollyer (1865-1943)

**Postcards illustrated include**
*Birn Brothers*
**Series 2401** (Childhood days) **[c.1905]**
*EW Savory*
**Series 686** In an Old Garden **[1917]**
(under pseudonym of Alice Martineau)
*Raphael Tuck*
**Art Glosso Series 9663** [nd]
**Christmas Series C1791 [1909]**
**Christmas Series C1796 [1909]**
**Christmas Series C1799 [1909]**
**Christmas Series C8705 [c.1914]**
**Birthday Series R2189** [nd]

## Eileen Hood (1892-1970)

**Postcards illustrated include**
*Henry Frowde and Hodder & Stoughton*
*Postcards for the Little Ones Series*
**Faithful Friends** (Dogs) **[1915]**
**Trusty and True** (Dogs) **[1915]**
*Humphrey Milford*
*Postcards for the Little Ones Series*
**Chums** (Children and dogs) **[1922]**
**Farm Babies** (Farm animals) **[1922]**
**The Farm Team** (Horses) **[1918]**
**Our Sporting Dogs** (Hunting dogs) **[1922]**
**Wild Life** (Wild animals) **[1922]**
*Also Geographia*

**Books illustrated include**
*Happy Billy Bunny* / Gross (Geographia nd)

## James Horrabin

**Postcards illustrated include**
*Davis & Carter*
*Toy Models Series*
**Series E14 [1919]**
**Series E16** Japhet's Model Theatre **[1919]**

**Books illustrated include**
*An Atlas of the USSR* / Gregory (Penguin Books 1945)
*Japhet & Happy's Annual*
*Some Adventures of the Noah Family including Japhet* (Cassell 1920)

## Sidney Hulme-Beaman (1887-1932)

**Postcards illustrated include**
*Humphrey Milford*
*Postcards for the Little Ones Series*
**Toytown Folk [1930]**

**Books illustrated include**
*Aladdin* (John Lane 1924)

*A Trusty Tale* / White (Collins 1938)
*Ernest the Policeman* (Milford 1930)
*John Trusty* (Collins 1929)
*Stories from Toytown* (Milford nd)
*Tales of Toytown* (Milford 1928)
*The Country Colouring Book* [with Dorothy Rees] (Dean 1927)
*The Easy Colouring Book* [with M Wilson] (Dean 1927)
*The Seven Voyages of Sinbad the Sailor* (John Lane 1926)
*The Smith Family* / Cradock (Nelson 1931)
*The Strange Case of Dr Jekyll...* / Stevenson (Bodley Head 1930)
*The Toytown Book* [A Cosy Corner Book] (Warne 1930)
*The Toytown Mystery* (Collins 1932)
*Wireless in Toytown* (Collins 1930)

***'Out of the Ark Books'***
*Grunty the Pig* (Warne 1927)
*Ham and the Egg* (Warne 1927)
*Jenny the Giraffe* (Warne 1927)
*Jimmy The Baby Elephant* (Warne 1927)
*Teddy's New Job* (Warne 1927)
*Wally the Kangaroo* (Warne 1927)

***'The Toyland Series'***
*Jerry and Joe* (Milford 1925)
*The Way to Toytown* (Milford 1925)
*The Wooden Knight* (Milford 1925)
*Trouble in Toyland* (Milford 1925)

***Annuals illustrated with others include***
*Blackie's Children's Annual; Cassell's Children's Annual; Chatterbox; Children's Golden Treasure Book; Chummy Book; Little Folks; Pip and Squeak Annual; Santa Claus Picture Book; The Bumper Book for Children; Tiny Tots Annual; Uncle Mac's Children's Hour Book;*

## Helen Jackson (1858-1911)

***Postcards illustrated include***
***Raphael Tuck***
**Series 45 Nos. 231-236** (Genre studies) **[1900] [Tuck France 958]**
**Series 46 Nos. 237-242** (Genre studies) **[1900] [Tuck France 958]**
**Art Series 1606** (Genre studies) **[c.1903] [Tuck France 627]**
**Art Series 1607** (Genre studies) **[c.1903] [Tuck France 627]**
**Art Series 6749** (Genre studies) **[1905]**
**Art Series 6750** (Genre studies) **[1905] [Tuck France 625]**
**Art Series 6751** (Genre studies)**[1905] [Tuck France 626]**
**Art Series 6752** (Genre studies)**[1905] [Tuck France 627]**
**Art Series 6753** (Genre studies) **[1905] [Tuck France 628]**
**Christmas Series C8011 Little Loves [c.1903]**
**Christmas Series C8029 [c.1903]**
**Also: W McKenzie & Co.**

***Books illustrated include***
*By the Light of the Nursery Lamp* (Tuck nd)
*Cat's Cradle* [et al] [Children's Gem Library] (Tuck nd)
*Effie's Little Mother* [et al] [Children's Gem Library] (Tuck nd)
*Jacks and Jills* (Tuck nd)
*Little Daisy's Painting Book* [et al] (Tuck 1893)
*Story Upon Story and Every Word True* [et al] / Nesbit (Tuck nd)
*The Ruby Fairy Book* [et al] / Vredenburg [ed] (Tuck nd)
*Tick Tock: Tales of the Clock* [et al] / Nesbit (Tuck c.1895)
*Treasures from Story Land* [No. 1530] (Tuck c.1897)

## Helen Jacobs (1888-1970)

***Postcards illustrated include***
***CW Faulkner***
**Series 1764** (Months of the year) **[1922]**
***J Henderson*** (Series or part series)
**Series K8 3243-3247 Kiddies [c.1920]**
**Series K9 3254-3259 Kiddies [c.1920]**
**Series K10 3303-3306 Kiddies [c.1920]**
***J Salmon*** (Series or part series)
**Card No. 3368 A Stitch in Time Saves Nine (1928)**
**Card No. 3387 It's an Ill Wind (1928)**
**Series 3597-3602** (humour) **(1928)**
**Card No. 3626 Tea for Two! (1929)**
**Card No. 3642 Chums! (1929)**

***Books illustrated include***
*Acting Games* / Collins (Univ. London Press 1946)
*Alice's Adventures in Wonderland* / Carroll (Martins Press c.1940)
*An Introduction to King's English* / Steel (Nisbet 1933)
*Betty and Bobtail at Pine Tree Farm* / Gask (Harrap 1920)
*Bim: A Boy in British Guiana* / Mead (Orion Press 1947)
*Chopsticks* / Codrington (CEZMS c.1931)
*Daffy Down Dilly* [Rag Book No. 180] (Dean c.1915)
*Farm and Factory in China* / Tayler (SCM 1928)
*Gracious is the Time* / Barber (Livingstone Press 1952)
*Hindu Fairy Tales* / Griswold (Harrap 1920)
*Jack and Me* / Forsey (Harrap 1919)
*Jesus in Palestine* / Collins (Univ. London Press 1948)
*Jolly Days in the Country* [et al] (Blackie c.1930)
*Life in Early Days* / Fraser (Nisbet 1932)
*Life in Later Days* / Fraser (Nisbet 1933)
*Magic London* [Royal Road Library] / Syrett (Butterworth 1922)
*Master Frisky* / Hawkes (Harrap 1920)
*Mitsu: A Little Girl of Japan* /Barnard (Edinburgh House 1928)
*Native Fairy Tales of South Africa* / Macpherson (Harrap 1920)
*Naughty Animals* / Seydewitz (Harrap 1934)
*New Friends – A Story of Malaya* / Izard (Highway Press 1955)
*Otto the Otter* [Nature's Pageant] / Davidson (Cassell 1932)
*Pow Wow Stories* / Collins (Univ. London Press 1948)
*Princes and Fairies* / Mead (Nisbet 1930)
*Ridge of Destiny* / Clinton (Edinburgh House Press 1956)
*Schoolgirl Humour* / Seydewitz (von BG Teubner 1934)
*Stepping Stones* (Mowbray 1948)
*Talks on Changing Africa* / Armstrong (Edinburgh House 1931)
*The Birthday Book of Balu* / Steedman (United Council 1920)
*The Book of Elves and Fairies* [et al] (Harrap 1919)
*The Brave Toy Soldier* (Bendix Pub. c.1940)
*The Foxglove Story Book* [et al] (Blackie nd)
*The Friendly Road* / Brown (Nisbet 1939)
*The Gingerbread House* / Mais (Harrap 1920)
*The Happy Folk* / Walker (Edinburgh House Press 1931)
*The Land of Happy Hours* / Mead (Nisbet 1929)
*The Land of Never Grow Old* / Mead (Newnes c.1930)
*The Land of Sunshine Primer I, II & III* / Pollard (Nisbet 1931/2)
*The Land Where Dreams Come True* / Mead (Nisbet 1932)
*The Land Where Stories Grow* / Mead (Nisbet 1929)
*The Land Where Tales are Told* / Mead (Nisbet 1930)
*The Old Willow Tree* [Royal Road Library] / Ewald (Butterworth 1921)
*The Pathway to the Hills* (Mowbray 1946)
*The Pedlar's Pack* / Garlick (Highway Press 1929)
*The Shining Way* / Mead (Univ. London Press 1941)
*The Taming of Tamsin* / Stuart (Harrap 1920)
*The Water Babies* / Kingsley (Philip and Tacey c.1937)
*The Wild Swans and Other Stories* (Philip and Tacey c.1936)
*Two Legs* [Royal Road Library] / Ewald (Butterworth 1921)
*Where Two Tides Meet* / Fairhall (Edinburgh House Press 1945)

***'The Land of Youth Series'***
*The Berries of Truth Series* / Clare (Nisbet 1934)
*The Saints of Kindness* / Fraser (Nisbet 1934)
*Tiff, Taff and Tuff* / Pollard (Nisbet 1934)
*Two Little Fish* / Pollard (Nisbet 1934)

***'Nature's Pageant Series'***
*Funny Bunny Bobtail* / Davidson (Cassell 1932)
*Henry & Hetty Hedgehog* / Davidson (Cassell 1932)
*Roland the Red Deer* / Davidson (Cassell 1932)
*Sandy Squirrel* / Davidson (Cassell 1932)
*The Weasel Family* / Davidson (Cassell 1932)

***'The Open Road Series'***
*Great Stories from Many Lands* / Mead (Nisbet 1936)
*Happy Ways* [Open Road Series] / Brown (Nisbet 1939)
*Paths in Storyland* / Mead (Nisbet 1937)
*The Friendly Road* / Brown (Nisbet 1939)
*The Roads of Dreamland* / Fraser (Nisbet 1939)
*The Ways of Wonderland* / Bayley (Nisbet 1937)
*Wayfaring in Many Lands* / Mead (Nisbet 1936)
*The Wings of the Morning* / Bayley (Nisbet 1936)

***'Round the World Series'***
*By River and Sea* / Entwhistle (Edinburgh House 1929)
*Fragrance and the Others* / Entwhistle (Edinburgh House 1928)
*On the Road* / Entwhistle (Edinburgh House 1926)
*The Call Drum* / Entwhistle (Edinburgh House 1927)

***'Round the World Stories'***
*Morning Light* / Mead (Univ. of London Press 1952)
*Golden Day* / Mead (Univ. of London Press 1952)
*Under the Sun* / Mead (Univ. of London Press 1952)
*Traveller's Joy* [et al] / Mead (Univ. of London Press 1952)

***Annuals illustrated with others include***
*Big Christmas Wonder Book; Bo-Peep's Bumper Book; Bubbles' Annual; Cassell's Children's Annual; Hullo Girls!; Joy Book Children's Annual; Partridge's Children's Annual; Pip and Squeak Annual; Little Folks; The Girl Guide Annual; The Wirelass Aunties' Annual; The Third Holiday Book; Treasure Trove for Boys and Girls; Uncle Mac's Children's Hour Book; Wilfred's Annual*

## Ivy Millicent James (1879-1965)

***Postcards illustrated include***
***CW Faulkner***
**Series 882 Little Comrades [1908]**
**Series 922 Joys of Winter** (Snow scenes) **[1909]**
**Series 1015 Early Loves** (Romance) **[1910]**
**Series 1070 Happy Hearts & Happy Faces [1910]**
**Series 1159** (Romantic couples in Dutch settings) **[1911]**
**Series 1191 So Jolly by the Sea [1911]**
**Series 1192** (Childhood days) **[1911]**
**Series 1194 From a Dutch Window [1911]**
**Series 1274 Our Children [1912]**
**Series 1425** (Childhood days) **[1914]**
**Series 1426** (Childhood days) **[1914]**
**Series 1582 Joys of Youth [1915]**
**Series 1628** (Childhood days) **[1918]**
**Series 1636 Little Lovers [1918]**
**Series 1676 Every Picture Tells a Story [1919]**
**Series 1698** (Gypsy children) **[1920]**
**Series 1699** (Dutch children) **[1920]**
**Series 1710** (Childhood days) **[1920]**
**Series 1734 On the Sands [1921]**
***Raphael Tuck***
**Series 9 Nursery Rhymes [c.1910]**
**Series C5040 Christmas Series** (Nursery rhymes) **[c.1910]**

***Books illustrated include***
*Little Lovers Postcard Painting Book* (Faulkner 1919)
*Our Children Postcard Painting Book* (Faulkner 1913)

## AE Kennedy (1883-1963)

***Postcards illustrated include***
**CW Faulkner**
**Unnumbered series Three Little Kittens [c.1911]**
**Series 1195 In Cat and Dog Land [1911]**
**Series 1215 Tubbies 1912**
**Series 1216 More Tubbies [with M Knight] [1912]**
**Series 1239** (Comedy toy dogs) **[with M Knight] [1912]**
**Series 1262** (Comedy cats & dogs) **[1912]**
**Series 1316 Mike [1913]**
**Series 1317** (Comedy cats & dogs) **[1913]**
**Series 1322** (Comedy dogs) **[1913]**
**Series 1338** (Comedy cats) **[with M Knight] [1914]**
**Series 1401** (Doggie games) **[1914]**
**Series 1404** (Comedy dogs) **[1914]**
**Series 1419** (Comedy dogs) **[1914]**
**Series 1424** (Comedy dogs) **[1914]**
**Series 1429 Dog Senses [1914]**
**Series 1494** (Comedy dogs) **[1915]**
**Series 1497** (Comedy dogs) **[1915]**
**Series 1507** (Comedy dogs) **[1915]**
**Series 1511** (Comedy dogs & cats) **[1915]**
**Series 1538** (Comedy dogs & cats) **[1916]**
**Series 1584** (Comedy dogs) **[1916]**
**Series 1585** (Comedy dogs) **[with M Knight] [1916]**
**Series 1592 Tales of Woe [1916]**
**Series 1613 Some Infants [1917]**
**Series 1626** (Childhood days) **[1918]**
**Series 1632** (Comedy dogs) **[1918]**
**Series 1633 Nursery Rhymes II Series [1918]**
**Series 1637** (Cat & dog portraits) **[1918]**
**Series 1646** (Comedy dogs) **[with M Knight] [1918]**
**Series 1656 Munitionette [with M Knight] [1919]**
**Series 1662** (Patriotic) **[1919]**
**Series 1687 Helping Mother [1919]**
**Series 1786 Lucky Black Cat [1922]**
**Series 1789** (Young pilot) **[1922]**
**Series 2055** (Nursery rhymes) **[oversize] [1935]**

***Books illustrated include***
*A Day in the Life of a Dog* / Cox (Faulkner 1920)
*Adventures of Tim Rabbit* / Uttley (Faber 1945)
*Another Funny Book* / Pope (Blackie 1917)
*Baby Animals* / Talbot (Nelson 1928)
*Denny of the Dingle* / Byron (Dean nd)
*Epaminondas & His Mammy's Umbrella* / Egan (Collins nd)
*Epaminondas & the Lettuces* / Egan (Collins 1940)
*Epaminondas & the Puppy* (Collins 1960)
*Fairy Tales and Rhymes* [et al] (Birn Bros c.1950)
*Farm Ways [No. 4]* [et al] (Dean 1927)
*Farmyard Friends* / Groom (Birn Bros nd)
*Frolicsome Friends* (Blackie 1915)
*Funniest Book of All* (Blackie 1914)
*Goo-Goo Eyes Postcard Painting Book* (Faulkner c.1920)
*Helping Mother* / Cox (Faulkner 1920)
*High Jinks* (McNair 1926)
*Holiday Friends* (Nelson 1932)
*Jolly Youngsters Books* [et al] (Dean 1927)
*Just a Funny Book* [verses] (Blackie 1922)
*Listen with Mother Tales [no. 6]* (Adprint c.1950)
*Little Brownies* (Dean nd)
*Macduff* / Uttley (Faber 1950)
*Merry-go-round* / Dean (Juvenile Prod. nd)
*Mother Goose* (Juvenile Prod. c.1945)
*Mrs Pretty Pussy's Play Book* [et al] (Milford nd)
*My Book of Pictures* [Ruth Cobb et al] (Blackie 1927)
*My Lovely Picture Book* (Collins nd)
*Nursery Ways [No. 2]* [et al] (Dean 1927)
*Pets and Pranks* (Blackie c.1950)
*Play Day Book* [with Dorothy Rees/Kay Nixon et al] (Dean 1927)
*Playful Pets Postcard Painting Book* (Faulkner 1917)
*Nursery Rhymes* (Faulkner 1920)
*Nursery Rhymes Postcard Painting Book* (Faulkner 1918)
*Poll & the Pussies* [with Kay Nixon] [Story Book No. 20] (Dean nd)
*Puppy Dogs* Playtime (Juvenile Prod. nd)
*Railways* [No. I of series] [with Kay Nixon et al] (Dean 1927)
*Round the Farm* [Rag Book No. 296] (Dean 1932)
*Teddy Bear* (Collins c.1940)
*Teddy Bear's Adventure* / Wickham (Collins nd)
*Ten Little Kittens & Ten Little Dogs* (Juvenile Prod. c.1954)
*The ABC Picture Book* [et al] (Collins nd)
*The Animal and Bird Colouring Book* (Dean 1927)
*The Big Coloured Picture Book* [et al] (Blackie 1924)
*The Big Book of Animals* (Blackie 1926)
*The China Dog Barks* / Duncan (Faber 1942)
*The Golliwog Book* [with Constance Wickham] (Collins 1940)
*The Teddy Bear Book* [with Constance Wickham] (Collins nd)
*The Three Bears* (Faulkner 1920)
*Two Little Friends* (Faulkner 1920)
*Young Ways [No .3]* [et al] (Dean 1927)
*Wizard Paint Book* [et al] (Collins c.1950)

***'AE Kennedy's Fun Books'***
*Dear Doggies* (Blackie 1915)
*Funny Friends* (Blackie 1914)
*Fun and Feathers* (Blackie 1914)
*Happy Families* (Blackie 1914)
*Old Friends* (Blackie 1915)
*Poor Pussies* (Blackie 1915)

***'Sam Pig Books'***
*Sam Pig and Sally* / Uttley (Faber 1942)
*Sam Pig and the Singing Gate* / Uttley (Faber 1955)
*Sam Pig at the Circus* / Uttley (Faber 1943)
*Sam Pig Goes to Market* / Uttley (Faber 1941)
*Sam Pig in Trouble* / Uttley (Faber 1948)
*Yours Ever, Sam Pig* / Uttley (Faber 1951)

## Jessie M King (1875-1949)

***Postcards illustrated include***
***Millar & Lang***
**The National Series Nursery Rhymes [1903]**

***Books illustrated include***
*A Book of Bridges* (Gowans & Gray 1911)
*A Book of Sundials* (Foulis 1914)
*A House of Pomegranates* / Wilde (Methuen 1915)
*A Little Book of Sundial Mottoes* (Foulis 1914)
*Aucassin & Nicolette* [with Kate Cameron] (Foulis 1913)
*Budding Life* (Gowans & Gray 1907)
*Cinderella & Co. Ltd.* / Thompson (Gowans & Gray 1930)
*Comus. A Masque* / Milton (Routledge 1906)
*Corners of Grey Old Gardens* (Foulis nd)
*Dwellings of an Old World Town: Culross...*(Gowans & Gray 1909)
*Everyman* (Gowans & Gray 1906)
*Friendship* / Emerson (Foulis nd)
*Glasgow the City of the West* (Foulis 1911)
*Guinevere* / Tennyson (Routledge 1903)
*Gulliver's Travels* / Swift (Routledge c.1906)
*How Cinderella Was Able to Go to the Ball* / (Foulis nd)
*Isabella, or the Pot of Basil* / Keats (Foulis nd)
*Kilmeny* / Hogg (Foulis 1911)
*Kircudbright* (Gowans & Gray 1934)
*Legends of Flowers* [with Walter Crane] (Foulis 1908)
*Littledom Castle* [et al] (Routledge 1903)
*Memories* (Foulis 1912)
*Mummy's Bedtime Story Book* (Palmer 1929)
*Nature Pictures* (Gowans & Gray 1908)
*Our Trees and How to Know Them* (Gowans & Gray nd)
*Poems* / Shelley (Caxton Publishing c.1910)
*Poems* / Spenser (Caxton Publishing c.1910)
*Ponts de Paris* / Arcambeau (Perche, Paris 1912)
*Songs from Byron* (Collins 1928)
*The Defence of Guinevere* (Lane 1904)
*The Enchanted Capital of Scotland* (Plaid Publishing nd)
*The Ettrick Shepherd* / Hogg (Foulis 1912)
*The Grey City of the North* (Foulis 1912)
*The Heroes* / Kingsley (Routledge nd)
*The High History of the Holy Grail* (Dent 1903)
*The Interlude of Youth* / Drinkwater (Gowans & Gray 1922)
*The Intruder* / Maeterlinck (Gowans & Gray 1913)
*The Legends of Flowers* / Montegazza (Foulis 1909)
*The Life of Saint Mary Magdalen* (Lane 1904)
*The Little White Town of Never-Weary* (Harrap 1917)
*The Morte d'Arthur* / Tennyson (Routledge 1903)
*Rubaiyat of Omar Khayyam* / Fitzgerald (Routledge 1903)
*Rubaiyat of Omar Khayyam* / McManus (De la More Press nd)
*The School of Poetry* (Collins 1927)
*The Seven Princesses* / Maeterlink (Musson Book Co. Toronto nd)
*The Werewolf* / Egerton (Gowans & Gray 1925)

## Ethel Larcombe (1876-1940)

***Postcards illustrated include***
***Liberty***
**Series** (Spring/summer/autumn/winter) **[c.1910]**
**Series** (Days of the week) **[c.1910]**
***EW Savory***
***Clifton Series***
**Clifton Series 412** (Victorian ladies) **[c.1915]**
**Clifton Series 567** (Mediaeval ladies) **[1917]**
**Clifton Series 912** (Ladies as flowers) **[1917]**
**Clifton Series 913** (Elegant ladies) **[1917]**

***Books illustrated include***
*A Heroine at Sea* / Marchant (Blackie nd)
*The Lances of Lynwood* / Young (Blackie nd)
*What Katy Did* / Coolidge (Blackie nd)
*The Clever Miss Follett* / Denny (Blackie nd)
*Epherimedes: An Almanack and Diary for 1902* (Dent 1902)
*Lollipop Lays* [Rag Book No. 152] (Dean 1915)
*Timmy the Elfin Taylor* [Pixie Series] / Rutley (Dean nd)

## Hester Margetson (1890-1963)

***Postcards illustrated include***
***Humphrey Milford***
***Postcards for the Little Ones Series***
**Fairy Wings** (Fairies) **[1930]**
***Valentine***
**Series 456-461** (At the seaside) **[1940]**
**Series 3906-3811** (Young girls / blossoms / children at play) **[1937]**
**Series 4742-4747** (Children at play) **[1939]**
***A Vivian Mansell***
**Series 1516** (Mermaids) **[1924]**
**Series 2116** (Fairy toadstools) **[1924]**
**Series 2127** (Water sprites in moonlight) **[1926]**
**Series 2129** (Woodland fairies) **[1926]**

***Books illustrated include***
*Delia the Dutch Doll* (Blackie nd)
*Granny's Wonderful Chair* (HF/H&S nd)
*The Admiral's Daughter* / Lane (Milford 1920)
*The Fairy Tale Book* [et al] (Nelson nd)
***Annuals illustrated with others include***
*Mrs Strang's Annual for Baby; Girl's Realm; Mrs Strang's Play Books; The Story Wonder Book; Wonder Book – A Picture Annual for Boys and Girls*

## HGC Marsh Lambert (1888-1981)

***Postcards illustrated include***
***Alpha Publishing***
**Series 940-95** (Childhood series) **[nd]**
***AM Davis***
**Series 514 Khaki Kiddies [c.1915]**
**Series 516 Britain and Her Allies [c.1915]**
**Series 518 Nursery Rhymes [c.1915]**
**Series 519 Flower Fairies [Set no 1] [c.1915]**
**Series 549 Flower Fairies [Set no 2] [c.1916]**
**Series 550 Nursery Rhymes [c.1916]**
**Series 552 Daphne, Dalia and Their Dolls [c.1916]**
**Series 553 Dutch Kiddies [c.1916]**
**Series 559 Old English Cries [c.1917]**
**Series 560 An Eventful Ride [c.1917]**
**Series 561 Round the Clock [c.1917]**
**Series 562 Children of the Empire [Set no 1] [c.1917]**
**Series 569 Seaside Kiddies [c.1917]**
**Series 577 Children of the Empire [Set no 2] [c.1918]**
***CW Faulkner***
**Series 961** (Boy meets girl) **[1909]**
**Series 962 Nursery Days [1909]**
**Series 1059 Chums [1910]**
**Series 1061** (At work and play) **[1910] [Dondorf 443]**
**Series 1086** (Playing in the snow) **[1910] [Dondorf 469]**
**Series 1128 Young Pretenders [1911]**
**Series 1135** (At the seaside) **[1912]**
**Series 1172** (Games & pastimes) **[1912] [Dondorf 516]**
**Series 1234 Rhymes for Little People [1912]**
**Series 1240** (Comic cats and dogs) **[1912]**
**Series 1400 I Do Believe in Fairies [1914]**
**Series 1508** (Letter writing) **[]1915]**
**Series 1510** (Little cherubs) **[with AE Kennedy] [1915]**
**Series 1531** (Patriotic) **[1916]**
**Series 1572** (Girls and their bonnets) **[1916]**
**Series 1576** (Little patriots) **[1916]**
**Series 1595** (Letter writing) **[1917]**
**Series 1635** (Illustrated proverbs) **[1918]**
**Series 1669** Illustrated proverbs **[1919]**
**Series 1677** (Games & pastimes) **[1919]**
**Series 1686** (Fairy tales) **[1919]**
**Series 1700** (Silhouettes) **1920**
**Series 1701** (London cries) **1920**
**Series 1714** (Proverbs) **1920**
***Gale & Polden***
**Series 1782-1793** (Months of year/birthstones) **[nd]**
**Series 2001-2006** (Birthday wishes/flowers) **[nd]**
**Series 2031-2036** (The children's day) **[nd]**
***E Mack***
**Series 387/401/477/478/479/480 [nd]**
***A Vivian Mansell***
**Series 387** (Romantic) **[1911]**
**Series 477-480** (Motoring) **[1911]**
**Series 2068** (Girl with doll) **1920]**
***Photochrom***
**Celesque Series 314-319** (Birthday series) **[nd]**
**Celesque Series 1034-1039** (Christmas series) **[nd]**
**Celesque Series 1160-1163** (Letter writing) **[nd]**
**Celesque Series 1457-1462** (Meaning of flowers) **[nd]**
**Celesque Series 1561-1566** (Christmas series) **[nd]**
**Celesque Series 1585-1590** (Flowers) **[nd]**
**Celesque Series 1712-1717** (Professions) **[c.1920]**
**Celesque Series 1790-1795** (Birthday series) **[nd]**
**Celesque Series 1886-1891** (Christmas series) **[nd]**
**Celesque Series 2155-2160** (Christmas series) **[nd]**
**Celesque Series 2161-2166** (Christmas series) **[nd]**
***J Salmon***
**Card No. 2068** (Girl with dolls) **[1921]**
***EW Savory***
**Clifton Series 868** (Seaside series) **[1920]**
**Clifton Series 869** (Christmas series) **[1920]**
***Advertising postcards***
**Ovaltine**
**185/186/187/188/189** + unnumbered card **[c.1926]**
**198/199/200/201/202/203 [c.1927]**
**Puritan Soap**
**Series 1 A-Z (26 designs) [c.1920]**

***Books illustrated include***
*ABC of Fairyland* [Painting book No. 1725] (Allday 1919)
*All About Little Spiffkins* (Dean c.1919)
*All Over the World ABC Book* (Collins 1920)
*Animal Fun* [with B Butler] (Art & Humour Co. nd)
*Babies Both* [with Edith Berkeley] [Rag Book No. 159] (Dean 1916)
*Baby Bunch* [The Merry Books] (Harrap 1920)
*Baby Bunting's Big Bedtime Book* (Ward Lock 1926)
*Baby Bunting's Big Book* (Ward Lock 1924)
*Baby Bunting's Bye Bye Book* (Ward Lock 1926)
*Baby Bunting's Book of Fairies* (Ward Lock 1925)
*Baby Bunting's Book of Games* (Ward Lock 1925)
*Baby Bunting's Big Play Book* (Ward Lock 1925)
*Baby Bunting's Book of Toys* (Ward Lock 1925)
*Baby Bunting's Easy Reading Book* (Ward Lock 1924)
*Baby Bunting's First Book* (Ward Lock 1924)
*Benjamin Brown Eyes* [Lambert's New Playbooks for 1921]
*Benny and Bunny* [Rag Book, No.172] (Dean 1916)
*Betty in the Country* [Embroidery book] (Art & Humour Co. nd)
*Betty by the Sea* [Embroidery book] (Art & Humour Co. nd)
*Boy Blue's Bazaar* [et al] / Royce [ed] (Collins c.1930)
*Chick-a-Biddy* [Lambert's New Playbooks for 1921]
*Dr Teddy Bear's School* [Painting book No. 1925] (Allday 1919)
*Fairy Tale Folk* [Lambert's New Playbooks for 1921]
*Goldilocks* [The Merry Books] (Harrap 1920)
*Jack and Jill's Easy Story Book* (Ward Lock nd)
*Little Bo-Peep's Animal Story Book* (Ward Lock 1927)
*Little Bo-Peep' Simple Story Book* / (Ward Lock nd)
*Little Bo-Peep's Big Nursery Story Book* (Ward Lock 1927)
*Me and Mike* (Gale & Polden c.1920)
*Merry Hours* [with Norman Hunter] (Warne nd)
*My Lady Betty* [with John Hassall] (Collins Cleartype nd)
*My Little Nature Book* [Follow the Dots Book] (Ward Lock 1926)
*My Playtime Book* [Follow the Dots Book] (Ward Lock 1926)
*Nursery Rhymes* (Ward Lock 1922)
*Nursery Verse* (Ward Lock 1923)
*Oh Susanah!* [The Merry Books] (Harrap 1920)
*Red Riding Hood* [The Merry Books] (Harrap 1920)
*Rock-A-Bye Rhymes* [Rag Book No. 203] (Dean 1917)
*Rhymes and Riddles* [Follow the Dots Book] (Ward Lock 1926)
*Some Jolly Games To Play* (Collins nd)
*Songs for the Wee Folk* [with Charles Lambert] (Gale & Polden 1919)
*Teddy Bears Travels* [The Merry Books] (Harrap 1920)
*Ten Little Niggers* [Rag Book No. 218] (Dean 1918)
*The Big Cosy Corner Story Book* (Ward Lock 1930)
*The Bonnie Big Story Book* (Ward Lock 1929)
*The Children's Playmate* [with Agnes Richardson] (Tuck nd)
*The Cobweb Dress* [Lambert's New Playbooks for 1921] (nd)
*The Diary of a Tomboy* (Art & Humour Co. nd)
*The Easy Reading Picture Book (ABC)* [et al] (Ward Lock nd)
*The Elfin Treasure* [advertising booklet] (Colgate c.1920)
*The Bo-peep Book* [The Merry Books] (Harrap 1920)
*The Little Shopkeepers* [Youngsters Picture Books] (Dean 1925)
*The Magicky Thread* (advertising booklet) (Sirdar Wools nd)
*The Nuts 'an May Story Book* (Ward Lock 1931)
*The Ovaltine Book of Puzzle Stories* [advertising booklet] (Ovaltine nd)
*The Rainy Day Book* [Follow the Dots Book] (Ward Lock) 1926)
*The Rascal's Book* [with Agnes Richardson] (Dean nd)
*Tick Tick Book* [Rag Book No.174] (Dean 1916)
*Tiny Tots School* [Rag Book No. 202] (Dean 1917)
*Toddles* [Rag Book No. 134] (Dean 1911)
*Ye Olde English Nursery Rhymes* (Davis nd)
***'Fluffy Tail Series'***
*The Story of Bad Little Billy Bear* (Chambers 1925)
*The Story of Little Blackie* (Chambers 1925)
*The Story of Mischievous Mops* (Chambers 1925)
*The Story of Peter Porkie* (Chambers 1925)
*The Story of Wee Willie Bear* (Chambers 1925)
***'Allday Series' (pub: 1919-1921)***
*Ann and the Goblins; Babes in the Wood; Bobby the Bold; Bunny Boy; Cookie Jane; Cross Patch; Dinky; Goldilocks; Jack and the Beanstalk; King of the Castle; Little Red Riding Hood; Mistress Mag and Little Midget; Molly and the Moon Fairies; Paddy, Pixiekin; Robin Red; Sleeping Beauty; The Holly Bush; The Story of Teddy Bear; The Mermaid; Tilda & Teddy*
***Annuals illustrated with others include***
*Blackie's Little One's Annual; Cassell's Annual for Boys and Girls; Little Folks; Little Frolic; Partridge's Children's Annual; Playbox Annual; Pleasure Book for Children; Prattle's Annual; Schoolgirl's Bumper Book; The Child's Own Magazine; The Bedtime Story Book; The Bumper Games Book; The Gladsome Book for Little Folk; The Infant's Magazine; The Joy Book; The Little One's Budget; The Story Wonder Book; Toddles Annual; Tot and Tim; Ward Lock & Co's. Wonder Book; Warne's Top-all Book for Children; Wonder Book*

## Joyce Mercer (1896-1965)

***Postcards illustrated include***
***CW Faulkner***
**Series 1894 Joyce Mercer's Fairy Series [1926]**
**Series 1896** (Nursery rhymes) **[1926]**
**Series 1894** (Fairy tales) **[1926]**
**Series 1960** (From Robert Herrick's poems) **[1926]**
***Advertising postcards***
**Pascall**
**Famous Advertisement Ser. No 1. The Pied Piper. [c1921]**

***Books illustrated include***
*Andersen's Fairy Tales* (Hutchinson 1935)
*Boy Blue's Bazaar* [et al] / Royce [ed] (Collins c.1930)
*Children's Golden Treasure Book* [et al] (Odhams 1935)
*Children's Playhour Book 1929* [et al] (Longmans Green 1928)
*Fairy Tales from Grimm* (Collins nd)
*Grimm's Fairy Tales* (Hutchinson 1935)
*Merry Mister Meddle* / Blyton (Newnes 1954))
*Mister Meddle's Mischief* / Blyton (Newnes 1940)
*Rachel and the Seven Wonders* / Syrett (Butterworth 1921)
*The Complete Edition of Andersen and Grimm* (New Century 1935)
*The Joyce Mercer Edition of Andersen and Grimm* (Hutchinson nd)
*Told in the Sunshine* / Vredenburg [ed] (Tuck c.1925)
*Vanity in Mayfair* [with D'Egville] / Sheridan (Palmer 1929)
***Annuals illustrated with others include***
*Blackie's Children's Annual; Bo-Peep's Bumper Book; Collins' Fairy Folks Annual; Collins' Toddlers Annual; Father Tuck's Annual; Girls' Own Paper; Partridge's Childrens' Annual; Favourite Wonder Book; Sunny Stories; The Big Christmas Wonder Book; The Chummy Book; The Golden Gift Book; The First War-time Christmas Book; The Prize; Toddles Annual; Tot and Tim Annual*
***Contributions to periodicals***
*Bystander; Illustrated London News; London Opinion; Punch; Sketch*

## Hilda Miller (1876-1939)

***Postcards illustrated include***
***CW Faulkner***
**Series 1690 Fairy Visions [1922]**
**Series 1746** (Grimms' Fairy Tales) **[1921]**
**Series 1748 Grimms' Fairy Tales [1921]**
**Series 1760** (Stories from Dickens) **[1921]**
**Series 1784 Little Folks' Rhymes [1922]**
**Series 1822 Peter Pan [1923]**
**Series 1823 Peter Pan [1923]**
**Series 1857** (Games & pastimes) **[1924]**
**Series 1897 Old Time Costumes [1926]**
**Series 1925** (Hans Andersen's Fairy Tales) **[1927]**
**Series 1926 Fairy Lovers [1927]**
**Series 1978** (Fairyland) **[1928]**
***Liberty & Co***
Signed but unnumbered and uncaptioned cards drawn between 1910 and 1918.

***Books illustrated include***
*A Garland of Legends* / Kenny (Univ. of London Press nd)
*Dulcibella and the Fairies* / Parker (Faulkner 1919)
*Lucy* / de la Mare (Blackwell nd)
*Shoes: A Story for Children* /Bentham (Duckworth 1920)
*The Butterflies' Day* / Koebel (Butterworth 1925)
*The Flame Flower* / Saunders (Butterworth 1922)
*The Pageant of Flowers* [with L Govey] / Koebel (Butterworth 1922)
*The Rose Fyleman Fairy Book* / Fyleman (Methuen 1923)
***Books illustrated with others include***
*Boys and Girls Wonder Book 1927* (Ward Lock nd)
*The Story Wonder Book* (Ward Lock 1937)
*Wonder Book* (Ward Lock 1920)

## Olwen Morgan (1896-1960)

***Postcards illustrated include***
***CW Faulkner***
**Series 1782** (Months of the year) (12 designs) **[1922]**
**Series 1850 A Week of Happy Days** (7 designs) **[1924]**

## Kay Nixon (1894-1988)

***Postcards illustrated include***
***CW Faulkner***
**Series 1819 Alice in Wonderland [1923]**

***Books illustrated include***
*Alice in Wonderland* / Carroll (Faulkner 1924)
*Animals and Birds in Folklore* (Warne 1969)
*Animal Legends* / (Warne 1966)
*Animal Mothers and Babies* / Foran (1960)
*Bird Studies in India* / (Oxford University Press 1928)
*Heyo! Brer Rabbit* / Blyton (Newnes 1938)
*Legend of the Sun and Moon* / Procter (Harrap nd)
*Little Folks at the Zoo* [Little Big Books] (Milford c.1926)
*Nature Stories* (Harrap 1922)
*Pindi Poo* (Warne 1957)
*Play Day Book* [with AE Kennedy/Dorothy Rees et al] (Dean 1927)
*Poll and the Pussies* [with AE Kennedy] (Dean nd)
*Poetry of Nature* [5 books] (1926)
*Poo and Pushti* (Warne 1959)
*Puck's Broom* / Gordon Browne (Harrap 1920)
*Pushti* (Warne 1955)
*Sentinels of the Wild* / Batten (Newnes 1938)
*Strange Animal Friendships* (Warne 1967)
*The Adventures of Binkle and Flip* (Newnes c.1949)
*The Bushy Tail Family* (Warne 1963)
*The Littlest One* [with Margaret Tarrant] / Webb (Harrap 1914)
*Whispers in the Wilderness* / Batten (Blackie 1960)
***Annuals illustrated with others include***
*Boys and Girls Annual; Boys and Girls Story Book; Mrs Strang's Annual for Baby; Sunny Stories; The Times of India*

## Ida Rentoul Outhwaite (1888-1961)

***Postcards illustrated include***
***The New Idea***
**The Ida Rentoul Series [1903]**
***A&C Black***
**Series 71 Elves and Fairies**
(4 from *The Enchanted Forest*. 2 from *Little Fairy Sister*) **[1926]**
**Series 71a Elves and Fairies** (6 from *Fairyland*) **[1926]**
**Series 72 Elves and Fairies** (6 from *Fairyland*) **[1926]**
**Series 73 Elves and Fairies** (6 from *Bunny & Brownie*) **[1926]**
**Series 74 Elves and Fairies** (6 from *Blossom*) **[1928]**
**Series 75 Elves and Fairies**
(2 from *The Enchanted Forest*. 4 from *Little Fairy Sister*) **[1927]**
**Series 76 Elves and Fairies**
(5 from *The Enchanted Forest*. 1 from *The Little Green Road*) **[1927]**
**Series 79 Elves and Fairies**
(2 from *The Enchanted Forest*. 2 from *The Little Little Green Road to Fairyland*. 2 from *Little Fairy Sister*) **[1927]**

***Books illustrated include***
*A Bunch of Wild Flowers* (Angus & Robertson 1933)
*A Fairy without Wings* (H&S c.1915)
*Australian Songs for Young and Old* / A Rentoul (Robertson 1907)
*Before the Lamps are Lit* / Quin (Robertson 1911)
*Blossom, A Fairy Story* (Black 1928)
*Bunny & Brownie* (Black 1930)
*Bush Songs of Australia for Young and Old* (Robertson 1910)
*Centenary Gift Book* [et al] / (Robertson & Mullens 1934)
*Chimney Town* / Daskein (Black 1934)
*Elves and Fairies* / Rentoul (Lothian 1916)
*Enchanting Isles* / Mellor (Howard Whyte 1934)
*Fairyland of Ida Rentoul Outhwaite* (Ramsay 1926)
*Gum Tree Brownie and Other Faerie Folk* / Quin (Robertson 1907)
*Mollie's Bunyip* / A Rentoul (Jolley 1904)
*Mollie's Staircase* / A Rentoul (Hutchinson [Aus] 1906)
*More Australian Songs...* / A Rentoul (Robertson 1913)
*Musical Nursery Rhymes Picture Book* (Murfett 1945)
*Nursery Rhymes* (Murfett 1948)
*Peter Pan: The Boy Who Wouldn't Grow Up* (Williamson 1908)
*Sixpence to Spend* / (Angus & Robertson 1935)
*The Enchanted Forest* / G Outhwaite (Black 1921)
*The Enchanted Seas* / Newell (Black 1937)
*The Fairy World of Ida Rentoul Outhwaite* / Muir/Holden (Black 1996)
*The Lady of the Blue Beads, Her Book* (Robertson 1908)
*The Little Fairy Sister* / Outhwaite (Black 1923)
*The Little Green Road to Fairyland* / Rentoul (Black 1922)
*The Other Side of Nowhere* / Quin (Robertson & Mullens 1934)
*The Red Witch* / Newall (Black 1937)
*The Sentry and the Shell Fairy* (Anderson Gowan c.1924)
*The Story of Peter Pan* / A Rentoul (Williamson 1908)
*The Story of the Pantomime Humpty Dumpty* / (Williamson nd)
***'Willie Winkie Zoo Books' by Mrs AR Osborn***
*Fuzzy, Wuzzy and Buzzy* / (Whitcombe & Tombs 1918)
*Peter's Peach* / (Whitcombe & Tombs 1918)
*Teddy Bear's Birthday* / (Whitcombe & Tombs 1918)
*The Guinea Pig that Wanted a Tail* / (Whitcombe & Tombs 1918)
*The Naughty Baby Monkey* / (Whitcombe & Tombs 1918)
*The Quarrel of the Baby Lions* / (Whitcombe & Tombs 1918)

## Phyllis Palmer (1893-1989)

***Postcards illustrated include***
***J Salmon***
**Series 2606-2610** (Childhood days) **[1924]**
**Series 4605-4610** (Humour) **[1938]**
**Series 4674-4678** (Humour) **[1939]**
**Series 4812-4822** (Humour) **[1941]**
**Series 4918-4921** (Childhood days) **[1944]**
**Series 4952-4963** (Boys and girls) **[1944]**
**Series 4994-4999** (Boys and girls) **[1948]**
**Series 5038-5043** (Humour) **[1949]**
**Series 5113-5118** (Romantic) **[1951]**
**Series 5119-5124** (Romantic) **[1951]**
**Card No. 5154** (Elves and pixies) **[1952]**
**Series 5209-5219** (Humour) **[1953]**
**Series 5243-5248** (Humour) **[1953]**
***A Vivian Mansell***
**Series 1150** (Girl humour) **[1920]**

## Ethel Parkinson (1868-1957)

***Postcards illustrated include***
***CW Faulkner***
**Series unnumbered** (Olden day snow scenes) **[c.1903]**
**Series 151** (Christmas series) **[1902]**
**Series 226 When George III was King [1902]**
**Series 352** (In the snow at sunset) **[1903] [Munk 195]**
**Series 358** (Olden day snow scenes) **[1903] [Munk 191]**
**Series 448** (Illustrated songs) **[1904]**
**Series 569 When the Heart is Young [1905] [Munk 233]**
**Series 570** (Young folk in the snow) **[1905] [Munk 232]**
**Series 580** (Mother and child in the snow) **[1905] [Munk 234]**
**Series 675 Happy Little Hollanders [1906] [Dondorf 126]**
**Series 699** (Christmas series) **[1907] [Munk 310]**
**Series 700** (Couples in the snow) **[1907]**
**Series 734 Little Dutchies [1907] [Munk 432]**
**Series 884** (Olden day snow scenes) **[1908]**
**Series 915** (Dutch children at work and play) **[1909]**
**Series 917** (Olden day snow scenes) **[1909] [Munk 531]**
**Series 941 The Arctic Series [1909] [Dondorf 395]**
**Series 951** (Dutch couples) **[1909]**
**Series 963** (Happy faces in the snow) **[1909] [Dondorf 433]**
**Series 1008** (Romantic couples and their moods) **[1910]**
**Series 1085** (Children in the snow) **[1910]**
**Series 1088** (Nursery rhymes) **[1910]**
**Series 1120** (Romantic Dutch couples) **[1911]**
**Series 1156** (Olden day children at play) **[1911]**
**Series 1157 Happy Days in Holland [1911]**
**Series 1167 Friends or Foes [1911]**
**Series 1168** (Young courtship) **[1911]**
**Series 1173** (Illustrated rhymes) **[1911] [Dondorf 517]**
**Series 1178** (Moonlight courtship) **[1911]**
**Series 1196** (Childhood days) **[1912]**
**Series 1261** (Days of the week) **[1913]**
**Series 1325** (Young children at play) **[1913]**
**Series 1509** (Young courtship) **[1915]**
**Series 1525** (Little patriots) **[1915]**
**Series 1549** (Dutch couples and their moods) **[1916]**
**Series 1580** (Dutch couples) **[1916]**
**Series 1674 Children's Carnival [1919]**
**Series 1683 Eve's Own [1919]**
***Hildesheimer & Co***
**Series 5426** (Greetings) **[nd]**
***Raphael Tuck***
**Christmas Series C276 [1908]**
**Christmas Series C277 [1908]**

***Books illustrated include***
*A Painting Book of Little Dutch Folk* / W Chapman (Blackie 1915)
*Dutchie Doings* / W Chapman (Blackie 1908)
*Fun and Frolic Postcard Painting Book* (Faulkner 1918)
*Little Folks from Holland* (Faulkner 1920)
*Sambo and Susanah* / Byron (Blackie 1907)
*Our Darlings* [et al] (Shaw nd)

## Rollo Paterson (1892-1978)

As Vera Paterson

***Postcards illustrated include***
***J Salmon***
**Card Nos. 4213/14** (Humour) **[1935]**
**Card No. 4224** (Humour) **[1935]**
**Card Nos. 4235-4241** (Humour) **[1935]**
**Card Nos. 4310-4313** (Humour) **[1936]**
**Card No. 4346** (Humour) **[1936]**
**Card No. 4356** (Humour) **[1936]**
**Series 5032-5037** (Humour) **[1949]**
**Series 5088-5093** (Humour) **[1950]**
**Series 5125-5129** (Humour) **[1951]**
**Series 5148-5153** (Humour) **[1952]**
**Series 5155-5160** (Humour) **[1952]**
**Series 5220-5225** (Humour) **[1952]**
**Series 5249-5254** (Humour) **[1953]**
**Also Carlton, Photochrom and Valentine**

## Susan Beatrice Pearse (1878-1980)

***Postcards illustrated include***
***Alpha***
**Series No. 2098** (Under the mistletoe) **[nd]**
**Series No. 2099** (Cupid) **[nd]**
**Series No. 2100** (Cupid) **[nd]**
**Series No. 2101 [nd]**
**Series No. 2102** (Tea with the vicar) **[nd]**
**Series No. 2108** (Gooseberry) **[nd]**
**Series No. 3072** (At the seaside) **[nd]**
***CW Faulkner***
**Series 798** (Childhood days) **[c.1907]**
**Series 984** (Childhood days) **[c.1909]**
**Series 1136 Happy Holidays [c.1912]**
**Series 1243** (Childhood days) **[c.1913] [Munk 727]**
**Series 1244** (Childhood days) **[c.1913] [Munk 727]**
**Series 1402** (Rhymes at bedtime) **[c.1914]**
**Series 1403** (Little girl with dolls) **[c.1914] [Munk 844]**
***Henry Frowde and Hodder & Stoughton & Humphrey Milford***
***Postcards for the Little Ones Series***
**By the Seaside [1915]**
**Christmastime [1915]**
**Dear Little Allies [1915]**
**For King and Country [1915]**
**From the Front [1915]**
**Our Baby [1916]**
**Our Darlings [1916]**
**Holiday Time [1917]**
**The Busy Day [1918]**
**Little Helpers [1920]**
**Odds and Evens [1920]**
**Jolly Games [1922]**
**Playmates [1922]**
***Hildesheimer & Co***
**Single card No. 80. Limpets**
***Kensington Fine Art Society***
**Series 201-218 Nursery Rhymes Silhouettes [c.1916]**
**Series 231-236 The Nativity Silhouette [c.1916]**
***A Vivian Mansell***
**Series 1030** (Patriotic children) **[1916]**
**Series 1088** (One, two, buckle my shoe) **[1917]**
**Series 1101** (Children's pastimes) **[1917]**
**Series 1172** (Fairy tales) **[1921]**
***M Munk***
**No. 563** (Romantic children) **[c.1910]**
**No. 629** (Romantic children) **[c.1910]**
**No. 635** (Studies of young girls) **[c.1910] (also Alpha)**
**No. 679** (Playing in the snow) **[c.1911]**
**No. 680** (Children and pets) **[c.1911]**
**No. 712** (Children at play) **[c.1912]**
**No. 713** (The children's day) **[c.1912]**
**No. 728** (Children at play) **[c.1913]**
**No. 844** (Seaside games) **[c.1914]**
**No. 856** (A girl and her dolls) **[c.1914]**
**No. 869** (Boy & girl on stile) **[c.1914]**
**No. 879** (Children in the snow) **[c.1914]**
**No. 922** (Children at play) **[c.1915]**
**No. 923** (Babies) **[c.1915]**
**No. 925** (Children and pets) **[c.1915]**
**No. 998** (Preparing for the date) **[c.1916]**
**No. 1111** (Romantic children) **[c.1917]**
**No. 1234** (Children at work and play) **[c.1919]**
***J Salmon***
**Series 1618-1622** (Playing with dolls) **[c.1919]**
**Series 1904-1909** (Playing on the sands) **[c.1920]**
***Valentine***
**Individual numbers 102 103 104 117 129 220 398 399 4009**

**Books illustrated include**
*Pam's Secret House* / Joan (Harrap 1927)
*The Twins and Tabiffa* / Heward (Harrap 1923)
*A Little Silver Trumpet* / Meade (Hodder & Stoughton 1909)
*Captain Boldheart ...* / Dickens (Constable 1916)
*Mother Goose Rhymes* [with Winifred Ackroyd] (Coker nd)
*Mother Goose's Rhymes* (Harrap 1920)
*Nursery Versery* / Strong (Muller 1948)
*The Pendleton Twins* / Jameson (HF/H&S 1908)
*The Trial for William Tinkling* / Dickens (Houghton Mifflin c.1914)
**'Ameliaranne Series' illustrated:**
*Ameliaranne and the Green Umbrella* / Heward (Harrap 1920)
*Ameliaranne Keeps Shop* / Heward (Harrap 1928)
*Ameliaranne Cinema Star* / Heward (Harrap 1929)
*Ameliaranne and the Monkey* / Heward (MacKay 1929)
*Ameliaranne in Town* / Joan (Harrap 1930)
*Ameliaranne at the Circus* / Gilmour (Harrap 1931)
*Ameliaranne and the Big Treasure* / Joan (Harrap 1932)
*Ameliaranne and the Magic Ring* / Farjeon (MacKay 1933)
*Ameliaranne's Prize Packet* / Farjeon (Harrap 1933)
*Ameliaranne's Washing Day* / Farjeon (Harrap 1934)
*Ameliaranne at the Seaside* / Gilmour (Harrap 1935)
*Ameliaranne at the Zoo* / Thompson (Harrap 1936)
*Ameliaranne at the Farm* / Heward (Harrap 1937)
*Ameliaranne Gives a Christmas Party* / Heward (Harrap 1938)
*Ameliaranne Camps Out* / Heward (Harrap 1939)
*Ameliaranne Keeps School* / Heward (Harrap 1940)
*Ameliaranne Goes Touring* / Heward (Harrap 1941)
*Ameliaranne and the Jumble Sale* / Heward (Harrap 1943)
*Ameliaranne Gives a Concert* / Gilmour (Harrap 1944)
*Ameliaranne Bridesmaid* / Morris (Harrap 1946)
*Ameliaranne Goes Digging* / Wood (Harrap 1948
*Ameliaranne's Moving Day* / Morris (Harrap 1950)
*The Ameliaranne Story Book* [compilation] / Heward (Harrap 1941)
**Books illustrated with others include**
*Crusoes of the Frozen North* [with CE Brock] (Blackie nd)
*The Flying Carpet* / Asquith (Partridge 1926)
*The Milk White Thorn* (Nelson c.1920)
**Annuals illustrated with others include**
*Arthur Mee's Gift Book; Blackie's Little One's Annual; Brighteyes Merry Book; Little Folks; Playbox Annual; The Chummy Book; The Graphic; Wonder Book – A Picture Annual for Boys and Girls*

## Gladys Peto (1890-1977)

**Postcards illustrated include**
***Alpha Celesque Series***
**Series 3993-3997** (Childhood days) **[1934]**
***Advertising postcard***
**Allenbury's Foods for Infants [1920]**

**Books illustrated include**
*A Fine Lady Upon a White Horse* / Leigh Hunt (Sampson Low 1929)
*Bedtime Pages for Boys and Girls* (Juvenile Prod. nd)
*Daphne and the Fairy and Other Tales* (Sampson Low 1924)
*Gladys Peto's Bedtime Stories* (Shaw 1931)
*Gladys Peto's Children's Book* (Sampson Low 1925)
*Gladys Peto's Girl's Own Stories* (Shaw 1933)
*Gladys Peto's Holiday Stories* (Shaw nd)
*Gladys Peto's Jolly Times* (Shaw nd)
*Gladys Peto's Merry Times* (Shaw nd)
*Gladys Peto's Storyland* (Shaw nd)
*Joan's Visit to Toyland* (Sampson Low 1924)
*Malta and Cyprus* (Dent 1928)
*Snow Man* (Sampson Low 1924)
*Summer Days* (Shaw nd)
*The China Cow* [et al] / Stokes (Sampson Low c.1929)
*The Egypt of the Sojourner* (Dent 1928)
*The Four-leafed Clover and Other Stories* (Juvenile Prod. 1937)
*Told in the Gloaming* (Shaw nd)
*Twilight Stories* (Shaw 1932)
**Annuals and periodicals illustrated with others include**
*Bystander; Gladys Peto's Children's Annual; Pearson's Magazine; Printer's Pie; The Sketch*

## Joyce Plumstead (1907-1986)

**Postcards illustrated include**
***A Vivian Mansell***
**Series 1004 Little People of the Seashore [1938]**
**Series 2126** (Woodland fairies) **[1936]**

**Books illustrated include**
*Giggles and the Spotted Donkey* (Dean 1965)
*The Monster Book for Children* (Dean c.1930)
*The Monster Book for Tinies* [et al] (Dean c.1933)

## Chloë Preston (1887-1969)

***For postcards illustrated see Chloë Preston & the Peek-a-Boos by Mary Hillier published by Richard Dennis 1998***

**Books illustrated include**
*A Duckling and Some Dogs* (Tuck c.1913)
*Cheerful Chubbies* [panorama book] (Tuck 1920)
*Cuddly Kittens* [panorama book] (Tuck 1920)
*Nursery Rhymes* (Nelson nd)
*Somebody's Darling* (Tuck nd)
*Tartar Tim* / Maclennan (Milford c.1921)
*The Bumper Book for Children* [et al] (Nelson 1929)
*The Busy Bo-Peeps* / Graydon (Blackie 1914)
*The Mischievous Pair* (Partridge 1925)
*Tootsie Wootsie Kiddies* [panorama] (Tuck c.1921)
**'Peek-a-Boos' books**
*The Peek-a-Boos* (HF/H&S 1910)
*The Peek-a-Boos in Winter* (HF/H&S 1911)
*The Peek-a-Boos Amongst the Bunnies* [with GH Vyse] (HF/H&S 1912)
*The Peek-a-Boos' Holiday* / Tom Preston (HF/H&S 1912)
*The Peek-a-Boo Japs* (HF/H&S 1912)
*The Peek-a-Boos in Town* / Byron (HF/H&S 1913)
*The Peek-a-Boos' Desert Island* /Hoyle (HF/H&S 1914)
*A Peek-a-Boo Adventure* (HF/H&S c.1915)
*The Peek-a-Boos at School* (HF/H&S 1915)
*The Peek-a-Boos at the Zoo* (HF/H&S 1915)
*The Peek a Boos in Camp* / Byron (HF/H&S 1915)
*The Peek a Boo Twins* (HF/H&S 1915)
*William & Woggs, A Peek-a-Boo Adventure* (HF/H&S 1915)
*The Adventures of Trooper Peek-a-Boo* / Byron (HF/H&S 1916)
*The Peek a Boos in War Time* / Byron (HF/H&S 1916)
*The Peek-a-Boos & Mr Plopper* [with GH Vyse] (HF/H&S 1917)
*The Peek-a-Boo Farmers* / Byron (Milford 1918)
*The Peek-a-Boos go Shopping* (Milford 1919)
*The Peek-a-Boo Circus* / Byron (Milford 1919)
*The Peek-a-Boo Christmas* / Byron (Milford 1920)
*Barbara Peek-a-Boo's Holiday* [with GH Vyse] (Milford 1921)
*The Peek-a-Boo Gardeners* (Milford 1921)
*The Peek-a-Boo Gipsies* / Byron (Milford 1922)
**Peek-a-Boo 'Playbooks' and 'Panoramas'**
*The Peek-a-Boos' Desert Island Playbook* (Milford 1927)
*The Peek a Boo Twins Playbook* (Milford 1927)
*The Peek-a-Boos in Winter Playbook* (Milford 1927)
*The Peek-a-Boos go Shopping & Gardening Playbook* (Milford 1928)
*The Peek-a-Boos in Town Playbook* (Milford 1928)
*The Peek a Boos in Camp Playbook* (Milford 1928)
*The Peek-a-Boos at the Zoo Playbook* (Milford 1931)
**'Peek-a-Booklets'**
*Peek-a-Boo AB* / Byron (HF/H&S c.1915)
*Peek-a-Boo Jane* / Byron (HF/H&S c.1915)
*Peek-a-Boo Jill* / Byron (HF/H&S c.1915)
*Peek-a-Boo Jim* / Byron (HF/H&S c.1915)
*Peek-a-Boo Pam* / Byron (HF/H&S c.1915)
*Peek-a-Boo Pat* / Byron (HF/H&S c.1915)
*Peek-a-Boo Patty* / Byron (HF/H&S c.1915)
*Peek-a-Boo Peter* / Byron (HF/H&S c.1915)
*Peek-a-Boo Polly*/ Byron (HF/H&S c.1915)
**'Peek-a-Boo Soldier and Sailor Booklets'**
*Admiral Peek-a-Boo* (HF/H&S 1913)
*Captain Peek-a-Boo* (HF/H&S c.1913)
*Peek-a-Boo Jacques* (HF/H&S c.1913)
*Peek-a-Boo Jack* (HF/H&S c.1913)
*Peek-a-Boo Jock* / (HF/H&S c.1913)
*Peek-a-Boo RN* / (HF/H&S c.1913)
*Peek-a-Boo Tommy* / (HF/H&S c.1913)
**'Peek-a-Boo Puppies'**
*Big Ben* (Milford c.1919)
*Bob the Bold* (Milford c.1919)
*Tartar Tim* (Milford c.1919)
**'Chunkies books'**
*The Chunkies* (HF/H&S 1916)
*The Chunkies' Adventures* (Milford 1921)
*The Chunkies at the Seaside* (Milford 1917)
*The Travels of Corporal Chunky* (Milford 1918)
*Five Bad Chunkies* / Byron (Milford 1920)
**'Chunkies Playbooks'**
*The Chunkies Playbook* (Milford 1931)
*The Bad Chunkies Playbook* (Milford c.1934)
**'Chunky Booklets'**
*Chunky Cottage* (Milford c.1921)
*The Chunkie Scouts* (Milford c.1921)
*The Chunky Store* (Milford c.1921)
*The Good Ship Chunky* (Milford c.1921)
**Annuals and periodicals illustrated with others include**
*The Chummy Book; The Peek-a-Boo Annual; Women's Pictorial*

## Eugenie Richards

**Postcards illustrated include**
***Boots Cash Chemist***
**Pelham Series** (Nursery rhymes) **[1910]**

**Books illustrated include**
*A Nursery Rhyme Rag Book* [Rag Book No. 161] (Dean 1916)
*Aladdin [Kiddieland Series]* (Dean 1915)
*Dog Toby By Himself* [Rag Book No. 47] (Dean c.1909)
*Fairies and Chimneys* / Rose Fyleman (Methuen 1918)
*Fairies and Friends* / Rose Fyleman (Methuen 1925)
*Forty Good Morning Tales* / Rose Fyleman (Methuen 1926)
*Puss in Boots* [Kiddieland Series] (Dean 1915)
*Seven Little Plays for Children* / Rose Fyleman (Methuen 1928)
*Teddy* [Kiddieland Series] (Dean 1915)
*The Fairy Flute* / Rose Fyleman (Methuen 1921)
*The Fairy Green* / Rose Fyleman (Methuen 1919)
*The First Book – Song & Story...* [et al] (Norland Press 1902)
**'Nursery Rhyme Readers'**
A. *Hey Diddle Diddle* (Sissons & Parker nd)
B. *The North Wind Doth Blow* (Sissons & Parker nd)
C. *Tom, Tom, the Piper's Son* (Sissons & Parker nd)
D. *Ding Dong Bell* (Sissons & Parker nd)
E. *Little Boy Blue* (Sissons & Parker nd)
F. *There Was a Little Man* (Sissons & Parker nd)
**'The Humpty Dumpty Books'**
1. *Humpty Dumpty's Tea Party*
2. *The Rose Fairy*
3. *The Fairy Ring*
4. *First Book of Fables (from Aesop)*
5. *Second Book of Fables (from La Fontaine)*
6. *Reynard the Fox*
7. *Harry's Dream Garden*
8. *Robin Hood and Little John*
9. *The Magic Glasses*
10. *The Cat Who Married a Mouse*
11. *The Mouse with the Green Eyes*
12. *The Wooden Horse of Troy*
13. *The King of the Castle*
14. *The Beggar's Gift*
15. *The Fairy of the Well*
16. *Finn & Far – a Celtic Folk Lore Story*
17. *The Four Brothers – a Danish Folk Lore Story*
18. *The King and the Bird*
**Annuals illustrated with others include**
*Our Children's Best Book*

## Agnes Richardson (1884-1951)

**Postcards illustrated include**
***Alpha*** (Individual card unnumbered)
**The Poor Little Flag Seller**
***Birn Brothers***
**Series E27 [nd]**
***Davidson Brothers*** (Individual cards unnumbered)
**Buttercups, Good-Morning, Good-Night, Telling the Time, The Busy Bees, The Little Lamb [nd]** (Set)
**I Wish We was Ducks, Les Miserables, Nice Weather for Ducks, Stormy, The Rain it Raineth Every Day, What's it Going to do Today? [nd]** (Set)
**Making it Up, Open Your Mouth and Shut your Eyes, The Lover's Token, The Quarrel [nd]** (4 of 6)
**Sweethearts, The Lover's Test, The Posy [nd]** (3 of 6)
***CW Faulkner***
**Series 974 [1909]**
**Series 996 [1909]**
**Series 1074 [1910]**
**Series 1155 The True Little Lovers [1911]**
**Series 1233 Dainty Little Maidens [1912]**
**Series 1264 Early Days and Early Ways [1912]**
**Series 1265 Love's Language of Flowers [1912]**
**Series 1568 [1915]**
**Series 1638 [1918]**
**Series 1781 [1922]**
**Series 1813 Happy Little Dutchies [1923]**
***Charles Hauff*** (Individual cards unnumbered)
**A Loving Design, Deserted, Making it Up, The Quarrel, The Serenade, When Three is Company [nd]** (Set)
**Mr Golliwog Good-night, My Turn Next, The Bogey Man, The Last in Bed..., Two Little Ducks, When Nobody's With Me I'm Always Alone [nd]** (Set)
***Inter Art***
**Artistique Series 1597-1602 [1916]**
**Artistique Series 1765-1770 [1917]**
**Artistique Series 1957-1962 [1917]**
**Artistique Series 1963-1968 [1917]**
**Artistique Series 2059-2064 (Children with pets) [1917]**
**Artistique Series 2197-2202 [1917]**
**Artistique Series 2215-2220 [1917]**
**Artistique Series 2263-2268 (Birthday series) [1918]**
**Artistique Series 2269-2274 [1918]**
**Artistique Series 2473-2478 [1918]**
**Comique Series 4291-4296 [1923]**
**Comique Series 4955-4960 [1924]**
**Comique Series 6758-6763 (Christmas children) [1929]**
**Comique Series 6763-6769 [1929]**
***A Vivian Mansell***
**Series 1114 [1916]**
***McLove & Co*** (Individual cards unnumbered)
**Who's the Lady – Tommy, Tommy in Captivity, Somewhere in France, On Short Leave, His First Engagement [nd]** (5 of 6)
***Millar & Lang***
***National series*** (Identified numbers)
**1003 1007 1009 1012 1013 1040 1042 1043 1044 1045 1047 1048 1050 1051 1054 1959 2075 2076 2082 2215 2220 3313 3315 3317 3318 3320 3321 3322 3323 3409 3412 3414 3415 3418 3419 3420 3424 3597 3598 3648 3764 3765 3766 3771 3772 3773 3812 4103 4466 4659 4660 4661 4662 4663 4941 4977 4978 4979 4980 4981 4982 5514**
***Birthday series***
**B653-658 B3312 B3316**
***Photochrom*** (Only numbered series listed)
**Celesque Series 224-229 [nd]**
**Celesque Series 308-313 [nd]**
**Celesque Series 554-559 [nd]**
**Celesque Series 560-565 [nd]**
**Celesque Series 584-589 [nd]**
**Celesque Series 590-595 [nd]**
**Celesque Series 668-673 [nd]**
**Celesque Series 746-751 [nd]**
**Celesque Series 776-781 [nd]**
**Celesque Series 1016-1021 [nd]**

**Celesque Series 1048-1053 [nd]***
**Celesque Series 1360-1365 [nd]**
**Celesque Series 1381-1386 [nd]**
**Celesque Series 1425-1430 [nd]**
**Celesque Series 1633-1638 [nd]****
**Celesque Series 1706-1711 [nd]**
**Celesque Series 1718-1723 [nd]**
**Celesque Series 1778-1783 [nd]**
**Celesque Series 1784-1789 [nd]**
**Celesque Series 2143-2148 [nd]**
**Celesque Series 2149-2154 [nd]**
**Celesque Series 2167-2172 [nd]**
**Celesque Series 2173-2178 [nd]**
**Celesque Series 2270-2275 [nd]**
**Celesque Series 2276-2281 [nd]**
**Celesque Series Novelty Cards Series 226-229 [nd]**
**Celesque Series Novelty Cards Series 408-411 [nd]**
**Coloured Glosso Birthday Series 303-308 [nd]**
**Celesque Series 519-524 War Humour Series [c.1942]**
**Celesque Series 525-530 Working for Winston [c.1942]**
**Celesque Series 1920-1926 Kute Komic Series [nd]**
**Series 107/1-107/12** (Humorous series) **[c.1942]**
* also reproduced under novelty cards
** also reproduced with no caption as an Easter series

***Celesque Series*** (part series identified)
**Cards 224-229**
**Cards 446-449**

***Regent Publishing*** (Individual cards unnumbered)
**For the Love of a Waac, I Love the Little Quackie Doodles, I Wish I was a Little Wackie Doodle, Let's Change Our Luck, The Quackie Doodles, [nd]** (5 of 6)
**For Home and Beauty, Good-night – We're All Dog Tired, I Love Little Pussie, School isn't Such Fun as I Thought, Six Little Ducks, Why Can't you Skip Kitty** (5 of 6)

***J Salmon***
**Series 4207-4212** (Humour) **1935**
Single cards or part series identified
**Cards 402-406 [1911]***
**Card 520 [1913]**
**Card 697 [1914]**
**Card 704 [1914]**
**Cards 745-749 [1914]**
**Card 754 [1914]**
**Card 764 [1914]**
**Card 767 [1914]**
**Card 991 [1916]**
**Cards 1146-1147 [1917]**
**Card 1814 [1920]**
**Cards 2901-2905 [1925]**
**Cards 2940-2944 [1925]**
* also bears E Mack imprint

***Raphael Tuck***
**Oilette Series 3244 Once Upon a Time [1920]**
**Oilette Series 3447 Once Upon a Time Series II [1920]**
**Oilette Series 3484 Little Pierrot and Wee Pierette [1924]**
**Oilette Series 3496 Ancient Egypt Up to Date [1924]**
**Oilette Series 8670 Our Kiddies Series I [1913]**
**Oilette Series 8671 Our Kiddies Series II [1913]**
**Oilette Series 8687 Duty's Call [1913]**
**Oilette Series 8688 Family Cares [1913]**
**Oilette Series 8740 We Can All Help [c.1914]**
**Oilette Series 8787 Our Kiddies Series III [c.1916]**
**Oilette Series 8788 Our Kiddies Series IV [c.1916]**
**Oilette Series 8894 When All is Young [c.1918]**
**Oilette Series 9982 Little Tots [1911]**
**Christmas Series C1420** (2 designs, 6 in pkt) **[nd]**
**Christmas Series C1421** (2 designs, 6 in pkt) **[nd]**
**Christmas Series C1422** (2 designs, 6 in pkt) **[nd]**
**Christmas Series C2004** (2 designs, 6 in pkt) **[nd]**
**Christmas Series C2005** (2 designs, 6 in pkt) **[nd]**
**Christmas Series C2006** (2 designs, 6 in pkt) **[nd]**
**Christmas Series C2012** (2 designs, 6 in pkt) **[nd]**
**Christmas Series C3119** (2 designs, 6 in pkt) **[c.1911]**
**Christmas Series C3120** (2 designs, 6 in pkt) **[c.1911]**
**Christmas Series C3121** (2 designs, 6 in pkt) **[c.1911]**
**Christmas Series C3603** (2 designs, 6 in pkt) **[c.1912]**
**Christmas Series C3604** (2 designs, 6 in pkt) **[c.1912]**
**Christmas Series C3605** (2 designs, 6 in pkt) **[c.1912]**
**Christmas Series C3606** (2 designs, 6 in pkt) **[c.1912]**
**Christmas Series C3609** (2 designs, 6 in pkt) **[c.1912]***
**Christmas Series C5002** (2 designs, 6 in pkt) **[c.1920]**
**Christmas Series C5003** (2 designs, 6 in pkt) **[c.1920]**
**Christmas Series C5056** (2 designs, 6 in pkt) **[c.1920]****
**Christmas Series C5060** (2 designs, 6 in pkt) **[c.1920]*****
**Christmas Series C7131** (2 designs, 6 in pkt) **[c.1912]**
**Christmas Series C7132** (2 designs, 6 in pkt) **[c.1912]**
**Christmas Series C7494** (2 designs, 6 in pkt) **[c.1913]**
**Christmas Series C7496** (2 designs, 6 in pkt) **[c.1913]**
**Christmas Series C7497** (2 designs, 6 in pkt) **[c.1913]**
**Oilette Card 3248 Sally & Our Alley [nd]**
**Oilette Card 8485 This is How We Feel [1912]**
**Oilette Card 8486 Back From the Front [1912]**
**Oilette Card 8487 Send Them Victorious [1912]**
**Oilette Card 8496 Daddy [1912]**
**Easter Series E1159 Joyous Easter [nd]**
* = reissue of C3119
** = reissue of C3120
*** = reissue of C3605

***Wildt & Kray***
**Series 5231** (Nursery rhymes) **[nd]**

***Books illustrated include***
*Arabian Nights. Puck's Sinbad Book* (Collins c.1930)
*Golden Locks and Pretty Frocks* / Gale/Floyd [et al] (1920)
*Holiday Times* [with M Bowley] / Vredenburg [ed] (Tuck nd)
*Joyful Stories* / Heward [et al] (Children's Press nd)
*Little Frolic* [with Louis Wain et al] (Shaw nd)
*Old Fairy Tales* [with AL Bowley] / Vredenburg[ed] (Tuck nd)
*Rêves d'Enfants (Children's Dreams)* (nd)
*Stories from Hans Andersen* (Geographia nd)
*The Children's Playmate* [et al] (Tuck nd)
*The Little Fairy Postcard Painting Book* (CW Faulkner (1913)
*The Way to Fairyland* [with M Attwell] [Welcome Gift Ser.] (Tuck nd)

***Annuals illustrated with others include***
*Big Book of Pictures and Stories; Blackie's Children's Annual; Blackie's Storytime Book; Father Tuck's Annual; Little Folks; Lots of Pictures; Santa Claus Picture Book; The Big Book of Pictures and Stories; Toddler's Annual; Toddles Annual; Wonder Book*

## Jennifer Rickard (b.1912)

**Postcards illustrated include**
***CW Faulkner***
**Series 2010** (Fairyland) **[1931]**

***Books illustrated include***
*Little Teddy Tales / Rhodes* (National Magazine Co. 1945)

***Annuals illustrated with others include***
*Sunny Stories*

## Freda Mabel Rose (1909-1987)

***Postcards illustrated include***
***J Salmon***
**Series 4400-4404** (Humour) **[1937]**
**Series 4544-4551** (Fairies) **[1938]**
**Also J Arthur Dixon**

## Harry Rountree (1878-1950)

***Postcards illustrated include***
***British Showcard & Poster Co.***
**Series 2. Shakespearean Play Titles [c.1905]**
**Unnumbered. Sporting Duckling [c.1905]**
***CW Faulkner***
**Series 236 Comic Bears [1903]**
***A Vivian Mansell***
**Series 1077** (Comic animals) **[1917]**

***Books illustrated include***
*A Book About Animals* (Blackie nd)
*A Great Adventure* [Little Tuppenny Series no 4] (Stevenson nd)
*Aesop's Fables* / Windsor [ed] (Ward Lock 1924)
*Alice's Adventures in Wonderland* / Carroll (Nelson 1908)
*Alice's Adventures in Wonderland & Through…*(Collins nd)
*Alice in Wonderland* [with Charles Pears] (Collins nd)
*Alice in Wonderland* (Children's Press nd)
*Animal Tales from Africa* / MacNair (Wells, Gardner 1914)
*Archibald's Amazing Adventure* / Hamer (Cassell 1905)
*A Wonderful Adventure* / Dearden (Heinemann 1929)
*Bruno Bear* / Gardner (Edmund Ward 1951)
*Bunny and Bobbie* (Cooke 1909)
*Cheepy the Chicken* [Menagerie Series] / Hamer (Cassell 1906)
*Children's Pets* [No. 533] (Birn Bros nd)
*Contes des Grimm* (Lafitte, Paris)
*Dicky Duck and Wonderful Walter* / L Rountree & Bradley (Warne nd)
*Enid Blyton's Book of the Year* / Blyton (Evans nd)
*Folk of the Wild* (Grant Richards 1911)
*Gervais and the Magic Castle* / Hamer (Simpkim 1920)
*Humpty Dumpty's Story Stall* [with Winifred Ackroyd] (Collins nd)
*Jungle Tales* (Warne 1934)
*Just Fancy* / Byron (Cooke c.1915)
*Lazy Lob & Other Stories* / Marlowe (Blackwell nd)
*Lickle Tickle* / Lang (Nelson 1914)
*Little Stories for Little People* [et al] (Nelson 1916)
*Me and Jimmy* / L Rountree (Warne 1929)
*Mr Punch's Book of Birthdays* (Punch 1906)
*My Book of Beautiful Legends* / Bayne (Cassell 1928)
*My Book of Best Fairy Tales* / Michael (Cassell 1922)
*My Book of Best Stories from History* / Michael (Cassell 1928)
*My Book of Best Stories from the Poets* / Michael (Cassell 1928)
*Peter Pink Eye* / Hamer (Nelson 1923)
*Pinion and Paw* / St Mars (Chambers 1919)
*Quackles Junior* [Menagerie Series] / Hamer (Cassell 1903)
*Rabbit Rhymes* (Stevenson 1917)
*Ronald, Rupert and Reg* [A Cosy Corner Book] (Warne nd)
*Rountree's Ridiculous Rabbits No. 1* (Stevenson nd)
*Rub-a-Dub Dub* (Nelson nd)
*Santa Claus* [Rag book No. 208] (Dean 1921)
*Stories from Grimm* (HF/H&S 1909)
*Sunday and Everyday Reading for the Young* [et al] (Wells Gardner 1915)
*Swiss Family Robinson* (Black 1924)
*Tales from the Woods and Fields* / Davidson (Wells Gardner 1950)
*Ten Little Pussycats [with music]* / Byron (Valentine 1910)
*The Adventures of Mabel* / Peck (Harrap 1917)
*The Adventures of Mr Mouse* [et al] (Collins nd)
*The Adventures of Peter Penguin* / Fry (Cassell 1920)
*The Adventures of Tootles and Timothy* / Seymour (Cassell 1922)
*The Animal Game Book* (Allen 1903)
*The Arkansaw Bear* / Paine (Harrap 1919)
*The Bold Brigands* [et al] (Dean nd)
*The Children of Cherry Tree Farm* / Blyton (Country Life 1950)
*The Children of Willow Farm* / Blyton (Country Life 1958)
*The Children's Song Book* [et al] (Andersons nd)
*The Doings of Dinky-Dandy* / Hayes (Cassell 1919)
*The Doings of Furry Mouse* / Watson (Cassell 1920)
*The Dumas Fairy Tale Book* / Spurr (Warne 1924)
*The Enchanted Wood & Other Stories* / Hamer (Simpkim 1920)
*The Forest Foundling* / Hamer (Duckworth 1909)
*The Fortunate Princeling* / Bright (Duckworth 1909)
*The Four Glass Walls* / Hamer (Simpkim 1920)
*The Golden Story Book* [et al] (Collins 1933)
*The Little Robinson Crusoes* / Avery (Nelson 1908)
*The Magic Wand* / Hamer (Duckworth 1908)
*The Mammoth Wonder Book* [et al] (Odhams Press 1935)
*The Milk White Thorn* [et al] (Nelson c.1920)
*The Odd Volume* [et al] (Nat Book Trade Prov. Soc. 1917)
*The Pirates of Pebble Pond* / Hayes (Cassell 1922)
*The Pond Mermaid* / Talbot (Cassell 1929)
*The Princess's Belt* [with A Rackham [et al] (Cassell 1914)
*The Ronuk Zoo Book* [advertising booklet] (Ronuk Polishes nd)
*The Secret Mountain* (Blackwell 1941)
*The Spell of the Open Air* (Foulis nd)
*The Story of Wicked Tim* / Hayes (Lithographing Co. 1930)
*The Strange Adventures of Billy Wilson* (Children's Companion nd)
*The Trapper's Foe* / Craig (Newnes 1917)
*The Wanderings of Roly Poly* / Wood (Cassell 1920)
*The Wiggly Weasel & Other Stories* / Marlowe (Blackwell 1925)
*The Wonderful Isles* / Hamer (Duckworth 1908)
*The Young Discoverers* [et al] (Cassell nd)
*The Young Gullivers* [The Menagerie Series] / Hamer (Cassell 1906)
*This Train for Storyland* [et al] (Cassell c.1915)
*This Way for Fun* [et al] (Cassell nd)
*Through the Looking Glass* / Carroll (Collins 1928)
*Toksikatem Castle or The Rescue…* / Ridge (Partridge nd)
*Uncle Remus* [with Rene Bull] / Harris (Lawrence & Co. nd)
*Uncle Remus* / Harris (Nelson 1908)
*Who's who at the Zoo* (Dean 1925)
*Wicked Tim* (Valentine nd)
*Wog and Wig* (Franklyn, Ward & Wheeler)

***'Little Tuppenny Series'***
*Little Miss Camill-Acuddle-Medoo* [No. 4] (Stevenson nd)
*The Disappearing Trick of Mickey & Morris* [No. 6] (Stevenson nd)
*Wonderkin* [No. 11] (Stevenson nd)

***'Farmyard Series' with transfer pictures***
*Brer Rabbit* / (WHC nd)
*The Farmyard in Spring* / Heslop (WHC nd)
*The Farmyard in Summer* / Heslop (WHC nd)
*The Farmyard in Autumn* / Heslop (WHC nd)
*The Farmyard in Winter* / Heslop (WHC nd)

***Annuals and periodicals illustrated with others include***
*Blackie's Children's Annual; Bo-peep; Cassell's Children's Annual; Chick's Own Annual; Children's Pets; Collins' Children's Annual; Daddy's Galloping Goat; Joy Street Annual; Little Folks; London Opinion; Playtime; Printer's Pie; Puck Annual; Punch; Radio Times; The Boy's Own Paper; The Bystander; The Captain; Cassell's Magazine; The Children's Wonder Book; The Flag; The Girls' Realm; The Graphic; The Humorist; The Jolly Book; The London Magazine; The Odd Volume; The Pall Mall Magazine; Pearson's Magazine; The Royal Magazine; The Sketch; The Strand Magazine; The Tatler; TocH Annual; The Windsor Magazine; The Wonder Book of Animals; The Wonder Book for Children; The Wonderland Annual*

## Hilda Dix Sandford (1875-1946)

***Postcards illustrated include***
***S Hildesheimer***
**No. 5261** (Seaside children) **[1905]**
**No. 5268** (Black children) **[1905]**

***Raphael Tuck***
**Oilette Series 2324 Egg-cellent [1906]**
**Oilette Series 2325 Egg-cellent [1906]**
**Oilette Series 8246 Christmas postcard [1905]**
**Oilette Series 8247 Christmas postcard [1905]**
**Oilette Series 8248 Christmas postcard [1905]**
**Oilette Series 8249 Christmas postcard [1905]**
**Oilette Series 9049 Happy Little Coons Series I [1906]**
**Oilette Series 9050 Happy Little Coons Series II [1906]**
**Oilette Series 9093 Curly Coons [1906]**
**Oilette Series 9102 Boys & Girls Come Out to Play [1906]**
**Oilette Series 9220 Girls & Boys [1906]**
**Oilette Series 9227 Happy Little Coons Series III [1906]**
**Oilette Series 9228 Happy Little Coons Series IV [1906]**
**Oilette Series 9229 Happy Little Coons Series V [1906]**
**Oilette Series 9307 When the World is Young [1906]**
**Oilette Series 9318 Seaside Coons [1906]**
**Oilette Series 9427 More Coons [1907]**
**Oilette Series 9428 Dark Girls & Black Boys [1907]**
**Oilette Series 9049 Happy Little Coons Series VI [1907]**
**Oilette Series 9468 Merry Winter [1907]**
**Oilette Series 9489 Dark Girls & Black Boys II [1907]**
**Oilette Series 9791 Young Egypt [1908]**
**Oilette Series 9968 Seaside Coons II [1911]** (from 9050/9318)
**Oilette Series 9969 Seaside Coons III [1911]** (from 9227/9229)
**Art Series 6700 [1905]**
**Art Series 6891 Happy Little Coons [1906]**
**Christmas Series 8438 Happy Little Coons [1906]**
**Christmas Series 6891 Happy Little Coons [1906]** (from 6891)
**Juvenile Series 6074 All in a Row [1905]**
**Juvenile Series 6082 Prude and Prim [1905]**

## Cecily Elmslie Shand (1898-1979)

*Postcards illustrated include*
*British Art Company*
**Unnumbered series**
A Birthday of Gaiety, A Dainty Partner, A Demure Maiden,
After the Ball, A Kiss for Bo-peep, A Little Persuasion,
An Eastern Maiden, Au Claire de la Lune, Bed Time,
Beginners, Blooms and Things, Butterflies, Carnival,
Fairy Time, Fine Feathers, Flowers of the East, Fun and Frolic,
Good Night, His First Proposal, Hollyhocks, Incense,
Kind of Risky, Lady of the Rose, Let's, Lonesome,
Loud Speakers, Madame Pom-Pom, May I Mais Oui!,
Miss Snowball, Moon and Two, My Lady Fayre,
Passive Resistance, Pierette, Rags, Ready for the Ball, Rivals,
Rival Suitors, Romance, Roses, Sitting Out, So Shy,
Springtime, Sunflowers, Suspense, The Bridesmaid,
The Cigarette, The Eternal Triangle, The Eastern Maiden,
The Flower Girl, The Introduction, The Intruder,
The Nautch Girl, The Old, Old Story, The Optimist,
The Serenade, The Tiff, Vanity, Ways and Means, Winter,
**Winter Cosiness**

## May Smith (b. 1904)

*Postcards illustrated include*
*Medici Society*
**Pkt 45/6322** (Children at play) **[c.1936]**
**Pkt 46/6321** (Children at play) **[c.1936]**
**Pkt 51** (Dogs) [c.1936]
*Valentines*
**Series 3339-3341** (Children at play) **[c.1936]**

*Books illustrated include*
*Billy Bob Tales* (Methuen 1938)
*Teeny Weeny's Holiday Book* (Milford 1935)
*The Man Who Caught the Wind* / Gibbs (Chapman & Hall 1936)
*Westwoods* / Farjeon (Blackwell 1930)
*Annuals and periodicals illustrated with others include*
*Joy Street; Radio Times*

## Millicent Sowerby (1878-1967)

*Postcards illustrated include*
*Chatto & Windus*
**Series from *Childhood* [1907]**
*Dondorf*
**Single card No.170** (Boy tosses petals into girl's lap) **[1907]**
*CW Faulkner*
**Series 568 Happy Childhood [1906]**
**Christmas series** (Unnumbered) **[1906]**
*Henry Frowde and Hodder & Stoughton / Humphrey Milford*
*Postcards for the Little Ones Series*
**Little Folk of Many Lands [1914]**
**The Children's' Day [1914]**
**Britain and Her Friends [1915]**
**Happy Days [1915]**
**Happy Little People [1915]**
**Little Jewels [1915]**
**Little Patriots [1915]**
**Playtime [1915]**
**Pleasant Days [1915]**
**Sons of the Empire [1915]**
**Favourite Nursery Rhymes [1916]**
**Favourite Nursery Stories [1916]**
**Bird Children [1920]**
**Fairies' Friends [1930]**
**Fairy Frolic Series [1926]**
**Farmyard Pets [1920]**
**Flower Fairies [1923]**
**Flowers and Wings [1920]**
**Golden Days (from *The Wise Book*) [1930]**
**Guides and Brownies [1924]**
**Happy as Kings [1921]**

**Merry Elves [1921]**
**Old Time Games [1921]**
**Peter Pan Postcards [1920]**
**Pretty Wings [1920]**
**Shakespeare's Heroines [1922]**
**Sky Fairies [1920]**
**Storyland Children [1924]**
**Woodland Games [1920]**
*The Fairy Frolic Play Book*, published by Milford [1926] is
comprised of pictures from Fairy Frolic Series and Pretty Wings.
*Meissner & Buch* (4 designs)
**Series 1427** (Children in Tudor settings) **[1906]**
*Misch & Co* (4 designs)
**Greenaway Girls [1907] [Dondorf 168]**
**In Greenaway Times [1907] [Dondorf 169]**
*Reinthal & Newman*
**Unnumbered** (Girls' names starting with 'P') **[1909]**
**Unnumbered** (The weather as in a child's mood) **[1909]**

*Books illustrated include*
*A Child's Garden of Verses* / Stevenson (Chatto & Windus 1908)
*Alice's Adventures in Wonderland* / Carroll (Chatto & Windus 1907)
*Alice's Adventures in Wonderland* / Carroll (HF/H&S 1913)
*Animal Stories for Tiny Folk* [Little Big Books] (Milford 1926)
*Childhood* / G Sowerby (Chatto & Windus 1907)
*Cinderella* (HF/H&S 1915)
*Cinderella's Play Book* (Milford 1927)
*Fairy Frolic Play Book* (Milford 1922)
*Fly Away Folk* (HF/H&S nd)
*For Teddy and Me* [et al] (Milford nd)
*Grimm's Fairy Tales* (Grant Richards 1909)
*Little Plays for Little People* / G Sowerby (HF/H&S c.1910)
*Little Rhymes for Little Folk* [A Little Big Book] (Milford 1926)
*Little Songs for Little People* / G Sowerby (HF/H&S c.1910)
*Little Stories for Little People* / G Sowerby (HF/H&S c.1910)
*Mrs Strang's Infant Readers* (Milford nd)
*My Birthday* / G Sowerby (Milford nd)
*Poems of Childhood* Githa Sowerby (HF/H&S 1912)
*The Angel of Love* / Meade (HF/H&S nd)
*The Bumbletoes* / G Sowerby (Chatto & Windus 1907)
*The Counterpane Book* / Byron (HF/H&S 1913)
*The Happy Book* / G Sowerby (Dent 1906)
*The Wise Book* / G Sowerby (Dent 1906)
*Yesterday's Children* / G Sowerby (Chatto & Windus 1908)
'Baby's Books'
*Rhymes for Baby* / Mrs Strang [ed] (HF/H&S nd)
*Stories for Baby* / Mrs Strang [ed] (HF/H&S nd)
*What Baby Reads* / Mrs Strang [ed] (HF/H&S nd)
*What Baby Sees* / Mrs Strang [ed] (HF/H&S nd)
'The Sowerby Books'
*The Bonnie Book* / G Sowerby (Milford 1918)
*The Bright Book* / G Sowerby (HF/H&S 1916)
*The Dainty Book* / G Sowerby (HF/H&S 1915)
*The Darling Book* / Joan (Milford c.1920)
*The Gay Book* / G Sowerby (HF/H&S 1915)
*The Glad Book* / Joan (Milford c.1920)
*The Joyous Book* / Joan (HF/H&S c.1920)
*The Merry Book* / G Sowerby (HF/H&S nd)
*The Pleasant Book* / G Sowerby (HF/H&S 1918)
*The Sunny Book* / Fyleman (Milford 1918)
*Books illustrated with others include*
*Curly Locks* [with Florence Hardy] (Milford nd)
*Fun* [with SG Hulme Beaman] (DLMS nd)
*Garlands Gay* / Mrs Strang [ed] (HF/H&S nd)
*Meadowsweet* / Mrs Strang [ed] (HF/H&S nd)
*Nuts in May* / Mrs Strang [ed] (HF/H&S nd)
*Other Plays of Fairy Days* [with G Lodge]/ M Lodge (Milford 1924)
*Pretty Maids* / Mrs Strang [ed] (HF/H&S nd)
*Seven Plays of Fairy Days* [with G Lodge]/ M Lodge (Milford 1923)
*The Hideaway Four* (Milford 1928)
*The Primrose Book* / Mrs Strang [ed] (HF/H&S nd)
*The Rose Book* / Mrs Strang [ed] (HF/H&S nd)
*Annuals illustrated with others include*
*Mrs Strang's Annual for Children;*
*Mrs Strang's Playbooks; The Big Book for Tinies; The Oxford Annual*
*for Baby; The Tiny Folks Annual*

## Lorna Steele (1902-1990)

*Postcards illustrated include*
*J Salmon*
**Series 4964-4969 Peeps at Pixies [1947]**
**Series 4970-4975** (Elves & fairies) **[1947]**
**Series 5006-5011** (Animals at play) **[1949]**
**Series 5012-5017** (Children & elves) **[1949]**
**Series 5050-5055 Famous Fairies [1949]**
**Series 5094-5099** (Fairyland) **[1950]**
**Series 5172-5177 Favourite Fairy Tales [1952]**

*Books illustrated include*
*The Adventures of Andy and Ann* (Partridge 1944)
*Caravan Boy* [Go-ahead Books] / Derwent (Univ. London Press 1942)
*I Will Repay* / Baroness Orczy (Univ. London Press 1945)
*Favourite Nursery Rhymes* [with Flora White] (J Salmon nd)
*Favourite Nursery Rhymes with Variations* (J Salmon nd)
*Magic Wood* / Jefferies (Collins nd)
*Miranda Mouse* / Lawson (J Salmon nd)
*Three Little Elves* (J Salmon 1944)

## Margaret Tarrant (1888-1959)

*Postcards illustrated include*
*Alpha*
**Series 4195-4200** (Children at the seaside) **[nd]**
*CW Faulkner*
**Series 923** (Flower fairies) **[1909]**
*Ward Lock*
**Nursery Rhymes**
(from Nursery Rhymes) [1914]
*Harrap*
**Months of the Year**
(from The Picture Birthday Book for Boys & Girls) [1916]
*Humphrey Milford & The Medici Society*
**The Sunbonnet Series [1925]**
**The Sunshade Series [1925]**
*The Medici Society*
**Pkt 1 Nursery Rhymes** (6 designs) **[c.1927]**
**Pkt 2 Magic of Childhood** (6 designs) **[c.1927]**
**Pkt 3 Devotional Series** (6 designs) **[c.1927]**
**Pkt 4 Fairies in Our Garden** (6 designs) **[c.1927]**
**Pkt 5 Fairy Hours** (6 designs) **[c.1927]**
**Pkt 6 Fairies of the Countryside** (6 designs) **[c.1928]**
**Pkt 7 Out o' Doors** (6 designs) **[c.1928]**
**Pkt 8 Joy of Heaven** (6 designs) **[c.1928]**
**Pkt 17 Sweet Fragrance** (6 designs) **[c.1928]**
**Pkt 18 Playtime** (6 designs) **[c.1928]**
**Pkt 21 Springtime of Life** (6 designs) **[c.1930]**
**Pkt 22 Elfin Series** (6 designs) **[c.1930]**
**Pkt 23 Sing Praises Series** (6 designs) **[c.1930]**
**Pkt 27 Flower of Dawn** (6 designs) **[c.1930]**
**Pkt 28 In Arcady** (6 designs) **[c.1930]**
**Pkt 30 In Arcady** (from Playtime Series) **[c.1932]**
**Pkt 31 Do You Believe in Fairies?** (from Fairy Hours) **[c.1932]**
**Pkt 32 Peter's Friends** (from Fairy Hours) **[c.1932]**
**Pkt 34 Thoughts of Youth** (from Springtime of Life) **[c.1932]**
**Pkt 35 Windflowers** (from Devotional) **[c.1932]**
**Pkt 36 Everybody's Brother** (from Devotional) **[c.1932]**
**Pkt 37 Love That Melts the Snows** (from Devotional) **[c.1932]**
**Pkt 41 The Little Son** (6 designs) **[c.1933]**
**Pkt 44 The Lilies of the Field** (from the Little Son) **[c.1933]**
**Pkt 47 Let Everything That Hath Breath**
(from the Little Son) **[c.1933]**
**Pkt 48 Baby's Grace** (from The Old, Old Rhymes) **[c.1933]**
**Pkt 49 Madonna of the Meadows [c.1933]**
**Pkt 50** (Flowers in vases) **[c.1933]**
**Pkt 53 The King of Love [c.1937]**
**Pkt 54 Pixie Time** (6 designs) **[c.1937]**
**Pkt 57 Blessing the Lamb [c.1939]**
**Pkt 58 Morning Carol [c.1939]**
**Pkt 62 Sing Heigh Ho! Unto the Green Holly [c.1939]**
**Pkt 74 He Prayeth Best [c.1939]**

**Pkt 103 Evening Blessing [c.1947]**
**Pkt 104 Angel Guides [c.1947]**
**Pkt 105 The End of the Day [c.1947]**
**Pkt 118 Stars in the Bright Sky [c.1948]**
**Pkt 119 Pixie Mail [c.1948]**
**Pkt 120 The Fairy Troupe [c.1948]**
**Pkt 122 Born the King of Angels [c.1948]**
**Pkt 129 Christ was Born Among the Lilies [c.1948]**
**Pkt 131 Grant to Little Children [c.1948]**
**Pkt 138 Joy to the World c1949**
**Pkt 149 Behold I Send You Forth [c.1950]**
**Pkt 150 Loving Shepherd of Thy Sheep [c.1950]**
**Pkt 151 All Things Wise and Wonderful [c.1950]**
**Pkt 152 The Star of Jerusalem [c.1950]**
**Pkt 153 The Fairy Way [c.1950]**
**Pkt 156 Little Hands Outstretched to Bless [c.1950]**
**Pkt 157 The First Flower Service [c.1950]**
**Pkt 161 The Gorse Fairies [c.1951]**
**Pkt 163 Fantasia [c.1951]**
**Pkt 164 There Must be Fairies Here [c.1951]**
**Pkt 165 Pixie Jazz Band [c.1951]**
**Pkt 171 Summer Dreams [c.1952]**
**Pkt 172 Elfin Chorus [c.1952]**
**Pkt 173 The Holy Child [c.1952]**
**Pkt 174 Summer Dreams [c.1952]**
**Pkt 180 Lighting Up Time [c.1953]**
**Pkt 181 Seashore Fairies [c.1953]**
**Pkt 182 Friends of the Woodland [c.1953]**
**Pkt 183 The Light of Light [c.1953]**
**Pkt 184 The Enchantress [c.1953]**
**Pkt 193 The Gorse Fairies [c.1953]**
**Pkt 194 Goblin Wood [c.1953]**
**Pkt 195 Sea Horses [c.1953]**
**Pkt 196 We Saw Him and We Blessed the Sight [c.1953]**
**Pkt 204 Spring Butterflies [c.1954]**
**Pkt 209 The Last Supper [c.1954]**
**Pkt 211 St Francis Preaching to the Birds [c.1954]**
**Pkt 212 The Garden Gate [c.1954]**
**Pkt 214 The Magic Palace [c.1954]**
**Pkt 215 Old Slowcoach [c.1954]**
**The Old, Old Rhymes** (6 designs) **[c.1933]**
**Britain's Heritage Series [c.1939]**
**Large format postcards $5^{7}/_{8}$ x $4^{1}/_{8}$ include:**
**Published between 1939 and 1956**
**971 Lesser Celandine**
**972 White Water Lily**
**973 Wood Anemone**
**974 Wild Hyacinth**
**996 Field Scabious**
**998 Yew**
**1001 Wild Crab Apple**
**1004 Hawthorn or May**
**1005 Scotch Thistle**
**1006 Blackthorn**
**1011 Harebell**
**1012 Common Squirrel**
**1013 Rabbit**
**1039 Iris**
**1041 The Picnic Party**
**1045 Britain's Treasure**
**1054 The Loving Shepherd**
**1057 How Beautiful Upon the Mountains**
**1068 Lift Up Your Hearts**
**1076 An Elf to Tea**
**1078 Spring Morning**
**1087 Bladder Campion**
**1088 Yew Wort**
**1089 Herb Robert**
**1090 Columbine**
**1091 Bull Rush**
**1093 Yellow Water Lily**
**1094 Common Butterwort**
**1096 Ribwort Plantain**
**1103 Betony**
**1104 Buck Bean**
**1105 Pasque Flower**

1106 Yellow Mimulus
1107 Meadow Sweet
1108 Wood Sorrel
1109 Winter Aconite
1110 Lords and Ladies
1111 Meadow Cranesbill
1112 Dark Mullein
1113 European Larch
1114 Bee Orchis
1115 Teasel
1116 Corn Marigold
1117 Elder
1121 Strawberry
1124 Cow Parsnip
1126 Viper's Bugloss
1127 Purple Loosestrife
1128 Musk Mallow
1129 Ragwort
1131 Common Broom
1132 Chicory
1133 Mistletoe
1134 Rock Rose
1135 Cotton Grass
1136 Dropwort
1137 Common Sea Lavender
1147 Fritillary
1148 Bugle
1149 Greater Stitchwort
1150 Colts Foot
1151 The Portrait Painter
1152 The Wandering Minstrels
1158 Silver Weed
1159 Sea Holly
1160 Yellow Toadflax
1162 Purple Clover
1173 Bramble
1174 Woody Nightshade
1220 Morning Blessing
1234 Woodland Hospital
1235 Arrowhead
1237 Deadly Nightshade
1270 Wall Pennywort

**Books illustrated include**
*Alice in Wonderland* / Carroll (Ward Lock c.1916)
*All the Old Nursery Rhymes* / Davidson (Pilgrim nd)
*An Alphabet of Magic* / Farjeon (Medici 1928)
*An Elf to Tea* (Medici Society nd)
*Animal Friends* / Golding (Ward Lock nd)
*A Picture Birthday Book for Boys & Girls* / Cole [ed] (Harrap 1915)
*A Story Garden for Little Children* / Lindsay (Harrap 1918)
*Autumn Gleanings from the Poets* (Allen 1910)
*Brighteyes Merry Book* [et al] (Coker c.1922)
*Contes de Perrault* / Fitzgerald (Librairie Flammarion 1910)
*Eliz'beth, Phil and Me* / Webb (Harrap 1918)
*Fairy Stories of Hans Andersen* (Ward Lock 1917)
*Fairy Tales* (Ward Lock nd)
*Favourite Fairy Tales* (Ward Lock nd)
*Games for Playtime and Parties* / Willman (Jack 1914)
*Gold Gorse Common* / Kaye (Collins c.1945)
*Hans Andersen's Fairy Stories* (Ward Lock nd)
*Hans Andersen's Fairy Tales* (Ward Lock nd)
*In Wheelabout and Cockalone* / Rhys (Harrap 1918)
*Joan in Flowerland* / Dutton (Warne 1935)
*Johann - the Woodcarver* / Wood (Warne 1949)
*Knock Three Times* / Webb (Harrap 1917)
*Lucy-Mary, or the Cobweb Cloak* / Herbertson (Blackie 1909)
*Magic Houses* / Todd (Medici nd)
*Margaret Tarrant & Her Pictures* / Gurney (Medici 1982)
*Margaret Tarrant's Birthday Book* (Medici 1932)
*Margaret Tarrant's Christmas Garland* / Hale 1942)
*Merry Animal Tales* (Harrap 1913)
*Mother Goose Fairy Tales* (Coker nd)
*Mother Goose Nursery Rhymes* (Ward Lock c.1925)
*Mother Goose Nursery Tales* (Harrap 1920)
*My Friend Phil* / Peacock (Ward Lock 1915)

*Nursery Rhyme Book* (Collins 1945)
*Nursery Rhymes* (Ward Lock 1914)
*Our Animal Friends* / Golding (Ward Lock 1930)
*Pinkie Mouse and Koko* (Collins 1947)
*Rhymes of Old Times* (Medici 1925)
*Songs the Letters Sing* [Primers] (Grant Educ nd)
*Songs with Music from 'A Child's Garden of Verses'* (Jack 1918)
*The Animal ABC* (Ward Lock 1930)
*The Book of Games* [with Nina Brisley] (Ward Lock 1920)
*The Book of the Clock* [with Nina Brisley] (Ward Lock 1920)
*The Book of Summer* (Allen 1910)
*The Book of Winter* (Allen 1910)
*The Book of the Seasons* (Allen 1910)
*The Children's Year* [A birthday book] (Cape 1922)
*The Child's Book of Verse* (Ward Lock nd)
*The Flowers and Trees of the Countryside* [with E Soper] (Medici 1942)
*The Girlhood of Famous Women* / Snell (Harrap 1927)
*The Gentle Heritage* / Compton (Ward Lock 1920)
*The Goblin and his Cap* [Simple Reading Steps] (Grant Educ.Co 1944)
*The Haliburton Primer* (Heath nd)
*The Jolly Book of Boxcraft* / Beard (Harrap 1918)
*The Little God* [with K Howard] (Harrap 1918)
*The Little One in Between* / Webb (Harrap 1929)
*The Little White Gate* / Hoatson (Harrap 1925)
*The Littlest One* [with Kay Nixon] / Webb (Harrap 1914)
*The Littlest One Again* [with D Newsome] / Webb (Harrap 1924)
*The Littlest One – His Book* / Webb (Harrap 1923)
*The Littlest One's Third Book* / Webb (Harrap 1928)
*The Magic Lamplighter* / Webb (Medici 1926)
*The Margaret Tarrant Birthday Book* / Cole (Medici nd)
*The Margaret Tarrant Nursery Rhyme Book* (Collins 1944)
*The Margaret Tarrant Story Book* (Collins 1947)
*The Pied Piper of Hamelin* / Browning (Dent 1912)
*The Songs the Children Sing* (Grant Educ. nd)
*The Songs the Letters Sing Book* (Grant Educ. c.1950)
*The Songs the Letters Sing Book II* (Grant Educ. c.1950)
*The Story of Christmas* / Bamfield (Medici 1952)
*The Story Wonder Book* [et al] (Ward Lock 1937)
*The Sunny Day Story Book* (Ward Lock nd)
*The Third Lamb* / Kyle (Medici 1938)
*The Tookey & Alice Mary Tales* / Rudolf (Harrap 1919)
*The Water Babies* / Kingsley (Dent 1908)
*The Wonder Book* [et al] (Ward Lock nd)
*Three Chums, Peggy, Prince and Bobby* (Chapman & Grimes 1939)
*Tim and the Twins* / Mais (Nelson nd)
*Verses for Children* / Golding [ed] (Ward Lock 1918)
*Wigley-an Elf* / Barnes (Ward Lock nd)
*Willie Winkie, The Tale of a Wooden Horse* / Golding (Ward Lock 1918)
*Within the Magic Gateways* / Saunders (Harrap 1919)
*Zoo Days* / Golding (Ward Lock 1919)

**'Margaret Tarrant's Flower Fairies' by Marion St John Webb**
*The Insect Fairies* (Modern Art Soc. 1924)
*The Flower Fairies* (Modern Art Soc. 1924)
*The Forest Fairies* (Modern Art Soc. 1924)
*The Heath Fairies* (Modern Art Soc. 1927)
*The House Fairies* (Modern Art Soc. 1926)
*The Insect Fairies* (Modern Art Soc. 1924)
*The Orchard Fairies* (Modern Art Soc 1928)
*The Pond Fairies* (Modern Art Soc. 1924)
*The Seashore Fairies* (Modern Art Soc. 1924)
*The Seed Fairies* (Modern Art Soc. 1923)
*The Twilight Fairies* (Modern Art Soc. 1927)
*The Weather Fairies* (Modern Art Soc. 1926)
*The Wild Fruit Fairies* (Modern Art Society 1924)

**'Old Favourite Toy Books'**
*A was an Archer* (Harrap 1920)
*Cinderella* (Harrap 1920)
*Cock Robin and The House that Jack Built* (Harrap 1920)
*Jack and the Beanstalk* (Harrap 1920)
*Jack and the Giant Killer* (Harrap 1920)
*Red Riding Hood* (Harrap 1920)
*The Three Bears* (Harraps 1920)
*Tom Thumb* (Harrap 1920)

**Annuals illustrated with others include**
*Boys and Girls Wonder Book; Wonder Book – A Picture Annual for Boys and Girls*

## Margaret Tempest (1892-1982)

**Postcards illustrated include**
**Medici Society**
Pkt 43/6265 Fun on the Ice [c.1937]
Pkt 43/6266 The Duet [c.1937]
Pkt 43/6267 The Evening Meal [c.1937]
Pkt 43/6334 Gruel [c.1937]
Pkt 43/6335 The Careful Mother [c.1937]
Pkt 52/6466 Dressing for the Party [c.1937]
Pkt 52/6482 Leap Frog [c.1937]
Pkt 52/6485 Bedtime [c.1937]
Pkt 52/6483 Christmas Pudding [c.1937]
Pkt 52/6484 The Bicycle Ride [c.1937]
Pkt 59/6815 His First Suit [c.1938]
Pkt 59/6826 The New Brother [c.1938]
Pkt 59/6827 The Explorers [c.1938]
Pkt 59/6835 Shelter from the Rain [c.1938]
Pkt 59/6836 Gardening [c.1938]
Pkt 61/6868 Down the Slope [c.1938]
Pkt 61/6987 Christmas Morning [c.1938]
Pkt 61/6988 The Explorers [c.1938]
Pkt 61/6997 King of the Castle [c.1938]
Pkt 61/6999 The Boat Race [c.1938]
Pkt 76/5131 Christmas Decoration [c.1938]
Pkt 77/5132 The Hurdy Gurdy [c.1938]
Pkt 78/6848 See Saw [c.1938]
Pkt 79/5129 The Boat Load [c.1938]
Pkt 80/5130 Blind Man's Buff [c.1938]
Pkt 85/6268 Jolly Sailors [c.1938]
Pkt 81 The Village School [1946]
Pkt 98 Fishing [1947]
Pkt 100 Sweet Apples [1947]
Pkt 106 The Stepping Stones [1947]
Pkt 108 What O'clock [1947]
Pkt 109 Teddy's Birthday Party [1947]
Pkt 110 The Village Pump [1947]
Pkt 111 Punch and Judy [1947]
Pkt 112 The Pick a Back Race [1947]
Pkt 113 The Patchwork Quilt [1947]
Pkt 145 Rock-a-Bye Baby [1950]
Pkt 155 The Toy Shop [1950]
Pkt 207 Cat-Astrophic [1953]
Pkt 208 Cats' Cradle [1953]

**Books illustrated include**
*ABC for You and Me* (Medici 1948)
*A Belief for Children* (Collins 1952)
*Black Bramble Wood* / Kaye (Collins nd)
*Gold Gorse Common* / Kaye (Collins 1945)
*Katinka's Travels to the Himalaya's* (1926)
*No Rubbish Here* / Evans (Collins 1936)
*Pinkie Mouse and Christmas Day* (Collins 1946)
*Pinkie Mouse and the Elves* (Collins 1947)
*Pinkie Mouse and Koko* (Collins 1947)
*Pinkie Mouse and the Rainbow* (Collins 1946)
*Potter Pinner Meadow* / Kaye (Collins 1937)
*The Doll's House* / Fyleman (1930)
*The Speckledy Hen* / Uttley (Collins 1945)
*Tittymouse and Tattymouse* / Valance (Muller 1946)
*Three Merry Madcaps* [et al] (Milford 1935)
*Willow Witches' Brook* / Kaye (Collins 1944)

**'Little Grey Rabbit Books' by Alison Uttley**
*The Squirrel, the Hare & the Little Grey Rabbit* (Collins 1929)
*How Little Grey Rabbit Got Her Tail Back* (Collins 1930)
*The Great Adventure of Hare* (Heinemann 1931)
*The Story of Fuzzypeg the Hedgehog* (Heinemann 1932)
*Squirrel Goes Skating* (Collins 1934)
*Wise Owl's Story* (Collins 1935)
*Little Grey Rabbit's Party* (Collins 1936)
*The Knot Squirrel Tied* (Collins 1937)
*Fuzzypeg Goes to School* (Collins 1938)
*Little Grey Rabbit's Christmas* (Collins 1939)
*Little Grey Rabbit's Painting Book* (Collins 1939)
*Moldy Warp the Mole* (Collins 1940)

*Little Grey Rabbit's Second Painting Book* (Collins c.1941)
*Hare Joins the Home Guard* (Collins 1942)
*Little Grey Rabbit's Washing Day* (Collins 1942)
*Water Rat's Picnic* (Collins 1943)
*Little Grey Rabbit's Birthday* (Collins 1944)
*Little Grey Rabbit to the Rescue* (Collins 1945)
*Little Grey Rabbit and the Weasels* (Collins 1947)
*Grey Rabbit and the Wandering Hedgehog* (Collins 1948)
*Little Grey Rabbit Makes Lace* (Collins 1950)
*Hare and the Easter Eggs* (Collins 1952)
*Little Grey Rabbit's Valentine* (Collins 1953)
*Little Grey Rabbit's Third Painting Book* (Collins c.1953)
*Little Grey Rabbit Goes to Sea* (Collins 1954)
*Hare and Guy Fawkes* (Collins 1956)
*Little Grey Rabbit's Paint Box* (Collins 1958)
*Little Grey Rabbit Finds a Shoe* (Collins 1960)
*Grey Rabbit and the Circus* (Collins 1961)
*Grey Rabbit's May Day* (Collins 1963)
*Hare goes Shopping* (Collins 1965)
*Little Grey Rabbit's Pancake Day* (Collins 1967)

**'Curly Cobbler Books'**
*Curly Cobbler and the Fairy Shoe* (Collins 1948)
*Curly Cobbler and the Snowfall* (Collins 1948)
*Curly Cobbler and the Happy Return* (Collins 1949)
*Curly Cobbler and the Cuckoo Clock* (Collins 1950)
*Curly Cobbler and the Robins* (Collins 1951)

**Annuals illustrated with others include**
*Lady Cynthia Asquith's Annual*

## GH Thompson (1853-1953)

**Postcards illustrated include**
**Ernest Nister**
Series 179 The Animals' Trip to Sea [1905]
Series 180 The Animals' Picnic [1905]
Series 181 The Animals' Rebellion [1905]
Card No. 320 Dog and pup with a bone [c.1902]
Card No. 330 Young rabbit having a haircut [c.1902]
Card No. 332 Jumping jumbo [c.1902]
Card No. 415 Kitten at school [c.1902]
Card No. 459 Ducklings going to school [c.1902]
Card No. 461 Tabbies accident in the kitchen [c.1902]
Card No. 465 Bear at an outfitters [c.1902]
Card No. 467 Dressed up goose [c.1902]
Card No. 468 Tabby kitten dressed up [c.1902]
**Stroefer (TSN)**
Series 265 (6 designs) from The Animals Touring Club

**Books illustrated include**
*Animal Frolics* (McLoughlin nd)
*Bright Eyes Story Book* [No. 2275] [et al] (Nister nd)
*Christmas in Animal Land*
*Froggy Would A-Wooing Go* [Nursery Series] (Tuck nd)
*Fun and Frolic* [with Louis Wain] (Nister nd)
*Funny Doings in Animaldom* / Bingham (McLoughlin c.1902)
*Funny Doings in Animal Land* / Bingham (Nister nd)
*Funny Friends* / Wood (Nister c.1889)
*Isn't it Funny* (Nister 1893)
*Les Animaux à la Mer* (Libraire Hachette Paris nd)
*Les Animaux Boy-Scouts* (Libraire Hachette Paris nd)
*Pussy's Mixture of Verse and Prose* / Bingham (Nister c.1898)
*Sports in Animal Land* / Bingham (Nister nd)
*Stories for all Times* [No. 3929] [et al] (Nister nd)
*The Animal's Alpine Club* / Bingham (Nister 1913)
*The Animal's Picnic* / Bingham (Nister c.1903)
*The Animal's Rebellion* / Bingham (Nister c.1903)
*The Animal's Trip to Sea* [No.616] / Bingham (Nister 1901)
*The Animal's Touring Club* / Braine (Nister c.1900)
*The Life & Strange...Adventures of Robinson Crusoe* [et al] (Nister nd)
*The Poet and Other Animals* / Richardson (Nister nd)
*The Three Bears* [No. 711a] (Nister c.1903)
*Transformation Pictures & Comical Fixtures* [movable] (Nister c.1895)
*What Fun!* [with Lawson Wood] (Birn Bros nd)

**Annuals illustrated with others include**
*Father Tuck's Annual; Nister's Holiday Annual; The Happy Book*

## Mary Tourtel (1874-1948)

*Postcards illustrated include*
(Dutch series 1) Sepia, also black & white [c.1934]
(Publisher anon)
*From Rupert in Dreamland*
    401 Rupert and Bill Badger walking through forest
    402 Rupert and Bill sitting for a photograph
    403 Rupert and BB on fairground ride
    404 Rupert running along country lane
    405 (Not known)
    406 Rupert sitting in garden reading
    407 Rupert and a seaman pointing
    408 Rupert riding a fish
    409 Rupert sitting at tea table with others
    410 Rupert cleaning shoes
(Dutch series 2) In colour; oversized postcards [c.1934]
NV Algemeen Handelsblad
    1 Rupert and dwarf inside castle
    2 Rupert and old lady in castle
    3 Rupert looking through doorway at Wise Old Goat
    4 Rupert standing with a wizard
    5 Rupert walking over bridge to the castle
    6 Rupert reaching for a box on a high shelf
(Dutch series 3) In colour [c.1931]
EH & Co
    Series A
    A1. Rupert with a pixie at a well
    A2. Rupert at the bedside of Wise Goat
    A3. Rupert at the tea table
    A4. Rupert and a reindeer
    A5. Rupert with a cat by a gate
    A6. Rupert with a princess
    Series B
    B1. Rupert with mother, father and an elephant
    B2. Rupert with Edward sitting on gate
    B3. (Not known)
    B4. Rupert in the forest with a knight
    B5. Rupert in the forest with a knight
    B6. Rupert by his front door with mother and Edward
    Series C
    C1. Rupert in car with Mr & Mrs Trunk and indian boy
    C2. Rupert and Edward on camels with indian boy
    C3. Rupert and Edward in a garden
    C4. Rupert and Edward sitting at table with lady
    C5. Rupert and Edward at home with Mr Trunk
    C6. Rupert at his home with mother and father
    Series D
    D1. Rupert with Beppo
    D2. Rupert and Mrs Bear with Beppo at table
    D3. Rupert with Beppo, Bill Badger and Edward Trunk
    D4. Rupert and Beppo at a shop with a lady
    D5. Rupert and Beppo at table with the lady
    D6. Rupert at his home with mother and father

*Books illustrated include*
*A Horse Book* [a Dumpy Book] (Grant Richards 1901)
*Little Bear and the Ogres* (Nelson 1922)
*Margot, the Midget and Little Bear's Christmas* (Nelson 1922)
*Old King Cole and Other Nursery Rhymes* (Treherne 1904)
*The Adventures of the Little Lost Bear* (Nelson 1921)
*Three Little Foxes* [a Dumpy Book] (Grant Richards 1903)
*Annuals illustrated with others include*
*Daily Express Children's Annual; Monster Rupert*

## Florence Upton (1873-1922)

*Postcards illustrated include*
Raphael Tuck
    **Golliwogg Art Series 1281** [1903] (blue edges)
    **Golliwogg Art Series 1282** [1903] (blue edges)
    **Golliwogg Art Series 1397** [1903] (blue edges)
    **Golliwogg Postcard 6065** [1904] (green edges)
    **Golliwogg Postcard 6066** [1904] (red/black edges)
    **Golliwogg Postcard 6067** [1904]

fromThe Golliwogg at the Seaside **(green/black edges)**
and The Golliwogg at War **(red/black edges)**
**Golliwogg Postcard 6068** [1904] (green edges)
**Christmas Postcard Series 1785** [1903] (blue edges)
Christmas/New Year overprint of 1282
**Christmas Postcard Series 1791** [1903] (blue edges)
Christmas/New Year overprint of 1281
**Christmas Postcard Series 1792** [1903] (blue edges)
Christmas/New Year overprint of 1281
**Christmas Postcard Series 1793** [1903] (blue edges)
Christmas/New Year overprint of 1282
**Christmas Postcard Series 8020** [1904] (green edges)
Christmas/New Year overprint of 6065
**Christmas Postcard Series 8063** [1903] (blue edges)
Christmas/New Year overprint of 1397
**Christmas Postcard Series 8064** [1903] (blue edges)
Christmas/New Year overprint of 1397
**Christmas Postcard Series 8095** [1904] (green black edges)
Christmas/New Year overprint of 6067
from the Golliwogg at the Seaside **(green/black edges)**
and the Golliwogg at War **(red/black edges)**
**Christmas Postcard Series 8096** [1904] (green edges)
Christmas/New Year overprint of 6068

Tuck also published the Golliwogg Series as greetings cards with
Christmas/New Year greetings overprints.

*Books illustrated include*
*Adventures of Borbee & the Wisp* (Longmans Green 1905)
*Florence Upton: Painter* / Lyttelton (Longmans 1926)
*Little Hearts* / Upton (Routledge 1897)
*Pax and Carlino* / Beckman (Fisher Unwin 1894)
*The Vegeman's Revenge* (Longmans Green 1897)
'The Golliwogg Books'
*The Adventures of Two Dutch Dolls* (Longmans Green 1895)
*The Golliwogg's Bicycle Club* (Longmans Green 1896)
*The Golliwogg at the Seaside* (Longmans Green 1898)
*The Golliwogg in War!* (Longmans Green 1899)
*The Golliwogg's Polar Adventures* (Longmans Green 1900)
*The Golliwogg's Auto Go-Kart* (Longmans Green 1901)
*The Golliwogg's Air-Ship* (Longmans Green 1902)
*The Golliwogg's Circus* (Longmans Green 1903)
*The Golliwogg in Holland* (Longmans Green 1904)
*The Golliwogg's Fox-Hunt* (Longmans Green 1905)
*The Golliwogg's Desert Island* (Longmans Green 1906)
*The Golliwogg's Christmas* (Longmans Green 1907)
*The Golliwogg in the African Jungle* (Longmans Green 1909)
*Annuals illustrated with others include*
*The Idler; Punch; The Strand Magazine*

## Louis Wain (1860-1939)

*We have included a short list of Louis Wain's classic
postcard designs for the nursery.*

*Alpha*
    Series 895 (Nursery rhymes)
CW Faulkner
    Series 454 (Games & pastimes)
    Series 515 (Games & pastimes)
*Raphael Tuck*
    Calendar series 297 (Nursery rhymes) [1902]
    Oilette series 3385 Dressing Dolls Series V [1922]
    Oilette series 3551 Louis Wain Mascots Series I [1925]
    Oilette series 3552 Louis Wain Mascots Series II [1925]
    Oilette series 3553 Louis Wain Mascots Series III [1925]
    Oilette series 3554 Louis Wain Mascots Series IV [1925]
    Art series 6721 The Nursery Series [1905]
    Art series 6723 (Fairy tales) [1905]
    Art series 6724 (Fairy tales) [1905]
    Christmas series 8123 The Nursery Series [1904]
    Christmas series 8125 The Nursery Series [1904]
    Christmas series 8126 (Nursery rhymes) [1904]
    Christmas series 8127 Fairy tales [1904]

## Ellen Welby (1851-1936)

*Postcards illustrated include*
Raphael Tuck
    **Series 99 Birds and Blossoms** [1900]
    **Series 124 Happy Childhood** [1901]

*Books illustrated include*
*By the Light of the Nursery Lamp* (Tuck nd)
*Culled from the Poets* (Tuck nd)
*Little Nightcaps [et al]* / Vredenburg [ed] (Tuck nd)
*Told by the Waterlilies* / Salmon (Tuck c.1890)

## Dorothy Wheeler (1891-1966)

*Postcards illustrated include*
A&C Black
    **Series 44 English Nursery Rhymes** [c.1924]
    **Series 44a English Nursery Rhymes** [c.1924]
    **Series 45 English Nursery Rhymes** [c.1924]
    **Series 45a English Nursery Rhymes** [c.1924]
J Salmon
    **Series 4611-4616** (Elves & woodland animals) [1938]
Bamforth
    **Fairy Secrets Series No 1** [c.1940]
    **Fairy Secrets Series No 2** [c.1940]
    **Woodland Secrets Series No 1** [c.1940]
    **Woodland Secrets Series No 2** [c.1940]

*Books illustrated include*
*A Pocketful of Silver* / Macdonald (Collins 1927)
*English Nursery Rhymes* / Walker (Black 1916)
*Further Adventures of Josie, Click.../*Blyton (Newnes 1952)
*Mr Pink-Whistle's Party* / Newnes nd)
*Mr Tumpy in the Land of Girls & Boys* (Sampson Low 1955)
*Sung by the Sea* /Macdonald (Black 1900)
*Tea, Toys and a Tale* / Kirkman (Black 1919)
*The Enchanted Wood* / Blyton (Newnes nd)
*The Magic Faraway Tree* / Blyton (Newnes 1946)
*The Folk of the Faraway Tree* / Blyton (Newnes nd)
*The Three Little Pigs* (Juvenile Publ. nd)
*Through the Green Door* / Macdonald (Blackwell 1924)
*Books illustrated with others include*
*Enid Blyton's Daffodil Story Book* [et al]
*Bo-Peep's Bumper Book;*
*Selfridges' Childrens's Story Book* (Selfridges nd)
*Sunny Stories* / Blyton (Newnes 1944)
*The Big Bedtime Book* / Blyton (Purnell nd)
*Annuals illustrated with others include*
*Sunny Stories Annual; Enid Blyton's Omnibus; The 10th Holiday Book*

## Flora White (1878-1953)

*Postcards illustrated include*
Photochrom (Full or part sets)
    **Celesque Series 236-241** [c.1914]
    **Celesque Series 1029-1040** (Patriotic) [1915]
    **Celesque Series 1060-1065** (Christmas) [1915]
    **Celesque Series 1096-1097** (Patriotic humour) [1915]
    **Celesque Series 1171-1172** (Patriotic humour) [1915]
    **Celesque Series 1206-1211 Doing Her Bit** [1915]
    **Celesque Series 1326-1331 Back to Blighty** [1916]
    **Celesque Series 1413-1418** (Christmas) [1916]
    **Celesque Series 1531-1536** (Christmas) [1917]
    **Celesque Series 1838-1843** (Ballet) [1917]
    **Celesque Series 1898-1903** (Games & Pastimes) [1918]
    **Celesque Series 1923-1928** (Childhood days) [1920]
    **Celesque Series 2055-2059** (Greetings) [1922]
    **Celesque Series 2061-2066** (Christmas) [1922]
    **Individual cards or part sets** 504 1010 1038 1096 1208 1347
    1372 1495 1529 1867 1984 1987 2110 2500 2520
Salmon (Full or part sets)
    **Series 013-018 Orchestra Series** [1916]*

**Series 034-039 Orchestra Series** [1916]*
**Series 1027-1034** (Greetings) [1916]
**Card No. 1084 Curly Locks** [1916]
**Card No. 1095 Mary Mary Quite Contrary** [1916]
**Card No. 1112 Ride-a-Cock Horse** [1916]
**Series 1148-1152** (Nursery rhymes) [1916] (1151 by Phlo)
**Series 1202-1213** (Months of the year) [1916]*
**Series 1313-1320** (Nursery rhymes) (1916)
**Series 1326-1332 Monday's chlid** [1917]*
**Series 1388-1391** (Patriotic) [1917]
**Series 1467-1472** (Fairy tales) [1918]
**Series 1489-1494** (Seaside humour) [1918]
**Card No. 1575** (Patriotic) [1919]
**Card No. 1575** (Greetings) [1919]
**Card No. 1651** (Greetings) [1919]
**Series 1715-1717** (Christmas) [1919]
**Series 1733-1738** (Greetings) [1920]
**Series 1778-1784** (Fairy tales) [1920]
**Card No. 1787** (Humour) [1920]
**Series 1794-1795** (Humour) [1920]
**Series 1798-1801** (Humour) [1920]
**Series 1835-1836** (Humour) [1920]
**Series 1847-1852** (Nursery rhymes) [1920]
**Series 1856-1861** (Baby humour) [1920]
**Series 1900-1903** (Piccanies) [1920]
**Series 1912-1916** (Fairy tales) [1920]
**Series 1917** (Nursery rhymes) [1920]
**Series 1952-1957** (Greetings) [1920]
**Series 2013-2018** (Christmas) [1920]
**Card No. 2084** (Greetings) [1921]
**Series 2189-2192** (Humour) [1921]
**Card No. 2277** (Humour) [1922]
**Series 2339-2344** (Pierrots & Romance) [1922]
**Series 2490-2491** (Humour) [1922]
**Series 2798-2803** (At the seaside) [1925]
**Series 2947-2948** (Seaside humour) [1925]
**Series 3106-3110** (Fairies) [1926]
**Series 3236-3240** (Fairies) [1926]
**Series 3332-3337** (Elves & Pixies) [1926]
**Series 3425-3428** (Christmas & New Year) [1927]
**Series 3818-3823** (Mermaids) [1930]
**Series 4201-4206** (Childhood days) [1933]
**Series 4339-4344** (Music making)
**Series 4417-4422** (Fairies) [1935]
Also: ETW Dennis
    *= E Mack series

*Books illustrated include*
*Dean's Catalogue for 1929* [ill wrapper by FW] (Dean 1928)
*Favourite Nursery Rhymes...* [with Lorna Steele] (Salmon nd)
*Little Folks at Play* [et al] (Collins nd)
*Original Nursery Rhymes* [with Lorna Steele] (Salmon nd)
*Peter Pan's ABC* (HF/H&S c.1915)
*Stories Told to Children* / Fairless (Duckworth 1914)
*The Blue Goblins* / Rutley (Dean nd)

## H Willebeek le Mair (1889-1966)

*Postcards illustrated include*
Augener
    **See panel on page 257**
*Drukkerij Benefelder*
    **Voor het Kind** (For the children) [1936]
    **3 Christmas designs in a large series by many artists.**
    These 3 designs first appeared in the Christmas number
    of *Ladies Home Journal* in December 1926
*Jobin & Cie*
    **Premiere Rondes Enfantines (30 designs)** [1904]

*Books illustrated include*
*A Child's Garden of Verses* / Stevenson (McKay 1926)
*A Gallery of Children* / Milne (Stanley Paul 1925)
*Birth Stories of the Prophets* (Fine Books 1978)
*Erste Levensjarenm* (Nygh & van Ditmar c.1910)
*Little People* / Elkin (Augener 1915)

*Little Songs of Long Ago* (Augener 1912)
*Old Dutch Nursery Rhymes* (Augener 1917)
*Our Old Nursery Rhymes* (Augener 1911)
*Premieres Rondes et Enfantines* (Sandoz, Jobin & Cie 1904)
*Schumann Album of Children's Pieces for Piano* (Augener 1913)
*The Children's Corner* (Augener 1914)
*The Flower Garden of Inayat Khan* (Fine Books 1978)
*Twenty Jataka Tales* / Inayat Khan (Harrap 1939)
*What the Children Sing* (Augener 1915)

***'Little Rhyme Books'***
*Auntie's Little Rhyme Book* (Augener c.1914)
*Baby's Little Rhyme Book* (Augener c1920)
*Daddy's Little Rhyme Book* (Augener c.1914)
*Grannie's Little Rhyme Book* (Augener c.1914)
*Mother's Little Rhyme Book* (Augener c.1914)
*Nursie's Little Rhyme Book* (Augener c1920)

## Madge Williams (1902-1986)

***Postcards illustrated include***

***Art & Humour***
**Series 6064 Our Darlings [nd]**
**Series 6071 Comic Dog Series [nd]**

***ETW Dennis (Full or part sets)***
**Series CS215-CS220** (Child humour) **[c.1928]**
**Individual cards or part sets 5696 5697 *CS162 CS164 CS187 CPC47/145 CPC47/152 TC48/172***

***Inter Art***
**Series 6123-6128** (Child humour) **[1927]**
**Series 6303-6308** (Child humour) **[1928]**

***Salmon (Full or part sets)***
**Card Nos. 2945-2946** (Child humour) **[1925]**
**Card No. 3157** (Child humour) **[1926]**
**Card No. 3174** (Child humour) **[1926]**
**Series 3242-3247** ((Child humour) **[1926]**
**Series 3430-3434** (Child humour) **[1927]**
**Series 3619-3623** (Child humour) **[1928]**
**Series 3778-3783** (Child humour) **[1930]**
**Card No. 3795** (Piccaninny humour) **[1930]**
**Series 3830-3833** (Child humour) **[1930]**
**Series 3998-4002** (Child humour) **[1931]**
**Series 4165-4170** (Child humour) **[1932]**
**Series 4423-4428** (Child humour) **[1935]**
**Series 4447-4452** (Child humour) **[1935]**
**Series 4523-4528** (Child humour) **[1935]**
**Series 4523-4524** (Child humour) **[1935]**
**Series 4636-4641** (Proverbs) **[1925]**
**Series 4728-4730** (Child humour) **[1935]**
**Series 4738-4743** (Elves & fairies) **[1939]**
**Series 4853-4858** (Patriotic) **[1942]**
**Series 4982-4987** (Child humour) **[1949]**
**Series 5000-5005** (Child humour) **[1949]**
**Series 5026-5031** (Child humour) **[1949]**
**Series 5064-5069** (Child humour) **[1949]**
**Series 5306-5311** (Elves & fairies) **[1957]**

***Raphael Tuck***
**Oilette Series 3632 Our Kiddies [1926]**
**Oilette Pinch & Squeak Novelty [c.1930]**

***Valentine***
**Series 6044-6049 Madge Williams Fairy Series [c.1940]**

## Alan Wright (1864-1959)

***Postcards illustrated include***

***Humphrey Milford***

***Postcards for the Little Ones Series***
**Pleased to See You [1930]** (3 by Lilian Govey)

***Regent Publishing Co.***
**Series 1010 (6 designs)**
from Mrs Bunnikins' Busy Day [1920]
**Series 1010 (6 designs)**
from Mrs Bunnikins' Busy Day [1920]
**Series 1042-1051 (12 designs)**
from The Tale of the Trail of a Snail [c.1921]

***Books illustrated include***
*Animal Stories for Tiny Folk* [et al] (Milford c.1926)
*Adventures of Dolly Dingle* / Wynne (Jarrolds 1920)
*Adventures of Dominie Dormouse* / MacNair (Dean nd)
*Adventures in Wallypug Land* (Pearson 1898)
*Baker Minor and the Dragon* / Farrow (Pearson 1902)
*Bingo and Babs. A Picture Story* (Blackie c.1919)
*Comic Sport & Pastime* [with Vernon Stokes] (Skeffington nd)
*In Search of the Wallypug* / Farrow (Pearson 1902)
*Little Teddy Bear* (Collins 1939)
*Mr Barker Bow* (Hodder & Stoughton 1920)
*Mr Poodle's Half Holiday* (Hodder & Stoughton 1920)
*Mr Bunnikins Builds a Bunglo* (Milford nd)
*Mrs Bunnikins Busy Day* (Jarrolds nd)
*My Little Dog* [with Clara Olmstead] (HF/H&S c.1909)
*My Picture Poetry Book* [with Clara Olmstead] (HF/H&S c.1909)
*Noah's Zoo* [Rag Book No. 79] (Dean 1910)
*Nan & Ken* [with AA May] / Wynnne (Nelson c.1919)
*Professor Philanderpan* / Farrow (Pearson 1904)
*Queen Victoria's Dolls* / Lowe (Newnes 1894)
*Rip Van Winkle* / Irving (Nelson 1921)
*Rural Life in England* [et al] / Irving (Routledge 1906)
*Tales of the Tuppeny Two* / Herbertson (Milford c.1926)
*The Book of Baby Birds* [with C Englefield] (Nelson 1936)
*Buttercups and Daisies* [with Clara Olmstead] (HF/H&S nd)
*The Christmas Book of Carols & Songs* (Routledge nd)
*The Dandy-Andy Book* (Nelson nd)
*The Enchanted Doll* / Lemon (Nelson 1921)
*The Great Mr Toad* (John Murray 1938)
*The Life of Queen Victoria* / Corkran (Jack 1910)
*The Little Panjandrum's Dodo* / Farrow (Skeffington 1899)
*The Magic Map Book* / Byron (HF/H&S c.1909)
*The Mandarin's Kite* / Farrow (Skeffington 1900)
*The New Panjandrum* / Farrow (Pearson 1902)
*The Story of the Saucy Squirrel* (Jacobs 1920)
*The Tale of Snoozleums* (Milford nd)
*The Tyrants of Kool-Sim* / Cobham (Henry 1897)
*The Wallypug at Play* (Tuck nd)
*The Wallypug Birthday Book* / Farrow (Routledge 1904)
*The Wallypug in Fogland* / Farrow (Pearson 1904)
*The Wallypug in London* / Farrow (Pearson nd)
*The Wallypug in the Moon or His Badjesty* (Pearson 1905)
*The Wonderful Tale of the Trail of a Snail* (Jarrolds c.1922)
*There was Once a Prince* / Mann (Henry 1897)
*Tony Twiddler, His Tale* [Bunnikins Series] (Jarrolds c.1921)
*Two Little Kittens* [et al] (HF/H&S c.1915)
*When Arnold Comes Home* / Mann (Henry 1897)

***Annuals illustrated include***
*Mrs Strang's Playbooks; My Big Book of Pictures; Blackie's Children's Annual; Blackie's Little One's Annual; Pip Squeak & Wilfred; Dome; Girl's Own Paper; Idler, Pall Mall; Parade; Strand; Sunday Pictorial; Wide World Magazine; Windmill.*

***'Dean's Youngsters' Picture Books'***
*A-Z in Rhymeland* (Dean nd)
*Fireside Stories* (Dean c.1925)
*Rambles Round the Farm* (Dean nd)
*The Picnic Book* (Dean 1925)
*The Pleasure Picture Book* (Dean 1925)
*The Youngster's Activity Book* (Dean 1925)
*Wheels, Wings and Water* (Dean 1925)

***'Never Wozzle Books'***
Never Wozzle Books, inspired by Alice in Wonderland show: 'how fir cones and feathers, acorns and poppy-heads may become with a little care and secotine, Dr Diplomadokus, the Fountain Penguin and a score of other but friendly creatures'.
*Oh, Nuttatall!* / St Leger (Universal Pubs. 1933)
*Under the U-Neversea* / St Leger (Universal Pubs. 1933)
*Under the Woodle Tree* / St Leger (Universal Pubs. 1933)

***'Little Giant Books'***
*Bubbles* [et al]/ Mrs Strang [ed] (Milford 1934)
*Mick and Me* [et al] / Mrs Strang [ed] (Milford 1926)
*Jack and Jill* [et al] / Mrs Strang [ed] (Milford 1930)
*The Birthday Party* [et al] / Mrs Strang [ed] (Milford 1927)
*The Hideaway Four* / Mrs Strang [ed] (Milford c.1927)
*The Red Umbrella* [et al] / Mrs Strang [ed] (Milford c.1927)

***See also: Anne Anderson for books illustrated jointly P267***

# Postcard listings by publisher

### CW Faulkner Series

This is a list of children's series of which we know the titles (only to be found on the original packets). We would like to hear of other titles that readers may know. Email: copecomms@demon.co.uk

72 J Hassall ***Fun & Frolic***
151 E Parkinson ***The Parkinson***
182 L Wain ***Louis Wain's Cats***
183 L Wain ***Louis Wain's Cats***
226 E Parkinson ***When George III was King***
236 H Rountree ***Comic Bears***
320 L Wain ***Comedy Dogs***
501 F Hardy ***Merry Little Folk***
568 M Sowerby ***Happy Childhood***
569 E Parkinson ***When the Heart is Young***
675 E Parkinson ***Happy Little Hollanders***
696 F Hardy ***The New Pierrots II***
731 S Barham ***Quaint Flower Land***
732 F Hardy ***Childhood's Happy Time***
734 E Parkinson ***Little Dutchies***
875 S Barham ***Beautiful Spring***
941 E Parkinson ***The Arctic Series***
996 A Richardson ***Agnes Richardson Series II***
1015 IM James ***Early Loves***
1049 K Feiertag ***Fair Julia***
1059 HGC Marsh ***Chums***
1070 IM James ***Happy Hearts & Happy Faces***
1073 E Ibbetson ***Boy Scouts***
1085 F Hardy ***Listening-in***
1101 K Feiertag ***My Teddy***
1128 HGC Marsh ***Young Pretenders***
1136 S Pearse ***Happy Holidays***
1155 A Richardson ***The True Little Lovers***
1157 E Parkinson ***Happy Days in Holland***
1167 E Parkinson ***Friends or Foes***
1190 S Barham ***Lantern Light***
1191 S Barham ***So Jolly by the Sea***
1194 IM James ***From a Dutch Window***
1195 AE Kennedy ***In Dog & Cat Land***
1215 AE Kennedy ***The Tubbies***
1216 AE Kennedy ***More Tubbies***
1217 S Barham ***Peter Pan***
1218 S Barham ***Where the Rainbow Ends***
1219 S Barham ***Memories of Pavlova***
1233 A Richardson ***Dainty Little Maidens***
1234 HGC Marsh ***Rhymes for Little People***
1241 AE Kennedy ***Fifi***
1263 D Pennion ***A Boy's Diary***
1264 A Richardson ***Early Days & Early Ways***
1265 A Richardson ***Love's Language of Flowers***
1268 S Barham ***The Chinese Lantern***
AE Kennedy ***Dancing Tubbies***
AE Kennedy ***Fifi (2nd Series)***
1316 AE Kennedy ***Mike***
1323 T Maybank ***Woodland Nymphs***
1324 C Stanton ***Things are not What they Seem***
1336 AE Kennedy ***The Three Bears***
1347 S Barham ***Where Pan Pipes***
1399 F Hardy ***Pierrot's Courtship***
1400 HGC Marsh ***I Do Believe in Fairies***
1505 HGC Marsh ***In Fairyland***
1531 HGC Marsh ***Little Soldier Boys***
1576 HGC Marsh ***Little Soldier Boy***
AE Kennedy ***Soldier Bear***
1582 IM James ***The Joys of Youth***
1592 AE Kennedy ***Tales of Woe***
1596 L Wain ***Happy Tabbies***
1630 P Purser ***Little Ducks***
1633 AE Kennedy ***Nursery Rhymes II Ser.***
1674 E Parkinson ***Children's Carnival***
1711 C Symonds ***Han's Andersen's Fairy Tales***
1731 S Barham ***The Pied Piper of Hamelin***
1734 IM James ***On the Sands***
1748 H Miller ***Grimm's Fairy Tales***
1784 H Miller ***Little Folks Nursery Rhymes***
1785 S Barham ***Pastorals***
1850 O Morgan ***A Week of Happy Days***
1859 S Barham ***Flower Fairies***
1958 C Symonds ***In the Land of Fairy Flowers***
1894 J Mercer ***Joyce Mercer's Fairy Series***

### E Mack 'Toy Town' Series of Working Toy Models

The 'Toy Town' Series No. 01
Six Pictorial Postcards
*Illustrator: George Piper*
***01*** ***Tudor cottage***
***02*** ***Girl in dress***
***03*** ***Tom, Tom, The Piper's Son***
***04*** ***Windmill***
***05*** ***Little Bo Peep***
***06*** ***Dick Whittington***

The 'Toy Town' Series No. 07
The 'Church' etc Packet
*Illustrator: George Piper*
***07*** ***Church***
***08*** ***Clown***
***09*** ***Roundabout***
***010*** ***The Original Punch and Judy Show***
***011*** ***Old Mother Hubbard***
***012*** ***The Old Woman who Lived in a Shoe***

A trial packet was printed for Toy Town Series 013, but a series of six postcards (013-018) by Flora White was issued in the Mack 'Orchestra' Series.

The 'Toy Town' Series No. 019
Wheelbarrow, Pump, etc Packet
1st edition - 5,000 - 1 May 1920
2nd edition published as Series No. 028.
*Illustrator: George Piper*
***019*** ***Child on Rocking Horse***
***020*** ***Little Red Riding Hood***
***021*** ***The Village Pump***
***022*** ***Humpty Dumpty***
***023*** ***See Saw Margery Daw***
***024*** ***The Model Wheelbarrow***

The 'Toy Town' Series No. 025
The 'Toy Shop' Packet containing 6 sheets to be made up into 3 pretty Model Shops in attractive colours. 1st edition - 10,000 printed 29 Jan. 1920
*Illustrator: WH Ellam*
***025*** ***Toys (Toyshop)***
***025A*** ***(Toyshop customers)***
***026*** ***Bones Butcher***
***026*** ***(Butcher, customers, etc)***
***027*** ***Mr Sprout Greengrocer***
***027A*** ***(Greengrocer's shop interior)***

The 'Toy Town' Series No 028
This is the 2nd printing of Series No 019
Published on 27 July 1920.
*Illustrator: George Piper*
***028 (Child on Rocking Horse)***
***029 Little Red Riding Hood***
***030 The Village Pump***
***031 Humpty Dumpty***
***032 See Saw Margery Daw***
***033 The Model Wheelbarrow***

A series of six postcards (034-039) by Flora White was issued in the Mack 'Orchestra' Series.

The 'Shadowgraph' Series No 040
A novelty cut-out series requiring a light to be shone through the cut out image and onto a screen behind.
*Illustrator: WH Ellam*
***040*** ***Beatty (Admiral Lord Beatty)***
***041*** ***L.G. (Lloyd George)***
***042*** ***HRH (Prince Edward)***
***043*** ***Doug (Douglas Fairbanks)***
***044*** ***Haig (Earl Haig)***
***045*** ***Charlie (Charlie Chaplin)***

The Cats' Academy Series No 046
(Not a Toy Town series).
*Illustrator: Louis Wain*
***046*** ***The Cats at Play***
***047*** ***The Dogs' Academy***
***048*** ***The Cats at Home***
***049*** ***The Cats at Home***
***050*** ***The Cats' Academy***
***051*** ***The Animals' Circus***

The 'Surprise' Packet
Series 052 of Working Toy Models
1st edition printed by Willis – 10,000 30.4.1920. 10,000 extra Charlie Chaplin postcards.
2nd edition – 5000 printed 28.7.1920
*Illustrator: George Piper.*
**Possibly by WH Ellam*
***052*** ***Monkey up a Stick****
***053*** ***Gollywog***
***054*** ***Charley's Aunt***
***055*** ***Charlie Chaplin***
***056*** ***Harlequin***
***057*** ***Policeman***

The 'Novelty' Packet.
Toy Town Series 058 of Mechanical Toys
*Illustrator: George Piper.*
**Possibly by WH Ellam*
***058*** ***Jumbo***
***059*** ***Pretty Polly****
***060*** ***Fido***
***061*** ***The Butterfly***
***062*** ***The Swing***
***063*** ***Pussy in Peace and War***

The 'National' Packet.
Toy Town Series 064 of 6 Mechanical Figures. *Illustrator: George Piper.*
**Possibly by WH Ellam*
***064*** ***Uncle Sam***
***065*** ***John Bull***
***066*** ***George Robey***
***067*** ***Charlie (Chaplin)***
***068*** ***Mary (Pickford)****
***069*** ***The Balancing Man***

Toy Town Series 064
was also issued as follows:
Printed by Willis - 5000 printed 13.8.1920
Printing blocks - Arc Engraving Company
*Illustrator: George Piper*

| 08 | *The Clown* |
| | (Card 08 from Packet 07) |
| 08 | *The Clown* |
| | (Card 08 from Packet 07) |
| 064 | *Uncle Sam* |
| | (Card 064 from Packet 064) |
| 064 | *Uncle Sam* |
| | (Card 064 from Packet 064) |
| 065 | *John Bull* |
| | (Card 065 from Packet 064) |
| 065 | *John Bull* |
| | (Card 065 from Packet 064) |

The 'Holiday' Packet. Toy Town Series 070
of Post Card Toy Models
Our Visit to the Seaside.
*Illustrator: WH Ellam*

| 070 | *Refreshment Tent* |
| 071 | *Refreshment Tent Counter* |
| 072 | *Beach Entertainment* |
| 073 | *(Not Known)* |
| 074 | *Beach Tent* |
| 075 | *(Not Known)* |

The 'Toy Town' Series No 076
My Zoo. Published 9 November 1920.
*Illustrator: WH Ellam*

| 076 | *Lion* |
| 077 | *Tiger* |
| 078 | *Bear* |
| 079 | *Camel* |
| 080 | *Elephant* |
| 081 | *Monkeys* |

The 'Doll's Furniture' Packet.
Toy Town Series 082. Complete Set of
Pretty Furniture. *Illustrator: WH Ellam*

| 082 | *Sofa* |
| 083 | *Easy Chair and Table* |
| 084 | *Piano (Music)* |
| 085 | *Wardrobe/Chair* |
| 086 | *Washstand* |
| 087 | *Bedstead* |

The 'Butterfly' Packet. Toy Town Series
No 088. Six beautiful Working Models
of Butterflies. *Illustrator: George Piper*

| 088 | *Blue Butterfly* |
| 089 | *(Not Known)* |
| 090 | *Green Butterfly* |
| 091 | *Blue/Orange Butterfly* |
| 092 | *Yellow Butterfly* |
| 093 | *Dragonfly* |

The 'Peter Pan' Packet.
Toy Town Series No 094.
*Illustrator: George Piper*

| 094 | *Peter Pan* |
| 095 | *Wendy* |
| 096 | *Captain Hook* |
| 097 | *Nana* |
| 098 | *Red Indian* |
| 099 | *Crocodile* |

The 'Jazz Top' Packet.
Toy Town Series 0100. Six Sheets of
Beautifully Coloured Tops.
*Illustrator: P Moring*

| 0100 | *Jazz tops* |

| 0101 | *4 Jazz Tops* |
| 0102 | *3 Jazz Tops* |
| 0103 | *4 Jazz Tops* |
| 0104 | *4 Jazz Tops* |
| 0105 | *Jazz Top* |

The 'Famous Buildings' Packet.
Toy Town Series No 106.
*Illustrator: WH Ellam*

| 0106 | *St Paul's* |
| 0107 | *The Tower* |
| 0108 | *Westminster Abbey* |
| 0109 | *Tower Bridge* |
| 0110 | *Horse Guards* |
| 0111 | *Nelson's Monument* |

The 'Motor' Packet.
Toy Town Series No 0112
*Illustrator: WH Ellam*

| 0112 | *The Taxi (Let's Take a Taxi)* |
| 0113 | *The Side Car (The Motor Cycle)* |
| 0114 | *Motor Fire Engine* |
| 0115 | *The Motor Car* |
| 0116 | *Motor Bus (Omnibus)* |
| 0117 | *Charabanc* |

The 'Doll's Furniture' II. Toy Town Series
No 0118. Complete Set of Pretty Furniture.
*Illustrator: WH Ellam*

| 0118 | *Kitchen Range (Range)* |
| 0119 | *Kitchen Dresser (Dresser)* |
| 0120 | *Bookcase* |
| 0121 | *Writing Desk (Bureau)* |
| 0122 | *Screen & Chair (Screen)* |
| 0123 | *Umbrella Stand (Umbrella)* |

The 'Toy Town Cinema' Series 0124
A Ten Reel Cinema. A Child can operate it.
One of the 6 cards is a Cinema Proscenium
with screen to be cut out. 5 other cards
each contain 2 reels of moving objects.
*Illustrator: WH Ellam*

| 0124 | *Toy Town Cinema (Proscenium)* |
| 0125 | *Record 1. Tumbler* |
| | *Record 2. Doing his Sum* |
| 0126 | *Record 3. Charlie Chaplin* |
| | *Record 4. How a Horse Runs* |
| 0127 | *Record 5. Tight Rope Dancer* |
| | *Record 6. Hey Diddle* |
| 0128 | *Record 7. Athlete's Long Jump* |
| | *Record 8. Little Miss Muffett* |
| 0129 | *Record 9. Pussy's Awakening* |
| | *Record 10. Bubbles* |

The 'Scout Packet'.
Toy Town Series No 0130.
*Illustrator: WH Ellam*

| 0130 | *(2 Scouts/Cart)* |
| 0131 | *(5 Scouts/Stretcher)* |
| 0132 | *(Not Known)* |
| 0133 | *(8 Marching Scouts)* |
| 0134 | *(1 Scout at attention, 1 with Bugle)* |
| 0135 | *(2 Scouts/Tent)* |

Toy Town Series No 0136.
*Illustrator: George Piper*

| 0136 | *Footballer* |
| 0137 | *Guardsman* |
| 0138 | *Penguin* |
| 0139 | *Pussy* |
| 0140 | *Jolly Jack Tar* |
| 0141 | *Kingfisher* |

The 'Children's Corner' Series 0200
Uncle Oojah, Don & Snooker.
No 1 of The Daily Sketch
Six Amusing Model Post Cards
*Illustrator: George Piper*
*Uncle Oojah of the Daily Sketch*
*Jerry Wangle Uncle Oojah's Merry Nephew*
*Rabby Bunnit from the Oojah Stories*
*Lord Lion Uncle Oojah's Friend*
*Don of the Oojah Stories*
*Snooker The Kitten Cat*

**Illustrators of the children's
postcards by A Vivian Mansell
by series number and artist**

1004 Joyce Plumstead
1005 Ethel Brisley
1014 Mary Horsfall
1015 Ethel Brisley
1016 Nina Brisley
1019 Clement Farmer
1022 Joyce Averill
1024 Joyce Averill
1029 Joyce Averill
1030 Susan Beatrice Pearse
1032 Joyce Averill
1033 Joyce Averill
1034 Nina Brisley
1035 Nina Brisley
1036 Nina Brisley
1037 Nina Brisley
1042 Linda Edgerton
1046 EF Sherie
1047 Joyce Averill
1052 EF Sherie
1057 Nina Brisley
1058 Nina Brisley
1059 Nina Brisley
1060 Joyce Averill
1064 Nina Brisley
1066 Nina Brisley
1067 Linda Edgerton
1069 Nina Brisley
1072 Linda Edgerton
1073 Nina Brisley
1074 Nina Brisley
1077 Harry Rountree
1087 Joyce Averill
1088 Susan Beatrice Pearse
1090 Ethel Brisley
1096 Linda Edgerton
1097 Howard Young
1103 Nina Brisley
1106 Ethel Brisley
1107 Linda Edgerton
1110 Linda Edgerton
1111 Linda Edgerton
1112 VM
1114 Agnes Richardson
1125 Nina Brisley
1126 Ethel Brisley
1127 Ethel Brisley

1140 Linda Edgerton
1141 Nina Brisley
1144 Nina Brisley
1146 Linda Edgerton
1147 Dorothy Braham
1150 Phyllis Palmer
1155 Linda Edgerton
1156 Joyce Brisley
1158 Linda Edgerton
1159 Linda Edgerton
1160 Linda Edgerton
1163 Linda Edgerton
1164 Elsie Maud Wood
1167 Linda Edgerton
1168 Nina Brisley
1170 Linda Edgerton
1171 Linda Edgerton
1172 Susan Beatrice Pearse
1175 Linda Edgerton
1179 Linda Edgerton
1185 Nina Brisley
1186 Linda Edgerton
1187 Linda Edgerton
1188 Linda Edgerton
1191 Linda Edgerton
1194 Linda Edgerton
1196 Nina Brisley
2105 Linda Edgerton
2106 Linda Edgerton
2107 Nina Brisley
2115 Florence Mary Anderson
2116 Hester Margetson
2117 Hester Margetson
2126 Joyce Plumstead
2127 Hester Margetson
2129 Hester Margetson

**Henry Frowde and Hodder &
Stoughton / Humphrey Milford
Postcards for the
Little Ones Series
(v) = vertical, (h) = horizontal**

**Barbara Briggs**
*The Busy Bees* (1930)
1. Bet likes her cracker cap... (v)
2. Goodnight Bridget... (v)
3. Rosamund knits... (v)
4. When John goes out to drive... (v)
5.
6.

*Our Dogs* (1923)
1. Entangled (v)
2. Knitting (v)
3. Left luggage (v)
4. The imp (v)
5. Too hot (v)
6. Windy weather (v)

*Our Terriers* (1923)
1. Irish Terrier (v)
2. Sealyham Terrier (v)
3. Scottish Terrier (v)
4. Skye Terrier (v)
5. West Highland White Terrier (v)
6. Wire-haired Fox Terrier (v)

**B Butler**
*Our Animal Friends* (1930)
1. Every day my watch I keep... (v)
2. 'Hullo, Mrs Moo, good day'... (v)
3. 'King of this lovely big castle I am' (v)
4. One morning these bunnies asked... (v)
5. Said Mrs Cart-horse to her foal... (v)
6. 'You pigs' cry the cats... (v)

**Rie Cramer**
*Joyous Days* (1930)
*Nos. 1,4,6 from 'In the Garden'*
*Nos. 2,3,5 from 'Little Mothers'*
1. In the hammock Sally swings... (v)
2. Jolly little Dutch boy Jan... (v)
3. Nan has needlework to do... (v)
4. October winds blow all around... (v)
5. Susan at the dressing table... (v)
6. They're ready Pamela and Pat... (v)

**Lilian Govey**
*A Day at the Zoo* (1925)
1. At 2pm the llamas arrive... (v)
2. For a camel ride, the keeper kind... (v)
3. Poor old Mr Macaw at the zoo... (v)
4. Quaint old birds, you're looking... (v)
5. The brown bear begs, jaws open ... (v)
6. The elephant is full of fun... (v)

*Dreams and Fairies* (1922)
1. Hugh and Hilda by the stream... (v)
2. Jack and the twins in golliwog's boat... (v)
3. The spinning wheel flies round... (v)
4. This is young Basil the brave... (v)
5. When children ought to be asleep... (v)
6. When Pussy and Jackie and Joan... (v)

*The Little Mouse Family* (1924)
1. A friend in need (v)
2. A tale of woe (v)
3. Fishing for the moon (v)
4. In disgrace (v)
5. Not on squeaking terms (v)
6. The old woman who lives in a shoe (v)

*The Mouseykins* (1924)
1. A flight of fancy (v)
2. Apple sauce (v)
3. How very rude (v)
4. The birthday cake (v)
5. The loud squeaker (v)
6. The picnic (v)

*Nursery Rhymes in Animal Land* (1930)
1. Hush-a-bye baby on the tree top... (v)
2. Little Tommy Tucker sang... (v)
3. Pussy-cat, Pussy-cat, oh! ... (v)
4. Three blind mice went for a spin... (v)
5. Three wise men of Gotham... (v)
6. Tom, Tom, the piper's son... (v)

**Lilian Govey and Alan Wright**
*Pleased to See You* (1930)
*2,3,6 by Lilian Govey*
*1,4,5 by Alan Wright*
1. 'Come in, come in', cries Mrs Bun... (v)
2. 'Good afternoon, friend Cockatoo...' (v)
3. Said Mrs Goose, 'how is your tea...' (v)
4. Said Mummy Bun, 'we make no fuss...' (v)
5. The Bobtails every year invite... (v)
6. 'You're welcome, Chips, my lad,...' (v)

**Lilian Price Hacker**
*Susan* (1923)
1. When Susan sews (v)
2. When Susan scowls (v)
3. When Susan's shy (v)
4. When Susan sings (v)
5. When Susan's smart (v)
6. When Susan swings (v)

**Norman Hartridge**
*A Child's Garden* (1923)
1. Earth greets cold winter ... (v)
2. Gay roses dangle overhead... (v)
3. My pidgeons flutter soft and sweet... (v)
4. My swan comes like a vessel gay... (v)
5. Sunshine makes a shadow finger... (v)
6. Three little gardeners here are seen... (v)

**Eileen Hood**
*Chums* (1922)
1. Now dogs attend to what I say... (v)
2. Of friends and pleasures small...(v)
3. Though I'm in charge of Bob... (v)
4. Though wolves are fierce... (v)
5. To guard you waking and asleep... (v)
6. To win a horse's heart, you'll find (v)

*Faithful Friends* (1915)
1. Belgian Mastiff (h)
2. British Bulldog (h)
3. Japanese Spaniel (h)
4. Russian Boarhound (h)
5. The French Wolf Dog (h)
6.

*Farm Babies* (1922)
1. Good morning. Calf (h)
2. Hungry chicks. Chickens (h)
3. Mother and Son. Foal (h)
4. Intruders. Pigs (h)
5. Spring Days. Lambs (h)
6.

*The Farm Team* (1918)
1. Two's company (h)
2. At the crossroads (h)
3. Mother and son (h)
4. On duty (h)
5. Sunday (h)
6.

*Our Sporting Dogs* (1918)
1. Cocker & Clumber Spaniels (h)
2. Foxhounds in full cry (h)
3. Greyhounds coursing (h)
4. Irish & English Setter (h)
5. Pointers (h)
6. Retriever (h)

*Trusty and True* (1922)
1. Canadian Sledge Dogs (h)
2. Retrievers (h)
3. Scotch Terriers (h)
4. Irish Terriers (h)
5. Scotch Deer Hounds (h)
6. Yorkshire Terriers (h)

*Wild Life* (1922)
1. The African Lion (h)
2. American Bisons (h)
3. The Eland (h)
4. Indian Tigers (h)
5. The Polar Bears (h)
6. Timber Wolves (h)

**Florence Jay**
***Our Puppies*** (1930)
1. Bruce is so eager and brave...(v)
2. Gyp found poor Teddy ... (v)
3. I'm brushed and combed...(v)
4. I taught my pups to play with ball...(v)
5. Poor Sealyham Sam cannot tell us...(v)
6. Sometimes these puppies have a fight...(v)

**Dora Leeson**
***Come out to Play*** (1916)
1. A wild beast show (v)
2. Battle royal (v)
3. Butterfly wishes (v)
4. Hide and seek (v)
5. Squad drill (v)
6. The voyager (v)

**Hester Margetson**
***Fairy Wings*** (1930)
1. Before the sun is very high...(v)
2. Hurry up, old bumble bee...(v)
3. In the middle of the night...(v)
4. My horse has crept to me up here...(v)
5. Now grasshopper you must be good... (v)
6. They've sent this tiger moth for me...(v)

**SG Hulme Beaman**
***Toytown Folk*** (1930)
1. Cowboy Mickey takes a ride...(v)
2. Hark! The drummer bangs his drum...(v)
3. Here's a clown on Toytown Neddy...(v)
4. Here's St George...(v)
5. Loud the toytown bagpipes play...(v)
6. Toytown Mother Hubbard goes...(v)

**Susan Beatrice Pearse**
***By the Seaside*** (1915)
1. A bite(v)
2. Ship ahoy! (v)
3. The fishers (v)
4. The look-out (v)
5. The voyagers (v)
6. What is it? (v)

***Christmastime*** (1915)
1. Christmas morning (h)
2. Hanging up the stocking (h)
3. Home from the party (h)
4. Santa Claus arrives (h)
5. The waits (h)
6. Under the mistletoe (h)

***Dear Little Allies*** (1915)
1. Brothers in arms (h)
2. Comrades (h)
3. Little sisters of the Red Cross (h)
4. Sons of the Empire (h)
5. Sunny south and snowy north (h)
6. Three little allies (h)

***For King and Country*** (1915) (4 designs)
1. Brothers in arms (v)
2. For king and country (v)
3. None but the brave deserve the fair (v)
4. Presents for the wounded (v)

***From the Front*** (1915)
1. A dug out (v)
2. Britannia rules the waves (v)
3. Can I help? (v)
4. Taking cover (v)
5. The wounded hero (v)
6. Who goes there? (v)

***Holiday Time*** (1917)
1. Along the road I rush and race... (v)
2. Hoppity-skip and skippety-hop... (v)
3. Leapfrog is a jolly game... (v)
4. The hare is running ever so fast... (v)
5. To ride my bike is what I like... (v)
6. We have such fun with hoop... (v)

***Jolly Games*** (1922)
1. Over, round and under... (v)
2. See-saw – on the trunk of a tree... (v)
3. Soap in the bowl, pipe in the hand... (v)
4. Swinging fast and high... (v)
5. The shuttlecock is light and small... (v)
6. When you start your kite... (v)

***Little Helpers*** (1920)
1. I am Bill the market man... (v)
2. I feed my pigs each morning early... (v)
3. In summer time we need no toys... (v)
4. I sow and plant and hoe and dig... (v)
5. Little lamb with smudgy nose... (v)
6. My ducklings are such funny things... (v)

***Odds and Evens*** (1920)
1. He's very stout and she is slim... (v)
2. Oh dear, that was a nasty fall... (v)
3. Our dog keeps snapping and snarling...(v)
4. Now Sir, don't fear, for while... (v)
5. You hold tight and you sit steady... (v)
6. You lost your sugar cake, I know... (v)

***Our Baby*** (1915)
1. His first bathe (v)
2. His first garden (v)
3. His first love (v)
4. His first party (v)
5. His first suit (v)
6. His first sum (v)

***Our Darlings*** (1915) (4 designs)
1. Love-a-dear (v)
2. My kiddlywink (v)
3. Piccaninny poppet (v)
4. So shy (v)

***Playmates*** (1922)
1. A careful hostess here you see (v)
2. Dobbin is very large and strong...(v)
3. Round the room we gaily go...(v)
4. So fast our feet keep flying!...(v)
5. This soldier and his fairy queen...(v)
6. We have built a golden castle...(v)

***The Busy Day*** (1918)
1. Mummy and Daddy take Joan...(v)
2. See the dollies snug and warm...(v)
3. Should the day be warm and fine...(v)
4. The hungry children wait...(v)
5. This teacher is not old...(v)
6. When children's frocks get torn...(v)

**Chloë Preston**
Other cards in this series
are by another artist,
as yet unknown to us.
***Hearts of Oak*** (1915)
1. Ready, aye ready (v)
2. True blue (v)
3.
4.
5.
6.

***Peek-a-Boo Gardeners*** (1924)
1. On market day the Peek-a-Boos...(h)
2. The Peek-a-Boo brings out... (h)
3. The Peek-a-Boos are holding out...(h)
4. The Peek-a-Boos with Peek-a-Pup...(h)
5. The Peek-a-Boos have picked...(h)
6. The Peek-a-Book is watering...(h)

***Peek-a-Boo Sportsmen*** (1926)
1. Says the Peek-a-Boo sportsman...(h)
2. The Peek-a-Boo hunter looks around...(h)
3. The Peek-a-Boos go driving...(h)
4. This Peek-a-Boo can swim...(h)
5. This Peek-a-Boo fisherman...(h)
6. This Peek-a-Boo gallops his horse...(h)

**Ruth Sandys**
***Old Street Cries*** (1927)
1. Knives and scissors to grind oh! (v)
2. Muffins and crumpet (v)
3. Sweep! Sweep! (v)
4. Who will buy my sweet blooming...(v)
5. Will you buy any milk today? (v)
6. Young lambs to sell (v)

**Amy Millicent Sowerby**
***Bird Children*** (1920)
1. Good gracious me... (v)
2. Kingfisher green and kingfisher blue (v)
3. Hark, Mr Owl! Tick tock, tick tock (v)
4. When Robin sings above the snow... (v)
5. When the first star begins to glow... (v)
6. With the first swallows... (v)

***Britain and her Friends*** (1914)
1. A little music. Portugal (v)
2. Give me some. Russia (v)
3. Off to the War. France (v)
4. Roast chestnuts. Belgium (v)
5. Wait till the clouds go by. England (v)
6. Work and play. United States (v)

***The Children's Day*** (1914)
1. Morning (v)
2. Noon (v)
3. Afternoon (v)
4. Night (v)
5. Just in time (v)
6. Just too late (v)

***Fairies' Friends*** (1926)
1. Oh bumble bee don't come too near...(v)
2. Poor bunny sobs...(v)
3. Safe in his pram the baby rides...(v)
4. This is a game called tail and touch...(v)
5. This water-lily elf is fond...(v)
6. Two weeny elves so plump and small...(v)

***Fairy Frolic Series*** (1926)
1. The summer elves are rather fond...(v)
2. This clever elf knows how to bend...(v)
3. This fay among the berries swings...(v)
4. This springtime fairy pipes so gay...(v)
5. When crocuses and snowdrops peep...(v)
6. When winter comes...(v)

***Farmyard Pets*** (1920)
1. I know you like some fruit... (v)
2. Little Bo-peep and her little pet lamb...(v)
3. Oh, Mrs Hen how kind it was...(v)
4. Mr Gobble-gobble turkey...(v)
5. My little foal is two weeks old...(v)
6. The little ducks upon the pond...(v)

***Favourite Nursery Rhymes*** (1916)
1. Little Bo-peep (v)
2. Little Jack Horner (v)
3. Little Miss Muffett (v)
4. Mistress Mary (v)
5. The piper's son (v)
6. Wee Willie Winkie (v)

***Favourite Nursery Stories*** (1916)
1. Beauty and the beast (v)
2. Cinderella (v)
3. Goldilocks (v)
4. Jack and the beanstalk (v)
5. Red Riding Hood (v)
6. The babes in the wood (v)

***Flower Children*** (1920)
1. Day lily (v)
2. Evening primrose (v)
3. King cups (v)
4. Love-in-a-mist (v)
5. Pansies (v)
6. Snowdrop (v)

***Flower Fairies*** (1923)
1. Come down, Mr Snailie, my dear...(v)
2. Here are the poppy boys...(v)
3. Says jolly Redcap in a tree...(v)
4. Says the spider, 'do give me a taste...'(v)
5. The apple blossom baby sleeps...(v)
6. This elf and field mouse play...(v)

***Flowers and Wings*** (1920)
1. By moonlight the wood fairies...(v)
2. Daddylonglegs, flying strong...(v)
3. Grasshopper, grasshopper...(v)
4. Oh bumble bee, you buzzing thing...(v)
5. Says Periwinkle Elf, 'I've heard...'(v)
6. This poor little elf with winglets...(v)

***Golden Days*** (1930)
1. Barbara Beck, pray where have...(v)
2. Down in the orchard...(v)
3. I know it always means good luck...(v)
4. Our broth is cooking in the pot...(v)
5. Poll, shall I undo your chain...(v)
6. The wind caught Moll...(v)

***Guides and Brownies*** (1924)
1. Climbing the ladder right up...(v)
2. In Spring a-gardening we go...(v)
3. In the garden after tea...(v)
4. Wearing aprons neat and white...(v)
5. We feed the poultry twice a day...(v)
6. When the weather's dry and fine...(v)

***Happy Days*** (1915)
1. A cracker's full of powder... (h)
2. I can't afford to waste one...(v)
3. In cold and wintry weather...(h)
4. These roses are so pretty...(h)
5. We've waited long to greet you...(v)
6. We want to pet and please you...(v)

***Happy as Kings*** (1921)
1. If rabbits, in a friendly way...(v)
2. Our golden fishes seem to be...(v)
3. Our kittens both look meek shy...(v)
4. Softly my pigeons shuffle round...(v)
5. We love our tiny terriers sweet...(v)
6. When Dicky sings, his yellow throat...(v)

***Happy Little People*** (1915)
1. Spring (h)
2. Summer (h)
3. Autumn (h)
4. Winter (h)
5. Comrades in arms (h)
6. Union is strength (h)

***Little Folk from Many Lands*** (1915)
1. A bargain. Italy (v)
2. Give me some. Russia (v)
3. Music hath charms. Turkey (v)
4. Out of reach.... North America (v)
5. Wait till the clouds roll by . England (v)
6. Open your mouth and shut... Holland (v)

***Little Jewels*** (1915)
1. Amethyst (v)
2. Emerald (v)
3. Pearl (v)
4. Ruby (v)
5. Sapphire (v)
6. Turquoise (v)

***Little Patriots*** (1915)
1. A night attack (v)
2. Dreadnoughts (h)
3. For the soldiers (v)
4. Lords of the sea (v)
5. None but the brave deserves the fair (h)
6. The winning side (h)

***Merry Elves*** (1921)
1. At dawn before the sun is hot...(v)
2. Hedgerow elves in roses sleep...(v)
3. This baby elf flew to the nest...(v)
4. This elf has found some grapes...(v)
5. Two dicky birds sat on a blackberry...(v)
6. When the mother bird flutters away...(v)

***Old Time Games*** (1921)
1. A hundred years or more ago...(v)
2. Peter Pan is afloat on a nest...(v)
3. The lost boys in the snowy weather...(v)
4. To the velvety tree-tops...(v)
5. Wendy and John and Michael look...(v)
6. Small Priscilla is fond of fruit...(v)

***Playtime*** (1916)
1. A three-legged race (h)
2. A tug of war (h)
3. Blind man's buff (h)
4. Leap-frog (h)
5. See-saw (h)
6. With bat and ball (h)

***Pleasant Days*** (1915)
1. A flight of rose leaves (v)
2. Christmas roses (v)
3. My lady's chair (h)
4. The duet (v)
5. The old love and the new (v)
6. They all love Jack (v)

***Pretty Wings*** (1920)
1. Red Admiral and caterpillar (v)
2. Peacock and caterpillar (v)
3. Clifton Blue and caterpillar (v)
4. Large White and caterpillar (v)
5. Orange Tip and caterpillar (v)
6. Brimstone and caterpillar (v)

***Shakespeare's Heroines*** (1922)
1. A maid so tender fair. Othello (v)
2. And she is fair. Merchant of Venice (v)
3. From East to Western Ind. As you like it (v)
4. My dear Lady Disdain. Much Ado (v)
5. The brightness of her cheek. Romeo (v)
6. What's done is done. Macbeth (v)

***Sky Fairies*** (1920)
1. On April days I'd like to have...(h)
2. This fairy got up in good time...(h)
3. To see-saw on a sunbeam...(h)
4. Two sky fairies are hiding...(h)
5. When fairies have a frolic...(h)
6. When Mr Dustman scatters...(h)

***Sons of the Empire*** (1915)
1. Australia (v)
2. Canada (v)
3. India (v)
4. New Zealand (v)
5. South Africa (v)
6. The West Indies (v)

***Storyland Children*** (1924)
1. Little Bo-peep (v)
2. Little Boy Blue (v)
3. Little Miss Muffett (v)
4. Mistress Mary, quite contrary (v)
5. Red Riding Hood (v)
6. Tom, the piper's son (v)

***Woodland Games*** (1920)
1. Listen Bun, we'll have some fun...(h)
2. Oh come and float on my lily boat... (h)
3. The rules of fairy leapfrog...(h)
4. This elf makes the squirrel his friend... (h)
5. To swing over poppies is nice...(v)
6. Two elves on the wing...(h)

**Margaret Tarrant**
***The Sunbonnet Series*** (with Medici) (1925)
1. A secret Polly tells to Prue...(v)
2. Polly and Prue are planting the beds...(v)
3. Polly and Prue each bought a balloon...(v)
4. Sunbonnet Poll and Sunbonnet Prue...(v)
5. The Sunbonnet sisters are fishing...(v)
6. When butterflies flutter by fast...(v)

***The Sunshade Series*** (with Medici) (1925)
1. A sudden wind came whistling by...(v)
2. Blue gown and gold with sunshades...(v)
3. Four friends are we who love to plan... (v)
4. Please put your little silver fish...(v)
5. With feast of rosy strawberries...(v)
6. With sunshades bright... (v)

**Dorothy Wheeler**
***A Day at the Fair*** (1930)
1. Here's the gipsy woman's stall (v)
2. Homeward go the girls and boys (v)
3. Hurry up children Hi! Hi! Hi (v)
4. Look at us all on the merry-go-round (v)
5. Now for a swingboat up in the air (v)
6. The children all come...(v)

***Snow Children*** (1926)
1. A Christmas carol (v)
2. A safe landing (v)
3. Hold tight (v)
4. Snow babies (v)
5. Snow flakes (v)
6. Tumbling down (v)

## Raphael Tuck Oilette Series of Cut Out 'Pastime' Novelty Picture Postcards

Oilette Series 3375
Birds on the Wing I – II
*Illustrator May Bowley*
'Six postcards of British Birds and their Eggs, reproduced in the famous Oilette process with the outlines perforated so that the wings may easily be bent upwards, giving the bird its natural flying appearance'.

Oilette Series 3381 Dressing Dolls
*Illustrator Margaret Banks*
1. Dolly Dimple & her Frocks
2. Jack at Play & his Suits
3. Little Pamela & her Frocks
4. Our Jimmy & his Suits
5. Pretty Peggy & her Frocks
6. Tommy Lad & his Suits

Oilette Series 3382
Dressing Dolls II
*Illustrator AL Bowley*
1. Baby Bunting
2. Little Bo-peep
3. Little Jack Horner
4. Little Miss Muffett
5. Mary, Mary, Quite Contrary
6. The Knave of Hearts

Oilette Series 3383
Dressing Dolls III
*Illustrator AL Bowley*
1. Handy Spandy Jack-a-Dandy
2. Little Betty Blue
3. Little Boy Blue
4. Simple Simon
5. The Queen of Hearts
6. Tom, Tom, The Piper's Son

Oilette Series 3384
Dressing Dolls IV
*Illustrator Margaret Banks*
1. A Little Bit of China
2. Little Miss America
3. Little Miss Britain
4. Little Miss Spain
5. The Little Dutch Girl
6. Vive La France

Oilette Series 3385
Fairy Tale Dressing Dolls
*Illustrator Louis Wain*
1. Aladdin, the Princess & the Magician
2. Beauty & the Beast
3. Cinderella
4. Dick Whittington & his Cat
5. Little Red Riding Hood
6. Robin Hood

Oilette Series 3386
Father Tuck's Fairyland Panorama
*Illustrator AL Bowley*
1. Beauty & the Beast
2. Cinderella
3. Jack & the Beanstalk
4. Little Red Riding Hood
5. Little Snow White
6. The Sleeping Beauty

Oilette Series 3387 Model Cottages
*Illustrator E Heatley*
'A charming and entertaining set of six postcards, each of which can be readily made up into a delightful cottage home, the row of six cottages everyone different making a most picturesque grouping'.

Oilette Series 3388 Model Cottages II
*Illustrator (Anon)*

Oilette Series 3390
Butterflies on the Wing Series I-V
*Illustrator Series I – (Anon)*
*Illustrator Series II – RJ Wealthy*
*Illustrator Series III – N Braby*
*Illustrator Series IV – Newton Braby*
*Illustrator Series V – Alice West*
'Six postcards of groups of British butterflies and moths reproduced in the famous 'Oilette' process with the outlines perforated so that the wings may be easily bent upwards giving the butterfly its natural flying appearance.'

Oilette Series 3394
Mechanical Dolls I
*Illustrator Margaret Banks*
1. A Little Welsh Maid
2. A Bonnie Highland Laddie
3. Somebody's Sweetheart
4. The Little Colleen
5. The Little Flower Girl
6. The Little Shepherdess

Oilette Series 3394
Mechanical Dolls II
*Illustrator (Anon)*
1. A Bonnie Hieland Laddie
2. A Little Fortune Teller
3. A Little Geisha
4. From the Sunny South
5. I'se Topsy
6. Minnehaha

Oilette Series 3396
The Window Garden Series
*Illustrator (Anon)*
1. Chrysanthemums
2. Crimson Rose Bush
3. Forget-me-Nots
4. Pink Rose Bush
5. Purple & Gold Pansies
6. Violets

Oilette Series 3397
The Zoo Zoo Series
*Illustrator (Anon)*
1. The Camelah
2. The Freakah
3. The Gallopah
4. The Jazzah
5. The Mascotah
6. The Snorzah

Oilette Series 3397
The Drawing Room Furniture Series
*Illustrator (Anon)*
1. Baby in Rocking Cradle
2. Drawing Room Cabinet
3. Drawing Room Chairs
4. Drawing Room Screen
5. Drawing Room Settee
6. Grandfather's Clock

Oilette Series 3399
Toy Rockers Series
*Illustrator (AL Bowley)*
1. Little Tee Wee went to sea
2. Here we go, up, up, up
3. Peter paddling his canoe
4. Pussy cat, pussy cat,
5. See a fine lady upon a white horse
6. This is the way the gentlemen ride

Oilette Series 3400
The Window Garden Series II
*Illustrator (Anon)*
1. Anemonies
2. Daffodils
3. Hyacinths
4. Poppies
5. Sweet Peas
6. Tulips

Oilette Series 3402
The Flower and Fruit Modelling ABC
*Illustrator (Anon)*
'An entertaining novelty for young folk. A letter of the alphabet is so arranged that when it is cut out it will stand up.'
1. A, B, C, D
2. E, F, G, H, I
3. J, K, L, M
4. N, O, P, Q
5. R, S, T, U, V
6. W, X, Y, Z

Oilette Series 3403
Merry Little Men
*Illustrator (Anon)*
1. Cheerful Chinese Conjurors
2. Good Sports
3. Here we are Again
4. Jolly Japanese Jumpers
5. Merry Music Makers
6. Nimble Niggers

Oilette Series 3404
Model Railway Engines
*Illustrator WH Ellam*
1. Great Western Railway
2. LMS Midland Section
3. LMS Caledonian Section
4. LMS London & North Western Section
5. LNER Great Northern Section
6. (Not known)

Oilette Series 3405
Swinging Dolls
*Illustrator possibly AL Bowley*
'Each card has a half doll seated on a swing; the lower legs and accessories are separate. When cut out and assembled, following the directions on the back of the card, it becomes a swing toy'.
1. Clown
2. Columbine
3. Harlequin
4. Joking Jock
5. Jolly Johny
6. Joyous Jenny

# Bibliography

*A Dictionary of British Artists 1880-1940*
J Johnson & Greutzner (ACC 1981)

*A Dictionary of British Artists 1900-1950*
Waters (Eastbourne Fine Arts 1975)

*A History of Children's Book Illustrators*
Whalley & Chester (Murray 1988)

*Arthur Rackham, A Life With Illustration*
Hamilton (Pavilion Books 1990)

*Artists of Northumberland* / Marshall Hall
(Marshall Hall Associates 1973)

*Australian Children's Book Illustrators*
Marcie Muir (Sun Academy Series 1977)

*British Children's Books in the Twentieth Century* / Frank Eyre (Longman 1971)

*Brush Pen and Pencil. The Book of Dudley Hardy* / AE Johnson (A&C Black 1909)

*Cecil Aldin: The Story of a Sporting Artist*
Ron Heron (Webb & Bower 1981)

*Chloë Preston & the Peek-a-Boos*
Mary Hillier (Richard Dennis 1998)

*Cicely Mary Barker and Her Art*
Laing (Frederick Warne 1995)

*Dictionary of British Book Illustrators*
Peppin/Micklethwait (Murray 1983)

*Dictionary of British Book Illustrators and Caricaturists* / Houfe (ACC 1978)

*Dictionary of 20th Century British Book Illustrators* / Horne (ACC 1994)

*Dictionary of Women Artists*
Gaze (Fitzroy Dearborn Publishing)

*Dictionary of Women Artists before 1900*
Chris Petty (GK Hall & Co 1985)

*Dorothy Wilding: The Pusuit of Perfection*
Pepper (National Portrait Gallery 1992)

*English Book Illustration*
R Sketchley (Kegan Paul 1903)

*English Female Artists*
Ellen Clayton (London 1876)

*Guide to Artists' Signatures & Monograms on Postcards* / Saleh (Minerva Press 1993)

*History of Children's Costume*
Elizabeth Ewing (Bibliophile 1977)

*Illustrators of Children's Books 1744-1945*
Mahoney, Latimer & Folmsbee
(The Horn Book Inc. 1947)

*Ivy Millicent James 1879-1965*
(Woodspring Museum 1981)

*John Hassall Lifestyle*
David Cuppleditch (Dilke 1979)

*Long Ago When I Was Young*
E Nesbit (Whiting & Wheaton 1966)

*Mabel Lucie Attwell* / Chris Beetles
(Pavilion Books 1988)

*Oxford Books for Boys & Girls 1927-28*
(Milford, OUP 1927)

*Painting Women: Victorian Women Artists*
Deborah Cherry (Routledge 1993)

*Picture Postcards and their Publishers*
Byatt (Golden Age Postcards 1978)

*Popular Arts of the First World War*
Jones & Howell (Studio Vista 1972)

*Randolph Caldecott – His Early Art Career*
Blackburn (Sampson Low 1886)

*The American Postcard Guide to Tuck*
Sally Carver (Carves Cards 1976)

*The Art of the Illustrator*
PV Bradshaw (Press Art School 1918)

*The Collectable World of Mabel Lucie Attwell*
John Henty (Richard Dennis 1999)

*The Enchanted World of Jessie M King*
Colin White (Canongate 1989)

*The Fairy World of Ida Rentoul Outhwaite*
Muir & Holden (A&C Black 1985)

*The Glasgow Girls*
Frances Page (Magna 1995)

*The History of the Christmas Card*
George Buday (Spring Books 1994)

*The History of the Royal Birmingham Society of Artists* / Hill & Midgley
(Birmingham 1922)

*The Illustrator and the Book in England 1790-1914* / Ray (OUP 1976)

*The International Book of Comics*
Denis Gifford (Hamlyn 1984)

*The Joyce Lankester Brisley Book*
Frank Waters (Harrap 1981)

*The London Sketch Club*
David Cuppleditch (A Sutton 1994)

*The Oxford Companion to Children's Literature* / Carpenter & Pritchard
(Oxford University Press 1984)

*The Portrait in Britain & America*
Robert Simon (Phaidon 1991)

*The Royal Academy of Arts Exhibitions 1769-1970* / Graves (Graves & Bell)

*The Royal Academy Illustrated* (Cassell)

*The Royal Scottish Academy Exhibitors 1826-1990* (Hilmartin Manor Press)

*The Society of Women Artists Exhibitors 1855-1996* / (Hilmartin Manor Press)

*The Treasures of Childhood* / Iona & Peter
Opie & Brian Alderson (Pavilion 1989)

*Time I Was Dead: Pages from My Autobiography* / Cecil Aldin (E&S 1934)

*Victorian Women Artists* / Pamela Gerrish
Nunn (Women's Press 1987)

*Women Artists* / Petersen & Wilson
(Women's Press 1978)

*Women, Art & Society* / Chadwick
(Thames & Hudson 1996)

*Women in Art* / Elizabeth Krull
(Studio Vista 1986)

*Women in the Fine Arts* / Clement
(Riverside Press 1904)

*Christian Science Monitor, Girl's Realm
Little Folks, The Art Journal, The Bookman,
The British Stationer, Pearson's Magazine,
The Stationery Trades Journal, The Studio,
The Year's Art*

# Index

THE "ALPHA" POSTCARD

Post Card

Post Card—Carte Postale
Universal Postal Union—Union Postale Universelle

BRITISH GOODS ARE B

TUCK'S CARTE

BOVEN IN DE
VLUGGERVER

FOR COMMUNICATION

Dear Mavis
mummy left her knitting
needle... I found it by the
front gate. so will take it
to Auntie's in the morning
love to you both from

S. K. Hathaway
28. Carlisle Ter
Tree Hoe
Plymouth

Miss M. Phillips
107 Elmwood
Wanstead

Miss Green
7, Mova Cottage

HALFPENNY

Copyright: The Medici Society Ltd., London
Art Publishers by Appointment to the late King
Engraved and printed in Great Britain

So sli
Take a sho
I can catch t
But Hare fell asle
So Tortoise passed
Said Tortoise to Hare
Steady and slow is advice